# Management Consultancy Insights and Real Consultancy Projects

G000069483

The field of management consultancy research has grown rapidly in recent years. Fuelled by the drivers of complexity and uncertainty, a growing number of organizations – both profit and third sector alike – are looking at management consultancy to assist in their aims for development and change. Consultants have become a common feature in organizational change initiatives, involved in both providing advice and in implementing ideas and solutions. However, despite this growing recognition and influence, management consultancy is still often misunderstood or criticized for its lack of theoretical underpinning.

The book seeks to address these issues by offering applied theoretical insights from academics that both teach and practice management consultancy. Written by recognized experts in their field, the contributors combine original insights with authoritative analysis. Uniquely, this book identifies emerging themes with critical discourse and provides rich empirical case study evidence to show the reader how management consultancy projects are implemented. Real-world international consultancy projects are featured as written up cases featuring organizations from multinational corporations to the public sector.

Written for graduate level managers or those who have practical leadership experience, this book will enable readers to apply management consultancy models beyond a classroom context.

**Dr Graham Manville**, CMC, MBA, PhD, is a Senior Lecturer in Business and Management and the Director of Employability and Enterprise for Norwich Business School, University of East Anglia, Norwich, UK. He has won several national and international awards in the fields of research and consulting. In addition, he is a Director of Longview Consulting Ltd.

**Dr Olga Matthias**, CMC, DBA, is Senior FME Fellow and a Senior Lecturer in Operations Management, School of Management, University of Bradford, UK. Previously, she had a long career at PA Consulting Group in the Business Operations and Performance practice. Olga is Head of the Operations and Information Management Department in the Faculty of Management and Law at the University of Bradford, UK. She holds a DBA, having researched how consulting firms can provide a more customised service to their clients. In addition she is a Certified Management Consultant. She has over 35 publications comprising international conferences, journals and book chapters. Olga is also a director of Capability Gap Limited, a boutique performance optimisation consultancy serving multi-sector clients..

**Julian Campbell**, MBA, is the Programme Director for the Executive MBA at the Norwich Business School, University of East Anglia, Norwich, UK. He is also a visiting Professor in Entrepreneurship at Vysoka Skola Ekonomicka in Prague. Prior to working in academia, he ran his own consultancy practice specialising in brand management with clients in Africa, Eastern Europe and the Middle East.

# Management Consultancy Insights and Real Consultancy Projects

Graham Manville, Olga Matthias and Julian Campbell

Routledge
Taylor & Francis Group

LONDON AND NEW YORK

First published 2018
by Routledge
2 Park Square, Milton Park, Abingdon, Oxon OX14 4RN

and by Routledge
711 Third Avenue, New York, NY 10017

*Routledge is an imprint of the Taylor & Francis Group, an informa business*

*British Library Cataloguing-in-Publication Data*
A catalogue record for this book is available from the British Library

*Library of Congress Cataloging-in-Publication Data*
A catalog record for this book has been requested.

ISBN: 9781472479297 (hbk)
ISBN: 9781138090132 (pbk)
ISBN: 9781315593425 (ebk)

Typeset in Bembo
by Apex CoVantage, LLC

# Contents

# Figures

# Tables

# Contributors

**Renae Agrey** is a researcher and an academic staff member at the University of Queensland's Business School, Australia. She has collaborated on publications in the areas of information systems, international business, and strategic management. She is the author and inventor of *Keeping the Records Straight!*™, an innovative bookkeeping apparatus for small business and has been a management consultant for over sixteen years in Australia and Canada's far north.

**Peter Allen** is the owner of Business Torque Systems Ltd, an industry leader in the application of governance principles to organisations wanting to begin or improve their governance. He creates governance development programmes for a wide range of industries and organisations, including Maori and Pacific cultures, based on his Governance Capability Development Model. He works with Massey University to deliver a programme aimed at training professionals to advise their clients in the development of good governance.

**Iouri P. Bairatchnyi** is a leading cross-cultural consultant and trainer with more than 15 years' experience of managing training programmes in the US and worldwide. Currently Adjunct Professor in the Faculty of Organizational Culture and Behaviour at Kent State University, his areas of expertise are organizational culture assessment, organizational learning and knowledge management. From 1994 to 2011 he was Programme Manager at the World Bank's Human Resources Department, where he managed institutional programmes on Language, Culture Training and Global Mobility.

**P. Matthijs Bal** is Professor of Responsible Management at the University of Lincoln, United Kingdom. Prior to joining Lincoln, he worked for the University of Bath, VU University Amsterdam and Erasmus University Rotterdam. His research interests concern workplace dignity, flexibility in the workplace, ideology, individualization at work and the role of fictional narratives at work. Recently, he published a book on workplace dignity, and he also edited two books, one on aging workers in the contemporary workplace, and one on idiosyncratic deals between employees and organisations. More information about his work can be found on his website www.matthijsbal.com.

**Hilmy Cader** is the International CEO of MTI Consulting, which is a boutique strategy consultancy with a network of associates across Asia, Africa and the Middle East. He operates from his dual bases in Bahrain and Australia. Under his leadership over the last 19 years, MTI has carried out over 520 assignments in 40 countries, across diverse industries. Hilmy is a Chartered Marketer and Fellow of the Chartered Institute of Marketing (UK), holds an MBA from the University of Colombo and received his executive education at Harvard Business School.

**Julian Campbell** is Programme Director for the Executive MBA course at the University of East Anglia, and provides support to all MBA students when completing their consultancy projects with external clients. He is former Director of Operations for Business Link, the government agency providing advice and support services to SMEs. Prior to working in academia, he ran his own consultancy practice specialising in brand management with clients in Africa, Eastern Europe and the Middle East.

**Chand Chudasama** is a strategic consulting manager at Price Bailey Group Limited, an award winning accountancy and business advisory firm serving private clients and regional, national and international business. He specialises in Strategy and Corporate Finance consulting for large corporations, and in disruptive early stage businesses. Prior to joining Price Bailey Group, he worked as a consultant in 40 countries, on all major continents. Chand also runs his own manufacturing and e-commerce business. He has an MBA from Newcastle University, UK.

**Jason Cordier** teaches and researches management as an assistant professor of management at SolBridge International School of Business in South Korea. Before entering academia he was a management consultant leading government and corporate projects in South East Asia, Europe, the Middle East, North Africa and the United States. Jason has published peer reviewed conference proceedings and journal articles in the areas of knowledge management, strategic practices and strategic human resource management.

**Simon B. de Jong** is Professor in Organizational Behavior and HRM at Maastricht University (The Netherlands). Throughout his career he has been interested in how organizational processes and structures can help (or hinder) employees and managers in their pursuit for improved well-being and performance. His work has been published in top scientific journals, such as *Journal of Applied Psychology*, *Organization Science*, *Human Relations*, *Journal of World Business*, *Journal of Management*, and *Journal of Management Studies*. After obtaining his PhD at the University of Groningen (NL) he worked as a human capital consultant at Deloitte. Subsequently, he held several academic roles at top-ranked universities, such as the University of St. Gallen (CH), EADA Business School (ESP), and the University of Bath and East Anglia (UK). Currently, he serves as an Associate Editor of the *European Journal of Work and Organizational Psychology*.

**Elissa Farrow** has extensive experience in strategy governance, design and transition, and is the founder of About Your Transition, a global consultancy practice. Elissa has masters-level academic qualifications that support her consultancy, coaching and facilitation services. She is an active contributor to governance bodies, including the Change Management Institute, and draws on 18 years of experience working with individuals, teams and organisations to deliver positive client outcomes. Elissa has a variety of YouTube videos and articles available at www.aboutyourtransition.com.au.

**Ian Fouweather** is a Lecturer in the Faculty of Management and Law at the University of Bradford, UK. He has taught a wide range of subjects from operations management to philosophy. His publications reflect his eclectic interests, with publications covering areas including: healthcare management, linguistics, industrial statistics, big data, eBusiness, the philosophy of sport and supply chain management. Ian has also run his own management consultancy for over a decade working in the FMCG sector with clients ranging from multinational corporations to microbusinesses and startups.

**Tahir Hameed** has been associated with SolBridge International School of Business in South Korea since 2012. He teaches undergraduate and graduate level courses in information systems and technology management. He obtained his PhD in Information Technology Management from KAIST in South Korea and his Master's in Computer Science from LUMS, Lahore. His research interests include the areas of technology standards, STI policy, information systems adoption, organizational knowledge management and health informatics. He has published extensively in prestigious journals and has presented several papers at leading conferences.

**Andrew Hine** is a partner at KPMG and leads the firm's UK public sector and healthcare businesses. Specialising in issues of strategy, performance and leadership of health and other public services, Andrew has undertaken a wide variety of consulting projects for governments and institutions in the UK, Europe and the Middle East. Andrew joined KPMG in 2004 and became a partner in 2006. Prior to joining the firm Andrew worked for 15 years in a variety of management and board-level executive roles in the NHS. Andrew is also a trustee and board member of the Refugee Council, a UK charity.

**Julie Hodges** is an associate professor at Durham University Business School in the UK. As well as being an academic, Julie is also an author and consultant. Her area of expertise is change in organizations, particularly the role and impact of people during transformations. Before entering the academic world Julie worked as a management consultant for over 20 years in several profit and non-profit organisations, including PwC. At PwC Julie was responsible for organisational change and management development in a number of companies, including Barclays, Shell, BBC, Lloyds and Reuters. Julie has also worked with Vertex where she set up and led a commercial consultancy team. Her first role was with the British Council where she was the Development Consultancy for East Asia. Julie has published in a number of international journals on change in organisations, leadership branding, and midlife women in business. She is the author of several books: *Managing and Leading People through Change* (London: Kogan Page); *Sustaining Change in Organizations* (London: Sage) and *Public and Third Sector Leadership: Experience Speaks* (London: Emerald). Julie's latest book is entitled *Consultancy, OD and Change* (London: Kogan Page).

**Elizabeth Kariuki** is a Director at Africa Policy Research Institute Limited (APRIL) a think tank, and a former PwC partner. She has worked in over 15 African countries on initiatives related to tax reform, public finance, public service reform and performance management. In 2011, she co-authored four chapters of a book entitled *Public Administration in Africa*. She completed her doctoral research in 2012 on performance measurement and tax administration at the University of Bradford's School of Management in the UK.

**Brett Knowles** is a long-time thought leader in the performance measurement space. Over the last 20 years he has worked with Drs. Kaplan and Norton and has had clients referenced in each of their books. Brett has assisted over 3,000 organizations from around the world and in all sectors from AT&T to Zeneca, from the IRS to the City of Kingston. His clients have had as many as 250,000 employees and as few as five. He is the co-founder of the first Balanced Scorecard application, has developed numerous measurement concepts around intangible assets, and has served on several editorial boards and conference constructs. Brett's clients have been profiled in the *Harvard*

*Business Review, Fortune,* and *Forbes.* There are over 20 business school cases covering the success of his clients. Three of Brett's clients have been placed on the Balanced Scorecard Hall of Fame by Drs. Kaplan and Norton.

**Caroline M. Lewis** is Director of Cross-Culture at Richard Lewis Communications, where she also delivers training and coaching in working effectively across cultures, with particular focus on Japan, Europe, Latin America and the US. Her diverse cultural and linguistic experience includes five formative years in Tokyo. She has a degree in Oriental Studies from the University of Oxford (Balliol College), and an MA in Comparative Literature from London University's School of Oriental and African Studies (SOAS).

**Richard D. Lewis** is Founder and Chairman of Richard Lewis Communications and one of Britain's foremost linguists and cross-cultural experts. Author of *When Cultures Collide* (1995, London: Nicholas Brealey), he pioneered the Lewis Model of Cross Culture now regarded as one of the most practical and intuitive approaches to cultural difference and interaction. His contribution to the field of cross culture has been recognised by many awards, including a Knighthood from the Government of Finland, and the SIETAR Founders' Award for 'outstanding commitment and service to the intercultural field', in 2015.

**Karen Lynas** was Managing Director of the National Health Service (NHS) Leadership Academy. As a founding member of the Academy, Karen has been instrumental in the vision to support and develop all leaders in the NHS, creating a climate of care and compassion and improving patient outcomes and their experience of the health service. To date, the Academy has offered leadership development to over 35,000 participants.

**Graham Manville** is Senior Lecturer in Business and Management and Director for Employability and Innovation in Norwich Business School at the University of East Anglia, UK. He holds a PhD in Corporate Performance Management from the University of Southampton (UK). In addition he also holds an MBA and is both an Incorporated Engineer and a Certified Management Consultant. He has won several research awards including the Best Knowledge Transfer Partnership (KTP) for the South West of England and an Emerald Literati Award for an Outstanding Journal Paper. His latest award was for a Best Developmental Paper at the BAM 2015 conference. Graham has more than 25 publications in international conferences, journals including two books and has guest edited a special issue international journal on performance management. Graham is also a Director of Longview Consulting Ltd, a boutique consultancy serving multi-sector clients.

**Olga Matthias** is Senior FME Fellow and Senior Lecturer in Operations Management. Olga is Head of the Operations and Information Management Department in the Faculty of Management and Law at the University of Bradford, UK. She holds a DBA, having researched how consulting firms can provide a more customised service to their clients. In addition, she is a Certified Management Consultant. She has had over 35 publications comprising international conferences, journals and book chapters. Olga is also Director of Capability Gap Ltd, a boutique performance optimisation consultancy serving multi-sector clients.

**Alejandra Marin** is an assistant professor focusing on management at SolBridge International School of Business. Her research interests centre on building and testing theory about organisations and organising collective processes in the early stages of their creation and implementation. To date, her research has appeared in entrepreneurship, leadership, business ethics, and innovation-related peer-reviewed journals. Alejandra is Colombian but she teaches and researches worldwide.

**Jason Paul Mika** is a Senior Lecturer in the School of Management, Massey University, Palmerston North, New Zealand, and is a director of Te Au Rangahau, the Māori Business & Leadership Research Centre. Jason is of the Tūhoe, Ngāti Awa, Whakatōhea, and Ngāti Kahungunu tribes. Jason is a former management consultant whose research interests centre on indigenous entrepreneurship, indigenous management theory and indigenous methodologies in business research. Jason's doctoral research was on the role of publicly funded enterprise assistance in Māori entrepreneurship in Aotearoa, New Zealand.

**Oliver Rodway** has been a learning and development manager in financial services for 16 years, and has worked an additional five years in the industry in operations management. Working for top-tier UK and global companies, he has specialised in developing training programmes for all levels of employees, from graduate intake to executive development. He has expertise in employee skill and behavioural development, having been a certified practitioner in De Bono's Six Thinking Hats, Myer Briggs Type Indicator and Neuro Linguistic Programming. He is a regular contributor to Industry Benchmark and working groups.

**Rod Scott** is a partner at Oakland Consulting and one of the founding members of The Oakland Institute for Business Research and Education. He has more than 20 years' experience helping organisations to improve the quality, cost and delivery of their products and services, primarily through Lean performance improvement, process-driven transformation, business model redesign and managing organisational change. Rod's consulting experience covers a wide range of clients across both the private and public sectors, including central and local government, executive agencies and private sector service providers to the public sector.

**Lorraine Warren** joined Massey University, New Zealand at the Manawatu campus in 2014 as a professor of innovation and entrepreneurship. Prior to that, she was Director of the Centre for Strategic Innovation at the University of Southampton's School of Management, also responsible for campus-wide strategic developments in entrepreneurship and innovation research, teaching and consultancy. She is an expert in systems-based consultancy, working with a wide range of organisations, large and small, public and private.

**Henry Xu** is a lecturer in the UQ Business School, The University of Queensland, Australia. He majored in mechanical engineering for his undergraduate and postgraduate studies, and obtained his PhD at Imperial College London with a research focus on supply chain management. His research interests include supply chain integration and coordination, disruption management in distributed supply networks and sustainable supply chains. His publications have appeared in the *International Journal of Production Economics*, *International Journal of Production Research* and *Journal of Manufacturing Systems*, among others.

# Foreword

As I write at the beginning of 2017, the global economy is contemplating the implications of enormous political and economic change. The outcome of the "Brexit" referendum in the United Kingdom, the US election of President Trump and possible results of elections in major European countries, are defying the expectations of policy experts and traditional market research methods.

The uncertainty around possible impacts could bring both opportunities and threats to organisations. Historic and long-negotiated trade deals no longer underpin the relative stability of current markets, and in this new era terms such as globalisation and national protectionism could take on new meaning and resonance.

The recently elected leaders of major governments will be setting policy directions which will certainly have a major impact on the already important aspects of doing business globally. Issues such as the freedom of movement of workers across Europe, access to markets and trade tariffs, and possible wholescale changes to regulations affecting business in local and international markets will likely change the business landscape for a generation.

In addition to these social and political changes, there is also the speed and impact of technological development, resulting in yet more new opportunities and challenges for organisations not only in terms of new value propositions, jobs and even greater prosperity, but also perhaps unfortunately in terms of uncertainty as a result of jobs disappearing and a new work revolution because of artificial intelligence or robotic technology.

The role of management consultancy has never been more important as a vehicle for enabling organisations to navigate their way through these uncharted waters.

Throughout this uncertainty, consultancy needs to remain true to "the practice of creating value for organisations", the definition offered by the Management Consultancies Association. Even as consultancy practices rise and fall as a result of their own economic success, the image of the profession remains dependent on delivering real value to clients, and consistent with the old consulting paradigm of Listen – Think – Consult – Act. The value in professional and personal relationships with clients will be tested as always, but good consulting practice demands that this remains both a thought-provoking and honest profession.

This book provides empirical insight for how management consultants have led and can continue to lead the way in an era of constant change. It is an exciting and thought-provoking edition to the field of management consultancy as it brings together both academia and practice in a unique way. The first part of the book provides the academic discourse written in a rigorous and yet accessible format by scholars at leading universities with consultancy backgrounds. The second part of the book provides compelling case studies from senior management consultants from around the world in a variety of sectors.

The management consultancy contributors vary from boutique consultancies to global management consultancy firms. The depth of analysis and the richness of the empirical evidence in these studies sets this book apart from others in this arena.

With its unique approach, this book will be useful for inquisitive managers, graduate students studying consultancy as part of their MBA and anyone engaging a management consultant for the first time. It also provides a unique contribution to academic theory as I believe this book bridges the academic community and the business world.

*Hans Groothius*
*Executive Director People Advisory Services, EY, Europe*

# Introduction

Since its inception towards the end of the nineteenth century, and its rapid growth throughout the twentieth century, management consultancy has come to permeate modern corporations and strongly influence their performance. It has become the aspirational career choice of many ambitious undergraduate and MBA students, such is its lure. Yet it was only in the 1990s that the study of management consulting began to gain concerted attention from academia.

The field of management consulting research has grown rapidly in the last twenty-five years. Fuelled by the drivers of complexity and uncertainty, a growing number of organisations are looking at the management consulting profession to assist them in navigating this pervasive change. The challenges that organisations face are both micro and geopolitical in nature. For example geopolitical factors relate to cultural assimilation of globalized organizations or the delivery of public services in a climate of rising expectations and ever-constraining budgets. Organisations also need to manage their core competencies and employee talent by addressing the challenges of a millennial (Generation Y) workforce.

During the 1960s, when consultancy became an international industry, the level of change was relatively incremental. Back then, the culture of a job for life and single employer careers was widespread. As this book goes to print in 2017, organizations are witnessing simultaneous technological innovation, globalization of business tempered with uncertainty and national protectionism from sovereign countries. The shifting kaleidoscope of the macro environmental factors such as politics, regulation, the economy, socio-cultural factors and technology are creating both opportunities and threats. At this uncertain and yet exciting time, the management consultancy profession has a pivotal role to play in helping their clients to navigate the organisations through safe passage whilst ensuring that their core competences have strategic renewal and invigoration in order to meet the challenges and opportunities that the twenty-first century offers to business. As we approach the first quarter of the century, the only thing we can say with great certainty is that throughout the twenty-first century, as previously, the only constant is change.

Management consulting is a multi-faceted business sector and is context dependent. The context is affected by size, sector, geography, linguistic culture and for-profit/not-for-profit; therefore consulting solutions are not a one-size-fits-all approach. Management consulting has flourished throughout the twentieth century by attracting the highest calibre graduates from leading universities. Despite this presence of talent, management consulting can often receive criticism from a number of viewpoints. From a practitioner perspective, management consultancy has not always delivered "what it said on the tin". Managing client expectation is just as important as the solution that the consultants provide.

In an academic context, particularly at research universities, there has been limited research that has provided symbiotic value to both the business community and academia. Often, it is viewed as a zero sum game — that is, one party benefits at the expense of the other. For example, with respect to management consultancy research, for publication in the higher ranking journals that renowned(?) academic researchers publish in, the language appears verbose and inaccessible to the business community, even to readers with an MBA. The consequence is that few business people read this research. Alternatively, the consultancy output is valued by the client/business community, but is deemed to be valued only by academia.

The published outputs of the practitioner community are commonly referred to as "airport books" where the solutions to business issues are prescriptive with a one size fits all and formulaic approaches. Another type of management consulting publication is the process-based approach to consulting, which provides methodological approaches to consulting but does not illustrate the different contexts and richness of management consulting.

This book seeks to bridge the gap between high quality academic research and case study research by providing impactful and insightful case studies in an accessible yet academically rigorous format. The book draws contributions from five continents: North America, Europe, Asia, Australasia and Africa, and brings together experts from the academic community who have the dual credibility of being researchers at respected university business schools and who have had long careers in management consulting.

The editors believe that this volume will be an essential read for academics, policy makers, MBA students and managers. The book is split into two sections; Part I is applied academic discourse on management consultancy with contributions from academics at leading universities who had previous careers in management consultancy. Part II provides a selection of case studies from the management consultancy profession. The international contributions are from a variety of contexts, and include leading consultancy practices, international boutique consultancies as well as large organizations and independent consultants.

# Part I

# Applied academic discourse

## Introduction to Part I

During the 1990s, the study of management consulting began to gain concerted attention from academia. Early research tended to be of the 'critical' school, largely because of the costs associated with consultants and their image as purveyors of dreams, dramaturgy, myths and story-making. Since then it has also become a highly researched industry, but little still exists that is observational, reflective or participative. This section addresses that gap and the chapters presented in this section provide a variety of perspectives on consultancy, including applied theoretical insights, that will hopefully encourage the reader to consider the profession and its practitioners in a new light, or possibly different lights.

The contributions are from academics who are, or have been, practising management consultants and who also teach management consultancy to university students, and from an invited selection of senior consultants from boutique, mid-size and global consultancy practices. The insights and shared practice by the contributors provide both a critical discourse about the industry today, a narrative considering practical implementation and the challenges and responses to that. Each contribution seeks to provide a unique perspective on the practice of management consultancy from a variety of contexts while contributing to and drawing from theoretical insights.

In the first chapter, Fouweather presents a positioning piece, considering consultancy through the lens of the gods of ancient Greece, specifically Hermes, the messenger and the god of travellers. It draws on the contradictory character of Hermes to create a mythically inspired bricolage that illuminates the 'Janus-faced reality' of consultancy: organisations seek out consultants to dispense wisdom and provide direction in the collective struggle for survival despite a dislike of the perceived use of a 'one size fits all' approach to clients. The many faces of management consultancy are explored in the chapters that follow. In Chapter 2, Agrey and Xu discuss the concept of stylised facts and how they influence the delivery of consultancy services, an approach to researching the industry and its constituent parts and as a mechanism for developing management consultancy theory. This should go some way to formalising a theoretical contribution regarding a sector which is still regarded as new. Bal and de Jong present an interesting discussion in Chapter 3 regarding adopting a human-oriented approach to consulting that could create value in a different way to present service delivery, where the focus is predominantly on standardisation and commodification. This of course has implications for knowledge accessing, acquisition, exchange and creation, all of which are key reasons why firms build or enter networks with other firms. Cordier, Marin and Cader discuss this at length in Chapter 4. Obviously, the role the client organisation plays in this, as well as their choice of consulting partner, influences method and outcome. As an internal consultant, knowledge accessing and creation plays a different role. Power and the nature of influencing the client cannot be the same, neither in reach nor depth. Yet, as Hodges explains in Chapter 5, there are unique features which make internal consulting a useful addition to the pantheon of delivery models. In Chapter 6, Scott and Matthias dissect current delivery models within the public sector and the multiple findings regarding success or otherwise in that arena. Their chapter ends with a number of proposals to improve commissioning, contracting and managing projects in the public sector for better outcomes. Chapter 7 examines the symbiotic relationship between the client, management skills of the consultant and the application and relevance of robust research methods to solve client problems in a value adding way. Manville Chudasama compares the research demands placed upon a conventional academic researcher and a consultant engaged on a typical assignment. Finally, Matthias and Campbell in Chapter 8 present how a consulting approach is adopted by MBA students for their learning, and how they later apply their newly learnt theory to practical situations provided by companies who work with universities for mutual benefit.

# 1 The management consultant

## The Hermes of our time

*Ian Fouweather*

## Abstract

Our need for certainty in an uncertain world is not new, but the narratives we choose must resonate with the times we imagine. In the twenty-first century, management discourses focus on rapid technological and societal changes to highlight a radically open future that is fundamentally different from the past. Where once oracles used the exploits of Zeus, Apollo and Dionysus to dispense wisdom and provide direction in our collective struggle for survival, we now look elsewhere. With the rise of scientific management in the early twentieth century, the corporate world and public institutions have looked to management consultants to provide the certainty they require. Not surprisingly with its rise, commentators and critics have sought to understand the nature of the industry and why it has become such a significant part of the business environment. Paradoxically, despite over twenty-five years of writing and many authoritative voices, the nature of the industry remains vague (Harvey et al., 2016). To shed light on why this might be this chapter draws on Greek mythology and the god Hermes, the fleet footed traveller dispatched from the heavens to dispense knowledge and wisdom to mortals on Earth - the first consultant

## Introduction

The consultant Merron (2005: 7) acknowledged that his clients often wanted him "to wave a magic wand over them". During the last forty years, the demand for corporate wand-waving has grown rapidly (Armbrüster, 2006; Poulfelt et al., 2010). Accompanying this rise has been a corresponding growth in writing on consulting practice (Pang et al., 2013). From describing and defining the industry, writers have moved on to evaluate the value and efficacy of the industry and/or profession (Hicks et al., 2009). Mainstream literature (typified by writers such as O'Shea and Madigan (1998) and Pinault (2000)) has highlighted the danger that consulting poses, exposing its murkier side. This chapter does not offer a magic wand, a theory of what consulting is or claim to expose the myth of consulting to which Clark (1995) alluded. Nor does it provide a totalising narrative written from the perspective of an industry expert or a scholarly academic who claims to provide the truth. As Heidegger (2013) acknowledged, Aletheia (or Veritas), the elusive goddess of truth, is misunderstood. She is not the arbitrator of the "correctness of vision" (truth as correspondence), but the one who discloses the nature of reality. Rather than providing certainty, this essay uses the often contradictory character of Hermes to create a mythically inspired bricolage that further illuminates the ambiguity of consulting, what Buono (2009) termed the "Janus-faced reality" of the industry.

## The power of the gods

The idea of stepping back into a magical past to explore the modern industry of management consultancy might be a paradox to some. Unconstrained by the apparent certainties that both consultants and academics strive to provide, ancient myths are awash with magic, the supernatural and contradictions. Yet there are parallels between the contemporary narratives that shape how we understand organizations and the flights of fancy found in much older stories. As Feibleman (1944: 118) has highlighted: "All knowledge is of the nature of partial truths, or myths, while so called myths are simply partial truths whose partial falsehood has been exposed". Academics, business writers and journalists may use different styles of writing in the twenty-first century, but many contemporary myths draw on a collective past. How many times has a corporate Icarus flown too close to the sun? Promethean metaphors are marshalled to explore the good and bad of technological innovation (Puschmann and Burgess, 2014) and the impact such innovation has on the global economic system (Landes, 2003). Successful entrepreneurs, innovators and speculators are bestowed with a Midas Touch. Similarly, our corporate titans are happy to draw their names from the ancient pantheon. Amazon, Mars, Nike, Olympus and Oracle all look to the gods, and what better name for a brand of luxury travel goods than Hermes the god of travellers? Yet the influence of classical mythology goes beyond selecting brand names and appropriating metaphors. As has already been acknowledged, Buono (2009) used the imagery of Janus, the two-faced Roman God of both time and contradiction, but Buono was not the first. Handy's (1978) *Gods of management: How they work, and why they will fail*, marshalled four Greek gods to shed new light on different forms of management. Two decades later Handy (1995) updated his ideas (though not his gods). Cowsill and Grint (2008) followed suit, employing Orpheus, Prometheus and Janus to explore contemporary leadership styles. Gabriel (2004) brought together several authors (including Gehmann, Grint, Guerrier, Höpfl, and Winstanley) in an attempt to show how a pantheon of mythical actors might shape our understanding of contemporary organizations. At the same time, Sturdy et al. (2004) and Clegg et al. (2004a, 2004b) created a scholarly dialogue exploring the nature of consulting from the (dis)comfort of a rather overcrowded *Procrustean Bed*. Procrustes was a mythical blacksmith, who was happy to offer passing travellers a bed for the night. The smith, who had made the bed from iron, found his guests did not fit his bed. To resolve the problem, Procrustes used his blacksmith's tools to amputate the limbs of those who were too tall, and stretched the limbs of those who were too short (as if on a medieval rack). As in so many myths, justice ensued. The heroic mortal Theseus killed the blacksmith, forcing him to lie in his own bed where he suffered the same treatment that his victims had suffered. The story draws attention to the tendency of consultants to apply predefined generic tools and techniques when working with clients. Just as with Procrustes, a "one size fits all" approach fails to embrace the needs of the particular client, with potentially dire consequences. Merron (2005) reused the same Procrustean metaphor to reinforce the shortcomings of the "one size fits all" approach to consulting.

Yet the question remains, why use ancient fantastical stories when we have modern research and empirical evidence at hand? Gabriel (2004: 20) asked: "But is it possible for fiction to be truer than reality?" Ancient myths, he argues, "reveal a deeper truth, that pertains to the general rather than the specific". Within such stories truth is revealed by drawing parallels with the present, in order to make sense of the current situation and to imagine how the future might unfold.

Yet the question remains, "Why Hermes?" Out of all the mythological characters, be they gods or titans, mortal heroes or mythical beasts, what makes Hermes the most suitable travelling companion? Whilst Buono (2009) used Janus with his two faces, the choice of characters available within the ancient pantheon is huge.[1] Procrustes has already been mentioned. Handy referred to Zeus, king of the gods. The all-powerful and omniscient Zeus might be a suitable choice for the big consulting firms offering strategic wisdom to the world's largest corporations. Apollo, god of reason and medicine, could represent the technical expert offering diagnoses and cures to ailing companies. In the titan Prometheus, who enraged Zeus with his repeated trickery, we can see the consultant who "steals your watch and then tells you the time" (Kihn, 2005). We might even want to embrace the harm that consultants can cause and look to Hades, god of the underworld and bringer of earthquakes, who according to Sophocles grew rich on the tears of mortals. Alternatively, to question the status of consultants as experts one could look to Koalemos, the spirit of stupidity and foolishness. All these characters have merit, but it is Hermes who best reflects the contradictory and sometimes confusing world of management consultancy.

## The many faces of business consulting

The growth and significance of management consulting is well documented (McKenna, 1995; Ernst and Kieser, 2002; Kipping and Clark, 2012; David et al., 2013), but quite what consulting involves is open to debate. A range of approaches have been adopted to attempt to make sense of consulting. Authors (such as Kipping, 2002) have created historical chronologies that describe the origins of the profession and its evolution. Topological approaches map the consulting terrain (Faulconbridge and Jones, 2012), establishing boundaries between a range of discrete functions. Similarly, typologies and frameworks disaggregate and aggregate the role of consultants and the different types of consultancy firms. Models of the client-consultant relationship have been developed to understand the function of consultants (see Nikolova et al., 2009). Elsewhere we find a host of metaphorical roles from rain makers, to brain surgeons, to mountain lions (Maister, 2007). Many "how to" books tap into the demand of aspiring consultants for practical advice. Typically, these present consultants as change agents skilfully using a range of (sometimes Procrustean) tools that claim to transform organizations. Although sometimes dismissed, such texts are significant in shaping our collective perception of consultants, and hybrid texts (Wickham and Wilcock, 2016) seek to combine the theoretical and the practical for a more intellectual readership. Critical evaluations of both the practices and efficacy of the profession add a further layer of understanding and complexity. Work by authors such as Clark and Greatbatch (2011) makes us aware of the performative or theatrical nature of consulting: the actors, the costumes and props, even the smoke and mirrors (Stewart, 2009) used by magicians (Fincham, 2000) or conjurors to draw their audience in. Whilst Sturdy and Gabriel (2000) present consultants relatively benignly as salesmen, Fincham and Clark (2002) call into question their wares, recognising their reputation as purveyors of snake oil. Clegg et al. (2004a) present consultants as parasites, and whilst this might allow for a benign (Jackall, 1988) or symbiotic relationship between client and consultant (Sturdy and Wright, 2011), these metaphors challenge less critical representations of the industry. Elsewhere the role of consultant as apolitical change agent (or as Maister, 2004 suggested, midwives of change) is questioned. Consultants are visionaries (Alvesson and Sveningsson, 2003), mystics and seers, and labels such as guru (Jackson, 2001; Groß et al., 2015), missionary (Wright and Kitay, 2004) and preacher (Whittle, 2005) implicitly question their knowledge claims and status. There are also many journalistic exposés that reveal the worst excesses of consulting (Mickelthwait and Wooldridge, 1997; O'Shea and Madigan, 1998; Ashford, 1998; Pinault, 2000; Craig, 2005; Kihn, 2005; Phelan, 2013).

   Whittle (2006: 434) goes some of the way to explain these multiple interpretations by introducing the concepts of repertoires, which acknowledges that consultants adopt a variety of roles that may not reflect "any underlying or stable stance, attitude or approach".

Perhaps as a result, it is not surprising that management consulting appears to have become a web of contradictions and paradoxes maintained by an ever-expanding polyphony of voices, whether they belong to academics or practitioners. Why an industry apparently built upon knowledge and founded upon the principles of scientific management, objective analysis and the application of theory should appear so varied might itself appear paradoxical. Conceptualising consultancy as a knowledge-based occupation (Muzio et al., 2011) in which knowledge is produced and distributed to customers might remove the contradictions and paradoxes.

However, rather than seeing these contradictions as problematic and urging consensus, it is possible to take a different position. Whitehead's (1938) Fallacy of the Perfect Dictionary problematises the quest to create a single definitive interpretation. If the truth of consulting is to be revealed, it may not be found by selecting one of these many voices, or distilling a single version from them all. Rather, it may be found in the space between them. Hermes, god of transitions and boundaries will guide the reader through this contested space.

## Step forward Apollo?

A perfect definition of consulting might be unachievable because to "consult" is simply to meet in order to obtain advice, as we might consult a lawyer or a doctor (Maister, 2004). Thus, a management consultant is someone to whom clients go when they are faced with a management problem and want information and advice in order to resolve it. Kipping (2002) offers an evolution of consultancy services, indicating that three strands of work have emerged within the industry. He suggests the industry now provides support for clients in operational improvement, strategic direction and project management. Although this recognises some diversification of role, Kipping's functionalist narrative suggests that the consultant remains the knowledgeable and trusted advisor. From this perspective, management consulting seems to owe more to Hermes's wiser elder brother Apollo, than to the mischievous silver-tongued traveller and cattle thief who skips between heaven and earth on winged sandals. Already acknowledged by Charles Handy (1978), Apollo is the god of knowledge, reason and rationality, the bringer of light and truth, dispenser of wisdom, mirroring the role of the archetypal consultant who provides "the latest management wisdom" (Engwall and Kipping, 2013: 86).

It should also be recognised that Apollo is the patron of doctors because of his ability to heal the sick. Echoing Turner (1982), Nikolova et al. (2009) emphasise the importance of consultants diagnosing client problems, whilst Zerfass and Franke (2013) explicitly use the term doctor referring to Broom and Smith's (1979) concept of an *expert prescriber*. Similarly Clegg et al. (2004a) and Mohe and Seidl (2011) refer to Schein's (1988) "doctor-patient" model suggesting that consultants act as metaphorical doctors treating sick businesses. Schein (1988) gives us the concept of *organisational therapists*. Fincham and Clark (2002) echo the medical metaphors, suggesting the role of the consultant might be "to diagnose organisational illnesses and prescribe appropriate remedies". It is, however, Maister (2004) who captures this concept most fully. Beginning with the medical metaphor of anatomy to explore the nature of consulting, he goes on to identify four discrete roles of consultants drawn from the healthcare profession. Depending on their specific role, consultants are pharmacists, nurses, brain surgeons and psychotherapists. And yet Maister's typology highlights that whilst these might be healing roles, they are not those of a diagnostic consultant. Each provides an intervention and hopefully a cure, but the healing must be preceded by a diagnosis. Fincham and Clark (2002) seem to mobilise their metaphors most effectively, echoing Turner (1982) and Schein's (1988) emphasis on clinical diagnosis, but even they concede that the doctor (or healer) metaphor only captures some aspects of consulting and that it can be found wanting.

By emphasising knowledge, reason and healing, Apollo might appear the epitome of the modern-day consultant. Yet advice is not knowledge (it can be given with little direct knowledge). Rather, advice is given (or emerges) from within a dialogic interaction. When effective, this process enables the client to make sense of the situation in which they find themselves. Thus understood, the consultant is not a modern-day Delphic oracle, a manifestation of Apollo who knows all and sees into the future. Rather, the consultant is a shrewd and persuasive messenger, bringing news from outside, a modern day Hermes bringing messages from the gods, including those from a wiser, but perhaps less convincing, Apollo. It is in Hermes, god of boundaries and transitions, who travelled from the heavens to walk among mortals bringing gifts that we have a companion with whom we might travel.

Apollo, god of Wisdom, should not be forgotten, however, because the sibling rivalry between the two brothers reveals much about our current understanding of consulting. As a number of academics (including O'Mahoney, 2007; Furusten, 2013; Frandsen et al., 2013) have acknowledged, there is a degree of tension between academics and consultants. McKenna (1995, 2006) indicates that, originally, business consultants were smart guys from the Ivy League Business Schools who saw an opportunity to make money helping businesses exploit the techniques and theories developed and formalised with academic endeavours. Although not always expressed directly, for some academic writers the status and authority of the learned academic as expert has been usurped by the sharp suit and slick presentations of the upstart management consultant. Perhaps understandably, this generates a degree of negativity, which might not always lead to impartial writing about the consulting industry. Despite a lack of direct empirical research on the consulting industry (Fincham and Clark, 2002), there is a huge amount of academic writing on the industry, and parts of it can often read like a concerted "demolition job" (Heller, 2002: 261). O'Mahoney and Markham (2013: 3) acknowledge that the success of the industry has created a "backlash amongst many journalists, academics and government watchdogs". Heller (2002: 262) suggests there are "very good reasons" why academics have "identified many anomalies, inconsistencies and deceitful procedures" within the industry. Whilst Heller's reasons may not be apparent, the tension is. In the ancient myths, the precocious infant Hermes hatches a devious plan to steal cattle from his elder and wiser brother Apollo. Hermes is confronted by his brother, but refuses to acknowledge the theft, and thus Apollo takes his brother to their father Zeus. Denying the charge, Hermes uses clever oratory to present himself as the falsely accused, innocent party. Omniscient Zeus is not fooled, ordering that Hermes return the cattle to their rightful owner. However, the young Hermes shows he is quick of mind and skilled in the art of barter as he immediately regains the cattle by trading them with Apollo for a lyre he has just made. In another tale, Hermes's kleptomania is evident when he steals Apollo's Golden Bow. Elsewhere, Hermes shows his business acumen and persuasiveness when he cuts a flute from the reeds and plays a sweet melody for his brother. Apollo is so infatuated with the music that he trades his golden wand for the flute. If Merron's (2005) anecdote is accepted, Apollo's wand is very much in demand and is used by the Hermes of our time. Heller (2002) acknowledges that, despite the tension, there is a symbiotic relationship between academics and consultants as creators and sellers of knowledge. There appears a similar relationship between Apollo, the lover of knowledge and music, and Hermes, his quick thinking younger brother. Apollo might not always like his younger brother's trickery, but he is enthralled and is perhaps just a little jealous of the wonderful noises that Hermes can make. For his own part, the mischievous Hermes seems to take delight in antagonising his elder, more learned and occasionally pompous, brother, but nevertheless he covets his possessions.

## Consultants: more than just tricksters

The image of consultants as tricksters, showmen, obscurants, illusionists or magicians (Clark, 1995; Clark and Salaman, 1998a; Ashford, 1998; Fincham and Clark, 2002; Gbada-mosi, 2005) is so well established that it cannot be ignored. Presented with the evidence the accused will be found guilty and punished (just as Zeus did when he fell victim to Prometheus' trickery), it is easy to paint consultants as silver-tongued thieves who have mastered the art of persuasion. Just as the archetypal consultant steals the client's watch to tell them the time (Kihn, 2005), so Hermes dupes the gullible Apollo. Hermes is a love-able rogue, a charmer, a romantic itinerant happy to bring a little mischief wherever he momentarily stops. But Hermes is also a guide and protector of those travelling in strange and unfamiliar lands. Like Hermes, the consultant has many tasks to perform. To try and fit the profession of consulting (if indeed it is one), into a Procrustean Bed is foolhardy. To some, consultants are one-trick ponies, rehashing the same old ideas wherever they find themselves, but one size definitely does not fit all when it comes to the practice of consulting.

## Hermes the traveller

Lift the lid on almost any organization and there is evidence of consultants and the stories they have woven. From hotels to hospitals, farms to foundries, banks to butchers, there seems no corporate corridor that the consultant has not walked. Nor is there a boardroom that has not echoed the sound of a consultant's self-assured voice. Clearly, the business consultant is an inveterate traveller, a peripatetic expert, with briefcase, overnight bag and laptop, ready to journey wherever he or she is needed – a travelling salesperson peddling wares from door to door.

Despite this intrinsic aspect of consulting, few writers seem to consider the significance of travel. Greenwood and Empson (2003), Corso et al. (2009) and Swan et al. (2016) recognise the peripatetic nature of the work, but there are few others. Whittle's (2008) work on flexible working does shed some light on the topic, but it is not exhaustive. In Gill's (2015: 314) empirical work, one respondent acknowledged with perhaps a degree of understatement that "You're away from home a lot of the time". One of Meriläinen et al.'s (2004) participants was more explicit: "There's a huge amount of travel". Despite these glimpses, the focus of most writers seems to be on mobility and impermanence of identity and career, which are often framed in terms of precariousness (Alvesson and Robertson, 2006; Sturdy et al., 2006; Alvesson et al., 2009). However, in O'Mahoney's (2007: 288) work, the writer reflects upon his time working in the profession and we do see the impact of travel:

> This geographical flexibility, whilst exciting for the first few months, was often cited by many consultants as their primary complaint about the work. Home, for many, became little more than an abstract notion. I was rarely home and even when I was there, I was generally asleep or working having eaten, exercised and socialised at the client site.

Like Hermes with his winged sandals, the idea of being stationary is alien to many consult-ants. They learn to jump between worlds, and they become addicted to the lifestyle. When the client calls, off they go. Whilst occasionally acknowledging the stress and challenges of travel, the alternative appears far worse. For O'Mahoney (2007: 289), this meant time on "'death row': a secure environment where, if you stayed for too long, you were likely to be dispatched". And yet whilst there are challenges in this nomadic career, there is ambivalence too (Kitay and Wright, 2007: 1637). Always "moving on" in search of new clients and new projects, travel takes the consultant to unfamiliar places offering both opportunities and threats. The absence of routine and the precarious identity (O'Mahoney, 2007) created by the requirement to constantly switch roles (Whittle, 2006) may generate existential pressure, but it is intrinsic to what consultants do. For some consultants perhaps change is a necessity as new clients and new locations open up the possibility of new adventures for the fleet-footed Hermes.

With travel comes movement and change. Kitay and Wright (2007) refer to it as a boundary-less career, both in terms of the precariousness of careers and the mobility required. However, drawing from the work of Whittle (2006) and Sturdy et al. (2009), it is not boundary-less but rather one in which multiple boundaries are maintained through constant renegotiation. Maister (2004: 36) acknowledges many practicing consultants are schooled in occupying the intellectual "high ground of detached, logical analysis", where a veneer of objective professionalism maintains a boundary between client and consultant. But as projects evolve, the client-consultant relationship may well change and adapt through an ongoing series of social interactions (Nikolova et al., 2009). Movement is constant. Boundaries are crossed and constantly redrawn. New clients, new roles and new locations mean that the consultant must be skilled at crossing boundaries and managing transitions, be they spatial or relational. Clients become colleagues, projects shift, personnel move on. Consultants might be midwives (Maister, 2004), delivering change within other organisations, but if we slightly alter the metaphor, they are also mothers of invention, constantly adapting to changes in their own working environments, establishing or reestablishing roles. The consultant needs Hermes at his side as he moves across boundaries and through transitions.

## Hermes the charmer

One of Hermes gifts was to give external voice to our inner thoughts. Hermes interpreted the laws of Zeus (logos) for mortals and so brought words to man. Thus he is the inventor of language and ruler of wise words as he was instructed by his father to reveal the truth to mortals. Yet this master communicator was also a devious and persuasive speaker whose clever use of oratory fooled his knowledgeable brother Apollo. The patron of poets, literature, wit and oratory, Hermes has a way with words. He is a charmer and uses words to do his bidding, happily walking the boundary between truth and lies, fact and fantasy. Whilst consultants are not simply silver-tongued tricksters, Hermes is an expert communicator who is willing to bend the truth to suit his own agenda. Like the archetypal sharp-suited consultants that Kihn (2005) describes, dressed in expensive sandals and carrying a designer satchel, Hermes can convince all (save Zeus) that day is night and black is white.

Just like Hermes, Pang et al. (2013) place great store on language and communication. They argue that there are two perspectives apparent within academic writing on the industry. There are functionalist writers who consider consultants as apolitical transmitters of information, and there are critical writers who focus on how consultants gain legitimacy and status. If Pang et al.'s (2013) dichotomy is accepted, then it might be reasonable to conclude that the first perspective focusses on the knowledge that experts communicate, whilst the more critical scholars focus on the discourses and narratives that grant consultancy its position. One perspective considers what is communicated, the other how is it communicated.

Although interesting, this theoretical dichotomy has to be used carefully, because whilst the abstraction may reflect academics' concerns, it is also rather simplistic. As management ideas change, the knowledge that consultants deploy will change. As commentators (Huczynski, 1993; Whittle, 2008) have highlighted, the fads and fashions of management that consultants embrace and employ are in a continual state of flux. Even when a Procrustian "one size fits all" approach is evident, how that is communicated to clients is context dependent, in order for the one size to be accepted by the client. Compared to theorists, technical experts and researchers working in a knowledge-intensive environment, consultants are not pure knowledge workers. The "what" of consulting often receives relatively little focus from clients. As Starbuck (1992: 731) pointed out, clients often "believe their own knowledge to be inadequate, so they cannot judge the experts' advice". The job of a consultant is to convince the client of their own authority; that they, or their company, are the ones who can diagnose and fix the problem. To fulfil this role, a consultant must have credibility, and the client must believe that the consultant has the wisdom and/ or knowledge they seek. Thus, a successful consultant (as opposed to a technical expert) needs to be a skilled communicator or social actor who is able to use a repertoire of linguistic practices to create a response that is both meaningful and credible to the client and the client's organization. It is only when the client has been convinced that they have a great magician (or at least a competent one) in front of them, that Merron's (2005) wand can be waved to create the requisite magic. The consultant must be able to present him or herself as a modern-day Hermes, a messenger who can disseminate the will of the gods to the mortals amongst whom he moves.

Sutter and Kieser (2015) build on Carlile (2002, 2004) to consider the knowledge boundaries that exist between organizations before exploring the linguistic barriers that exist between the "different thought worlds" (Carlile, 2004: 442) of the client and consultant. Using Orlikowski (2002) and Luhmann's theory of communication (Mohe and Seidl, 2011), Sutter and Kieser (2015) conceptualise the client and the consultant organization as two discrete social systems. The transfer of knowledge between such systems is far from straightforward (Werr and Stjernberg, 2003) because, put simply, the two do not *speak the same language*. Although both may share the same formal language or use and be conversant in a common language, syntactic, semantic and pragmatic barriers (Carlile, 2004) exist and make things far more difficult than they might appear. The first of these barriers is encountered when words that one party uses are not familiar to the other. The second, when words are used in different ways. And the third barrier relates to differing priorities between the parties. All three are common when working as a consultant. Within an unfamiliar organization, an outsider may hear the equivalent of Chomsky's (1956) "colorless green ideas sleep furiously". Whilst the clients are clearly speaking English, all of Carlile's three barriers conspire against the consultant so that whilst the individual words are recognised, establishing the meaning of the utterances becomes impossible. As Kieser and Wellstein (2008: 504) acknowledged, whilst the "consultants stay inside the client firm for a certain time and form teams with members of the client organization they remain part of the client's environment". Sensitivity to these barriers is essential for a consultant, and learning how to appreciate the subtleties of language and communication (whether it be their own or those of others) is a key skill. Like any seasoned traveller, the experienced consultant becomes a skilled communicator, sensitive to linguistic boundaries and having the ability to step over them with relative ease by using appropriate or common language (Werr and Stjernberg, 2003) that can bridge the linguistic gaps between two systems. Additionally, the consultant must possess the ability to listen (or perhaps appear to listen) to the client and to respond accordingly, giving appropriate advice that the client finds credible.

However, just like Hermes, the consultant is known for his use of rhetoric (Kitay and Wright, 2007) not necessarily his listening skills, and it is here that the literature has much to reveal. Academics have often focused on how consultants manage and shape perceptions using language. Several works provide examples of how language is deployed to influence clients: Kaarst-Brown (1999), Werr and Styhre (2003), Sturdy et al. (2009), Alvesson et al. (2009) and Sutter and Kieser (2015). Writers including Kornberger and Brown (2007), Styhre et al. (2010) and Alvesson and Sveningsson (2011), explore how the individual (consultant) uses language to shape his own *presentation of self* (Goffman, 1959, 1990) and thus how he projects himself to clients. Elsewhere, Clark and Salaman (1998a) explore "impression management," which focusses on the ongoing client-consultant interactions, and the "symbols of expertise" (Starbuck, 1992), which consultants rely upon – such as statistical analysis, testimony of other experts, jargon, appearance and demeanour – to influence how they are perceived by clients. Although the last of these may not appear to be linguistic, the quality of a suit communicates information about an individual, and the skilled rhetorician knows this, whether he or she is a politician or consultant.

By the same token, these "tricks of the trade" become ammunition for the more critical observer. The social commentator Will Rogers suggested that an expert is "a man fifty miles from home with a briefcase," emphasising both the importance of impression management and the need to maintain professional distance and boundaries. Distance confers status, proximity removes it. Under the microscope, the symbols and signs used to manage impressions become the tools of the con artist. Under such scrutiny, the apparently knowledgeable expert might be reimagined as a parasite (Clegg et al., 2004b), bringing a plague upon the organisation.

Communication and language are thus cast as both hero and villain (Bosma et al., 2016). Language provides an imperfect boundary between two social systems, that of the client and the consultant. Without effective language skills, the consultant cannot communicate knowledge in a way that is meaningful to the client. Without using language to charm and persuade, the consultant will not be invited to cross the boundary and enter into the client's organisation. At the same time, the plasticity and ambiguity of language can make consultants appear as sophists (Czarniawska-Joerges et al., 1990) or charlatans (Bloomfield and Danieli, 1995; Groß et al., 2015) to a critical onlooker. Indeed, as Starbuck (1992) acknowledged, consultants often knowingly use jargon to obscure their meaning – as if deliberately using an incomprehensible language that only the gods (of management) can understand – and in doing so create an air of expertise.

Thus whilst Armbrüster (2006) draws our attention to the two perspectives seen in writing on consultants, disambiguating the two is impossible because they are inseparable within practice. The "what" and the "how" of consulting are enmeshed, and whilst the "how" is far more important than the "what", the consultant must weave the two together seamlessly. It is through skilled oratory and presentation that they are woven together, creating a language "for representing mutually acceptable ways of knowing, defining and talking about management, managers and organisations" (Clark and Salaman, 1998b: 147). Without this skill, consultants would find their work impossible.

Like it or not, the consultant must therefore have a silver tongue and be able to weave stories that an audience of mortals can understand and believe (or at least buy into). Focusing purely on the truth content of the consultant's stories is a failure to embrace the mythical nature of all our stories (Feibleman, 1944). Clegg et al. (2004a) point towards the work of Nietzche's (2006: 114):

> What then is truth? A movable host of metaphors, metonymies, and anthropomorphisms: in short, a sum of human relations which have been poetically and rhetorically intensified, transferred, and embellished, and which, after long usage, seem to a people to be fixed, canonical, and binding. Truths are illusions which we have forgotten are illusions – they are metaphors that have become worn . . .

Hermes does not fall in to the trap of differentiating truths from illusions; rather, he understands that they are pieces within Wittgenstein's *language-games*. Like their patron Hermes, effective and successful consultants are skilful players in this game of symbols and signs. It is these skills that allow consultants to cross the many boundaries they must negotiate and enter into the client's world, bringing the sort of stories that the client can believe in.

## Conclusion

Whether for good or for bad, management consultants have been around for over a century, and they look set to remain a feature of businesses and organisations for some time. Their prevalence may ebb and flow, as may their status, but our ongoing need for certainty means that organisations will seek advice and support (or diagnosis and cure) from outsiders professing to be experts.

As highly rewarded change agents, management consultants will always receive a hostile reception in some quarters, whilst being feted in others. This essay has not sought to arbitrate the value of consultants, or to disentangle the truth from the lies of consulting. Rather, it has embraced the contradictions and paradoxes of the "Janus-faced reality" of consultancy (Buono, 2009).

Whilst Apollo is the patron of knowledge and virtue, Hermes provides a character who reflects the many contradictions of consulting practice. With his winged sandals and rhetorical skills, Hermes represents the archetypal consultant, simultaneously a cattle thief and a skilled herdsman. Whether he is stealing or protecting Apollo's assets, is a matter of interpretation. An itinerant storyteller, he reveals both truths and lies, blurring the boundaries between heaven and earth, dreams and reality. A silver-tongued travelling salesman, his command of language can unlock doors and make the impossible seem probable. Even the knowing Apollo, god of reason, is taken in by his sweet-talking brother, only to be infuriated when his trickery and guile come to light.

Judging consultants is like judging Hermes. They display similar talents and neither hangs around in any one place for long, but as they travel through the world they mess around with established orders and as a result things change. Whether this represents a positive or negative is often unclear, but they'll probably be long gone by the time the dust settles. Both use poetic words to charm and beguile, but whether their words reveal the truth depends upon their audience

No wonder both are loved and hated in equal measure for, like Janus, they each have two faces, each presenting a different self. Like Apollo, we find it hard knowing what to make of this precocious trickster.

# Note

1 See Theoi.com, for an extensive list of the characters mentioned.

# References

Alvesson, M., Kärreman, D., Sturdy, A., and Handley, K. (2009). Unpacking the client(s): Constructions, positions and client – consultant dynamics. *Scandinavian Journal of Management*, 25(3), 253–263.

Alvesson, M., and Robertson, M. (2006). The best and the brightest: The construction, significance and effects of elite identities in consulting firms. *Organization*, 13(2), 195–224.

Alvesson, M., and Sveningsson, S. (2003). Good visions, bad micro-management and ugly ambiguity: Contradictions of (non-)leadership in a knowledge-intensive organization. *Organization Studies*, 24(6), 961–988.

Alvesson, M., and Sveningsson, S. (2011). Identity work in consultancy projects: Ambiguity and distribution of credit and blame. In C. N. Candlin and J. Crichton (eds.), *Discourses of deficit*. New York: Palgrave Macmillan, pp. 159–174.

Armbrüster, T. (2006). *The economics and sociology of management consulting*. Cambridge; New York: Cambridge University Press.

Ashford, M. (1998). *Con tricks: The shadowy world of management consultancy and how to make it work for you.* New York: Simon & Schuster.

Bloomfield, B. P., and Danieli, A. (1995). The role of management consultants in the development of information technology: The indissoluble nature of socio-political and technical skills. *Journal of Management Studies*, 32(1), 23–46.

Bosma, B., Chia, R., and Fouweather, I. (2016). Radical learning through semantic transformation: Capitalizing on novelty. *Management Learning*, 47(1), 14–27.

Broom, G. M., and Smith, G. D. (1979). Testing the practitioner's impact on clients. *Public Relations Review*, 5(3), 47–59.

Buono, A. F. (2009). *Emerging trends and issues in management consulting: Consulting as a Janus-faced reality*. Charlotte, NC: IAP.

Carlile, P. R. (2002). A pragmatic view of knowledge and boundaries: Boundary objects in new product development. *Organization Science*, 13(4), 442–455.

Carlile, P. R. (2004). Transferring, translating, and transforming: An integrative framework for managing knowledge across boundaries. *Organization Science*, 15(5), 555–568.

Chomsky, N. (1956). Three models for the description of language. *IRE Transactions on Information Theory*, 2(3), 113–124.

Clark, T. (1995). *Managing consultants: Consultancy as the management of impressions*. Managing work and organizations series. Buckingham; Bristol, PA: Open University Press.

Clark, T., and Greatbatch, D. (2011). Audience perceptions of charismatic and non-charismatic oratory: The case of management gurus. *The Leadership Quarterly*, 22(1), 22–32.

Clark, T., and Salaman, G. (1998a). Creating the 'Right' impression: Towards a dramaturgy of management consultancy. *The Service Industries Journal*, 18(1), 18–38.

Clark, T., and Salaman, G. (1998b). Telling tales: Management gurus' narratives and the construction of managerial identity. *Journal of Management Studies*, 35(2), 137–161.

Clegg, S. R., Kornberger, M., and Rhodes, C. (2004a). Noise, parasites and translation: Theory and practice in management consulting. *Management Learning*, 35(1), 31–44.

Clegg, S. R., Kornberger, M., and Rhodes, C. (2004b). When the saints go marching in: A reply to Sturdy, Clark, Fincham and Handley. *Management Learning*, 35(3), 341–344.

Corso, M., Giacobbe, A., and Martini, A. (2009). Designing and managing business communities of practice. *Journal of Knowledge Management*, 13(3), 73–89.

Cowsill, R., and Grint, K. (2008). Leadership, task and relationship: Orpheus, Prometheus and Janus. *Human Resource Management Journal*, 18(2), 188–195.

Craig, D. (2005). *Rip-off! The scandalous inside story of the management consulting money machine*. Bournemouth: Original Book Company.

Czarniawska-Joerges, B., Gustafsson, C., and Björkegren, D. (1990). Purists vs. pragmatists: On protagoras, economists and management consultants. *Consultation*, 9(3), 241–256.

David, R. J., Sine, W. D., and Haveman, H. A. (2013). Seizing opportunity in emerging fields: How institutional entrepreneurs legitimated the professional form of management consulting. *Organization Science*, 24(2), 356–377.

Engwall, L., and Kipping, M. (2013). Management consulting: Dynamics, debates, and directions. *International Journal of Strategic Communication*, 7(2), 84–98.

Ernst, B., and Kieser, A. (2002). In search of explanation for the consulting explosion. In K. Sahlin-Andersson and L. Engwall (eds.), *The expansion of management knowledge: Carriers, flows, and sources*. Stanford, CA: Stanford University Press, pp. 47–73.

Faulconbridge, J., and Jones, A. (2012). The geographies of management consultancy firms. In M. Kipping and T. Clark (eds.), *The Oxford handbook of management consulting*. Oxford: Oxford University Press, pp. 225–246.

Feibleman, J. (1944). The mythology of science. *Philosophy of Science*, 11(2), 117–121.

Fincham, R. (2000). Management as magic: Reengineering and the search for business salvation. In D. Knights and H. Willmott (eds.), *The reengineering revolution*. London: Sage, pp. 174–91.

Fincham, R., and Clark, T. (2002). Management consultancy: Issues, perspectives, and agendas. *International Studies of Management & Organization*, 32(4), 3–18.

Frandsen, F., Johansen, W., and Pang, A. (2013). From management consulting to strategic communication: Studying the roles and functions of communication consulting. *International Journal of Strategic Communication*, 7(2), 81–83.

Furusten, S. (2013). Commercialized professionalism on the field of management consulting. *Journal of Organizational Change Management*, 26(2), 265–285.

Gabriel, Y. (2004). *Myths, stories, and organizations: Premodern narratives for our times*. Oxford: Oxford University Press.

Gbadamosi, G. (2005). Ritualism, symbolism and magic in consultancy practice: An exploratory investigation. *Management Decision*, 43(9), 1129–1146.

Gill, M. J. (2015). Elite identity and status anxiety: An interpretative phenomenological analysis of management consultants. *Organization*, 22(3), 306–325.

Goffman, E. (1959/1990). *The presentation of self in everyday life*. London: Penguin.

Greenwood, R., and Empson, L. (2003). The professional partnership: Relic or exemplary form of governance? *Organization Studies*, 24(6), 909–933.

Groß, C., Heusinkveld, S., and Clark, T. (2015). The active audience? Gurus, management ideas and consumer variability. *British Journal of Management*, 26(2), 273–291.

Handy, C. B. (1978). *Gods of management: How they work, and why they will fail*. London: Souvenir Press.

Handy, C. B. (1995). *Gods of management: The changing work of organizations*. New York: Oxford University Press.

Harvey, W. S., Morris, T., and Müller Santos, M. (2016). Reputation and identity conflict in management consulting. *Human Relations*, 70(1), 1–27. Published online before print May 5, 2016. doi:10.1177/0018726716641747.

Heidegger, M. (2013). *The essence of truth: On Plato's cave allegory and theaetetus*. London: Bloomsbury Academic.

Heller, F. (2002). What next? More critique of consultants, gurus and managers. In T. Clark and R. Fincham (eds.), *Critical consulting: New perspectives on the management advice industry*. Oxford: Blackwell, pp. 260–272.

Hicks, J., Nair, P., and Wilderom, C. P. M. (2009). What if we shifted the basis of consulting from knowledge to knowing? *Management Learning*, 40(3), 289–310.

Huczynski, A. A. (1993). Explaining the succession of management fads. *The International Journal of Human Resource Management*, 4(2), 443–463.

Jackall, R. (1988). *Moral mazes: The world of corporate managers*. Oxford: Oxford University Press.

Jackson, B. (2001). *Management gurus and management fashions: A dramatistic inquiry*. London: Routledge.

Kaarst-Brown, M. L. (1999). Five symbolic roles of the external consultant – integrating change, power and symbolism. *Journal of Organizational Change Management*, 12(6), 540–561.

Kieser, A., and Wellstein, B. (2008). Do activities of consultants and management scientists affect decision making by managers? In W. H. Starbuck and G. P. Hodgkinson (eds.), *Oxford handbook of organizational decision making*. Oxford: Oxford University Press, pp. 495–516.

Kihn, M. (2005). *House of lies: How management consultants steal your watch and then tell you the time*. New York: Warner Business Book.

Kipping, M. (2002). Trapped in their wave: The evolution of management consultancies. In T. Clark and R. Fincham (eds.), *Critical consulting*. Oxford: Oxford University Press, pp. 28–49.

Kipping, M., and Clark, T. (2012). Researching management consulting: An introduction to the handbook. In M. Kipping and T. Clark (eds.), *The Oxford handbook of management consulting*. Oxford: Oxford University Press, pp. 1–36.

Kitay, J., and Wright, C. (2007). From prophets to profits: The occupational rhetoric of management consultants. *Human Relations*, 60(11), 1613–1640.

Kornberger, M., and Brown, A. D. (2007). Ethics' as a discursive resource for identity work. *Human Relations*, 60(3), 497–518.

Landes, D. S. (2003). *The unbound Prometheus: Technological change and industrial development in Western Europe from 1750 to the present*. Cambridge: Cambridge University Press.

Maister, D. H. (2004). The anatomy of a consulting firm. In C. J. Fombrun and M. D. Nevins (eds.), *The advice business: Essential tools and models for management consulting*. Upper Saddle River, NJ: Pearson Prentice Hall.

Maister, D. H. (2007). *Strategy and the fat smoker: Doing what's obvious but not easy*. Boston, MA: The Spangle Press.

McKenna, C. D. (1995). The origins of modern management consulting. *Business and Economic History*, 24(1), 51.

McKenna, C. D. (2006). *The world's newest profession*. Cambridge: Cambridge University Press.

Meriläinen, S., Tienari, J., Thomas, R., and Davies, A. (2004). Management consultant talk: A cross-cultural comparison of normalizing discourse and resistance. *Organization*, 11(4), 539–574.

Merron, K. (2005). *Consulting mastery: How the best make the biggest difference*, 1st ed. San Francisco, CA: Berrett-Koehler Publishers.

Micklethwait, J., and Wooldridge, A. (1997). *The witch doctors: What the management gurus are saying, why it matters and how to make sense of it*. London: Mandarin.

Mohe, M., and Seidl, D. (2011). Theorizing the client – consultant relationship from the perspective of social-systems theory. *Organization*, 18(1), 3–22.

Muzio, D., Kirkpatrick, I., and Kipping, M. (2011). Professions, organizations and the state: Applying the sociology of the professions to the case of management consultancy. *Current Sociology*, 59(6), 805–824.

Nietzche, F. (2006). On truth and lies in a nonmoral sense (1873). In K. Ansell Pearson and D. Large (eds.), *The Nietzche reader*. Oxford: Blackwell Publishing.

Nikolova, N., Reihlen, M., and Schlapfner, J.-F. (2009). Client – consultant interaction: Capturing social practices of professional service production. *Scandinavian Journal of Management*, 25(3), 289–298.

O'Mahoney, J. (2007). Disrupting identity: Trust and angst in management consulting. In S. C. Bolton and H. Maeve (eds.), *Searching for the human in human resource management: Theory, practice and workplace contexts, management, work and organisations*. Basingstoke: Palgrave Macmillan, pp. 281–302.

O'Mahoney, J., and Markham, C. (2013). *Management consultancy*. Oxford: Oxford University Press.

O'Shea, J., and Madigan, C. (1998). *Dangerous company: Management consultants and the businesses they save and ruin*. New York: Penguin Books.

Orlikowski, W. J. (2002). Knowing in practice: Enacting a collective capability in distributed organizing. *Organization Science*, 13(3), 249–273.

Pang, A., Frandsen, F., Johansen, W., and Yeo, S. L. (2013). A comparative study of crisis consultancies between Singapore and Denmark: Distant cousins of the same destiny? *International Journal of Strategic Communication*, 7(2), 149–164.

Phelan, K. (2013). *I'm sorry I broke your company: When management consultants are the problem, not the solution.* San Francisco, CA: Berrett-Koehler.

Pinault, L. (2000). *Consulting demons: Inside the unscrupulous world of global corporate consulting,* 1st ed. New York: Harper Business.

Poulfelt, F., Greiner, L., and Bharmbri, A. (2010). The changing global consulting industry. In L. Greiner and F. Poulfelt (eds.), *Management consulting today and tomorrow.* London: Routledge, pp. 5–32.

Puschmann, C., and Burgess, J. (2014). Big data, big questions| metaphors of big data. *International Journal of Communication,* 8.

Schein, E. H. (1988). *Process consultation volume I: Its role in organization development.* Reading, MA: Addison-Wesley Publishing Company.

Starbuck, W. H. (1992). Learning by knowledge-intensive firms. *Journal of Management Studies,* 29(6), 713–740.

Stewart, M. (2009). *The management myth: Debunking modern business philosophy.* New York: W.W. Norton.

Sturdy, A., Clark, T., Fincham, R., and Handley, K. (2004). Silence, procrustes and colonization: A response to Clegg et al.'s 'Noise, parasites and translation: Theory and practice in management consulting'. *Management Learning,* 35(3), 337–340.

Sturdy, A., Clark, T., Fincham, R., and Handley, K. (2009). Between innovation and legitimation – boundaries and knowledge flow in management consultancy. *Organization,* 16(5), 627–653.

Sturdy, A., and Gabriel, Y. (2000). Missionaries, mercenaries or car salesmen? MBA teaching in Malaysia. *Journal of Management Studies,* 37(7), 979–1002.

Sturdy, A., Schwarz, M., and Spicer, A. (2006). Guess who's coming to dinner? Structures and uses of liminality in strategic management consultancy. *Human Relations,* 59(7), 929–960.

Sturdy, A., and Wright, C. (2011). The active client: The boundary-spanning roles of internal consultants as gatekeepers, brokers and partners of their external counterparts. *Management Learning,* 42(5), 485–503.

Styhre, A., Olilla, S., Wikmalm, L., and Roth, J. (2010). Expert or speaking-partner? Shifting roles and identities in consulting work. *Leadership & Organization Development Journal,* 31(2), 159–175.

Sutter, M., and Kieser, A. (2015). How consultants and their clients collaborate in spite of massive communication barriers. *International Journal of Business Communication,* 1–29. doi:10.1177/2329488415613340.

Swan, J., Scarbrough, H., and Ziebro, M. (2016). Liminal roles as a source of creative agency in management: The case of knowledge-sharing communities. *Human Relations,* 69(3), 781–811.

Turner, A. N. (1982). Consulting is more than giving advice. *Harvard Business Review,* 60(5), 120–129.

Werr, A., and Stjernberg, T. (2003). Exploring management consulting firms as knowledge systems. *Organization Studies (01708406),* 24(6), 881–908.

Werr, A., and Styhre, A. (2003). Management consultants – friend or foe? Understanding the ambiguous client-consultant relationship. *International Studies of Management & Organization,* 32(4), 43–66.

Whitehead, A. N. (1938). *Modes of thought.* New York: Macmillan.

Whittle, A. (2005) Preaching and practising 'flexibility': Implications for theories of subjectivity at work. *Human Relations,* 58(10), 1301–1322.

Whittle, A. (2006). The paradoxical repertoires of management consultancy. *Journal of Organizational Change Management,* 19(4), 424–436.

Whittle, A. (2008). From flexibility to work–life balance: Exploring the changing discourses of management consultants. *Organization,* 15(4), 513–534.

Wickham, L., and Wilcock, J. (2016). *Management consulting: Delivering an effective project.* Harlow, Essex: Pearson.

Wright, C., and Kitay, J. (2004). Spreading the word: Gurus, consultant and the diffusion of the employee relation paradigm in Australia. *Management Learning,* 35(3), 271–286.

Zerfass, A., and Franke, N. (2013). Enabling, advising, supporting, executing: A theoretical framework for internal communication consulting within organizations. *International Journal of Strategic Communication,* 7(2), 118–135.

# 2 The challenges and opportunities of stylized facts for management consulting modeling and theory development

*Renae Agrey and Henry Xu*

## Abstract

To improve the ability to influence practice for greater impact, this chapter addresses the knowledge gap for better practical and theoretical understanding of the relevance of stylized facts for management consulting. This literature review explores the usefulness of stylized facts and in the answering of our research questions we identify three definitions for stylized facts based on an economic, business or information system orientation. We discover that stylized facts are used as a classification, as a mechanism for modeling and theory development and as an emerging type of literature review. With its business-oriented theme, our discoveries map methodology and process for stylized facts practices, and observe that the stylized facts literature is riddled with challenges, strategies, goals and recommendations as utilities in the establishment of policy. The use of stylized facts, though limited in "management consulting" specific literature, is not a new phenomenon and instead we see it has become a source of competitive advantage in its technical evolution. The trend of its use is increasing, as is its usefulness.

## Introduction

As we experience the third wave of communication and information (Curnow and Reuvid, 2003), its disruption and the second coming of the Internet and big data, a large base of knowledge has become more readily available for many disciplines thus furthering their advancement founded in science and on facts. A fact, as a true piece of information, is something that has an actual existence (Merriam-Webster, 2016).

A stylized fact on the other hand is a fact that is not true in every case (Heine et al., 2005). This creates an interesting challenge for researchers and practitioners. As general patterns are observed with the accumulation of evidence, the concept of the stylized fact is rooted in the field of economics in its understanding of the phenomenon of economic growth for theory development. Economic modeling is a tool used by economists to advance scientific practice by enhancing the usefulness of descriptive statistical frameworks (Kremer, 1993). For the formulation of theory, mathematical models are used in three different ways: to "fit" theories to the world, as theorizing and as investigative instruments to learn more about economic theory and the world (Boland, 1994). Economists construct models to reproduce empirical regularities which can then be used for interpretation and recommendation purposes (Solow, 1970). Modeling has led to, as an example of a stylized fact, the discovery of knowledge that there is a tendency for the flow of all factors of production to cluster together (Lucas, 1988).

Trade theory and macroeconomic policy are continuing elements in business decisions and the real world. Because stylized facts are based in the real world, they are of importance to

*Figure 2.1* Prevalence of the increased trend of stylized facts in literature
Source: Scopus. Chart developed by authors.

the practices of management consulting. Figure 2.1 portrays a historical representation of the total increase in stylized fact interest and of their use in business, management and accounting.

In management literature, the definition for a stylized fact refers to economic literature as an accumulation of evidence (observations made in many contexts) that points to empirical regularities (empirical truths) to provide a more generalized understanding of the world to which theories must fit (Helfat, 2007; Boland, 1994). Similar to the nebulous and difficult to define concept of "consulting" (Ajmal et al., 2009), the stylized fact concept plays an important role in the economic literature even though there is little analysis of the characterization and use of the term in management consulting. Following Mingers's (2000) approach, we critique the tradition, authority, objectivity and rhetoric of the literature with the goal of answering the following research questions: What are stylized facts? How have they helped advance research efforts for management consulting? What are the problems or issues of concern with them? Are we able to determine best practices for the application and use of stylized facts?

In this chapter, we investigate, present and discuss stylized facts and explore their potential for researchers in management consulting models and theory development. This literature review follows Tranfield et al.'s (2003) three step methodology (planning, executing and reporting) to ensure a replicable, scientific and transparent process. First, we introduce the stylized fact concept. Second, we contrast research approaches and theoretical perspectives of stylized facts for theory building and development, highlighting the advantages and disadvantages in research. Third, we conduct a keyword analysis for more detail and understanding of the management consulting stylized facts literature. Fourth, as a contribution, we offer a synthesis of standardized methods for structuring stylized facts, including recommendations for further guidance. We then conclude the chapter.

## Research method

Literature reviews have been gaining more importance with their systemic approach to investigation and understanding of the phenomenon under study (Tate et al., 2015). This integrative (Torraco, 2005) literature review follows Tranfield et al.'s (2003) three-step methodology: planning, executing and reporting. The literature review process is a key tool in management research because it can manage a variety of information sources that are specific to the academic inquiry (Tranfield et al., 2003). Literature reviews of the stylized facts should be completed with every use or determination of a stylized fact (Houy et al., 2015). The following highlights the spectrum of methodological approaches used with stylized facts.

In the management research relevant to consultants, there are three overlapping types of research: theory building (inductive), theory testing (deductive) and problem centered/practical research (methodical pluralism) (Gill and Johnson, 1997). Stylized facts can be used for both theory development and testing (Houy et al., 2015), and will often be used in combination to address the "what" and "why" of the question at hand (Phillips and Pugh, 1987). In the course of scientific practice, methodical pluralism is context-sensitive in its use of not only multiple theoretical models but also multiple methodological approaches (Lancaster, 2005).

Aggregating both qualitative and quantitative data from different empirical methods by following a systematic process is one approach to derive stylized facts from empirical evidence (Heine et al., 2005). Other possible approaches include surveying experts (Mohe, 2007), or by using the statistical analysis of large data sets (Cont, 2001). Litner's (1956) research on firm dividend policy was based on interviews with corporate managers. The field study result provided useful guidance for subsequent research and the use of stylized facts. For example, Marsh and Merton (1986) draw on Litner's analysis and stylized facts for the development of their analytical modeling of dividend variance.

Wagner (2011) recommends the use of meta-analysis to understand why empirical results differ across space and time, and to uncover stylized facts that can inform theoretical modeling and policy debates. The need to integrate findings from many studies ensures that meta-analytic outcomes include more precise estimates, and with the large body of research now being generated, the conduct of research becomes more feasible (Mendritzki, 2014).

Although they may not fully support structural estimation, cross-section data can yield interesting stylized facts to guide both the general theorizing and empirical analysis of specific industries ("Scatter acorns . . .", n.d.). Instead of attempting structural analysis, Schmalensee's (1981) search for stylized facts focused on the importance of various effects, not just with coefficient signs and t-statistics. For a "quick method" to identify stylized facts, they used a simple analysis variance framework to avoid specific hypotheses and measurement issues.

Houy et al. (2015) note that a goal of stylized facts is comparison by using them as language-based artefacts. Ittner and Larcker (2002) use the words "restrictions", "contradictions" and "difficulties" to describe their stylized facts. As a starting point for further empirical and theoretical research (Solow, 1956), stylized facts are observed as "intuitive notions that are conceptually ambiguous" (Mendritzki, 2014: 1). Stylized facts are statements about the outcome of some abstract social or economic process and are not about the outcome of any concrete or real process (Arroyo Abad and Khalifa, 2015). For example, a stylized fact in the high-growth firm literature is the inability to predict their growth episodes (Coad et al., 2014).

However, according to Ferraro et al. (2005), there is a limitation in how theories in economics discourse become dominant when their language is used widely, and assumptions (harmful or beneficial) become accepted and normatively valued, regardless of their empirical validity. As a result, this can lead to forms of organizational stupidity (Alvesson and Spicer, 2012).

*Table 2.1* Stylized facts partiality of representation

| Scope Hypothesizing Strategy | | Pooling Strategy | |
|---|---|---|---|
| **Procedural stylization:** Information is gradually discarded from rather concrete representations | | **Violation stylization:** Begins by assuring generality by having a broad data set and then moving to finding partial correspondences | |
| This strategy starts from assuring partial correspondences and then moving to argue why the particular narrow subset of targets chosen might be representative | | This strategy generates partial correspondences in a way that violates the procedural definition. It starts with assuring generality by having a broad data set and then moves to find partial correspondences | |
| *Advantages* | *Disadvantages* | *Advantages* | *Disadvantages* |
| Grounding (it minimally does well in representing one member of the set) | Having to assume that scope expansion is capturing similar targets | Demonstrates a relationship | In not knowing if the similar elements are those that are most relevant for explaining any particular system |

Source: Adapted from Mendritzki (2014) by the authors.

In terms of a strategy of use with stylized facts, Mendritzki (2014) notes that stylization as a strategy can reduce comprehensiveness (i.e. ignoring some of the operating factors), and proposes an approach (Table 2.1) depending on the partiality of representation as a push for justification. An example of its use is Hansen and Hughes's (2005) model. As a partial representation of the impact of licensing of management consulting innovations, future study of licensing may generate a body of knowledge with spill over to other consultants.

The difficulty with this approach is that both strategies can claim that they desire to address their own deficits in the long term. Boland (1997: 245) identifies a possible methodological problem with stylized facts in "the potentiality of circular argument when purporting to explain stylized facts and the situation that they define". In the case of stylized facts, if a model corresponds to a set of stylized facts and a set of stylized facts corresponds to some targets, then the model corresponds to the targets (Mendritzki, 2014).

To improve outcomes, the underlying measurement method for stylized facts is purported to be triangulation (Houy et al., 2015). According to Luyt (2012), the concept of triangulation has a long and formative history in mixed methods literature because multiple viewpoints lead to greater accuracy of measurement. Its use develops a clearer understanding of phenomena through "convergence, corroboration, and correspondence of results across the different method types" (Caracelli and Greene, 1993: 196). Triangulating quantitative and qualitative results can result in positive effects (Houy et al., 2015).

## Sample selection

Literature reviews today are generally undertaken through the use of a simple keyword and database analysis. The scope of our review is limited to published, peer-reviewed scholarly journals (Mainela et al., 2014). With this we have identified a large and relatively untapped base of potential research opportunities through the use of stylized facts. Following Tranfield et al.'s, (2003) three-step evidence-based process, our search within the online literature databases used the Boolean search string "stylized facts" and "management consulting" as our conceptual boundary for triangulation.

Table 2.2 Management consulting stylized facts Scopus literature base: document characteristics and classification map

| No. | Type | Study | Research Method | Purpose | Stylized Facts | Keywords Used | JEL General Classification★★ | JEL Secondary Classification★★ | Citations |
|-----|------|-------|-----------------|---------|----------------|---------------|------------------------------|--------------------------------|-----------|
| **1.** | Book Chapter | Cohendet P., Meyer-Krahmer F. (2005) | Generative | Discusses the conceptualization of knowledge production based on the notion of community | Describes how knowledge intensive communities can compensate for some of the learning failures of markets and organizations | n.a. | n.a. | n.a. | 3 |
| 2. | Journal Article | Lim K.-P. (2007) | Quantitative | Demonstrates via rolling sample approach that market efficiency evolves over time | Nonlinear dependence in stock returns is localized in time. Market efficiency evolves over time. Nonlinear dependence in stock returns also evolves over time | nonlinear dependence, bi-correlation, market efficiency | n.a. | n.a | 50 |
| 3. | Journal Article | Nielsen C.K. (2008) | Qualitative | This paper links rational beliefs to the presence of overconfidence | The stylized facts of diversity of beliefs and overconfidence are replicated by rational belief models | rational beliefs, WAMS Markov processes, continuous state space, rational overconfidence | D – Microeconomics | D01 – Microeconomic Behavior: Underlying Principles D84 – Expectations; Speculations | 4 |
| 4. | Review | Sloan F.A., Wang Y. (2008) | Mixed Method, Conceptual | Discusses three alternative conceptual frameworks used by economists to study addictive behavior | Short-term rates are higher than long-term rates for both smoker and non smokers which is consistent with hyperbolic discounting | addiction, cigarette prices, hyperbolic discounting, impulsivity, rationality, risk preference, time preferences, smoking | n.a. | n.a | 11 |
| 5. | Journal Article | Ormerod P., Heineike A. (2009) | Quantitative | Examines global recessions as a cascade phenomenon | International transmission across countries is a feature of recessions under capitalism | cascades, recessions, international transmission, interacting agents | C – Mathematical and Quantitative Method | C69 – Mathematical Methods; Programming Models; Mathematical and | 1 |

(Continued)

Table 2.2 (Continued)

| No. | Type | Study | Research Method | Purpose | Stylized Facts | Keywords Used | JEL General Classification★★ | JEL Secondary Classification★★ | Citations |
|---|---|---|---|---|---|---|---|---|---|
| | | | | | | | E – Macroeconomics and Monetary Economics N – Economic History | Simulation Modeling: Other E32 – Business Fluctuations; Cycles N10 – General, International, or Comparative | |
| 6. | Conf. Paper | Zhong J., Zhao X. (2011) | Quantitative | This paper compares multifractal models for assets returns from four aspects of economic perspective: ability of reproducing stylized facts, support of economic theory, accuracy of forecasting and explaining, mathematical elegancy and computational parsimony | Multifractal models have better forecasting performance and more excellent ability to reproduce stylized facts. Efficient Market Hypothesis, Adaptive Market Hypothesis | economic perspective, multifractal models for assets returns, multifractality of financial time-series, stylized facts | n.a | n.a | 0 |
| 7. | Journal Article | Becchetti L., Pelloni A. (2013) | Quantitative, Qualitative | Determines the economic value of what we are learning from life satisfaction literature | "Quazi-stylized" facts of happiness (i.e. the positive effect of religion, marriage, income), short run effects. The impact (sizeable in magnitude) of self-reported health on subjective well-being | life satisfaction, shadow value of non-market goods, unemployment/ inflation trade-off | A – General Economics and Teaching D – Microeconomics | A13 – Relation of Economics to Social Values D64 – Altruism; Philanthropy | 4 |

| # | Type | Authors | Method | Description | Keywords | JEL Classification | JEL Codes | Count |
|---|------|---------|--------|-------------|----------|--------------------|-----------|-------|
| 8. | Journal Article | Larson D.J., Maxcy J. (2013) | Conceptual | Not explicitly stated – builds on own prior work to corroborate that cycling coaches be hired by the athletes not their teams to create more value. | n.a | J – Labor and Demographic Economics L–Industrial Organization | J22 –Time Allocation and Labor Supply J24 – Human Capital; Skills; Occupational Choice; Labor Productivity L23 – Organization of Production L83 – Sports; Gambling; Restaurants; Recreation; Tourism | 2 |
| 9. | Book Chapter | Angiellari-Dajci F., Lawless W.F., Agarwal N., Oberleitner R., Coleman B., Kavoossi M. (2013) | Mixed method | The authors discuss new developments in telehealth for diagnostic evaluation and ASD treatment in the US | They build a theoretical model to capture telehealth system's potential in reaching market equilibrium under the constraint of full utilization of provider hours and other stylized facts. | n.a | n.a | n.a | 0 |
| 10. | Journal Article | Bianchi S., Pianese A. (2014) | Literature review | Surveys a large class of stochastic processes – The Gaussian processes with pseudo differential elliptic operators–providing a generalization of fractional Brownian motion (fBm) | The fact that very large and sudden downward variations tend to occur only when the Hölder exponent is much larger than 1/2, while the reverse is much less frequent and tends to appear only immediately after the falls. | multi-fractional processes, efficient markets, behavioural finance, stylized facts | n.a | n.a | 2 |

*(Continued)*

Table 2.2 (Continued)

| No. | Type | Study | Research Method | Purpose | Stylized Facts | Keywords Used | JEL General Classification** | JEL Secondary Classification** | Citations |
|---|---|---|---|---|---|---|---|---|---|
| 11. | Report | Sornette D, (2014) | Generative, Qualitative | *A short review presenting a selected history of the mutual fertilization between physics and economics* | *Financial markets are reproduced only when agents are overconfident and mis-attribute the success of news to predict return to the existence of herding effects. The multifractal structure characterized by a continuous spectrum of exponents of the power law relaxation of endogenous burst of volatility.* | *finance, econophysics, Ising model, phase transitions, excess volatility puzzle, adaptive markets, bubbles* | *n.a* | *n.a* | 22 |
| 12. | Journal Article | Heller Y. (2014) | Quantitative, Qualitative | Investigates the evidence suggesting that people tend to be overconfident in that they overestimate the accuracy of their private information | Hard-easy effect: the degree of overconfidence depends on the difficulty of the task. False certainty effect: people are often wrong when they are certain in their private information. People should be risk averse with respect to aggregate risk and risk neutral with respect to idiosyncratic risk. Cascade interactions: herds eventually arise, but the probability of herding on the wrong action is lower than with a rational rule. | n.a. | D – Microeconomics | D81 – Criteria for Decision-Making under Risk and Uncertainty D82 – Asymmetric and Private Information; Mechanism Design | 0 |

| No. | Type | Authors | Method | Description | Findings | Key terms | JEL category | JEL code | Count |
|---|---|---|---|---|---|---|---|---|---|
| 13. | Journal Article | Houy C., Fettke P., Loos P. (2015) | Literature Review Quantitative, Qualitative | Points out the potential of stylized facts in information systems research | Event-driven process chains are easy to understand | Stylized facts, literature review, research synthesis, cumulative research, theory development | n.a. | n.a. | 1 |
| 14. | Journal Article | Gnann T., Plötz P. (2015) | Conceptual | Reviews models of combined AFV and refuelling infrastructure market diffusion to point out gaps | Mature markets develop initial refuelling infrastructure before vehicles gain larger market shares | Alternative fuel vehicles, refuelling infrastructure, interaction modeling | n.a. | n.a. | 7 |
| 15. | Journal Article | Levich R.M., Poti V. (2015) | Quantitative, Qualitative | Studies the predictability in currency markets over the period 1972–2012 | Predictive regressions of currency returns. Periods of high and low predictability tend to alternate. Challenges Fama's (1970) Efficient Market Hypothesis. Consistent with Lo's (2004) Adaptive Market Hypothesis coupled with a slow convergence toward efficient markets | Foreign exchange, predictability, filter rules, market efficiency | n.a. | n.a. | 1 |
| 16. | Journal Article | Kaiser U., Müller B. (2015) | Qualitative | Studies how start-up teams are assembled in terms of team member human capital characteristics to generate stylized facts on team heterogeneity | Observed substantial increase in team heterogeneity over time. Startups from knowledge-intensive sectors become more heterogeneous over time relative to other startups | Entrepreneurship, start-ups, skill heterogeneity, team dynamics | C – Mathematical and Quantitative Methods  D – Microeconomics  J – Labor and Demographic Economics  L – Industrial Organization | C10 – Econometric and Statistical Methods and Methodology: General  D22 – Firm Behavior: Empirical Analysis  J22 – Time Allocation and Labor Supply  J24 – Human Capital; Skills; Occupational Choice; Labor Productivity | 0 |

Source: Scopus and ⋆⋆ www.aeaweb.org/jel/guide/jel.php. JEL uses a "top down" hierarchical classification system. Table developed by the authors.
*Shading*: these studies should be removed from the sample as per Wang and Chugh (2014).

As an initial measure of the breadth of the literature base, we began our search with Google Scholar. This returned "about" 112,000 results and then "about" 15,000. JSTOR returned 13,775 for "stylized facts" and then exploded to 182,744 with the addition of "management consulting", which was the same result for just "management consulting". EBSCOhost and the Web of Science returned thousands of results for "stylized facts" but nothing for both sets of keywords. Elsevier's Scopus returned a result of 2,543 with 16 stylized facts documents for "management consulting" at the time of the sample. While some would consider a sample of 16, reduced to 11 journal articles – and then to four to focus specifically on business, management and accounting – small in scope (Table 2.2), the literature indicates that it is an average size for use with stylized facts in new areas (Linder, 2016).

## Findings

An initial assessment of the stylized facts data resulted in the following discoveries. The subject areas of the Scopus output included nine subject areas (Appendix 1, Table 2.3). From this we identified 160 keywords that were used 4,104 times throughout all the stylized facts documents. Of the 16 management consulting documents, we identified 106 keywords and found that only ten were from the original 160 keywords (Appendix 2, Table 2.4). Of these ten we observe that some of the keywords were above average in use for the whole management consulting sample when compared to the total use in the database (Figure 2.2).

While the number of management consulting articles in the Scopus database is increasing, the quantity of the articles with the keyword "management consulting" as the topic has decreased from one (Cohendet and Meyer-Krahmer, 2005) to none. Surprisingly, none of the articles used the words "management consulting" anywhere in its text leaving us to wonder what identifies and classifies the documents as management consulting literature. We did find a set of 12 keywords specific to the business, management and accounting literature (Figure 2.3), which indicated that market efficiency in our sample is below the average of all the documents in the database.

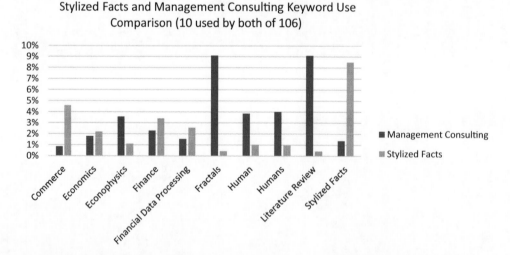

*Figure 2.2* Comparative analysis of keyword use for all stylized facts vs. management consulting use

Source: Scopus. Chart developed by authors.

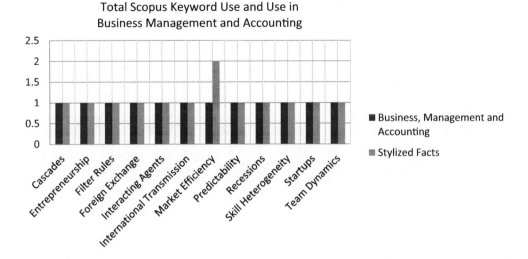

*Figure 2.3* Comparative analysis of keyword use for all stylized facts vs. business, management and accounting

Source: Scopus. Chart developed by authors.

While interesting in their classification, we found that these keywords did not reflect the words and themes used in the articles themselves. We then proceeded to conduct another keyword analysis based on a review of the literature. We compiled a list of 130 keywords, of which 90 were evident in at least two of the articles. Again, notable patterns are observed. While conducting a literature review is important for the determination of the stylized facts, 11 of the 16, then eight of the 11 have "literature review" reflected in the keyword results, but only two of the four have business, management and accounting specific articles.

When we reduce it further to the 11 journal articles and then to a focused four articles specific only to business, management and accounting (Wang and Chugh, 2014), the only keyword that remains above average in all instances was "literature review", which identifies both a document classification type and a type of research method in Scopus (Table 2.2).

No. 13, the one article from the field of information systems, is the only record to have a definition for stylized facts. This study is different in how stylized facts are defined as a form of literature review and is placed in the middle between a narrative review and a meta-analysis. Here, the purpose of stylized facts is to "identify broadly supported phenomena and relationships focusing on the relevant characteristics of a phenomenon" (Houy et al., 2015: 10). Study no. 5 was the only article in the sample to return "phenomenon".

We also discovered that all 2,453 documents indicated the keyword "how". The keywords "model", "management" and "consulting" were clustered for all 16 of the Scopus documents. When reduced to 11, "economics" then became part of the keywords for all the sample articles. Our keyword search returned only five documents for "triangulation" and two for "formative" of the total Scopus results. None of the management consulting literature indicated its use.

The use of the word "fit", like most of the keywords, was below the total Scopus keyword use averages. Of the total 2,243 results, 198 identified "fit" and 94 for "art" and, within this, four papers of each were identified in our sample. Interestingly, none of the documents identified both "fit" and "art".

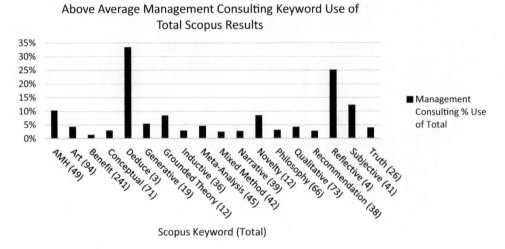

*Figure 2.4* Above average keyword use for initial sample of 16

Source: Scopus. Chart developed by authors.

The keyword "art" is remarkable in that although there is only one sample of four in the 16, it represented a higher than average use for management consulting when compared to total use of the word for all the Scopus documents (Figure 2.4). Model formation is an art in its instrumentation (Heine et al., 2005). If we follow Wang and Chugh (2014) and reduce the results specific to the subject area of business, management and accounting, all four results return "fit" and not "art". Figure 2.4 presents the above average keyword use of the 130 terms derived from the literature.

"Truth" is notable in how we see it as above average for the 16 samples, but then it does not appear in the 11 sample articles (Figure 2.5). The challenge with such a small sample size is that one instance can tip the scale. For example, while "reflective" is observed in the 16, we find that the one record is a book chapter pertaining to management consultants (no. 1).

A review of the literature resulted in the observation of three key themes. All the documents had some element of markets (e.g. open or specific), time (e.g. linear or ways to save it) and capital (e.g. human and other) even though the keyword result may not have indicated so. While the keyword search indicates the inclusion of stylized facts, only three articles (no. 6, 10, 13) include the words as keywords in the article itself (Table 2.2). In no. 16, the empirical results do and do not subscribe to Parker's (2009) model prediction of the state dependence of firm heterogeneity. With the intertwining of fields of study (e.g. Econophysics), no. 11 identifies some of the most studied stylized facts and models as part of a comparative analysis in its observation of stylized facts "in financial time series, such as excess volatility, high trading volume, temporary bubbles and trend following, sudden crashes and mean reversion, clustered volatility and fat tails in the returns distribution" (Sornette, 2014: 18). No. 11 scored highest in use of our keyword terms in the analysis.

The strength of a stylized fact is its ability to meld evidence from different types of sources into something meaningful. Hansen and Hughes (2005) note that the use of technology and sale of software are becoming integral parts of practice. Information and technology are now factors of production, and in their use wealth is created. With its exponential growth, levels of data production are getting big and its management has become an issue. The challenge is determining how the data may or may not be relevant to a

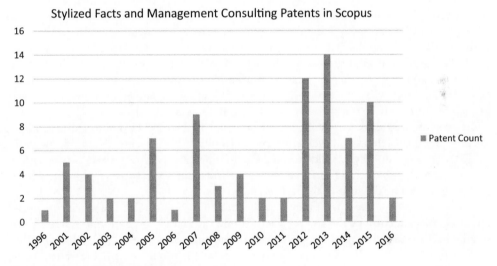

**Above Average Management Consulting Keywords (sample of 11)**

■ Total SCOPUS Use

■ Management Consulting Use

*Figure 2.5* Above average keyword use in the sample of 11

Source: Scopus. Chart developed by authors.

**Stylized Facts and Management Consulting Patents in Scopus**

■ Patent Count

*Figure 2.6* Patent evidence in Scopus

Source: Scopus. Chart developed by authors.

specific situation, and the "sift and search" method is very time consuming (BCG, 2010). A review of the Scopus database as "a network technology" indicates 84 patents with our search string, and its trend seems to be increasing (Figure 2.6).

With a review of the patent databases we observe parallels in both the literature and patent databases. Statistical analysis, networks, clustering, typology and classification are all keywords, and their patterns of use are growing. Technology has influenced easier and cheaper ways to do sequencing, extractions and duplications. For example, abstractions from evidence-based practice and the use of technology have resulted in the mapping of the human genome. With its limited use at the time of the study, the opportunity of the emerging stylized facts data in the field of management consulting encourages an increase in discussion and further exploration.

## Discussion

Kaldor (1961: 178) proposed an "as if" conceptualization for stylized facts as a starting point for theoretical models. Other than the direction left to us by Kaldor (1961: 178) – such as "to concentrate on broad tendencies, ignoring individual detail" and proceed with the "as if" method (i.e. to construct a hypothesis that accounts for the stylized facts without committing to the historical accuracy or sufficiency of the facts or tendencies thus summarized)" – and by others' practical application and reporting of stylized facts (e.g. Wagner, 2011; Moreno, 2015), a standardized approach to stylized facts has become a basis for debate. Mäki (1998) reports many "as if" versions in literature.

For the purpose of this review, the aggregation of our research initially leaves us with a three-step economic approach as directed by Kaldor, and Wagner (2011) contributes recommendations for model formation. Simulation studies employ a five-step generative research strategy (Epstein, 2006), which is similar to Kaldor's "as if" method. Stylized facts are used in many different contexts, but in their effort to realize scientific consensus, a successful model is expected to explain the stylized facts (Boland, 1994).

Stylized facts are theory independent (Houy et al., 2015). They can be used to test and compare the explanatory power of existing theories, and in their use they identify and measure scientific progress (Heine et al., 2005). Theoretical models should be established with "realistic assumptions that inform policy debates in an evidence-based way" (Wagner, 2011: 2). The usefulness of theory is in how it can make sense of data or help diagnose a problem, in addition to generating value, considering options or making decisions (Evans et al., 1992). With stylized facts, decisions are subjective and dependent on the objectivity of the literature and the transparency of results (Houy et al., 2015).

To assess stylized facts statements for quality, Linder (2016: 554), outlines a method to measure the quality based on Weißenberger and Löhr's (2007) point system. Houy et al. (2015) propose taxonomy to validate and confirm their value. This approach assesses direct quotations of the stylized facts from the literature and scales them by level. Not one of the 16 studies used a quality test of the stylized facts.

A major challenge we encountered in the literature was the lack of clarity in presentation and reporting of the stylized facts. While distinctive to economics, there is no standardized approach for development and reporting of stylized facts, although the coding process should be developed in a transparent manner as with the retrieval of sources and their analysis to realize the advantage of granularity of research results (Houy et al., 2015). The third element of the three-step methodology is the reporting of results (Tranfield et al., 2003). The following section highlights the stylized fact method to fulfil this final step.

### Proposed steps for reporting stylized facts

To develop further understanding we use Hansen and Hughes (2005) to illustrate the use of a synthesized five-step method as a tool for management consultants. We include the thinking of Kaldor's (1961) "as if" approach, Heine et al. (2005) to allow for a comparison of results for the pooling of knowledge, Wagner's (2011) recommendations for a holistic understanding of the stylized fact method in use and discuss each element as we step through the method. To begin:

**Formulate the research question**. What is the problem? The research question is formulated for construct and context identification with a literature review.
"How are innovations disseminated and gains shared with a learning-by-doing externality and a bargaining game?"

**Step 1: Identify the stylized facts**. The empirical investigations start with a thorough identification of stylized facts. What are the assumptions?

Step 1: Examine recent findings in the literature to develop an overview of the topic and related theory. "We begin by characterizing optimal licensing fees when the consultant enters engagements sequentially. There has been considerable prior research on innovation (e.g. cost reduction) and licensing."
Assumption: "The industry setting is a two-period Cournot duopoly . . ."

*Recommendation:* Use different data sets from published research so that the work can be re-examined for scientific replication.

**Step 2: Explain the stylized facts**. Develop a series of structural models to formulate and estimate the stylized facts.

Step 2: ". . . Kamien and Tauman [1986] consider whether an R&D firm can extract more rents from oligopolistic producers for an innovation through per-unit royalties or lump-sum fees. Our model reflects many stylized facts of the management consulting industry (Greiner and Metzger [1983], Maister [1993])."
Model development: "In the Nash bargaining game, the consultant has bargaining power $\beta$ and each client firm has bargaining power $\alpha$ where $(\alpha=1-\beta)$."

*Recommendation:* Never consider results based on one sample, one firm, one country or from one period as a stylized fact. Work with other teams in other countries towards a unified approach for capturing data.

**Step 3: Determine empirical superiority**. A model that explains more stylized facts than its rivals should be preferred because it is empirically superior (Mendritzki, 2014).

Step 3: "The choice between sequential engagements (delayed dissemination of innovation with learning by doing) and concurrent engagements (immediate dissemination of innovation) is considered."

**Step 4: Identify the contribution**. How do the stylized facts impact the results?

Step 4: "The contribution of our analysis rests with imbedding learning by doing externality and a bargaining game to determine how innovations are disseminated and gains from innovation are shared."

**Step 5: Report the results**. Did the results support or contradict the stylized facts?

Step 5: "Our analysis of equilibrium licensing agreements raises the interesting prospects that either the licensee or licensor may become the industry's low-cost producer. More generally, we provide plausible conditions under which either immediate or delayed dissemination may be optimal from the constant's perspective depending on both the extent of her learning by doing and her bargaining power."

Offering: Proof of propositions

*Recommendation:* Make your work available for replication and extension. Do this as an author, an editor and as a referee.

## Conclusion

As an expanding phenomenon, this chapter introduces the concept of the stylized fact in its use specific to management consulting. As an exploratory investigation, we constructed a historical perspective through a review of the literature. We then conducted an examination of findings and reported our findings as the answers to our questions. As our contributions, we first conducted a comprehensive review of stylized facts in relation to management consulting. Then, we synthesized the knowledge and offered a proposed approach to the presentation in the reporting of stylized facts for management consulting.

The challenges we encountered were many. First, we discovered that there is no unified definition of a stylized fact. Next, our scope was limited to one database and a small sample size. Then, we discovered a singularity of the facts and a potential lack of relevance. Finally, a lack of clarity of presentation hindered our research efforts to ascertain the stylized facts. However, the opportunities this chapter provided are also numerous.

Our findings provided a refined understanding of the concept of the stylized fact in its various uses and forms. We then observed patterns with the accumulation of the data that can assist the development of management models. Three main themes were identified as well as key indicators specific to management consulting literature. As new sources of information, the implications for further research is encouraging although there are limitations. We found that while there is a flaw in how the use of assumptions can be self-fulfilling, evidence-based assumptions can provide an opening in their presentation as enablers to theory and model development. Further, stylized facts are not true in every instance. Even so, with their strength in their ability to handle a diversity of evidence-based knowledge, and with the increasing use of technology, we observe that their use has become a source of competitive advantage.

## References

Ajmal, M., Nordstrom, F., and Helo, P. (2009). Assessing the effectiveness of business consulting in operations development projects. *International Journal of Productivity and Performance Management*, 58(6), 523–541.

Alvesson, M., and Spicer, A. (2012). A stupidity-based theory of organizations. *Journal of Management Studies*, 49(7), 13–33.

Arroyo Abad, L., and Khalifa, K. (2015). What are stylized facts? *Journal of Economic Methodology*, 22(2), 143–156.

Boland, L. A. (1994). Stylized facts. In *The new dictionary of economics*. London: Macmillan, pp. 535–536.

Boland, L. A. (1997). *Critical economic methodology: A personal Odyssey*. London: Routledge.

The Boston Consulting Group (BCG) (2010). *United States Patent 7,672,950*. Eckardt, III et al. March 2.

Caracelli, V. J., and Greene, J. C. (1993). Data analysis strategies for mixed-method evaluation designs. *Educational Evaluation and Policy Analysis*, 15(2), 195–207.

Coad, A., Daunfeldt, S-O., Johansson, D., and Wennberg, K. (2014). Whom do high-growth firms hire? *Industrial and Corporate Change*, 23(1), 293–327.

Cohendet, P., and Meyer-Krahmer, F. (2005). Technology policy in the knowledge-based economy. In P. Llerena and M. Mireille (eds.), *Innovation policy in a knowledge-based economy: Theory and practice*, Berlin: Springer Berlin Heidelberg, pp. 75–112.

Cont, R. (2001). Empirical properties of asset returns: Stylized facts and statistical issues. *Quantitative Finance*, 1, 223–236.

Curnow, B., and Reuvid, J. (2003). *The international guide to management consultancy: The evolution, practice and structure of management consultancy worldwide*, 2nd ed. London; Sterling, VA: Kogan Page.

Epstein, J. M. (2006). *Generative social science*. Princeton, NJ: Princeton University Press.

Evans, B., Reynolds, P., and Cockman, P. (1992). Consulting and the process of learning. *European Industrial Training*, 16(2), 7–11.

Fact. (2016). *Merriam-Webster.com*. Available from www.merriam-webster.com/dictionary/fact [Accessed April 30, 2016].

Ferraro, F., Pfeffer, J., and Sutton, R. (2005). Economic language and assumptions: How theories can become self-fulfilling. *Academy of Management Review*, 30(1), 8–24.

Gill, J., and Johnson, P. (1997). *Research methods for managers*, 2nd ed. London: Paul Chapman Publishing.

Hansen, S. C., and Hughes, J. S. (2005). The dissemination of management consulting innovations and the pace of technological improvements. *Journal of Institutional and Theoretical Economics*, JITE, 161(3), 536–555.

Heine, B-O., Meyer, O., and Strangfeld, O. (2005). Stylised facts and the contribution of simulation to the economic analysis of budgeting. *Journal of Artificial Societies and Social Simulation* [online], 8(4). Available from http://jasss.soc.surrey.ac.uk/8/4/4.html [Accessed April 8, 2016].

Helfat, C. E. (2007). Stylized facts, empirical research and theory development in management. *Strategic Organization*, 5(2), 185–192.

Houy, C., Fettke, P., and Loos, P. (2015). Stylized facts as an instrument for literature review and cumulative information systems research. *Communications of the Association for Information Systems*, 37, 225–256.

Ittner, C., and Larcker, D. (2002). Empirical managerial accounting research: Are we just describing management consulting practice? *European Accounting Review*, 11(4), 787–794.

Kaldor, N. (1961). Capital accumulation and economic growth. In F. A. Lutz and D. C. Hague (eds.), *The theory of capital*, reprint ed. 1968. London: Macmillan, pp. 177–222.

Kremer, M. (1993). The O-ring theory of economic development. *Quarterly Journal of Economics*, CVIII, 551–575.

Lancaster, G. (2005). *Research methods in management - a concise introduction to research in management business consultancy*. Oxford: Elsevier Butterworth Heinemann.

Linder, C. (2016). Embeddedness and the international workforce: Stylized facts and future research directions. *Global Business Review*, 17(3), 541–565.

Litner, J. (1956). Distributions of incomes of corporations among dividends, retained earnings and taxes. *The American Economic Review*, May, 97–113.

Lucas, Jr., R. E. (1988). On the mechanic of economic development. *Journal of Monetary Economics*, 22, 4–42.

Luyt, R. (2012). A framework for mixing methods in quantitative measurement development, validation, and revision a case study. *Journal of Mixed Methods Research*, 6(4), 294–316.

Mainela, T., Puhakka, V., and Servais, P. (2014). The concept of international opportunity in international entrepreneurship: A review and a research agenda. *International Journal of Management Reviews*, 16(1), 105–129.

Mäki, U. (1998). As if. In J. B. Davis, D. W. Hands and U. Maki (eds.), *The handbook of economic methodology*. Cheltenham; Northampton, MA: Edward Elgar, pp. 25–27.

Marsh, T., and Merton, R. (1986). Dividend variability and variance bounds tests for the rationality of stock market prices. *The American Economic Review*, 76(3), 483–498.

Mendritzki, S. (2014). To stylize or not to stylize, is it a fact then? Clarifying the role of stylized facts in empirical model evaluation. *Economic Methodology*, 21(2), 1–18.

Mingers, J. (2000). Variety is the spice of life: Combining soft and hard OR/MS methods. *International Transactions in Operational Research*, 7(6), 673.

Mohe, M. (2007). Perspectives on management consulting research. *Arbeit*, 16(3), 255–264.

Moreno, F. (2015). Entrepreneurial growth: Individual, firm, and region high-growth firms: Stylized facts and conflicting results. In *Advances in entrepreneurship, firm emergence, and growth*, Vol. 17. Bingley, UK: Emerald Group Publishing Limited, pp. 187–230.

Parker, S. C. (2009). Can cognitive biases explain venture team homophily? *Strategic Entrepreneurship Journal*, 3(1), 67–83.

Phillips, E. M. and Pugh, D. S. (1987). *How to get a PhD: Managing the peaks and troughs of research*. Philadelphia: Open University Press.

Scatter acorns so that oaks may grow. (n.d.). MIT Institute Archives & Special Collections. Available from http://libraries.mit.edu/archives/exhibits/adlittle/history.html [Accessed March 22, 2016].

Schmalensee, R. (1981). Risk and return on long lived tangible assets. *Financial Economics*, 9, 185–205.

Scopus. The University of Queensland Libraries. (n.d.). Available from http://search.library.uq.edu.au/primo_library/libweb/action/search.do?vl(freeText0)=scopus&ct=facet&rfnGrpCounter=1&frbg=&&indx=1&fn=search&dscnt=0&scp.scps=scope%3A(61UQ)%2Cprimo_central_multiple_fe&vl(1UIStartWith0)=contains&tb=t&vid=61UQ&mode=Basic&ct=search&srt=rank&tab=61uq_all&vl(D75285834UI0)=any&fctExcV=newspaper_articles&mulExcFctN=facet_rtype&rfnExcGrp=1&fctExcV=reviews&mulExcFctN=facet_rtype&rfnExcGrp=1 [Accessed June 1, 2016].

Solow, R. M. (1956). A contribution to the theory of economic growth. *The Quarterly Journal of Economics*, 70, 65–94.

Solow, R. M. (1970). *Growth theory: An exposition*. New York: Oxford University Press.

Sornette, D. (2014). Physics and financial economics (1776–2014): Puzzles, Ising and agent-based models. *Reports on Progress in Physics*, 77(6), 1–28.

Tate, M., Furtmueller, E., Evermann, J., and Bandara, W. (2015). Introduction to the special issue: The literature review in information systems. *Communications of the Association for Information Systems*, 37(5), 103–111.

Torraco, R. J. (2005). Writing integrative literature reviews: Guidelines and examples. *Human Resource Development Review*, 4(3), 356–367.

Tranfield, D., Denyer, D., and Smart, P. (2003). Towards a methodology for developing evidence-informed management knowledge by means of systematic review. *British Journal of Management*, 14(3), 207–222.

Wagner, J. (2011). From estimation results to stylized facts twelve recommendations for empirical research in international activities of heterogeneous firms. *De Economist*, 159, 389–412.

Wang, C., and Chugh, H. (2014). Entrepreneurial learning: Past research and future challenges. *International Journal of Management Reviews*, 16(1), 24–61. Business Source Alumni Edition, *EBSCOhost* [viewed 19 March 2016].

Weißenberger, B., and Löhr, B. (2007). Planung und Untersuchungserfolg: Stylized facts aus der empirischen: Controllingforschung im deutschsprachigen Raum von 1990–2007. *Zeitschrift für Planung & Unternehmenssteuerung*, 18(4), 335–363.

# Appendix

*Table 2.3* Appendix 1: Scopus literature cross-over by subject area

| Study No. | Document Title | Economics, Econometrics and Finance | Business, Management and Accounting | Decision Sciences | Medicine | Health Professions | Mathematics | Physics and Astronomy | Computer Science | Energy |
|---|---|:---:|:---:|:---:|:---:|:---:|:---:|:---:|:---:|:---:|
| | | 8 | 5 | 3 | 3 | 2 | 2 | 2 | 1 | 1 |
| 1. | Technology policy in the knowledge-based economy | ★ | ★ | | | | | | | |
| 2. | Ranking market efficiency for stock markets: A nonlinear perspective | ★ | | | | | ★ | ★ | | |
| 3. | On rationally confident beliefs and rational overconfidence | ★ | | ★ | | | | | | |
| 4. | Economic theory and evidence on smoking behaviour of adults | | | | ★ | | | | | |
| 5. | Global recessions as a cascade phenomenon with interacting agents | ★ | ★ | | | | | | | |
| 6. | A comparison of multifractal models for asset returns in economic perspective | ★ | | | | | ★ | | | |
| 7. | What are we learning from the life satisfaction literature? | ★ | | | | | | | | |
| 8. | The industrial organization of sport coaches: Road cycling as a distinguished case | | ★ | ★ | ★ | ★ | | | | |
| 9. | Telehealth-based systems for diagnosis, management and treatment of autism spectrum disorders: Challenges, opportunities, and applications | | | | ★ | ★ | | | | |
| 10. | Multifractional processes in finance | ★ | | ★ | | | | | | |
| 11. | Physics and financial economics (1776–2014): Puzzles, Ising and agent-based models | | | | | | | ★ | | |
| 12. | Overconfidence and diversification | ★ | | | | | | | | |
| 13. | Stylized facts as an instrument for literature review and cumulative information systems research | | | | | | | | ★ | |
| 14. | A review of combined models for market diffusion of alternative fuel vehicles and their refuelling infrastructure | | | | | | | | | ★ |
| 15. | Predictability and "good deals" in currency markets | | ★ | | | | | | | |
| 16. | Skill heterogeneity in start-ups and its development over time | | ★ | | | | | | | |

★ Shaded rows are the article as per the Wang and Chugh (2014) reduction method to focus on "business" articles only (no. 1 is a book chapter and was then removed for a final sample of four)

Source: Scopus. Table developed by the authors.

*Table 2.4* Appendix 2: Scopus keywords for the management consulting literature base

| | | |
|---|---|---|
| Adaptive Markets | Financial Data Processing | Natural Gas Vehicles |
| Addiction | Forecasting Performance | Nonlinear Dependence |
| Adult | Foreign Exchange | Phase Transitions |
| Aged | Fractals | Plug-in Electric Vehicles |
| Aged 80 and Over | Fuel Cell Electric Vehicle | Predictability |
| Alternative Fuel Vehicles | Fuel Cells | Rational Beliefs |
| Alternative Fuels | Gas Fuel Analysis | Rational Overconfidence |
| Application Examples | Hardware | Rationality |
| Behavioral Finance | Health Care Policy | Recessions |
| Bicorrelation | Health Policy | Refueling Infrastructure |
| Bubbles | Human | Related Drawbacks |
| Carbon Dioxide | Humans | Research Synthesis |
| Cascades | Hyperbolic Discounting | Review |
| Choice Behavior | Impulsive Behavior | Risk Factors |
| Cigarette Prices | Impulsivity | Risk Preference |
| Cigarette Smoking | Information Systems | Sampling |
| Commerce | Interacting Agents | Scientific Knowledge |
| Competitive Intelligence | Interaction Model | Shadow Value of Non-market Goods |
| Conceptual Framework | Interaction Modeling | Skill Heterogeneity |
| Continuous State Space | International Transmission | Smoking |
| Controlled Study | Ising Model | Smoking Cessation |
| Costs And Cost Analysis | Life Satisfaction | Startups |
| Cumulative Research | Literature Review | Statistical Mechanics |
| Current Situation | Literature Reviews | Stock Markets |
| Diffusion | Market Development | Stylized Facts |
| Economic Aspect | Market Efficiency | Team Dynamics |
| Economic Perspective | Middle Aged | Theory Development |
| Economic Theories | Models | Time Factors |
| Economics | Multi Frequency | Time Preferences |
| Econophysics | Multifractal Models | Tobacco Dependence |
| Efficient Markets | Multifractal Models For Assets Returns | Transport Sectors |
| Empirical Studies | Multifractality | Unemployment/inflation Trade-off |
| Entrepreneurship | Multifractality of Financial Time-series | Vehicles |
| Excess Volatility Puzzle | Multifractional Processes | WAMS Markov Processes |
| Filter Rules | Mutual Interaction | |
| Finance | Natural Gas | |

Source: Scopus. Table developed by the authors.

# 3 Create more value for all

## A human dignity oriented approach to consulting

*P. Matthijs Bal and Simon B. de Jong*

### Abstract

This chapter explores how consultants may address societal and business challenges which have become increasingly more manifest since the economic crisis of 2008. These issues range from bankruptcies and corporate scandals to increased burnout amongst employees. We argue that in contrast to the contemporary utilitarian approach of perceiving people as instrumental to company goals and of focusing on the maximum amount of short-term profit for a select few, consultancy can be designed on the philosophy of humanism and human dignity so that it provides more value to all stakeholders. First, the concept of human dignity is introduced and we highlight that people should not be treated as means to an end, but rather as ends in themselves. Then, we argue that one practical way of achieving human dignity is to increase organizational democracy. Subsequently, the concepts of human dignity and organizational democracy are applied to three main phases of the consulting process, namely 1) the starting phase (includes entry, diagnosis, and planning); 2) the 'doing' phase (includes action, engagement, and delivery); and 3) the final phase (includes evaluation and termination). The chapter ends by concluding that an inclusive, democratic way of running consultancy projects is likely to pay off in the long run, not only for employees and society, but also for companies and shareholders as well as consultants themselves, as it strengthens human and organizational capabilities to effectively manage the uncertain circumstances which characterize contemporary businesses and societies.

## Introduction

Since the financial crisis, it has become increasingly clear that there are fundamental problems underlying contemporary societies, our economic systems, and our business practices (Seymour, 2014). Key indicators for this are that inequality and poverty have increased as have unemployment and underemployment (George, 2014). Additionally, health problems such as higher employee burnout (Leiter et al., 2014) and worker abuse (Lucas et al., 2013) have gone up, as have depressions and suicides (Kentikelenis et al., 2014; Seymour, 2014). Some commentators have attempted to whisk these facts away by arguing that this is a necessary evil of doing business and that this is the only way to create value (which is then often narrowly defined as company or shareholder value or profit). However, a quick glance at the news shows that many organizations are facing financial, innovational, and/or reputational challenges. For example, organizations which were once common household names have recently gone into bankruptcy, such as BHS in the UK, RadioShack in the US, or V&D in the Netherlands. Additionally, as Lazonick has shown in his 2014 *Harvard Business Review* article, many CEOs are now taking out so much money from their organizations (e.g., via stock buy backs) that innovation and long-term sustainability are put at risk. Lastly, once reputable organizations such as global banks or car manufacturers have been plagued by scandals, government bailouts, and enormous fines (Rhodes, 2016). The issues have now become so apparent that even established pro-business news outlets, such as Bloomberg, are asking for a rethink of how we conduct business as well as contemplate what governments should, and should not, do (e.g., 'Bloomberg Editorial Letter', March 12, 2013). All these facts indicate that there is something fundamentally wrong with how we have come to think about business and management. This conclusion is further reinforced if we take into account the current unsustainable use of planetary resources (Klein, 2014).

Luckily our societies contain various institutions and organizations which might contribute to solving these problems. Invaluable societal assets, such as a free press and independent universities contribute to this, as well as various NGOs who attempt to represent society at large. However, we will argue in this chapter that one sector appears to be overlooked when it concerns potential solutions to societal problems, namely (internal and external) business and management consulting. In our opinion, the consulting sector might play an important part as consultants are requested when companies do not have the time or expertise to deal with complex topics. Additionally, due to their relatively high fees, consultants tend to be used for projects which have substantial impact, such as strategic (re-)designs or change management programs. Moreover, consultants tend to consult at various organizations, sometimes at the same time, sometimes in rapid succession. The key is thus that consultants are often in unique positions of influence and can also 'cross-pollinate' ideas by facilitating the transfer and adoption of 'best practices' across organizations and industries as well as between science and practice. Hence, we argue that if our societies could change the way we engage in consulting, there might be substantial benefits to everyone, and such change might occur quite rapidly due to the nature of consulting.

More specifically, we argue that the current challenges mentioned in the opening paragraph could be resolved or significantly reduced via consultancy work. Consultants play an important role in the shaping of contemporary organizations (for example, via strategy or organizational design or process consulting), yet with this role also comes an inherent responsibility to the (societal) systems and the organizations which provide the ecosystem for consultancies to flourish in. This responsibility is thus actually in line with consultants' own interests. But as indicated in the introduction, the current systems show many symptoms of illness, and solving these issues might be beneficial for all stakeholders, including the consultants themselves. For example, the costs in Europe of employee burnout have been calculated to be over £77 billion (Evans-Lacko and Knapp, 2014), and estimates for the damages caused by global warming and the unsustainable use of resources range even higher (Klein, 2014). Hence, there is plenty of work available and consultants may actually fulfill a crucial role in alleviating societal problems whilst at the same time help their clients and themselves.

However, to alleviate such problems, it is essential to analyze the underlying causes of the flaws in the economic system and the increasing social injustice (George, 2014; Harvey, 2005; Seymour, 2014). If not addressed at the core, superficial 'improvements' might be implemented or, even worse, Corporate Social Responsibility (CSR) 'greenwashing' might be used to give an aura of sustainability without any actual real change (cf. Porter and Kramer, 2011). Hence, we need to look more deeply at the current neoliberal capitalist society and acknowledge that it has been focusing too much on (short-term) profit maximization for individual firms and individual actors (e.g., the enormous bonuses of individual top managers: Lazonick, 2014), and has done so through a dominant approach which views labor as purely instrumental. For example, often at the advice of consultants, organizations have adopted management practices which focus on short-term gains, and narrow the employee relationships towards a pure transactional relationship by making jobs more insecure (Thompson, 2013). However, this transactional relationship has not really benefitted most workers, as most workers get little to no bonus, while executive pay and bonuses have rapidly increased since the 1980s, in line with the increasing inequality in society (Desai, 2012). This instrumentality has undermined employee commitment, engagement, and trust (Chartered Institute of Personnel and Development [CIPD], 2012), and has put employee, team, and organizational learning, development, and growth at risk (Lazonick, 2014). The question is thus how consultants may address the inherent problems of the current form of capitalism; problems which have become increasingly more manifest since the economic crisis of 2008. We argue that in contrast to the contemporary utilitarian approach of perceiving people as instrumental, or as resources to be used and to be expended, consultancy can be designed based on the philosophical alternative of humanism and human dignity (Kant, 1785).

Human dignity, according to Immanuel Kant, postulates that people can never be treated as means to an end, but rather should be treated as ends in themselves. When human dignity is introduced as an alternative paradigm for consultancy, all aspects of the consulting process should be changed and updated. We argue that there are two main roles for 'human dignity' consultants: 1) through their work, consultants can contribute to greater dignity in the workplace and thus dignity should become a clear outcome of any project; but 2) beyond dignity as an outcome, it may also sit at the heart of the work of a consultant, especially when a consultant takes on the synergist or champion role (Caldwell, 2001). As such, in offering organizations advice, consultants could focus on taking a less instrumental and transactional approach (e.g., focus less on maximizing shareholder interests), and consult more in a dignified way and via a more dignified process (e.g., focusing on protecting and promoting all stakeholder interests).

The current chapter will explain both ways in greater detail, and we will discuss how human dignity can be applied to the different phases of a consulting project. We will first give an overview of human dignity, followed by a section on why human dignity could provide a suitable foundation for consulting activities. This is followed by a section on workplace and organizational democracy, which we will argue can be a valuable tool for bringing more dignity into the consulting process. We then apply these theories and concepts to the established consulting model of Kolb and Frohman (1970) by focusing on three main phases of the consulting process, namely: 1) the starting phase (includes entry, diagnosis, and planning); 2) the 'doing' phase (includes action, engagement, and delivery); and 3) the final phase (includes evaluation and termination). The chapter ends with overall conclusions.

## Overview of, and the importance of, human dignity

Human dignity has not been used widely in the field of management. This is surprising given that it has a long tradition in philosophy, and has also been used in law, as indicated by the inclusion of human dignity in Article 1 of the Universal Declaration of Human Rights. Hence, human dignity has global relevance, and it is only recently that management studies have started to explore the role of human dignity at work (Pirson and Lawrence, 2010). The philosopher Immanuel Kant, in the eighteenth century, postulated the dignity of the human being as central to life. This contrasts with the utilitarian perspective that strives for the greatest benefit for the largest number of people, which has been used to defend an instrumental approach to people in organizations. In a utilitarian view, it could be 'logical' to allow a few people to suffer, so that the majority can achieve greater benefits. Human dignity, however, sees the individual human being as central to the organizing principle. Human dignity indicates that all individuals are equal and that dignity represents an existential value (Kateb, 2011). This means that every human being has a dignity which does not have to be earned. While there is no prevailing definition of human dignity, in the current chapter we define human dignity as the unalienable right of each individual human being to self-respect and get respect from others, to set one's own standards and principles of living, and to live accordingly (Bal, 2015; Bal and Lub, 2015).

Human dignity does not only entail *the right* for people to be treated with dignity, but also *the duty* of people to behave dignified and treat others with dignity (Rosen, 2012). Dignity is therefore essentially relational, and it binds people together in exchange relationships, where people commit to each other by treating others in a dignified manner, while themselves behaving in a dignified way. More specifically, dignified treatment means that people respect themselves and are free to set their own standards, but at the same time respect others who are also free to set their standards. In reciprocal exchange relationships, people can only live and work together when they respect each other's dignity. Therefore, dignity should be respected, protected, and promoted (Pirson and Dierksmeier, 2014). People should respect the dignity of others, which means they provide other people the freedom to set their own standards. Moreover, people should protect the dignity of others, which means that they strive not to violate the dignity of other people (or allow or encourage others to do so). Finally, people should promote the dignity of others, which means that people actively contribute to upholding dignity standards within and across organizations and social life. Hence, human dignity contains both rights and duties and focuses on respecting, protecting, and promoting the dignity of all.

## Using human dignity as a basis for consulting

Human dignity can inform the way organizations are founded and managed (Pirson and Dierksmeier, 2014), and can thus also be a basis on which consultancy can take place. This replaces the current instrumentalist, individualistic, and short-term profit focused approach stemming from contemporary capitalist and investor-centric approaches for doing business (cf. Lazonick, 2014; Porter and Kramer, 2011). As a fundamental principle, it should be publically acknowledged that all stakeholders will be treated in a dignified way during the consulting process itself as well as in the final end product (cf. Bridoux and Stoelhorst, 2014). This includes all people involved, such as sellers, buyers, governmental institutions, investors, future generations, and so forth. As these relationships become the center of consulting, the aim becomes how these parties can engage in a meaningful exchange that is focused on respect, protection, and promotion of human dignity for all. This does *not* suggest that business concerns, such as profits, are no longer relevant. Organizations can only be sustainable when they retain a (long-term) positive balance sheet and create some surplus for investments and unforeseen circumstances.

However, the current practice of myopically focusing on short-term profits and transferring profits to top managers and shareholders (Lazonick, 2014), without acknowledging the dignity of all the other stakeholders, has been shown to have such adverse outcomes such as (semi-)slavery, inequality, and other forms of dignity violations (Kaufmann et al., 2011). Moreover, this 'value extraction' is likely to undermine the long-term viability of the organization by hindering 'value creation', whilst also negatively affecting the relationship with key stakeholders. For example, utilitarian and neoliberal business strategies can encourage offshoring profits to tax havens, cheating customers, misleading investors, or creating environmental pollution (Rhodes, 2016). In contrast, with a human dignity approach the aim of organizing, and thus also of consulting, becomes the art of retaining a balance between the (long-term) interests of various stakeholders, whilst acknowledging that each of these parties have their dignity which should not be violated by overly satisfying one stakeholder above the others (e.g., giving investors some quick dividend). Balance, therefore, is of crucial importance for successful 'dignified' consulting (Bal, 2015; Pirson and Lawrence, 2010).

The implication of having human dignity underlying business and consulting is that it changes the meaning people attribute to their jobs as well as the meaning which organizations have in society. Human dignity acknowledges that people become part of organizations to create and produce, and to be a member of a group, and through being part of organizations gives meaning to their lives (Bal, 2015). Reasons of existence for organizations therefore need to be redefined to enhance the potential to this 'meaning making' for employees, as well as other stakeholders. Hence, organizations have to become more than just simple money-making machines for a select few (cf. Lazonick, 2014), and become drivers for the promotion of human dignity and progress across the world. Some companies already aim to do so. For example, the German outdoor equipment producer Vaude claims to be "dedicated to making (y)our world a better place' (Vaude, 2015). Through an inclusive approach (e.g., investment in the local community) and sustainable practices (e.g., production under ethical standards), this company strives for a more dignified process of organizing. Other examples include Semco in Brazil, Sekem in Egypt, Happy Computers in the UK, Mondragon in Spain, Buurtzorg in the Netherlands, and SMUD in the US. By putting certain values forward – such as economical, ecological, and social sustainability and responsibility – these companies aim to be more than profit-making organizations, and they strive to find a 'dignified' balance. Hence, various business cases can be found where a more dignified approach to business has paid large (societal) dividends, and consulting can use those cases as a starting point and convince companies of the need to take this approach. However, once companies have been convinced and agree to strive to put human dignity at the heart of their business, a new question arises: *How to use the principles of human dignity during a consulting project?* We explain how the concepts of workplace democracy and representation provide useful tools to integrate human dignity throughout the key phases of a consulting project (Kolb and Frohman, 1970).

## The importance of democracy and representation

Workplace democracy can be one practical way through which organizations achieve the respect, protection, and promotion of human dignity for all stakeholders (Sauser Jr, 2009; de Jong and Van Witteloostuijn, 2004). Applied to consultancy, the idea of workplace democracy may indicate the ways in which consultants deliver advice to clients. As a central notion of human dignity pertains to the equality of people within the organization, it should be realized that the product of a consultant for an organization is not a neutral or 'objective' one; rather, it is always embedded within the relationships existing within an organization (as well as outside the organization). In other words, the consultant's product interacts with the ways of organizing in a company. If the advice of a consultant, or a team of consultants, is enforced top-down through the hierarchy of an organization, it is more likely to neglect the role of human beings in the organization than when all stakeholders in the organization are represented and involved in the process. Research has shown that such 'voice' is very important. For example, in 2010, the CIPD reported that 'voice' was the third most important aspect for creating engagement in a company after 'meaningful work' and 'leadership' (both of which should be improved as well via a dignified and human-oriented approach to consulting). Hence, a democratic way of consulting, through the inclusion of all stakeholders based on the idea of equality of everyone, will be more likely to deliver a product that respects the dignity of the people involved.

The reason why democracy is important here is that it indicates that power is redistributed across the organization, from managers to workers, and this contributes to more equitable relationships. Research supports this notion, as it has been shown that when people within the organization trust each other due to strong relational ties, employees will be more committed to the organization and more willing to contribute in a positive way (Rousseau, 2012). One way to commit employees to an organization or a consulting project is ownership (Rousseau and Shperling, 2003). When employees feel ownership of a project, they are likely to be more committed to the long-term viability and performance of the organization. Thus, democracy aligns with human dignity not only because of its respect for fair and equal relationships, but also because democracy protects and promotes the responsibility of each individual as a member of the organization.

In conclusion, taking the above reasons together, consultancy projects which take into account the human dignity of all stakeholders will not only increase organizational functioning (e.g., growth, learning, innovation), but also positively contribute to society and thus increase the company brand in the eyes of customers and potential employees, and also reduce risks of being fined by governments or being the target of campaigns by NGOs. To achieve all these benefits, we must resolve how consulting projects could be adapted to be more aligned with dignity and democracy principles. In the next section, we discuss how this can be done across the main phases of consulting (Kolb and Frohman, 1970).

## Human dignity and democracy across the main phases of consulting

Consulting firms use many tailor-made frameworks to capture the key phases of a consulting project (e.g., Werr et al., 1997). We choose to simplify the well-known model of Kolb and Frohman (1970) into three main phases. In phase 1, there is still no concrete project, and as such the entry strategy, problem diagnosis, and project planning all need to be established. We then focus on phase 2 where actions are undertaken in the project and where the consultant(s) are engaging with the client and stakeholders to deliver results. Lastly, we focus on phase 3 where the project has been delivered and it is time to evaluate. The sections below are meant as illustrations of how the principles of human dignity and democracy could be implemented from the start to finish of a consulting project, and can thus be adapted to any framework. Naturally, the specific details will have to be custom-made for each specific consulting project.

### Phase 1: Entry, diagnosis, and planning

Often a single stakeholder (or its representative) contacts the consulting firm regarding a potential project, yet this person might (inadvertently) not represent the interest and dignity of all stakeholders involved. This could, for example, simply be because the client has not yet thought about the broader impact. Hence, at the very start of the project, the consultant should actively collect the views of *all* stakeholders (not just the internal stakeholders at the client's office or factory) because it is only in this way that the full impacts can be assessed and proactively managed. For example, the project could be notified via internal messaging boards, so that people can declare an interest by responding within a given time frame and select any representatives if desired or ask for periodic updates. Externally, local communities can be contacted via councils or representatives and customers can be asked via Customer Relationship Management (CRM) activities, whilst representation of others can be achieved via discussions with NGOs. By truly incorporating all stakeholders at the very start, the project plan can proactively incorporate all stakeholders in its work flows. In contrast to a '*max. profit*' analysis for a small group of stakeholders, the analysis should (also) include a '*min. hurt*' analysis for all stakeholders. In other words, it needs to be assessed who is to gain from the project and who is going to lose – and if that loss is acceptable. This might also help with the ultimate role of a consultant, namely to assess the 'real' problem underlying those that manifest themselves for management. For instance, management might have asked a consultant to increase motivation as there is much (short-term) sickness and high rates of absence in the company, yet this absence may be resulting from a company culture that pressures people and violates the dignity of the workers and/or customers (e.g., aggressive phone sales techniques). It is the role of the consultant to assess and address these 'real' causes, not only to help the workers (e.g., less sickness), but also to help the company (e.g., retain talent and customers) as well as society (e.g., fewer workers who are [partially] disabled due to burnout and need to claim benefits). By involving all stakeholders early in the process, and taking all of their dignity into serious consideration, a consultant is much more likely to find the real problem facing the organization and to find a balanced and long-term solution.

From a (short-term) utilitarian perspective this might seem to be cumbersome and time consuming. Yet, from a broader and longer-term perspective, the time spent on getting broader buy-in at the start will smooth the work in other phases. For example, obstacles will be noted earlier, and more ideas will be generated from internal stakeholders and importantly also from other stakeholders who are (or might become) customers or employees – otherwise they might become vocal activists *against* the new changes once they are communicated to the outside world (e.g., when plans have unforeseen societal or environmental impacts). By guarding the human dignity of all at the beginning of the project by giving all some democratic representation, these issues can be avoided or reduced.

For instance, if customers would have had more insight into 'exotic' financial products, it could be argued that banks would not have needed government bailouts, fewer companies would have gone bankrupt, fewer customers would be in debt, and fewer banking employees would now be made redundant. Or, if regulators would have had more insight into the 'fuel efficiency' procedures at Volkswagen, billion dollar claims could have been avoided, the environment could have been spared, and the reputation of car makers and Germany as a country could have been preserved (Rhodes, 2016). In the long-term, it has now become apparent that what was needed was a culture where cheating was disapproved, and where employees had more options to 'blow the whistle' about potential morally questionable practices. Yet, the short-term focus prevailing in many companies underestimates (or even completely ignores) the benefits of such cultures. Lastly, to make it even more concrete, BP's oil spill in the Gulf of Mexico has been so costly ($50+ billion) that *only* preventing this accident (and there have been many more . . .) could have enabled the company to spent *more than $500 million a year* (in 2016 terms) extra on human dignity, democracy, and sustainability during its *entire 100+ year existence* and still be better off financially as well as have a better reputation. In addition, workers would have worked in safer conditions and the environment would not have been polluted. Surely, with numbers and outcomes such as these, it should not be too hard to make a sound business case to challenge contemporary assumptions underlying business and consulting. One difficulty in making these business cases is that it is often overlooked that even shareholders are made up of quite different groups, such as the very long-term view of government and pension funds versus the very short-term view of some private equity firms. As such, a business or a consulting project might explicitly exclude some forms of capital because their short-term focus makes them prone to violate the human dignity of other stakeholders. Excluding these 'non-dignified' sources of capital can enable companies to (re)gain economic, reputational, worker-related, environmental, and societal benefits.

Overall, these high-profile incidences show that it pays of *in the long-term* to get it right the first time, and a human-dignified approach to business and consulting can more easily achieve this as it has a much longer and broader perspective than the current narrowly focused utilitarian view of neoliberal capitalism, which ignores many stakeholders and therefore has a high risk of violating the dignity of others and thus, ultimately and ironically, undermining the sustainability of its own practices (as indicated in our introduction and, for example, in the editorial articles in *Bloomberg* in 2013). Concretely, in the very first phase of consulting, the benefits (and risks) the project brings to all stakeholders should be clearly acknowledged, whilst ensuring that everybody's dignity is maintained (even if this means lower maximum profit for some shareholders). To do so adequately, mostly likely an iterative process is needed to incorporate all the views into the final document.

### Phase 2: Action, engagement, and delivery

In the first phase, all stakeholders are identified and their views are heard and balanced via a democratic process. Yet, this is not a guarantee that their dignity will also be protected, promoted, and developed during the project. To safeguard this, a clear 'voicing' or feedback mechanism is needed (e.g., CIPD, 2010, 2012), so that key stages of the project are not just signed off by the client or key stakeholders or their representatives. For small projects, this could imply that one person is chosen to perform a 'devil's advocate' role and s/he voices the concerns of minority or vulnerable stakeholders. This could, for example, be an internal manager, but could also be an external and independent party, such as a lawyer, union member, or an academic who specializes in the particular field. Another way to safeguard human dignity is to truly acknowledge the possible impacts on others by being as transparent and open as possible during the engagement and delivery phase. Crowdsourcing and open source projects are now increasingly common for technological, scientific, and environmental projects, and these ideas could be translated into business consulting projects as well. For example, instead of having focus group sessions only for consumer products, it would be possible to get similar feedback on key consulting projects as well. This could be facilitated and anonymized via online survey providers, such that the specific trade secrets of the client company and consulting firm are protected.

The above ideas can be implemented in a staged approach throughout the project engagement phase and can be tailor-made to each group of stakeholders. For example, vulnerable or minority groups might require full anonymity (e.g., via online surveys or a representative), yet customers' opinions might be less sensitive and could be obtained via face-to-face meetings. The voice of some other groups (e.g., short-term focused private equity) might need to be lowered and put into perspective (e.g., long-term focused pension funds). The timing of when to ask certain stakeholders is also dictated by the concern for their dignity, with those who will have the most negative (long-term) impact needing to be prioritized. This is the reverse of many current practices where those with the most (short-term) benefits are giving the most attention. These groups will make their views known quite easily and vocally, and the difficulty is thus in getting the other views and then accounting for them in a balanced way. Without explicit democratic representation early on in the project, and without some form of regular and iterative feedback during the project and its delivery, the strong voice of the few who benefit in the short-term will be heard, putting other stakeholders at risk. Yet, it is because of the long-term stakeholders that the company will thrive in the future (e.g., employees or funders who are willing to stick with the company in difficult times, instead of taking their capital and labor to the competitors). This must be emphasized because there is an increasing mountain of evidence that the instrumental and short-term way of working is no longer viable (Klein, 2014). Thus, a more fundamental change is needed to stop the scandals and bailouts of the financial sector, the safety violations of oil companies, and the cheating by large car manufacturers as well as the current practice of ignoring the 'social dilemmas' underlying the unsustainable use of resources to the short-term benefit of a few, but to the long-term detriment of us all.

### Phase 3: Evaluation and termination

As many textbooks (e.g., Armstrong, 2012) and professional reports (e.g., CIPD, 2007) will state, evaluation is imperative for effective decision making and for truly learning from consulting and change management activities. However, a clear evaluation plan (or an overall exit strategy) is often lacking in consulting projects, with the result that lessons learned are not transferred to other projects, key knowledge is not retained in the company, and companies are then doomed to repeat the same mistakes over and over again. A key driver causing this seems to be the neoliberal and utilitarian belief that the next project is more important as it brings in short-term resources, yet this viewpoint ignores that for the long-term sustainability of both the client and consulting company it is important to truly reflect and learn from each project and to adequately document this for future use. For example, by doing so the client could learn how to avoid these problems, thus reducing the need to call in expensive consultants again. The consultancy could learn how to more effectively deliver a project, thus reducing burdens on consulting staff (and lower burnout and turnover rates) and increasing viability. It should be realized that there is an underlying asymmetry: whilst a consulting firm might use the new knowledge soon and thus retain some (implicit) insights, the client might only use this knowledge many years from now (e.g., normally one does not do a fundamental strategic change or a complete overhaul of ICT systems each year). Hence, the utility for the consultancy firm and the client firm are not in sync. The same outcome occurs between the consultancy firm and the consulting team who did the actual work. It would be in the consultants' long-term interest to truly learn from the project and thus increase their competencies. This would increase the human resources available to the consultancy firm and thus also increase the firm's long-term viability. Yet current performance management practices are heavily biased towards short-term profit for shareholders (cf. Desai, 2012), not to long-term learning, growth, and development. This bias puts consultants and their consulting companies at risk.

Not surprisingly, if the key stakeholders involved with a consultancy project already have so many problems with evaluating and getting the most out of a consulting project, a neoliberal and utilitarian perspective is even worse for other stakeholders. Many of the 'lean' and 'efficiency' programs have traded short-term gains, for long-term costs, resulting in lower average pay, higher stress, less free time, less creativity and development, etcetera. (Bal, 2015). When all firms take similar actions, the total 'societal pie' available to all shrinks, as the lower-paid or stressed-out employees from one firm do not have the money or energy to invest in other activities provided by other organizations. This leads the latter firms to lower their employee offerings and investments (Lazonick, 2014), putting more stress on workers who then can spend even less and so forth. This spills over beyond the business world, as depleted people cannot engage in learning and development activities or engage in societal activities, such as raising the next generation or being well-informed democratic citizens. Ultimately, and ironically, even the goals of the ones the neoliberal/utilitarian viewpoint is supposed to promote (e.g., shareholders) are put at risk, as shareholders will see ever diminishing returns if societies do not have the ability, motivation, or opportunity to explore new opportunities (cf. Lazonick, 2014). Hence, a sound 'post-project' strategy and a true evaluation involving all stakeholders are needed for the long-term benefit of us all, even though this is very difficult to argue for in the current utilitarian, neoliberal, and max-profit philosophy. However, if businesses and consultancies change their underlying paradigm to a humanistic approach, which takes into account the human dignity of all, the above suddenly starts to make a lot of sense.

## Conclusion

The current chapter investigated the role of dignity in consulting projects. Contemporary organizations are in a state of uncertainty, as current neoliberal and utilitarian capitalist practices have run out of their relevance for society, making it increasingly clear that they are not an optimal way for society to function (cf. Porter and Kramer, 2011). Consultancy may play a very important role in alleviating these problems and changing the rules of the game, and we have introduced human dignity (Kant, 1785) as a key paradigm to build a new way of doing consultancy projects. Dignity may inform not only the outcomes of a consulting project (i.e., a more dignified organization that contributes not only to its own viability but also to societal functioning), but also the ways in which consulting projects are executed. We have described three key steps of the consultancy project and how dignity may inform these steps (Kolb and Frohman, 1970). In general, we propose an inclusive, democratic way of running consultancy projects, which includes the views and interests of all stakeholders to arrive at balanced solutions where the minimum amount of hurt is taken into consideration, not only the maximum amount of profit for a select few (cf. Lazonick, 2014). This approach is likely to pay off in the long run, not only for employees and society but also for companies and shareholders, by strengthening organizational capabilities to effectively manage the uncertain circumstances which characterize the contemporary workplace. A key reason for this is that democracy empowers employees across the organization, enhances commitment, and identifies risks (CIPD, 2010, 2012).

In sum, a focus on human dignity allows companies to be organized in a different, more humane way and to be better able to create spaces where people flourish rather than where they are forced to conduct work in an ever more intense and 'soulless' way. An easy reminder might be the old saying, 'Do unto others as you would have them do unto you', when engaging in consulting work. At each stage of the consulting project, consultants (and other stakeholders) could ask themselves: Would *I* want to work in this job/team/organization after they followed my advice? Perhaps even more insightful, one could even ask: Would I want my *children and grandchildren* to work in this job/team/organization after they followed my advice? It is important that consultants keep asking questions such as these (and change their behaviors accordingly), as they can (or perhaps even should) play a crucial role in bridging societal, company, and employee interests and aligning these different needs for a more future-oriented workplace that respects the dignity of all of its stakeholders.

## References

Armstrong (2012). *Armstrong's handbook of human resource management practice*. London: Kogan Page Limited.

Bal, P. M. (2015). Voorbij neoliberalisme in de arbeids- en organisatiepsychologie: menselijke waardigheid en organisatiedemocratie [Beyond neoliberalism in work and organizational psychology: Human dignity and workplace democracy]. *Gedrag en Organisatie*, 28, 199–218.

Bal, P. M., and Lub, X. D. (2015). Individualization of work arrangements: A contextualized perspective on the rise and use of i-deals. In P. M. Bal and D. M. Rousseau (eds.), *Idiosyncratic deals between employees and organizations: Conceptual issues, applications, and the role of coworkers*. London: Psychology Press, pp. 9–23.

Bridoux, F., and Stoelhorst, J. W. (2014). Microfoundations for stakeholder theory: Managing stakeholders with heterogeneous motives. *Strategic Management Journal*, 35, 107–125.

Caldwell, R. (2001). Champions, adapters, consultants and synergists: The new change agents in HRM. *Human Resource Management Journal*, 11(3), 39–52.

CIPD (2007). *The changing HR function*. London: CIPD.

CIPD (2010). *Creating an engaged workforce*. London: CIPD.

CIPD (2012). *Where has all the trust gone?* London: CIPD.

de Jong, G., and Van Witteloostuijn, A. (2004). Successful corporate democracy: Sustainable cooperation of capita and labor in the Dutch Breman Group. *Academy of Management Executive*, 18, 54–66.

Desai, M. A. (2012). The incentive bubble. *Harvard Business Review*, 91, 124–133.

Evans-Lacko, S., and Knapp, M. (2014). Importance of social and cultural factors for attitudes, disclosure and time off work for depression: Findings from a seven country European study on depression in the workplace. *PloS One*, 9, e91053.

George, J. M. (2014). Compassion and capitalism: Implications for organization studies. *Journal of Management*, 40, 5–15.

Harvey, D. (2005). *A brief history of neoliberalism*. Oxford: Oxford University Press.

Kant, I. (1785/2002). *Groundwork for the metaphysics of morals*. New Haven, CT: Yale University Press.

Kateb, G. (2011). *Human dignity*. Boston, MA: Harvard University Press.

Kaufmann, P., Kuch, H., Neuhäuser, C., and Webster, E. (2011). Human dignity violated: A negative approach – introduction. In P. Kaufmann, H. Kuch, C., Neuhäuser and E. Webster (eds.), *Humiliation, degradation, dehumanization*. Netherlands: Springer, pp. 1–5.

Kentikelenis, A., Karanikolos, M., Reeves, A., McKee, M., and Stuckler, D. (2014). Greece's health crisis: From austerity to denialism. *The Lancet*, 383, 748–753.

Klein, N. (2014). *This changes everything: Capitalism vs. the climate*. New York: Penguin Books.

Kolb, D. A., and Frohman, A. L. (1970). An organization development approach to consulting. *MIT Sloan Management Review*, 12(1), 51–65.

Lazonick, W. (2014). Profits without prosperity. *Harvard Business Review*, 92, 1–11.

Leiter, M., Bakker, A., and Maslach, C. (2014). The contemporary context of job burnout. In M. Leiter, A. Bakker and C. Maslach (eds.), *Burnout at work: A psychological perspective*. New York: Psychology Press, pp. 1–9.

Lucas, K., Kang, D., and Li, Z. (2013). Workplace dignity in a total institution: Examining the experiences of Foxconn's migrant workforce. *Journal of Business Ethics*, 114, 91–106.

Pirson, M. A., and Dierksmeier, C. (2014). Reconnecting management theory and social welfare: A humanistic perspective. *Academy of Management Proceedings*, 2014(1), 12245. Academy of Management.

Pirson, M. A., and Lawrence, P. R. (2010). Humanism in business – towards a paradigm shift? *Journal of Business Ethics*, 93, 553–565.

Porter, M. A., and Kramer, M. R. (2011). Creating shared value. *Harvard Business Review*, 89, 62–77.

Rhodes, C. (2016). Democratic business ethics: Volkswagen's emissions scandal and the disruption of corporate sovereignty. *Organization Studies*, 37(10), 1501–1518.

Rosen, M. (2012). *Dignity: Its history and meaning*. Boston, MA: Harvard University Press.

Rousseau, D. M. (2012). Free will in social and psychological contracts. *Society and Business Review*, 7, 8–13.

Rousseau, D. M., and Shperling, Z. (2003). Pieces of the action: Ownership and the changing employment relationship. *Academy of Management Review*, 28(4), 553–570.

Sauser Jr, W. I. (2009). Sustaining employee owned companies: Seven recommendations. *Journal of Business Ethics*, 84(2), 151–164.

Seymour, R. (2014). *Against austerity*. London: Pluto Press.

Thompson, P. (2013). Financialization and the workplace: Extending and applying the disconnected capitalism thesis. *Work, Employment & Society*, 27(3), 472–488.

Vaude. (2015). *Vaude: Experience vaude*. [Online]. Available from www.vaude.com/en-GB/Experience-VAUDE/ [Accessed: August 4, 2015].

Werr, A., Stjernberg, T., and Docherty, P. (1997). The functions of methods of change in management consulting. *Journal of Organizational Change Management*, 10(4), 288–307.

# 4 The role of client knowledge in consulting projects

## Explorative, exploitative and ambidextrous approaches

*Jason Cordier, Alejandra Marin and Hilmy Cader*

### Abstract

Management consulting remains one of the most knowledge-intensive professions. Consultants need to be knowledgeable enough to be awarded projects, yet they also need to build on their clients' knowledge to provide valuable solutions. In this chapter, we use ambidextrous approaches to cast light on how consultants balance the creation of new knowledge with the existence of knowledge provided by their clients. We use the narratives of industry consultants to understand the varying approaches consultants use to manage knowledge when engaged in consulting projects. We found that in most contextual situations, consultants deliberately employ learning strategies as they use knowledge management strategies and draw heavily upon their client's knowledge in an explorative manner. Our findings also illustrate the limitations of exploitative knowledge management on projects. More important than possessing the required knowledge for elements of projects themselves, consultants need to know who else might be an expert in that area. Social capital therefore becomes very relevant within the consulting profession. Our chapter explores a number of other areas pertaining to explorative and exploitative knowledge practices, providing a concise review of the extant literature. We then provide additional conclusions and recommendations from our own empirical findings.

## Introduction

Knowledge is a valuable strategic resource for professional organisations (Anand et al., 2007), and nowhere is this more the case than in management consulting. Within the professional services domain, management consulting remains one of the most knowledge-intensive professions (Van den Bosch et al., 2005; Von Nordenflycht, 2010; Muzio et al., 2011). Accordingly, for management consultants, knowledge accumulation is a critical component for maintaining market relevance and competing. How consulting firms and consultants learn, transfer knowledge both internally and externally and engage with and deliver value to their clients has consequently been the focus of considerable scholarly activity. By what manner the consultant gains, and subsequently delivers, knowledge to the client remains far from a straightforward linear transaction. "Knowledge transfer" from consultant to client is what many envision when thinking of consultancy, which represents the dominant prescriptive definition (Fincham, 2002). However, as is often the case, there is an ideal state and then there is reality. The socio-political nature of organizations, actors having their own agendas, and consultants not necessarily possessing all the knowledge necessary to complete a project, all move the actual practices surrounding consulting further away from a rational consultant-to-client transaction.

For consultants, knowledge exists in different forms across varying levels inside and outside of the consulting firm. Consciously or unconsciously, individual and collective knowledge, knowledge sharing routines and practices and whether or not to use existing knowledge or create new knowledge all play critical roles in how with whom and where consultants are able to deliver value. Within this context, being able to simultaneously engage in the acquisition of *exploitative knowledge*, or "things already known", and *exploration*, "the development of new knowledge" (Levinthal and March, 1993:; Lavie et al., 2010), is seen to be critical to organizational success. The ability to engage in these two distinctive forms of knowledge accumulation at the same time is known as *organizational ambidexterity* (March, 1991), and while it represents a highly desirable state it is also very difficult to achieve (Andriopoulos and Lewis, 2009; He and Wong, 2004; Raisch and Birkinshaw, 2008; Bednarek et al., 2015).

In this chapter we use organizational ambidexterity (March, 1991) as a means to understand how consultancy firms balance the creation of new knowledge with the use of existing knowledge when delivering value to clients. Particularly, we focus on the client-consultant relationship in which clients can act as a rich source of knowledge from which consultants can draw. Our chapter uses a *strategy-as-practice* framework (Whittington, 1996; Jarzabkowski, 2000, 2005) to understand the interconnection of practices, praxis (micro actions) and practitioners (Reckwitz, 2002; Jarzabkowski and Spee, 2009) when using a client-consultant relationship as a means to gather knowledge. We not only discuss the sources of client knowledge (Im and Rai, 2008) in the consulting domain, but also view how knowledge is obtained and is subsequently used (Bednarek et al., 2015). As a means to achieve this, we use the narratives of industry consultants across a multitude of countries to understand the approaches and interactions they undertake when acquiring and using client knowledge.

This chapter consists of three sections. First, we provide a general discourse surrounding consulting firms' use of knowledge by placing them within the domain of knowledge-intensive firms (KIFs). This section provides an overview of the characteristics of KIFs as well as the difficulties faced by consultancy firms when sharing and managing knowledge in general. We also offer a broad overview of the value proposition consultants present to clients as KIFs, and the value clients accordingly seek. Here we pay particular attention to how this influences the dynamics of the client-consultant relationship, as the nature of one's relationship with a client has significant implications for accessing client knowledge. In our second section, we discuss the structures that *exploitative and explorative knowledge* takes, and in what spaces such positions place consulting firms. We seek here to offer a summary of the mechanisms and configurations to manage knowledge. Finally, we illustrate the dynamics of ambidexterity in the client-consultant relationship.

### *Consulting firms as knowledge-intensive organizations*

#### *Knowledge-intensive workers*

Hand-in-hand with the emergence of the knowledge-based economy has come the knowledge-intensive firm. The rise of both has led many to claim that knowledge is now one of the highest valued commodities available. Concurrently, the proliferation and explosive growth of consulting services has accompanied the expansion of the knowledge economy (Powell and Snellman, 2004). The expansion of consulting has stemmed from consulting firms having benefited significantly from trends in organizations downsizing and from in-house activities being externalized (Werr and Styhre, 2002). Typically consulting firms are defined as KIFs because in consulting practices and activities, knowledge has a greater importance than other inputs such as financial capital (Alvesson, 2001). Here consultants compete with knowledge rather than resources, such as access to financial capital (Teece et al., 1997; Zack, 1999). As a means for consultancy firms to leverage knowledge, they rely heavily on human capital in which the competencies and capacities of those who have knowledge-sets are highly valued, making those who engage in consulting knowledge-intensive workers (Starbuck, 1992). That is, people working within a consulting firm use what they know to work towards achieving organizational goals and outcomes. The resource-based view (Barney, 1991) and dynamic capabilities perspective (Teece et al., 1997) frame knowledge, and the manner in which knowledge is shared, in consultancy firms as a rare and sustainable advantage over competitors, rather than a company's ability to "ride the wave" of an attractive industry (Dunford, 2000). However, knowledge-sharing is a complex phenomenon, and in reality the process is fraught with obstacles and challenges. As such, a high reliance on what people know can bring significant challenges when attempting to manage and transfer knowledge.

### Characteristics of knowledge within consulting firms

The characteristics of consulting knowledge are arguably reflective of a contrast between *explicit* or *articulate* knowledge and *tacit* knowledge. The former is represented by documents and databases, while the latter is held in the minds of consultants and analysts and relies on personal interaction for knowledge to be shared. Explicit and tacit knowledge can be viewed from two positions: Knowledge as theory and knowledge as practice (Werr and Stjernberg, 2003). From the *knowledge as theory* perspective, it is believed that knowledge can be disconnected from the actor, codified and subsequently made available to other actors. From this standpoint member's *acquire, maintain and accumulate* knowledge, and then disseminate their knowledge to the remainder of the organization. A focal point for the consultancy here would be to identify information suitable to synthesize, and then encourage and motivate other employees to take on this knowledge (Werr and Stjernberg, 2003; Dunford, 2000).

When treating *knowledge as a practice*, knowledge is regarded mainly as tacit and situated. Knowledge is viewed as being attached to its context and does not exist separately from the situation and person using it. Accordingly, knowledge is *generated, maintained and accumulated* (Werr and Stjernberg, 2003). People that share situated knowledge on a regular basis may form a community of practice. The challenges for the consulting firm come from understanding that an organization's knowledge is always in the making, and that individuals attempt to manage tensions between different expectations, dispositions and local conditions (Tsoukas, 1996).

Consultancy firms deal with complex problems, and are exposed to a diverse set of interests that exist among its different knowledge workers. Thus, scholars from both perspectives of knowledge (i.e., theory and practice) have documented several challenges people in consultancy jobs face when sharing knowledge. Strategy tools and concepts such as Porter's Five Forces and SWOT analysis may be widely available, yet the manner by which they are selected and applied, and the agency of actors who choose tools or concepts over each other (Jarzabkowski and Kaplan, 2015), influence how actors approach a strategic issue.

Additionally, the commodification of knowledge in the knowledge supply chain for consultants is fraught with obstacles. Some scholars conceive commodification as a process of social interaction between different actors that operate "backstage" (Clark and Greatbatch, 2004). While developing new knowledge ideas into marketable commodities is seen as linear and unproblematic, it is intrinsically a challenging process for consulting firms as internal elements enable or hinder the commodification process (Heusinkveld and Benders, 2005). More specifically, in the process of introducing new knowledge products, already existing knowledge frameworks tend to be seen as old and less attractive (Heusinkveld and Benders, 2005). From a knowledge-practice standpoint, people cannot be detached from the knowledge they use or possess, and therefore tensions might arise when new frameworks emerge and old ones are discarded.

Donnelly (2008) paints a clear picture of the difficulties associated with sharing knowledge internally within a consulting firm as illustrated in Figure 4.1. His research identified eight difficulties of sharing knowledge for consultants. Among the most significant obstacles mentioned is the tendency for people to be protective of their knowledge and to keep it for themselves. In part, this is driven by the fact that consultants can be seen to compete based on the knowledge they possess, and therefore knowledge can be perceived as something people need to hold on to in order to get ahead in their careers. In other words, keeping knowledge close to one's chest can result in increased perceived personal power. In this way, codification of knowledge tends to suffer because people are reluctant to share their expertise. Thus, more traditional approaches, such as face-to-face interactions, were found to be more effective sharing mechanisms (Donnelly, 2008).

Consultants, as knowledge-workers, operate in environments with high levels of ambiguity (Glückler and Armbrüster, 2003). Plagued by uncertainty at varying stages of a project – particularly in larger projects – consultants need to draw not only upon their own knowledge and experiences, but also on internal and external knowledge. Thus, the possible directionalities of knowledge flow within a consulting project; they occur internally and extra-organizationally, as well as between client and consultant. Internally, there can be a high reliance on leveraging the knowledge of other consultants as well as codified knowledge, such as how similar projects were approached and overcome. Outside knowledge can be drawn from a host of areas, such as free and publically available information found on the web, databases and reports (which often incur subscription fees or charges to access), or external specialists who are capable of dealing with a specific element of the project that is either highly specialized or for which the firm has no skills to address.

The transference of knowledge is also able to occur extra-organizationally. While consultants can pass knowledge to clients, so too can clients pass knowledge to the consultants. Thus, a significant source of external knowledge comes from the clients themselves. Clients possess large volumes of knowledge about their business, their customers and the external environment in which they operate. As one consultant from a large international consulting firm noted "we can't know the clients' business or domain anywhere to the degree they know it themselves. We, however, need to leverage their knowledge."

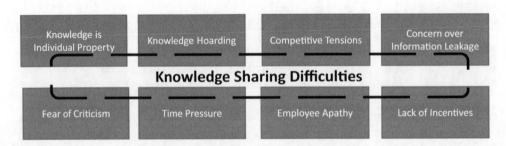

*Figure 4.1* Difficulties of sharing internal consulting knowledge

Source: Adapted from Donnelly (2008).

*The nature of the client-consultant relationship*

Central to extra-organizational knowledge flow in the practice of management consulting is the client–consultant relationship (Werr and Styhre, 2002). A *functional perspective* of the client–consultant relationship (Fincham and Clark, 2002) focuses on the consultant passing information to the client without concern for all the other motives that exist for using a consultant. Consultants foster solutions that draw from a knowledge base (Greiner and Metzger, 1983) by leveraging the notion that they are capable of delivering what the client is unable to deliver or deems too costly or difficult to deliver internally. Consultants have superior knowledge to offer, but the client maintains control and keeps the consultant at an arm's length, treating them as a service provider who is expected to have superior knowledge (Werr and Styhre, 2002).

A *critical perspective* of the client–consultant relationship sees consultants as legitimating client knowledge in situations in which clients need external stamps of approval in order to validate the clients' knowledge (Sturdy et al., 2009). Important aspects in this approach are the consultants' status as organizational outsiders, as independent experts based on the brand of the firms and the status of its clients (Glückler and Armbrüster, 2003). According to this perspective, it is not so much what consultants know, but whom they know and whether they are trustworthy partners in the clients' eyes.

**Explorative and exploitative knowledge**

As a means to address delivering value, consulting firms, like any organization, can position themselves within the market to leverage their capabilities, while in some cases also seek out additional opportunities to develop new capabilities. Embracing these occasions can result in additional financial prospects, access to new markets or legitimacy benefits (see Benner and Tushman, 2003). In essence, the realm of strategic challenges center around where to place oneself in the consulting spectrum. Where and with whom to do business and how to do so depends on a firm's capabilities and capacity, and on the sought value of the client. Moving between or engaging in additional innovation and spaces, and offering enhanced or new services, involves elaborate knowledge management (Subramaniam and Youndt, 2005). Using the knowledge of the client, however, can be a means to obtain both explorative and exploitative knowledge for KIFs (He and Wong, 2004; Levinthal and March, 1993; Bednarek et al., 2015). As Atuahene-Gima (2005) describes, exploitation is incremental in nature and seeks gradual extensions of knowledge upon what is already known. Under these circumstances, this means that consulting firms or practices leverage *routine recipes* (Franklin, 2001). Essentially, the particular client problem is one that is familiar to the consultant (Maister, 2012; Van den Bosch et al., 2005). The development of new knowledge comes more as a result of an exploration process, where more radical innovation is needed. This may include pursuing new knowledge (such as abilities or market capability) or entering new markets or product categories (Lavie and Rosenkopf, 2006). Before we move into the final section of this chapter and understand how consulting firms use external client knowledge as a source of ambidexterity, it is worth understanding the pathways towards ambidexterity, and the implications for consulting firms positioning themselves in the market. Or, in the words of Van den Bosch et al. (2005: 26), to "distinguish a spectrum of consulting practices related to different clients' problems". Figure 4.2 shows the characteristics of both exploitative- and explorative-positioned firms. The nature of these two different environments requires disparate approaches and capabilities to meet the demands of either position. Accordingly, being ambidextrous requires managing significant

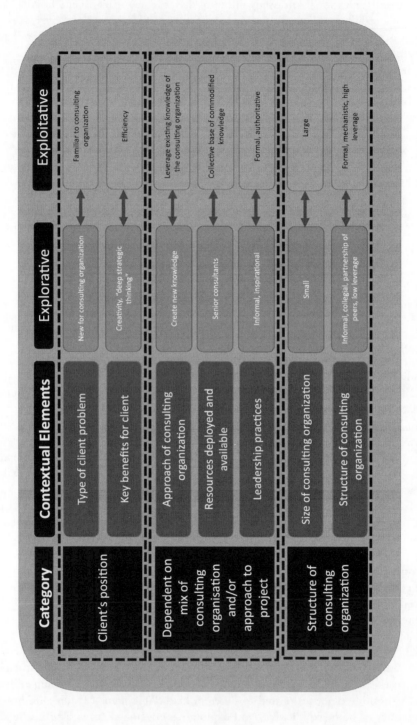

*Figure 4.2* The spectrum of strategy consulting practices and the conflicting requirements

Source: Adapted from Van den Bosch, Baaij, and Volberda (2005).

conflicting tensions when producing both new knowledge and utilizing existing knowledge. However the rewards for successfully managing this knowledge are considerable, and have been found to offer substantive competitive advantage (Van den Bosch et al., 2005) and act as a base for dynamic capability (Birkinshaw and Gibson, 2004)

To manage these conflicting tensions, Birkinshaw and Gibson (2004) offer the organizational forms of structural and contextual ambidexterity. In the case of the former, organizational structure to support both exploratory and exploitative practices is largely determined top-down. Senior management define what time and energy will be spent on either position. In the case of the latter, however, knowledge workers – the consultants themselves – have autonomy in how and what to focus their time on. Arguably, this would require the consulting firm to have a degree of experience and confidence with a greater portion of more senior resources that have the experience base to determine what projects to pursue.

### Consultant's approaches and their narratives

#### Deliberately learning as we go

Explorative knowledge as we have discussed is not incremental, but rather uncertain and unfamiliar. Consequently, consulting firms positioning themselves in ambidextrous or explorative spaces need a method for acquiring new knowledge in domains or realms that are currently beyond their capabilities and expertise. From a structural perspective of ambidexterity, consulting firms can deliberately and strategically use clients as a rich and deep source of knowledge to migrate into new consulting domains. Strategically accessing this new knowledge occurs in several ways. A country manager and senior consultant from a medium-sized firm operating across multiple international markets remarks:

> When we bid on a project, we decide our price based on whether it is a "learn, earn or churn" project. Depending on the prospective client, we will offer a discount for a learning project, but I cannot recall a situation where we have made a loss, or offered a significant price adjustment just because we want to learn.
>
> Senior Consultant and Country Manager for medium boutique international consulting firm with offices in multiple markets

Here the consulting firm has developed positions in which pricing differentials occur as a means to achieve sought strategic objectives. Engaging in *learn* projects considers the knowledge available from the client for the strategic purpose of increasing skills and knowledge in order to migrate into new areas of consulting, while the *earn* position seeks to maximize revenue. *Churn* projects apply accepted bodies of knowledge such as Total Quality Management and Six Sigma that exist largely as explicit knowledge, but require some finesses in tailoring these approaches to the client's context to ensure effective implementation. A senior consultant from a "big four" firm in Canada responds in this way to the question, "Does his firm deliberately take on learning projects?":

> Absolutely! There are different drivers to take on engagements. We can take on engagements purely from a learning context where we have not delivered a solution like that or you have not worked in that industry before. This adds to what you have delivered and your experience base. There are a lot of projects you would take on that are only projected to break even as a means to develop future revenue streams as well

as what might come from that particular client in the future . . . the learning you gain, rather than just monetizing a relationship needs to be considered.

> Senior consultant working in a Canadian big four firm
> who previously worked across multiple markets in Asia

In many industries, research and development comes at a cost, sometimes a significant one. It stands to reason then that consultancy firms need to invest in their capabilities. Yet, there is a toll that must be paid here as well. In these two cases, however, structural perspectives did not result in the firms taking a loss, although it is wholly possible for this to occur. From a contingent perspective where knowledge workers have more autonomy, firm level structure, strategy and perhaps even politics play a lesser role in consultants seeking new projects. The autonomous knowledge worker, in their most pure form, is a sole-proprietor consultant. They work by themselves, and although they can often align themselves with a larger consulting firm to offer panel or expert advice, their decision matrix towards an ambidextrous position is wholly theirs to make. Yet strategic positioning is of significant importance here as well, as the importance to future projects is not only the knowledge the client has but also the success on that particular engagement. The following quotations bear this out:

> This [project] has not been easy for me. But, as this will give me access to local governments and NGOs, it is strategically important to widen my network because [undertaking this project results in it being] easier to make new networks.
>
> Individual management consultant in the Netherlands who
> previously worked in related industries

> Currently, I am working on a project – it is into micro finance. Now, even though I have been doing work in banking and the financial sector, I have had no previous experience in micro finance. In that particular situation it is essential that I obtain that information from the client, because I don't have that exposure. How I drive the project is I request the client to provide a certain number of dedicated resources who will have a very good understanding of their business. Because at the end of the day it is a system to run their business and they are the best people to draw knowledge from. The value addition for my part is to play the catalyst role.
>
> Individual management consultant operating in Sri Lanka who has
> transitioned from ITC to management consulting through exploration

From a contingent position, personal agency and motivations do play a bigger part in decision making because the agency of an individual knowledge worker takes a more central role in deciding what projects to pursue. Here, their own personal interests are a basis for decision making. In the case of an individual consultant these interests are a strong driver towards contingent ambidexterity:

> Learning is enjoyable and there is something new to be learned from every project, especially when it comes to domain knowledge. Taking on new projects is not only for commercial purposes, it is using that for a credibility. Given the choice, I opt for new learning experiences to develop myself.
>
> Individual management consultant operating in the Middle East

A sole practitioner consultant contrasts these views, clearly preferring to operate in an exploitative setting due to the consultant being very aware of legitimacy issues, feeling that to deliver value he must be a domain expert. This may be indicative of not having a team of knowledge workers to make sense of ambiguity and collectively draw upon each other through social structure to navigate the unknown (Marin et al., 2016). The consultant notes:

> I have been really focusing on the manufacturing area because the companies I have managed are from the manufacturing sector. As a result, I focus on these because that is my experience. I don't think any consultant should deliberately undertake a project to purely learn something he [or she] does not know. In the first place, [they] should not have been there in my opinion. I have never done that, and in my opinion the majority of consultants don't do this just to learn.

This consultant, however, had previously discussed the great importance of using client knowledge to develop a solution, but the knowledge in question was referred to in a doctor-patient metaphor where the consultant needs to learn the symptoms of the illness in order treat the patient in a familiar domain. Keeping with the metaphor, the consultant would only deal with cardiology problems, using patient knowledge to determine the treatment for heart related issues, but would not be prepared to use the patient as a means to migrate beyond cardiology – to oncology, for instance.

*Knowing what we need to know*

In the creation of new strategic knowledge, patterns of visual interactions offer a means to understand how new strategy tools have been created. Paroutis et al. (2015) showed how actors generate new knowledge by "visually interact[ing] with strategy tools", and how working in groups has been used to create new strategies and new knowledge. For consultants, this use of visual reference can be an effective tool to draw out client knowledge and enable exploration. One of the consultants we interviewed articulated the importance of this as she works with clients to draw deep strategic knowledge that they are unable to link to the organizational environment themselves.

> I like to use participatory tools and activities in order to draw information out, rather than it being a one-to-one conversation. . . . I like to use documents, and one of the things I like to do is try to help the client focus on a document review. This is to use things like a matrix of the area to be explored and the questions to be answered, with the matrix outlining the sources to draw on as a means to help them draw [out relevant information], not just have them give me all the information they might have which I don't have time to read. . . . [This] also help[s] them to see where their information gaps are.
> Consultant from a New Zealand consulting firm

Additionally, when seeking knowledge from a client – often *down the line* – strategic knowledge exists embedded within employees and line managers. Indeed, what is planned and what occurs are often two different things, and during strategic implementation it can be those closest to the periphery that influence strategy (Regnér, 2003; Mintzberg and Waters, 1985) or have critical knowledge the consultant does not have.

> Especially when there is a younger crowd at the bottom, that is where you see those new and creative ideas come in, because they have knowledge on technology.
> Independent consultant operating in Sri Lanka

I can't prioritize the importance of information at levels. Equally important knowledge comes from each level, although you need to often work a little bit harder to access [information] down the line as people start to protect themselves.

Senior consultant operating globally in an international firm

Drawing appropriate knowledge from further down the line can be different from that at the formal strategic and middle management levels. As one moves further away from the center, individuals may lack exposure to the broader organizational environment and firm level strategic rationale (Truss et al., 2002). Here it becomes essential not to become bogged down in details, but also draw out relevant information from which new knowledge can be consolidated and created.

### Knowing who knows what

Previous literature has recognized the importance of social networks as mechanisms for consultants to engage in organizational ambidexterity (Rogan and Mors, 2014). Across our interviews, we also find that an important capability, especially when consultants are engaging in more exploratory practices, is to know who else can support domain specific knowledge if needed. In situations in which consultants explore new terrain, it is highly likely that they face gaps in their knowledge base. Knowing, and especially having access to, other consultants with higher levels of expertise is key to overcoming possible challenges due to knowledge gaps in front of a client.

Some of this is relationship based, learning from the people around us, being able to know whom to ask. Some other aspects are more formal, we could use a panel approach. We could use a panel of experts of subject matter, who are not necessarily at the core, but that we identify as people that we can ask.

Consultant from a New Zealand consulting firm

Here we can see similarities to cognitive explanations related to social interaction and knowledge management. In particular this links to the concept of *transactive memory* (Ren and Argote, 2011). This results in groups of people developing transactive memory systems to ensure that important information can be remembered, retrieved and accessed. Central to this system is a shared awareness of who knows what when deficits in one's own knowledge emerge, being comfortable not possessing knowledge themselves and turning to other people for help (Moreland, 1999).

When consultants were asked about exploratory practices in which they lack core expertise, an important tool to overcome possible challenges was to identify who could provide additional domain specific information, suggesting the development of transactive memory systems. Interviewed consultants largely felt comfortable not knowing technical information as long as they had mentally referenced a source to address knowledge gaps. Such sources, as earlier discussed, could also come from the client where legitimacy is not a concern. In the earlier quotation where a consultant acknowledged their lack of experience in microfinance but felt comfortable in the banking space, resulted in a transactive memory reference drawn from the client themselves. The client and consultant were open to acknowledging where specific expertise existed in their partnership, and addressed this when the client provided dedicated resources to deal with technical microfinance elements about which the consultant lacked knowledge. While the sole propriety consultant did not have the ability to draw from the transactive memory of internal consulting firm resources, he was able to leverage a strong relationship with the client as a reference point for accessing knowledge.

An important characteristic articulated by consultants that influences the exploration process was the level of strength and comradery existing between the parties involved. As explorative practices might be perceived as involving higher risk, consultants used strong relationships with other consultants to be open about their challenges and to find not only professional support but also personal support. These relationships can be conceived as "backstage" to their roles – that is, among other consultants.

Relationships between consultant and client also influence the extent to which the consultant can explore, especially at the beginning of the project. Here we saw different approaches. Some consultants have had previous projects or connections with clients, which were then used to introduce the consultants to new projects. Leveraging these relationships can present an opportunity to enter projects from an exploratory position, facilitating access that would be very hard to achieve otherwise.

> We are always trying to stretch our boundaries. Our general approach is that we have a network, access to people. So we can bring people to solve almost any problem as long as it is related to strategic management . . . but it depends on the relationships with the client. With some clients we can be very honest, saying we do not know but we can speak to such [sic] expert and we define our roles clearly.
>
> Senior consultant in north Asia working for an international consulting firm

Other consultants took a "ground-zero" knowledge approach, indicating to clients that they were not domain experts, and as such the consultants needed to be educated in domain knowledge first. According to the consultant whose firm uses this approach, his clients tended to feel less defensive and more integrated during the project.

> Each client we have comes from a different industry with domain expertise, which obviously we do not claim to understand. In that situation we take the ground-zero knowledge approach in which the client would educate us. So we do not take any knowledge baggage that we have. We learn whatever we can from the client, but we then compare and contrast. Going with the approach of "we know the industry" puts the client in a defensive mode and it would limit their level of openness to share their knowledge.
>
> Consultant in regional consulting firm in Sri Lanka

Here, coming across as too knowledgeable about a project was perceived as being counterproductive to accessing client knowledge. A consultant from New Zealand also noted that while appearing to speak the lingo of the industry added legitimacy to one's self as a valued partner, this must be balanced with not seeming too knowledgeable about the client's business domain for fear of the client starting to treat the consultant as a technical insider. She notes that core knowledge is skipped over if members of the client's organization come to believe the consultant is a highly technical domain expert.

Additionally, the manner by which one is able to access knowledge was indicated to be different between mature and developing markets. Consultants from Canada and Australia who have spent considerable time in developing markets – such as southeast Asia, the Middle East and North Africa – both noted that mature markets are more accepting of consultants and treat them as partners in which they are initially more forthcoming in the transfer of knowledge to the consultant. However, time was noted to be a precious commodity within mature consulting markets, with consultants receiving only a limited amount of it from client stakeholders.

> Unlike in emerging markets, you have to come to the meeting well prepared, having done your homework. The time for a scheduled meeting is what you get and you might not get another chance. So, you want to make sure what you spend your time on is value-adding [actions where information] is not easily accessible somewhere else.
>
> Senior consultant working in a Canadian big four firm who previously worked across multiple markets in Asia

> My experience in developing markets is people are unclear of the value consultants bring to the process and hold back on their knowledge. However getting access and spending time with stakeholders is easily done, as culturally the clients are open to meeting. We then can draw knowledge out over time, focusing a lot of our learnings on the client as we have time to draw it out of them. In Australia, no one has the time to do that.
>
> Consultant working in Australia

## Conclusion

This chapter has looked at the role knowledge plays in delivering value to the consultant-client relationship. We framed this position by first discussing the forms knowledge takes, and then the challenges encountered when transferring knowledge. We then discussed the structural and contingent forms of ambidextrous organizations and the implications for such positions when seeking business and delivering value on projects. By providing the narratives of consultants across varied markets we then came to understand how explorative and exploitative knowledge can be negotiated between the client and the consultant, with the way value is framed being important in how consultants are able to access knowledge from the client (i.e., legitimacy vs. obtaining unknown concepts).

We also outlined the value of social capital in exploration and how strong personal relationships grant access to the backstage. At the senior management level, relationships open the door for quality information, but consultants still must develop strong relationships with actors down the line. Finally, we have offered a perspective on how the accumulation of knowledge by individual consultants is not always needed or sought. By using both internal consultant relationships as well as external sources of knowledge to reference where to find information, transactive memory can support exploratory knowledge practices.

The insights provided in this chapter do not seek to offer an exhaustive understanding of knowledge management for consulting firms, as this field is far-reaching with many competing ideas. Rather, we offer the reader an overview of the importance of knowledge-related aspects as they pertain to *exploiting* and *exploring* knowledge. This came from drawing on the work already done in this field that aligns to a *practice perspective,* in addition to bringing new insights from a spectrum of consultants operating in international, regional and national settings. Consultants' narratives were drawn from consulting operations including "big four", medium-sized and boutique firms, as well as consultants working as individual practitioners, with contrasts between mature and developing markets illustrated.

# References

Alvesson, M. (2001). Knowledge work: Ambiguity, image and identity. *Human Relations*, 54, 863–886.

Anand, N., Gardner, H. K., and Morris, T. (2007). Knowledge-based innovation: Emergence and embedding of new practice areas in management consulting firms. *Academy of Management Journal*, 50, 406–428.

Andriopoulos, C., and Lewis, M. W. (2009). Exploitation-exploration tensions and organizational ambidexterity: Managing paradoxes of innovation. *Organization Science*, 20, 696–717.

Atuahene-Gima, K. (2005). Resolving the capability – rigidity paradox in new product innovation. *Journal of Marketing*, 69, 61–83.

Barney, J. (1991). Firm resources and sustained competitive advantage. *Journal of Management*, 17, 99–120.

Bednarek, R., Burke, G., Jarzabkowski, P., and Smets, M. (2015). Dynamic client portfolios as sources of ambidexterity: Exploration and exploitation within and across client relationships. *Long Range Planning*, 49(3), 324–341.

Benner, M. J., and Tushman, M. L. (2003). Exploitation, exploration, and process management: The productivity dilemma revisited. *Academy of Management Review*, 28, 238–256.

Birkinshaw, J., and Gibson, C. (2004). Building ambidexterity into an organization. *MIT Sloan Management Review*, 45, 47.

Clark, T., and Greatbatch, D. (2004). Management fashion as image-spectacle the production of best-selling management books. *Management Communication Quarterly*, 17, 396–424.

Donnelly, R. (2008). The management of consultancy knowledge: An internationally comparative analysis. *Journal of Knowledge Management*, 12, 71–83.

Dunford, R. (2000). Key challenges in the search for the effective management of knowledge in management consulting firms. *Journal of Knowledge Management*, 4, 295–302.

Fincham, R. (2002). The agent's agent: Power, knowledge, and uncertainty in management consultancy. *International Studies of Management & Organization*, 32, 67–86.

Fincham, R., and Clark, T. (2002). Introduction: The emergence of critical perspectives on consulting. In R. Fincham and T. Clark (eds.), *Critical consulting: New perspectives on the management advice industry*, pp. 1–20.

Franklin, P. (2001). Guest editorial: From routine recipes to deep strategic thinking: Strategy making as an intellectual challenge. *Strategic Change*, 10, 359–365.

Glückler, J., and Armbrüster, T. (2003). Bridging uncertainty in management consulting: The mechanisms of trust and networked reputation. *Organization Studies*, 24, 269–297.

Greiner, L. E., and Metzger, R. O. (1983). *Consulting to management*. Englewood Cliffs, NJ: Prentice-Hall.

He, Z.-L., and Wong, P.-K. (2004). Exploration vs. exploitation: An empirical test of the ambidexterity hypothesis. *Organization Science*, 15, 481–494.

Heusinkveld, S., and Benders, J. (2005). Contested commodification: Consultancies and their struggle with new concept development. *Human Relations*, 58, 283–310.

Im, G., and Rai, A. (2008). Knowledge sharing ambidexterity in long-term interorganizational relationships. *Management Science*, 54, 1281–1296.

Jarzabkowski, P. (2000). Putting strategy into practice: Top management teams in action in three UK universities. PhD thesis, University of Warwick.

Jarzabkowski, P. (2005). *Strategy as practice: An activity based approach*. London: SAGE Publications.

Jarzabkowski, P., and Kaplan, S. (2015). Strategy tools-in-use: A framework for understanding 'technologies of rationality' in practice. *Strategic Management Journal*, 36, 537–558.

Jarzabkowski, P., and Spee, A. P. (2009). Strategy-as-practice: A review and future directions for the field. *International Journal of Management Reviews*, 11, 69–95.

Lavie, D., and Rosenkopf, L. (2006). Balancing exploration and exploitation in alliance formation. *Academy of Management Journal*, 49, 797–818.

Lavie, D., Stettner, U., and Tushman, M. L. (2010). Exploration and exploitation within and across organizations. *The Academy of Management Annals*, 4, 109–155.

Levinthal, D. A., and March, J. G. (1993). The myopia of learning. *Strategic Management Journal*, 14, 95–112.

Maister, D. H. (2012). *Managing the professional service firm*. New York: Free Press, Simon and Schuster.

March, J. G. (1991). Exploration and exploitation in organizational learning. *Organization Science*, 2, 71–87.

Marin, A., Cordier, J., and Hameed, T. (2016). Reconciling ambiguity with interaction: Implementing formal knowledge strategies in a knowledge-intensive organization. *Journal of Knowledge Management*, 20(5), 959–979.

Mintzberg, H., and Waters, J. A. (1985). Of strategies, deliberate and emergent. *Strategic Management Journal*, 6, 257–272.

Moreland, R. L. (1999). Transactive memory: Learning who knows what in work groups and organizations. In L. L. Thompson, J. M. Levine and D. M. Messick (eds.), *Shared cognition in organizations: The management of knowledge*. Mahwah, NJ: Erlbaum.

Muzio, D., Hodgson, D., Faulconbridge, J., Beaverstock, J., and Hall, S. (2011). Towards corporate professionalization: The case of project management, management consultancy and executive search. *Current Sociology*, 59, 443–464.

Paroutis, S., Franco, L. A., and Papadopoulos, T. (2015). Visual interactions with strategy tools: Producing strategic knowledge in workshops. *British Journal of Management*, 26, S48–S66.

Powell, W. W., and Snellman, K. (2004). The knowledge economy. *Annual Review of Sociology*, 30, 199–220.

Raisch, S., and Birkinshaw, J. (2008). Organizational ambidexterity: Antecedents, outcomes, and moderators. *Journal of Management*, 34(3), 375–409.

Reckwitz, A. (2002). Toward a theory of social practices a development in culturalist theorizing. *European Journal of Social Theory*, 5, 243–263.

Regnér, P. (2003). Strategy creation in the periphery: Inductive versus deductive strategy making. *Journal of Management Studies*, 40, 57–82.

Ren, Y., and Argote, L. (2011). Transactive memory systems 1985–2010: An integrative framework of key dimensions, antecedents, and consequences. *The Academy of Management Annals*, 5, 189–229.

Rogan, M., and Mors, M. L. (2014). A network perspective on individual-level ambidexterity in organizations. *Organization Science*, 25, 1860–1877.

Starbuck, W. H. (1992). Learning by knowledge-intensive firms. *Journal of Management Studies*, 29, 713–740.

Sturdy, A., Clark, T., Fincham, R., and Handley, K. (2009). Between innovation and legitimation – boundaries and knowledge flow in management consultancy. *Organization*, 16, 627–653.

Subramaniam, M., and Youndt, M. A. (2005). The influence of intellectual capital on the types of innovative capabilities. *Academy of Management Journal*, 48, 450–463.

Teece, D. J., Pisano, G., and Shuen, A. (1997). Dynamic capabilities and strategic management. *Strategic Management Journal*, 18, 509–533.

Truss, C., Gratton, L., Hope-Hailey, V., Stiles, P., and Zaleska, J. (2002). Paying the piper: Choice and constraint in changing HR functional roles. *Human Resource Management Journal*, 12, 39–63.

Tsoukas, H. (1996). The firm as a distributed knowledge system: A constructionist approach. *Strategic Management Journal*, 17, 11–25.

Van den Bosch, F. A., Baaij, M. G., and Volberda, H. W. (2005). How knowledge accumulation has changed strategy consulting: Strategic options for established strategy consulting firms. *Strategic Change*, 14, 25–34.

Von Nordenflycht, A. (2010). What is a professional service firm? Toward a theory and taxonomy of knowledge-intensive firms. *Academy of Management Review*, 35, 155–174.

Werr, A., and Stjernberg, T. (2003). Exploring management consulting firms as knowledge systems. *Organization Studies*, 24, 881–908.

Werr, A., and Styhre, A. (2002). Management consultants-friend or foe? Understanding the ambiguous client-consultant relationship. *International Studies of Management & Organization*, 32, 43–66.

Whittington, R. (1996). Strategy as practice. *Long Range Planning*, 29, 731–735.

Zack, M. H. (1999). Developing a knowledge strategy. *California Management Review*, 41, 125–145.

# 5 To be or not to be an internal consultant

*Julie Hodges*

## Abstract

Internal consultancy is often characterized as the poor cousin of its external counterpart. Although there are some who support this view there are also those who point to the value of internal consultancy. In order to consider these conflicting views, this chapter explores the nature of internal consultancy. It begins with a review of the literature, which draws out the differences in terms of the role, impact and positioning of internal consultancy. The discussion that follows highlights the changing role of internal consultancy and, in particular, the blurring of the division between management and internal consultancy. The chapter concludes by arguing that the nature and boundaries of internal consultancy are shifting and highlights the need for organizations and researchers to recognize the impact that this may have.

## Introduction

Internal consultancy is traditionally characterized as the 'poor cousin' of its external counterparts (Subbiah and Buono, 2013). Internal consultancy can take a variety of forms such as 'independent subsidiaries or as departments embedded in the corporate hierarchy; as centralized headquarters functions or as decentralized, local staff; as profit centers billing market prices or as free internal services' (Armbrüster, 2006: 113). Whatever form internal consultancy takes, it is becoming increasingly important and indeed viewed as an alternative option to external consultancy for organizational change and transformation (Sturdy et al., 2016). Indeed, as Armbrüster (2006) points out, the establishment of an internal consultancy may well signal that an organization is not content with external advice but has a strong focus on implementation, which in turn signals readiness for change and organizational adaptability.

The majority of the literature on consultancy tends to focus on the activities of consultancy firms (e.g. McDonald, 2015) and external consultants (e.g. Buono, 2015; Howlett and Migone, 2013). In contrast, internal consultancy is an under-researched area (Sturdy and Wylie, 2011). It is unclear why this should be the case, although it would seem likely that external consultancy is generally perceived as the higher status activity as well as being more visible (Sturdy et al., 2013). The external consultant is usually viewed as having higher levels of expertise, experience and credibility (Kubr, 2002). Paying for external services also implies the output is better or more valued (Kitay and Wright, 2007). In addition to these perceived advantages, externals are considered as being more up-to-date on the latest business ideas and ways of working, and as bringing the added value of a broader base of experience (Ramsden and Bennett, 2005). Although there are many who agree with this view, there are also those who highlight the advantages of internal consultancy. Advocates point out that internal consultants have just as much expertise as external consultants (Armstrong, 1992), and have the additional advantage of knowing the business – its culture, language and processes – from the inside (Kenton and Yarnall, 2012). Internal consultants are also considered to be well positioned to counsel their colleagues against hasty adoption of pre-designed solutions, which critics suggest are often offered by external consultants (Buono, 2015). The fact that internal consultants are 'around in an organisation' is considered of benefit as it 'allows [them] exposure to organizational intelligence and the organizational memory which can help to build a picture which is useful' (Mottram, 2016: 147). There are, therefore, a variety of opinions on whether or not internal consultants are the poor relations in the consultancy profession.

This chapter explores the role of internal consultancy and the challenges it faces in its identity. It begins by reviewing the literature that draws out the differences of internal consultancy from external consultancy in terms of role, impact and positioning. The discussion suggests that some caution is needed in interpreting or accepting some of the standard definitions of internal consultancy, as there is an on-going blurring of the demarcation between internal consultancy and management. The chapter concludes by arguing that the nature and boundaries of internal consultancy are changing, and highlights where the focus might be for future research in order to gain greater clarity about the role of internal consultancy. In this way, the chapter contributes to the existing literature on internal consultancy.

### Definition of internal consultancy

Definitions of consultancy vary in the literature. The most common are the exclusion and inclusion definitions (Kubr, 2002). The former, often favored by professional associations, views consultancy as a special service where specific qualifications or capabilities are required to identify and analyze client issues and recommend solutions '*in an objective and independent manner*' (Greiner and Metzger, 1983: 245). In this way, consultancy is a key '*generator and distributor of new knowledge*' (Thrift, 2005: 35). Such a perspective is largely in keeping with the identity of consultancy as a '*distinctive occupation*' (Kitay and Wright, 2007: 1615) compared to management. In particular, this definition proposes that consultants are specialist advisors in organizational change, whereas managers focus on its implementation (Armbrüster and Kipping, 2002). Although such a view might be considered rather traditional, it is in accordance with definitions that distinguish consultancy from other management activities.

The second definition is the inclusive one and it originates largely from the humanistic and process consultancy traditions (i.e. Schein, 1988). It emphasizes the approach of providing help towards organizational improvement so that anyone can be a consultant regardless of their role in the organization. This means that 'a manager can also act as a consultant if he or she decides to give advice and help to a fellow manager, or even to subordinates rather than directing them or issuing orders to them' (Kubr, 2002: 3). This contradicts the first definition, which defines consultancy as exclusive and distinct from other roles. In practice, Sturdy and Wylie (2011) point out that both approaches may co-exist and be selectively applied.

### Benefits of internal consultancy

Researchers vary in their views of the benefits of internal consultancy. Those who tend to support consultancy identify the benefits as helping to develop creativity and achieve radical organizational innovation or the '*disruption of dominant orders*' (Clegg et al., 2004: 36). In particular, Tisdall (1982) identifies consultancy as providing expertise, extra staff and the facilitation of organizational change. To this can be added the role of legitimizing knowledge and decisions (McKenna, 2006). Such benefits tend to fall broadly into the categories of perspective, people, process and politics (Czerniawska and Toppin, 2010). These characteristics relate to consulting projects and are client focused. However, researchers also point out that it is important to recognize that consultancy occurs at the margins of projects and beyond them (Sturdy, 2011). So, for instance, consultancy can also involve the research and development (R&D) of products and services, what is termed 'commodification' (Anand et al., 2007; Suddaby and Greenwood, 2001), as well as the diagnosis of the root causes of issues (Anderson, 2012). Such activities provide expertise and the facilitation of organizational change.

Researchers who are more critical highlight how consultancy has had an impact on the developing character of organizations and contributes to millions of people having to adjust to new ways of working (Fincham and Clark, 2002) and thinking (O'Mahoney, 2010: 2). Others point out how consultancy has long been associated with securing efficiencies through job losses so that 'a significant percentage of the staff soon find that their services are surplus to requirements' (Craig and Brooks, 2006: 106) – although the extent to which this is the case is debated (Armbrüster and Gluckler, 2007). More critically, Grint and Case argue that, in certain contexts, 'the consultant's briefcase harbors the managerial equivalent of the great white shark' (1998: 560). A further critique is aimed at the non-legitimate or opaque influence of consultancy on decision-making (Sturdy, 2011) as democratic or rational decision-making processes are bypassed through elite personal relationships (Jones, 2003). Thus, there are various criticisms against the approach of consultants.

Regardless of which side of the fence they are on, both popular and academic commentators seem largely to agree that internal consultants, and the ideas they purvey, are highly significant (McKenna, 2006). O'Mahoney (2010) points out that they can exert enormous influence. So the impact that internal consultants have cannot be denied.

### The identity of internal consultants

The impact of internal consultants is influenced by their identity. A key part of their identity is the role that they play in an organization. Researchers tend to agree that the internal consultant's aim is to lead and influence change through supporting clients (Anderson, 2012). To achieve this, Buono and Subbiah (2014) suggest that the roles of internal consultants be comprised of: trouble-shooter, sensor, research analyst, coach and mentor, implementation supporter, adviser and critic. Since internal consultants are part of an organization, they have the opportunity to engage in such roles over the long term (van Aken, 2004) whereas external consultants typically have shorter interactions (Kitay and Wright, 2004). This dimension of the role of internal consultants is what Sturdy et al. (2016) describe as 'internal-outsiders'. The 'internal-outsider' role is valued notably when the internal consultant is seen to operate outside of standard reporting structures (Sturdy and Wylie, 2011). This gives internal consultants a dual status whereby they can be both embedded in the organization, but also outside of, or detached from, the immediate or daily operational concerns. Despite this apparent paradox, the dual status is often considered fundamental to the contribution that internal consultants can make. In particular, it allows internal consultants to emphasize their relative independence or objectivity, and to argue that they have a broader view of the organization which goes beyond the immediate departmental concerns.

In contrast, other studies point out the limitations of internal consultants. For instance, Buono and Subbiah (2014) found that although internal consultants are likely to be well socialized into the norms and beliefs of the organization and more sensitive to behaviors, they may be more subjective than objective with certain people. Critics point out that the ability of an internal consultant to see things with the fresh eyes of someone unfamiliar with the organization is limited, and they may be unaware of the blind spots which can plague those who are too close to a situation (Mottram, 2016). Researchers highlight this especially when it comes to organizational politics as an internal consultant tends to be enmeshed within an organization's political system (Barnes and Scott, 2012). On the one hand, this is advantageous in that it enables them to have clear insight into who holds political power among the key stakeholders and how to manage them. However, on the other hand, they might also be driven by the organizational politics and relationships that exist, and there is a strong probability that they may become ethnocentric after several years of being in the role (Sherrit, 2016). Buchanan (2016) stresses that the consultant who is not willing to play politics will fail, sooner or later, and probably sooner. Or, as Louis Frankel says, 'if you don't play, you can't win' (2014: 19).

The literature highlights that the internal consultant is confronted with various tensions in their role. This is especially evident when they are faced with the dilemma that the best help that they can give may not be aligned with the manager's agenda (Appelbaum and Steed, 2005). Block (2011) recognizes such tensions and describes how line managers may see internal consultants as being constrained by the same forces and madness that impinge on themselves. As a consequence, managers may be slower to trust internal consultants and also to recognize that they have something of value to offer.

The skills and attributes which internal consultants bring to the role are often over-looked by managers when they are looking for support. Scott and Barnes (2011) suggest that this can result in internal consultants being given mundane operational tasks while external consultants are given the more challenging, strategic change projects. This side-lining of internal consultants is, according to Kenton and Moody (2003), due to several factors including: the lack of understanding of the role of the internal consultant within the business; the poor credibility of the consultants themselves and their lack of power to action projects. There appears, therefore, to be a lack of clarity and understanding about the role of internal consultants.

### Reactive and proactive position

One approach for clarifying the role of internal consultancy is to examine whether the consultant is proactive or reactive – are they taking the lead and suggesting to the manager that a particular situation should be examined, or are they following the manager's lead, for example, the manager gives the consultant all the work (Hodges, 2016). The positioning of an internal consultant is illustrated in Figure 5.1. The horizontal access shows the type of role the consultant is expected to play. This can range from expert to facilitative.

The expert role involves providing knowledge to solve a problem defined by the client. The client defines the issue and asks the consultant to solve the problem (Schein, 1988). In this context, the consultant's currency is their expertise. Once in this role, attempting to get the client to accept ownership and responsibility for the issue can be tricky, and attempts by the consultant to release themselves from this expert role may cause anxiety for both the consultant and the client (Appelbaum and Steed, 2005). For the client, supervision of the consultant's work can be challenging since the consultant's specialized knowledge is usually greater than the client's (Freedman and Zackrison, 2001). For this approach to work effectively, the client must have already conducted an accurate assessment of the issues and clearly defined the problem and indicated what they expect from the consultant.

In contrast to the expert approach, the facilitative approach involves the consultant being an expert in process consulting rather than specific content areas (Czerniawska,

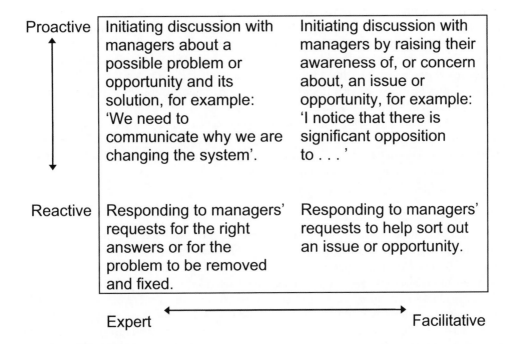

*Figure 5.1* Reactive and proactive roles

Source: Adapted from Hodges (2016).

2002). Compared to the expert approach which often involves 'off the shelf' solutions that may have general validity, but in fact are not the best option for the organization, facilitative consultancy has the advantage of being by its nature customized to specific situations (Kenton and Yarnall, 2012). Similarly, whereas the expert approach will provide a toolkit of good practice methods, the facilitative approach will ensure that the tools which are employed will best fit the organization's needs.

In practice, internal consultancy involves employing a mix of expert and facilitative approaches, with the consultant adapting their approach depending on the context in which they are working.

The majority of internal consultants begin their consultancy careers in the lower (reactive) half of the diagram in Figure 5.1, and it is usually the aspiration of almost all of them to move upwards so that, at least for some of the time, they are taking the initiative and helping to move the organization forward. This is a positive strategy because it is in the proactive area that they potentially offer the organization the greatest value, as they may well alert managers to an external or internal opportunity or issue before anyone else does so. But it is also the area of greatest risk since to confront senior managers, and to seek to change their thinking, especially from a position lower down the hierarchy, is uncomfortable and potentially dangerous. That is why internal consultants require exceptionally well-developed interpersonal skills and self-awareness (Mottram, 2016).

Internal consultants need to know where their skills and energy lie on the spectrum, running from providing advice at one end to being a facilitator at the other, and they need to understand whether there is a need for them to be proactive or reactive depending on the context in which they are working.

Internal consultants can help an organization sustain successful change. Determinants of that success, however, are embedded in a full understanding of the organization, the internal and external drivers for change, the views of employees, the organization's needs and its political and sociocultural realities (Hodges and Gill, 2015). By ensuring that staff, from senior management to front line employees, are knowledgeable about the challenges and opportunities faced by the organization, internal consultants can help reduce the uncertainty involved in the change process (Buono and Subbiah, 2014). Internal consultants can help the organization develop and deploy an approach that interweaves understanding of issues and solutions, organizational development, resource needs and infrastructure support, with interventions that provide social and emotional support for employees and a facilitative culture that supports change (Hodges, 2016).

### Management as consultancy

The stance taken by internal consultants (reactive or proactive) is being affected by transformations in the role of management. Management can be seen to have changed in as much as it, in some areas, resembles consultancy. Research indicates that the boundaries between internal consultancy and management are becoming less distinct (Sturdy and Wylie, 2011). In particular, organizational change has become a more explicit imperative for management activity to the extent that it has become less of a specialism (Sturdy and Grey, 2003). Likewise, formal and structured approaches to organizational changes and their management are more familiar to managers, in part due to the growth of formal management education, such as MBAs, but also due to the recruitment of former external consultants into management positions (Sturdy and Wright, 2008). In addition, project working and program management has extended well beyond its initial focus in engineering and IT and has resulted in the 'projectification' and 'programmification' of management work (Maylor et al., 2006).

A more explicit reshaping of management into consultancy is evident in the way in which consultancy has been taken on by various management occupations and professions over the years (Sturdy and Wylie, 2011). This is especially evident in Human Resource Management (HRM), which has adopted a consultancy model as part of its desire for greater credibility and impact as 'business partners' (Vosburgh, 2007; Wright, 2008). Such changes undermine claims of consultancy being an exclusive occupation, as management is carrying out consultancy alongside internal consultants, thus blurring the boundaries between the two.

### Consultancy as management

There are changes in internal consultancy itself which indicate that it appears to be moving closer to management. Consultants have become increasingly involved in implementing change as well as diagnosing the need and readiness for change and designing interventions (Morris, 2000). There is also an increasing use of consultants as an extra 'pair of hands' or 'body shops' – in other words, as a reserve army of management rather than as expert advisors (Scott and Barnes, 2011). A further change is the recruitment of experienced managers into some areas of consultancy, rather than appointing, for example, new graduates or MBAs (O'Mahoney, 2010). This has shifted the role of managers. Randall and Burnes (2016) point out that managers are brokering change and exercising the facilitation skills that were once the preserve of a consultant. This has the effect of further breaking down the barriers between managers and consultants (Sturdy et al., 2009). Finally, in certain contexts, an explicit and distinctive consultancy identity is being played down or becoming less prominent or visible. In relation to this, Clegg et al. (2007) highlight that coaching is defining itself in opposition to consulting. Alternative labels are also being used in some organizations to replace 'consultancy', such as 'business transformation', 'business improvement' or 'change management' (Sturdy, 2011).

Whether or not internal consulting is moving into some form of identity crisis, it appears that its distinctiveness, from other parts of management, is under threat of erosion due to the blurring of the boundaries between management and consultancy.

## Discussion and future research

Internal consultancy is ultimately about facilitating change. At the most basic level, it requires helping management by analyzing, diagnosing, researching, advising, implementing and evaluating change interventions (Hodges, 2016). Through proactively, rather than reactively, enacting consultancy for change, an internal consultant can bring benefits. There is value in having 'inside' agents who understand what is going on, who have strong, established relationships and who are skilled in their interventions (Czerniawska, 2002). Performing such an internal consultancy role can, however, be difficult, since internal consultants appear to operate in a highly equivocal space. They are permanent employees but also operate outside the traditional activities and structures of the business organization (Wright, 2009). While external consultants must also bridge organizational boundaries (Kitay and Wright, 2004), this process is intensified for internal consultants. External consultants can always walk away, while internal consultants have to stay and maintain relationships with their colleagues (Mottram, 2016).

The position of internal consultants is becoming more ambiguous as the boundaries between consultancy and management are becoming less defined. The rise of the consultant-manager, the former consultant now occupying what may be a very senior position in a client organization, is becoming increasingly ubiquitous (Czerniawska, 2011) and may reshape the role of internal consultancy.

There are a number of areas in which internal consultancy would benefit from future research. First, internal consultancy is seen to play an important role in delivering and facilitating change projects and programs in organizations across a range of sectors (Sturdy and Wylie, 2011). However, it does so without there being an established model or even understanding of what is internal consultancy. Given that most understandings of internal consultancy derive from a comparison with its more prominent external cousin, there is a need for research into an alternative view in the hope of developing insight as to what it should be like in the future. For instance, for internal consultancy to retain its distinct position, there may be scope for the emergence of a transformation specialism that simply eschews the title of 'consultant' and focuses more on not only facilitating transformation but also sustaining it. Second, as internal consultancy evolves, there may also be benefit in research focusing on the more distinctive features of internal consultancy in order to understand its impact. For instance, there is a lack of comparative research that explores the role of internal consultancy during organizational transformation. Such research would shed some light on the impact of internal consultancy on organizational effectiveness. Third, there is scope for research into the capability and capacity required by internal consultancy during transformations. Until now, it has been sufficient to transfer those attributes considered sufficient for external consultants to those operating internally.

Finally, research into the issue of the distinction between management and consultancy would be of benefit in order to help individuals decide 'to be or not to be an internal consultant'.

## References

Anand, N., Gardner, H. K., and Morris, T. (2007). Knowledge-based innovation: Emergence and embedding of new practice areas in management consulting firms. *Academy of Management Journal*, 50(2), 406–428.

Anderson, D. L. (2012). *Organization development: The process of leading organizational change*. London: Sage.

Appelbaum, S. H., and Steed, A. J. (2005). The critical success factors in the client-consulting relationship. *Journal of Management Development*, 24(1), 68–93.

Armbrüster, T. (2006). *The economics and sociology of management consulting*. Cambridge: Cambridge University Press.

Armbrüster, T., and Gluckler, J. (2007). Organizational change and the economics of management consulting: A response to Sorge and van Witteloostuijn. *Organization Studies*, 28(12), 1873–1885.

Armbrüster, T., and Kipping, M. (2002). Types of knowledge and the client-consultant interaction. In K. Sahlin-Andersson and L. Engwall (eds.), *The expansion of management knowledge – carriers, flows and sources*. Stanford, CA: Stanford University Press.

Armstrong, M. (1992). How to be an internal consultant. *Human Resources*, Winter 1992/3, 26–29.

Barnes, B. K., and Scott, B. (2012). The influential internal consultant. *Industrial and Commercial Training*, 44(7), 408–415.

Block, P. (2011). *Flawless consulting*, 3rd ed. San Francisco, CA: Jossey Bass/Pfeiffer.

Buchanan, D. (2016). I couldn't disagree more. In B. Burnes and J. Randall (eds.), *Perspectives on change: What academics, consultants and managers really think about change*. Routledge Studies in Organizational Change and Development. London: Routledge, pp. 5–21.

Buono, A. F. (2015). An introduction to management consultancy. *Academy of Management Learning & Education*, 14(1), 144–147.

Buono, A. F., and Subbiah, K. (2014). Internal consultants as change agents: Roles, responsibilities and organizational change capacity. *Organization Development Journal*, 32(2), 35–53.

Clegg, S. R., Kornberger, M., and Rhodes, C. (2004). Noise, parasites and translation: Theory and practice in management consulting. *Management Learning*, 35(1), 31–44.

Clegg, S. R., Rhodes, C., and Kornberger, M. (2007). Desperately seeking legitimacy: Organizational identity and emerging industries. *Organization Studies*, 28(4), 495–513.

Craig, D., and Brooks, C. (2006). *Plundering the public sector*. London: Constable.

Czerniawska, F. (2002). *Value-based consulting*. New York: Palgrave.

Czerniawska, F. (2011). *Consultant-managers: Something else to worry about*. Available from www.sourceforconsulting.com/blog/2011/05/03/consultantmanagers-something-else-to-worry-about/ [Accessed May 22, 2016].

Czerniawska, F., and Toppin, G. (2010). *The economist: Business consulting: A guide to how it works and how to make it work*. Suffolk: Profile Books.

Fincham, R., and Clark, T. (2002). Introduction: The emergence of critical perspectives on consulting. In T. Clark and R. Fincham (eds.), *Critical consulting: New perspectives on the management advice industry*. Oxford: Blackwell, pp. 1–18.

Frankel, L. (2014). *Nice girls don't get the corner office: Unconscious mistakes women make that sabotage their careers*. London: Hachette.

Freedman, A. M., and Zackrison, R. E. (2001). *Finding your way in the consulting jungle*. San Francisco, CA: Jossey Bass/Pfeiffer.

Greiner, L. E., and Metzger, R. O. (1983). *Consulting to management*. PTR: Prentice Hall.

Grint, K., and Case, P. (1998). The violent rhetoric of re-engineering: Management consultancy on the offensive. *Journal of Management Studies*, 35(5), 557–577.

Hodges, J. (2016). *Managing and leading people through change*. London: Kogan Page.

Hodges, J., and Gill, R. (2015). *Sustaining change in organizations.* London: Sage.

Howlett, M., and Migone, A. (2013). Policy advice through the market: The role of external consultants in contemporary policy advisory systems. *Policy and Society,* 32(3), 241–254.

Jones, A. (2003). *Management consultancy and banking in an era of globalization.* Houndsmills: Palgrave/Macmillan.

Kenton, B., and Moody, D. (2003). *The role of the internal consultant.* London: Roffey Park Institute.

Kenton, B., and Yarnall, J. (2012). *HR: The business partner.* London: Routledge.

Kitay, J., and Wright, C. (2004). Take the money and run? Organizational boundaries and consultants' roles. *The Service Industries Journal,* 24(3), 1–18.

Kitay, J., and Wright, C. (2007). From prophets to profits: The occupational rhetoric of management consultants. *Human Relations,* 60(11), 1613–1640.

Kubr, M. (2002). *Management consulting: A guide to the profession.* London: International Labour Organization.

Maylor, H., Brady, T., Cooke-Davies, T., and Hodgson, D. (2006). From projectification to programmification. *International Journal of Project Management,* 24(8), 663–674.

McDonald, D. (2015). *The firm: The story of McKinsey and its secret influence on American business.* London: OneWorld.

McKenna, C. (2006). *The world's newest profession.* Cambridge: Cambridge University Press.

Morris, T. (2000). From key advice to execution? Consulting firms and the implementation of strategic decisions. In P. Flood, T. Dromgoole, S. Carroll and L. Gorman (eds.), *Managing strategic implementation: An organizational behaviour perspective.* Oxford: Blackwell, pp. 125–137.

Mottram, E. (2016). Dilemmas, doubts and decisions. In B. Burnes and J. Randall (eds.), *Perspectives on change: What academics, consultants and managers really think about change.* London: Routledge, pp. 144–156.

O'Mahoney, J. (2010). *Management consultancy.* Oxford: Oxford University Press.

Ramsden, M., and Bennett, R. J. (2005). The benefits of external support to SMEs: 'Hard' versus 'soft' outcomes and satisfaction levels. *Journal of Small Business and Enterprise Development,* 12(2), 227–243.

Randall, J., and Burnes, B. (2016). Managers as consultants. In B. Burnes and J. Randall (eds.), *Perspectives on change: What academics, consultants and managers really think about change.* Routledge Studies in Organizational Change and Development. London: Routledge, pp. 203–206.

Schein, E. (1988). *Process consultation: Its role in organization development,* Vol. 1. Reading, MA: Addison Wesley.

Scott, B., and Barnes, B. K. (2011). *Consulting on the inside: A practical guide for internal consultants.* Alexandria, VA: American Society for Training and Development.

Sherrit, D. (2016). Is OD just a big bag of interventions? In B. Burnes and J. Randall (eds.), *Perspectives on change: What academics, consultants and managers really think about change.* Routledge Studies in Organizational Change and Development. London: Routledge, pp. 245–266.

Sturdy, A. (2011). Consultancy's consequences? A critical assessment of management consultancy's impact on management. *British Journal of Management,* 22(3), 517–530.

Sturdy, A. J., Clark, T., Fincham, R., and Handley, K. (2009). *Management consultancy, boundaries and knowledge in action.* Oxford: Oxford University Press.

Sturdy, A., and Grey, C. (2003). Beneath and beyond organizational change management: Exploring alternatives. *Organization,* 10(4), 759–770.

Sturdy, A., and Wright, C. (2008). A consulting diaspora? Enterprising selves as agents of enterprise. *Organization,* 15(3), 427–444.

Sturdy, A., Wright, C., and Wylie, N. (2016). Managers as consultants: The hybridity and tensions of neo-bureaucratic management. *Organization,* 23(2), 184–205.

Sturdy, A., and Wylie, N. (2011). *Internal consultants as agents of change.* London: Economic & Social Research Council.

Sturdy, A., Wylie, N., and Wright, C. (2013). Management consultancy and organizational uncertainty: The case of internal consultancy. *International Studies of Management & Organization,* 43(3), 58–73.

Subbiah, K., and Buono, A. F. (2013). Internal consultants as change agents: Roles, responsibilities and organizational change capacity. In *Academy of management proceedings,* January, Academy of Management, 10721.

Suddaby, R., and Greenwood, R. (2001). Colonizing knowledge – Commodification as a dynamic of jurisdictional expansion in professional service firms. *Human Relations*, 54(7), 933–953.

Thrift, N. (2005). *Knowing capitalism*. London: Sage.

Tisdall, P. (1982). *Agents of change*. London: Heinemann.

van Aken, J. (2004). Management research based on the paradigm of the design sciences: The quest for field-tested and grounded technological rules. *Journal of Management Studies*, 41(2), 222–246.

Vosburgh, R. M. (2007). The evolution of HR: Developing HR as an internal consulting organization. *People and Strategy*, 30(3), 11.

Wright, C. (2008). Reinventing human resource management: Business partners, internal consultants and the limits to professionalisation. *Human Relations*, 61(8), 1063–1086.

Wright, C. (2009). Inside out? Organizational membership, ambiguity and the ambivalent identity of the internal consultant. *British Journal of Management*, 20(3), 309–322.

# 6    Consulting in the public sector

*Rod Scott and Olga Matthias*

## Abstract

The chapter explores the current landscape in the public sector, considering complications and constraints inherent in delivering service and performance improvement. Cost challenges are key factors for all departments, as are wider societal changes, and have led to changes to delivery models. UK government cuts have already been the biggest in the G7 group of major developed economies, and more are planned. Departmental structure, culture and behaviour, as well as the scale of service delivery, present operational challenges not just internally but also to the consultants engaged to help. Consideration is also given to commercial constraints which govern the contracting process and how that in turn affects consultants, client interaction and outcomes. Taking into account the salient features that must be overcome, the chapter concludes by suggesting how the constraints and complications can be minimised or mitigated by adopting alternative approaches more attuned to operating within a public service environment.

## The current public sector landscape

Political, epidemiological and economic uncertainties have always shaped the public sector landscape, affecting both strategic and tactical responses. Changing demographics, the impact of Brexit, the continued threat of global recession, the impact of the migrant crisis in Europe and a political desire to reduce the size of the UK's public sector are just some of the current challenges government departments need to contend with while delivering across the board public services.

Official population projections suggest that the number of people aged over 85 will increase from 2.4% to 7.4% of the UK population in the next 50 years. Resulting from improving health care and healthier lifestyles, this is a welcome trend, albeit one that brings significant financial cost. The Office for Budget Responsibility (OBR) projects that spending on health will increase by 10%, spending on long-term care will double and spending on state pensions will increase by a third in relation to GDP as a result of age-related pressures over the next 50 years (Office_for_Budget_Responsibility, 2015). At the same time, the UK government's cuts in public spending since 2010 have been the biggest in the G7 group of major developed economies, relative to GDP, with a reduction of 400,000 public sector jobs, and a further reduction of 400,000 jobs between 2015 and 2020 (Chynoweth, 2015). All government departments, both protected (Health, Education and Police) and unprotected (the rest), face funding challenges in real terms. Coupled with this, the government's ambition is to improve the provision of public services for evermore informed and demanding citizens and not simply to accept a reduction in services commensurate with reduced funding. This has been called the 'more for less' agenda (Arnaboldi et al., 2015; Matthias and Brown, 2016), and further increases pressure on the already delicate balance of service delivery and expenditure.

### Societal changes influencing the public sector

At the same time, as cost challenges demand changes to the way the public sector works and delivers its services, changes to society in general impact the public's rights, expectations and perceptions.

### Freedom of information

A belief that openness is fundamental to the political health of a modern state led to the Freedom of Information Act (FOIA) in 2000. Based on the principle that people have a right to know about the activities of public authorities, the Act enshrines access to information held by public authorities by obliging publication of certain information regarding their activities, and by allowing individuals to request information (an FOIA request). Indirectly, the Act encourages transparency, and as such is impacting the culture of the public sector because of consideration as to the potential release of information (Wallace, 2016).

### Citizen expectations

Coupled with government's desire for more transparency in their working, are the increased and still growing expectations of 'excellent service' in the UK. Citizens can share problems and access solutions through social media and other digital channels through which information is shared. It is not difficult for the interested citizen to build a picture of the services they are expecting and assess whether they are being delivered.

Feedback on the service received is generally a key ingredient for effective continuous improvement, but it is yet another aspect that raises the bar on the improvement required across the whole public sector, thus adding to the complexities departments face.

### Perceptions, pressure and projects

National infrastructure requires public consultation, which brings with it the impact of pressure groups, lobbying and social media exposure to any idea, making it possible for schemes to be effectively 'filibustered' through endless appeals. A number of major infrastructure projects illustrate the problems faced:

*   A Public Enquiry for the new Hinckley Point C Reactor started in 1988/89. The key contract was only signed in September 2016, close to 30 years later.
*   The White Paper regarding a third runway at Heathrow was published in December 2003, with plans for completion within 12 years. Following a public consultation document published in November 2007, there was a flurry of anti-runway activity. Public protests, European Union warnings that a third runway would significantly breach air pollution guidelines, a legal challenge launched by Councils, residents and environmental groups in April 2009, formal withdrawal of the plans in 2010, and in September 2016 the possibility that approval may be obtained through an open vote in Parliament.
*   Regionally, planning uncertainty is one of the biggest risks to the overall plan for UK Rail Enhancements. Farmers can fight temporary works, defined under the 1986 British Railways Act, on their land, which can delay rail improvements by years and cost millions of pounds.

A softly-softly approach to engender public support conflicts with creating confidence in the ability to deliver such schemes. Similarly, pre-2008 bodies – such as the Office for Standards in Education, Children's Services and Skills (Ofsted) and the Care Quality Commission (CQC), which regulates the public sector – predominantly adopted a softly-softly approach to regulation. After the global financial crisis of 2007–2008, regulators have become more interventionist, although questions remain about what 'good regulations' are and what regulators roles ought to be. Should they be customer (citizen) champions, safety authorities, technical authorities, 'score-keepers', decision-makers or lobby groups? Whilst the answer has not yet been determined, regulators are likely to have an increasing influence on the delivery of public sector services.

## Government responses to the societal and financial challenges

To help departments respond to the operational challenges created by the financial and societal changes outlined, government has adopted a number of what are best described as standard business approaches. New service delivery models are being introduced to try and reduce the pressures on departments. There has been a push towards the digitalisation of services. Outsourcing has been extended, joint ventures embarked upon and benchmarking enriched. Whilst appearing straightforward, such operational changes compound the operational uncertainties raised by the strategic changes (Helfat et al., 2007; Winter, 2012). Each is discussed in turn.

### Digitalisation of services

The Government Digital Strategy sets out the ambition of 'digital services being so straightforward and convenient that all those who can use them will choose to do so' (Cabinet_Office, 2012). The high-level principles are to 'help make government digital services and information simpler, clearer and faster, putting users' needs before the needs of the government'. Actions include moving government information provision to a single website (www.gov.uk/) and enabling online transactional services for such processes as applications, taxes, licensing and payments. The Digital Transformation Programme started with the ambition to make 25 major services digital by default. The seven departments[1] which handle the majority of central government transactions were required to agree on three exemplar service transformations and implement them by March 2015. By this deadline, 20 of the exemplar services were publicly available, with five still in development.

This responds to public need for convenience and to self-manage, where possible, as well as produce the associated savings that were estimated at £1.7 and £1.8 billion a year (ibid). Nonetheless, the potential for further reducing costs and re-engineering the relationship between the citizen and government is enormous and largely untapped.

### Outsourcing

Government outsourcing is not new, having started in the 1980s with compulsory competitive tendering first introduced for construction, maintenance and highways work, and represents an explicit effort to inject private sector management practices into public service delivery (Alonso et al., 2015). In 1997, the concept of 'Best Value' became widespread to counter (legitimate) concerns of a focus on cost over quality. By 2015, outsourcing has extended from 'traditional' back-office services, through business process outsourcing, to delivery of front line services. Authors such as Hood (1991), Osborne and Brown (2005), Hood and Dixon (2013), Ayres and Pearce (2013) and Alonso et al. (2015) have all researched the phenomena pertaining to cost-cutting and modernisation. Whilst measurable financial and service quality gain is broadly unsubstantiated, the progression of outsourcing scope and scale has compounded complexity and risk.

There is a substantial gap between the efficiency rhetoric of the modern outsourcing industry and the reality of delivery. Media's selective reporting of fiascos and the paring of service delivery does not help public perception (Bowman et al., 2015). Despite this gap, the drive to outsource more of the public sector continues (King and Crewe, 2014; Froud and Leaver, 2015).

### Joint ventures

A variation on outsourcing is the joint venture initiative. Where fundamental reengineering is required, some traditional consulting organisations take complex problems entirely off the government's hands. These models exist in the private sector, for example helping banks to manage caseloads for Payment Protection Insurance (PPI) and changes in consumer regulation, and are gaining traction in the public sector.

### Decentralisation

The Conservative-Liberal Democrat coalition government (2010–2015) made a commitment to decentralisation to create the conditions for sustainable growth, better public services and a stronger society (Clark, 2012: 3). This decentralisation extends the longer-running devolution of power to the Scottish Parliament, the National Assembly of Wales and the Northern Ireland Assembly, devolving powers on agriculture, education, environment and health and housing, to name but a few. This empowerment of regions, cities, local authorities and service deliverers has changed many delivery models, although different levels of enthusiasm for decentralisation across and within Whitehall departments undermines a more cohesive approach (Ayres and Pearce, 2013). Laffin et al. (2014) further assert that there is no weakening of vertical linkages. Instead, bureaucratic and hierarchical structures remain pervasive and power remains highly centralised.

### Benchmarking

Decentralisation means more variety in the way in which services are delivered. As the devolved and decentralised entities report at the field level on the outputs and costs of their services, performance and value for money reporting becomes more distinct, allowing better comparison, competition and learning between organisations (Andrews, 2014). Helpfully, citizens can use performance information to hold politicians to account, particularly when public organizations are perceived to be performing poorly (ibid).

## The public sector and consultants

The required changes are complex. As well as having to downsize in numbers and restructure, there are challenges in terms of reform under time pressure and public scrutiny, and with continuing reductions in staff numbers. The skills needed to deliver the changes are not present in the Civil Service. The consulting market is one of the 'normal' routes to acquire these skills, especially in instances when there is not an enduring need for the capabilities being brought in.

Figure 6.1 shows central government annual expenditure on consultancy decreasing after 2009–10, reflecting the effects of the global financial crisis flowing through to government spending, but renewed growth thereafter.

The Management Consultancies Association (MCA), whose members represent around 60% of the total UK consulting industry, estimates 2015 fee income across the whole public sector at £1,123 million (Figure 6.2).

This represents a significant proportion of the £5.5 billion fee income MCA members earned in 2015. Figure 6.3 shows the nature of public sector spending on consultancy services. Practical, operational skill and knowledge input account for close to 80% of consulting activity, with digital and technology consulting unsurprisingly the most significant.

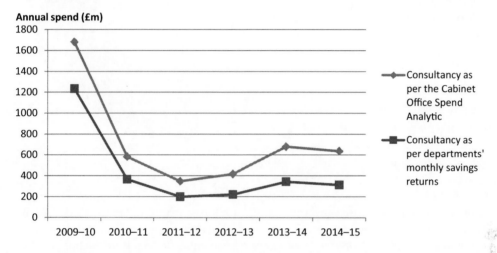

*Figure 6.1* Departments' spend on consultancy, 2009–10 to 2014–15

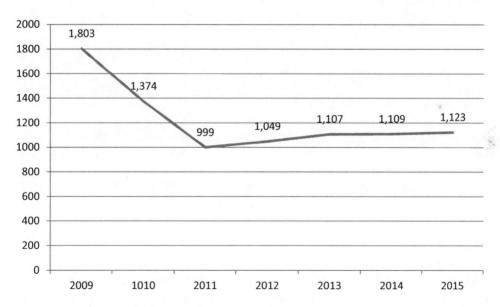

*Figure 6.2* Aggregate public sector consulting fee income (£000s)

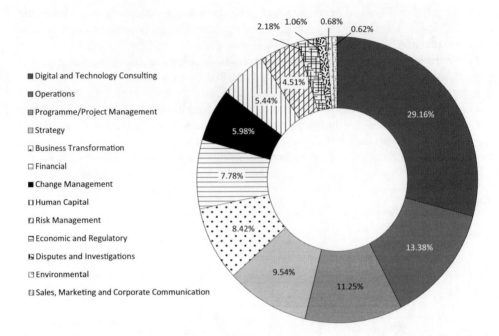

*Figure 6.3* Public sector service lines

Unsurprisingly, these areas mirror public sector reform priorities (Kerslake, 2012). Whilst these figures suggest a public sector dependency on management consultancy, this dependency is mutual since the consulting industry derives so much income from the public sector.

### Consultants working in the public sector

In 1998, Schmenner and Swink wrote about the 'law of cumulative capabilities', which expresses operational responses to market requirements, allowing maintenance or improvement of performance in line with market changes as well as the requirements for developing operational capability. They emphasised the interaction between people, systems and processes. Sections 1 and 2 of this chapter have outlined the 'market changes' and the operational responses to deal with them. This section seeks to discuss the particularly significant capability areas the public sector and its consulting partners have to address in order to have successful interaction between people, systems and processes to deliver the stated ambitions. They are: the scale of the delivery challenge; public sector structure, culture and behaviours and commercial constraints. These specific characteristics challenge the requirements, methods and type of consulting work required as well as the relationship that public sector clients have with their consultants.

### Scale of the delivery challenge

Project-based delivery is increasingly important, especially through 'major projects'. The Infrastructure and Projects Authority (IPA) has oversight of the Government Major Projects Portfolio, which contains the biggest and riskiest changes in the public sector. In June 2015, their portfolio contained 149 projects with a whole-life cost of £511 billion.

Successful delivery for 34% of these projects was assessed as in doubt or unachievable unless action was taken. Of the 149 projects in portfolio, 95 were transformation, service delivery and ICT projects, changing how the government operates, modernising 'back office' activities, improving delivery of services to the public and developing new digital technologies to reduce costs and provide better access to services.

The size, volume and ambition of individual projects present significant operational challenges magnified by a misalignment between the required funding cycle and the political decision-making cycle. Most large (capital) projects take longer than a single parliament. Frequently, even the initial planning, scoping and investment case takes longer than a parliament. The consequences range from projects being cancelled at the last minute, early (often substantial) development funding being wasted or significant scope changes (with the associated cost impact).

A number of recurring issues lead to poor project delivery:

- an absence of portfolio management at both the departmental and government level
- lack of clear, consistent data with which to measure performance
- poor early planning
- lack of capacity and capability to undertake a growing number of projects, especially in specific areas such as risk management and behaviour change
- lack of clear accountability for leadership of a project (Morse, 2015).

In addition, 'Departments often overlook whether the project has realised the intended benefits' (ibid). Departments are responsible for monitoring and reporting benefits, and they often do not rigorously do this.

### Public sector structure, culture and behaviours

As with all clients, the public sector has a number of traits that are important to understand if change is to be successful. Natural Civil Service – 'small c' conservatism – has always been needed to balance ministerial whims but impacts change. 'Small c' conservatism refers to an opposition or resistance to change, important in the public sector to stop or slow seismic swings in policy from one administration or minister to another. This predilection towards conservatism variously impacts all change involving the public sector, and is not helped by the complexity of the interacting, indirect and multiple-group membership of stakeholders – the general public, service users, local government, national government, opposition parties, lobby groups, activist groups and even competing consultants. This complexity needs to be recognised, accepted, understood and taken into account – especially for those charged with delivering change.

### Multi-layered 'blockers' and change constraints

All organisations experience difficulties when initiating and implementing change. However, as already mentioned, the public sector has certain unique features that make its difficulties significantly greater.

#### Organisational structure and culture

A feature of many public sector organisations, especially central government departments, is their scale and number of layers from top-to-bottom. The 'management chain' is strong and multi-layered. The multitude of different services provided by some of the bodies make it difficult for top management to really understand every aspect of their organisation in depth. Moreover, many of the outputs are hard to measure or quantify. The culture in many parts of the public sector is to adhere to the management chain. Information gets communicated up and down this chain and distorted – sometimes unintentionally, sometimes intentionally. Top-down initiatives never fully reach the front line, as messages are distorted and stopped through the middle management layers. Bottom-up initiatives impact quickly on front line services, but are never fully understood at top-management levels and therefore wither and die, rather than spreading throughout the organisation. This impacts the ability of those at both the 'top' and the 'bottom' of the organisational structure to understand clearly what is going on. Combined with natural conservatism, these features can be killers for real organisational transformation.

Managing poor performance, to discipline or remove individuals from the public sector, can be a thankless task. The process can be so time consuming and cumbersome that poor performance is ignored or accommodated. People are often moved sideways rather than removing them from the organisation. Research by the Chartered Institute of Personnel and Development (CIPD) (Chynoweth, 2015), showed that public sector managers are more reluctant to discipline or sack poor performers. On average, there was one formal disciplinary case per 364 employees each year, compared with 119 among private services employers, and 72 employees among manufacturing and production organisations. Moreover, when they do decide to formally discipline staff, public sector managers spend far longer than their private sector counterparts: an average of 21 days of management time on every formal disciplinary case, compared to 11.5 days for private sector organisations. Such working relations are also not conducive to transformational change.

*Professional allegiances*

Multiple public service organisations, especially Health, Education, Defence and the Judiciary, involve two, sometimes conflicting, allegiances for individuals. The 'bureaucratic hierarchy' of management, administration and service delivery on which organisational structures and reporting lines are typically built have already been discussed. The 'professional hierarchy' provides training and accreditation, a value-set, social identity and status and creates greater cultural allegiance to the profession than the employer (Carr-Saunders and Wilson, 1964; Mintzberg, 1983). Constant reform has played its part in creating a functional and conflict-based approach (Muzio et al., 2013; Brock and Saks, 2016). The NHS is frequently in the media because of this clash between professional allegiance and bureaucratic demands (Crosson, 2003; Nash et al., 2003; Kyratsis et al., 2017). In recent years, their relationship has been described as 'fraught' and 'tense' (Cramer, 2015). For both mangers and consultants wanting to drive change, this presents another complicating factor.

*Silo working, integrated services*

Citizen expectations do not align with the traditional department structure. Because it exists elsewhere, people expect a fully integrated service, taking for granted:

• single login for online services
• a joined-up service (be it welfare, health, or the justice system).

Having said that, there is increasing evidence of inter-department/agency work:

- NHS Trusts and commissioning groups are collaborating with local authorities, meaning entire local health economies are working hard on integrated approaches to delivery of care
- inter-agency work to safeguard and promote the welfare of children through Local Safeguarding Children Boards (LSCBs), involving local authorities, the police, the NHS, youth offending teams, National Probation Service etc.

Much of this is driven by front-line staff and managers who identify the need and try to take the necessary action. Integration is also required 'vertically' through the supply chain with clear internal customer/supplier accountabilities and boundaries. Yet, inter-department/agency work is hindered by 'political disagreements, a lack of clarity about policy and budgetary responsibility and insufficient flexibility in planning across government' (Morse, 2016a: 15). Moreover, Morse's report continues, government manages the departmental funding allocation by process rather than an overarching strategic framework for achieving government's objectives and achieving an appropriate balance between short-term political drivers and long-term value for money. This is a significant weakness in the framework for planning and managing public sector activity in the UK (ibid).

### Commercial constraints

Most commercial contracting processes with consulting organisations clash with the results required and the dynamic responses needed to rapidly adjust to a changing world. As part of the drive for greater control of government spending, 'stronger' approvals processes have been introduced with departments, requiring Cabinet Office approval before they appoint consultants for assignments that extend beyond nine months and cost more than £20,000. Given spending on consultants in 2015 was estimated at £1,123 million (Figure 6.2), it can be assumed that the approval process has become more expensive by an order of magnitude. The recent NAO report on the use of consultants and temporary staff (Morse, 2016b) noted that:

- The proportion of assignments based on fixed prices increased from 30% in 2010 to 56% in 2014–15. However, in practice, contracts are priced on the basis of daily rates, and these are often extended once the fixed price is reached.
- There was no evidence of formal evaluation of performance or feedback to suppliers – for any of 31 sample assignments examined.
- Of 60 consultancy assignments let or extended by CCS on behalf of departments between April and October 2015, 43% had limited or no competition:

  - 34 (57%) were let competitively
  - 11 (18%) were single-tender actions at the department's request,
  - 15 (25%) assignments were extended (without competition).

Risk and reward is often discussed, but rarely used, as it does not match with the certainty that public sector budgeting typically demands.

Only 40% of tenders attracted the target of five bids. Lack of pre-tender contact by departments, short timescales for tenders and the cost of bidding unsuccessfully for contracts (ranging from 2% to 25% of their total government fee income) were factors in suppliers' decisions not to bid.

Of particular concern is the lack of genuine understanding, measurement and discussion around benefits and hence value for money. This applies equally to the public sector and the consulting industry. If the real total cost of a project (external consultants, internal resources etc.) is £1 million and the results save £5 million (taking into account the total impact across government) then surely undertaking more of these is a good thing. If the real total cost outweighs the benefits across government, then this should also be taken seriously and things done differently to avoid such outcomes.

*Choices for and about consultancy services*

Adding to the complexity is the fact that many departments require external organisations to choose between 'client-side' advisory and 'supply-side' delivery when new commercial frameworks are established. To avoid those who advise public sector management positioning their own organisations favourably when supply contracts are let, as more work is outsourced, such choices must be made. This impacts consultancies trying to move into the outsourced provision of public services and supply organisations trying to move into advisory work.

The target of 25% of procurement spending on SMEs by 2015, set in 2010, was exceeded, reaching 27% in 2014–15. A new target, to reach 33% by 2020, is now in place. The overall SME position thus appears strong. SME consulting firms do not mirror this success. Between 2009–10 and 2014–15, consulting SME's share of the Crown Commercial Service (CCS) consultancy agreement rose from 6% to 9%, but their share of all consultancy spend fell to 5%. In contrast, the largest six consultancy firms[2] won 75% of the work let through the CCS consultancy agreement in the same period. The intention to bring consulting SMEs into the public sector is to bring new thinking and different viewpoints. Most departments and public bodies still have a long way to go in that regard. The current procurement processes and frameworks have not helped. SMEs have reacted to the onerous procurement processes variedly. Many have sub-contracted into the larger consultancies to participate in the procurement process, thereby distancing themselves from the framework and the potential clients. Others have banded together to form SME consortia to submit credible bids, while some others have gone alone, with limited success. More recently Lord Young reported on public procurement reform,[3] which tries to reduce the burdensome commercial processes by:

- removing a pre-qualification stage for procurements below the EU thresholds
- requiring contracting authorities to include provisions to ensure prompt payment through the supply chain
- a requirement to advertise public sector opportunities in one place.

## New thinking and new working for public services

Having outlined the current public sector landscape and broad complications that impact the approach to consulting in the public sector, this section seeks to explore potential improvements not just to client-consultant relationships but also to problems themselves. Whilst consulting tools and methods apply equally to public and private sectors, there are specific areas where consultants can guide and encourage their public sector clients to focus on specific concepts that will add value and on specific opportunities to work with the public sector system rather than against it.

### Customer thinking?

The concept of customer value, or putting the voice of the customer at the heart of the business, has been a core concept of operational excellence and improvement approaches over the last 50 years. Total Quality Management (TQM), Toyota Production System (TPS), Lean, Lean Six Sigma and Continuous Improvement are familiar terms. The classic characteristic of customers is their ability to choose between different products and service providers, and spend their money where they believe they are getting best value. For many businesses and industries, these philosophies have had transformational effects on the quality, cost and delivery of the products and services the organisations provide. The public sector customer does not easily conform to the general definition. At a transactional customer-service level, such as telephone queries or online applications, the same criteria are valid and customers can and do expect the same service quality as elsewhere. At a broader level, the customer is society, so assessing value is more difficult (Moore, 1995; Bryson et al., 2015).

Many public sector organisations have implemented programmes of various shapes and sizes based on these approaches; for example, Lean and Continuous Improvement, especially over the last 15 years (Martin, 2010; Beuster, 2011; Radnor and Johnston, 2012; Matthias and Buckle, 2016). While there are plenty of examples of success at the individual process level, the extent to which there has been organisational-wide transformation and fundamental changes in the way of thinking is much more questionable (Carter et al., 2011, 2013; Radnor and Osborne, 2013; Procter and Radnor, 2014). Certainly, the concept of 'customer', whether as individual or citizen, is notable by its absence.

Two other characteristics of the public sector have impacted the (lack of) systemic operational excellence transformation:

- In response to reducing budgets, many parts of the public sector can make a choice to reduce the range or quality of services they provide precisely because the public has no choice about usage.
- Whilst volume and demand are predictable in many areas (e.g. tax returns, school enrolments), migration, natural disasters (such as the floods of 2014 and 2015) and public health scares inject unpredictable variety.

A citizen-centric view to transforming services should be adopted by public sector leaders, with a clearly defined view of what 'public' (or 'citizen') value is; and better understanding leads to optimising performance. The consultants that work with them can use this as a lever to reject drops in service as an acceptable response to budget cuts whilst transforming services.

### Accelerating digital technology service delivery

Digital technology should simultaneously improve service to the citizen and reduce costs.

Yet, for example, the cessation of paper road-tax discs in October 2014, was expected to simplify and harmonise the application process, make enforcement easier and save £10 million annually. In November 2015, the Department for Transport reported that this change could be the major contributor to a £80 million loss in Vehicle Excise Duty (VED) revenue, as the percentage of unlicensed vehicles in the UK rose from 0.6% in 2013 to 1.4%.

Digital technology has a massive role to play in public sector transformation, but fully thought through business cases are required, and an appetite and method to learn from previous projects.

### Systems thinking and demand management

As external change agents, it is clearly important for consultants to help public sector clients think more broadly than their own department and consider the wider system. The nature of public service provision is often demand-driven, so understanding, analysing and managing demand is important. This chapter has highlighted numerous examples of 'departmentalised silos' and explained how insufficient consideration of the end-to-end impact of change causes unwanted outcomes.

For example, 78% of police emergencies in 2013–14 were connected with anti-social behaviour, or other incidents like mental health issues, rather than crime. There is a direct correlation to this increase in demand with the reduction in mental health funding in the same period. Similarly, 30% of Accident & Emergency (A&E) visitors belong to other services but go there because they are looking for responsiveness, which they feel is absent elsewhere. Good decisions can only be made using whole-systems thinking. Service delivery is not just about building the capacity where it is required. It is also about clearly signposting the public to the right destination, offering reliable service in a timely manner.

The commissioning of offender management and the transformation of rehabilitation are examples of longer-term programme development that combine policy objectives and service reforms with more efficient delivery models to deliver better outcomes – less reoffending, less spending. With their prospect-mining and modelling capabilities, consultants in the public sector can help clients identify such opportunities for public value.

### 'Assumption busting'

The rules that determine how the public sector is designed and operates can exist in the form of explicit policies, or, more often, in the routines and behaviours of the people who operate the processes. Such unwritten rules are the product of assumptions about the environment, developed over many years, and often emerge from uncertainties surrounding policy, relationships, capabilities, resources or authority.

The eight-step approach to Assumption Busting (Figure 6.4) is a specific concept that aims to identify and challenge the rules that dictate how organisations run. It can add value in the public sector by changing some of the underlying assumptions to create breakthrough improvement.

### Collaboration

Improved cross-departmental working and improved (and different) relationships with the private sector have been themes throughout this chapter. Policy often states that that collaboration is necessary but provides no guidance on how to overcome barriers. Specific challenges to overcome, especially in collaboration between the public sector and private sectors are:

- The ability to manage risk. The private sector is relatively mature at not accepting uncosted risk. In many cases, the cost of such risks are prohibitive and hence they are retained by government, even if they do not have the means to control or mitigate the risk.

# Assumption Busting

*Figure 6.4* Assumption-busting transformation

- Ensuring value for money. BS11000 promotes collaboration and transparency, as do other collaboration models. However, many of the commercial behaviours, on both the supply and client side, are distinctively combative, which reduces the relationship to a transactional one based on old forms of contracting.
- Making collaboration genuine. It takes huge energy to form a genuine alliance and much of this effort needs to be at the front-end if the collaboration is to work and deliver maximum value. Early on in a relationship there needs to be a conscious decision as to which route to take.

Network Rail Infrastructure Projects was an early adopter of BS11000, as they sought a framework to drive the policies, processes, culture and behaviours required for continuous improvement with its partners. The need was to:

- respond to the rail industry challenge to deliver greater value for money,
- redefine the partnering approach with the supply chain to improve levels of performance, introduce greater levels of innovation and deliver cost efficiencies,
- deliver a significant and growing capital works programme in a safer, quicker and more efficient manner to provide better value for money for the fare-paying passenger and the taxpayer.

Establishing a collaboration model with all interested parties adds value in terms of working and outcomes.

## Shaping a new public sector landscape

As discussed throughout this chapter, the public sector landscape is turbulent. Consultants are used extensively as part of a concerted effort to respond to the social and operational demands. Yet, many problems remain, both with the nature of the challenges (the projects and their execution) and with the way consultants contribute. Given known areas of consultant expertise, there is much that can be done to improve scope, definition, involvement and outcomes. This section suggests a number of specific aspects that can be used advantageously to kick-start beneficial change.

### Decentralisation as a performance lever

From a Lean perspective anything that brings the service provider closer to the customer is a good thing. The decentralisation agenda creates natural opportunities to deliver services differently, as spending increasingly devolves to regions and communities. The new generation of local government leaders will need to become system thinkers, not just organisational leaders, working across different agencies and competing interests. This will be an enormous challenge for many local authorities and their leaders. They will need more help than they have done in the past to ensure that decentralisation has a positive not negative impact on public services.

### Project benefits realisation

Currently, assessment of any project, be it consulting or major, is a cost vs. benefit equation. Costs are normally captured fairly thoroughly in the public sector. The benefit/impact capture is weak. Improving the focus on benefits realisation and reporting will improve the assessment of value for money and benefit delivery, which are core objectives of any project. However, this seems to be an area of recurrent difficulty in the public sector. Once projects are established and timelines in place, project leaders and their teams often lose sight of the real purpose of the work being undertaken and adopt a milestone-driven approach to project management. If milestones are expressed in terms of outcomes (benefits) this is fine, but usually they are not. Teams are driven hard by the governance arrangements to adhere to timescales. The quality of the outcome (the benefits) can be obscured and pushed into a distant second place as projects slowly lose sight of why they were initiated. Delivering late and/or over budget are easy concepts to understand, measure and communicate. Too often these aspects of delivery completely dominate the thinking. After all, full benefits assessment could be years down the line, if it happens at all, so the project will have closed and people moved on by then.

Consultants can help project leaders and their teams consider benefits throughout the full project lifecycle in the following way:

- At **project initiation,** benefits are a key component of the business case. If projects are strongly policy driven, a balanced, comprehensive view on benefits is required. There is great temptation to include information which substantiates policy and exclude information that does not.
- At **project start-up,** the processes for benefits measurement need to be established, clear accountability for benefits allocated and the delivery of benefits fully modelled. The benefits modelling should be worked into the project plans so that milestones are benefits-based as well as activity-based.

- During **project delivery,** as benefits realisation begins. Early benefits milestones need to be assessed and realisation plans updated as required.
- **Project close.** On the premise that projects are about delivering benefits, project close should only happen when the benefits have been delivered as forecast, or a variation to the benefits profile has been documented and accepted. Too often projects are closed prematurely and realisation handed over to operations.

### Solutions that can adapt to the reality of public sector decision making

Far from all decisions made in the public sector are logical, especially those that involve politics. Personal views and statements from 'The Minister' and senior public servants can cause real disruption to a project. Another significant impact is the two- to three-year role rotation that is popular in many parts of the public sector. A new arrival takes time to settle in and understand the situation. They then want to 'make their mark', which does not necessarily align with the current direction of travel. In extreme cases, this can mean severe braking or even reverse gear.

Developing solutions that have deep roots and a strong underlying infrastructure means that they are much more likely to continue and prosper when the new broom sweeps through. Ensuring broad-based support, fact-based benefits measurement, and clear linkages to policy goals are all vital to make solutions stick.

### Managing in complex delivery structures

Assurance (i.e. to provide confidence that project requirements will be fulfilled) is a key element in all project delivery, but especially those projects that are large, complex, multi-year and span a number of departments. Currently the impact of the Infrastructure and Projects Authority assurance regime on project delivery within its scope is variable (Morse, 2015). Some departments state that the assurance process does add value but that some review teams lack the seniority to influence experienced project teams.

Typically, public sector assurance processes take the classic programme/project management approach, focusing (naturally) on the programme or project in question. PRINCE2[4] is the de facto standard adopted by the UK Government for project management, which states that: "Assurance is about checking that the project remains viable in terms of costs and benefits (business assurance), checking that the users' requirements are being met (user assurance) and that the project is delivering a suitable solution (specialist or technical assurance)" (PRINCE2). However, these project-based considerations are rarely the reasons for project failure.

For the classic risk management approach to work well (i.e. a 2x2 matrix looking at likelihood and impact), there needs to be accurate assessment. For large complex projects, especially in their early stages, management consultants can help the public sector better understand and cope with the concept of 'Knightian Uncertainty', which is risk that is both immeasurable and not possible to calculate (Knight, 1921). This is exemplified by the 'messes' at the start of large, complex public sector projects, because the issue is generally complex and not well-formulated or defined (Figure 6.5).

Gerald Ashley, a risk and behaviour expert, elaborated, stating, "One of the greatest mistakes that can be made when dealing with a mess is to carve off part of the mess, treat it as a problem and then solve it like a puzzle – ignoring its links with other aspects of the mess" (Ashley, 2016).

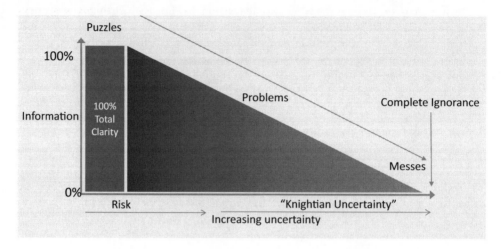

*Figure 6.5* From certainty to ignorance

A better assurance process that can provide real assurance is one that focuses equally on how the underlying delivery organisation(s) function and the underlying risks in the delivery organisation(s). In reality, pure project-based risks are pretty dull. The collection of data to measure and report risk is delegated to junior members of the project team. Often, they collect poor data, which is then poorly aggregated. Senior management look at the results and take action on what has been reported. The recent Hendy Report (2016) on the replanning of Network Rail's Investment Programme highlighted that, for many projects, people optimise their own (project) silos and omit the end-to-end risk. The required solution is not to 'just get better data'; rather, it is to inculcate a different, broader way of thinking about risk and a broader approach to assurance that looks end-to-end, outside the normal project boundaries. This is a clear opportunity for the consulting industry to add value to the assurance process.

### Normal consulting rules still apply

The requirements for successful consulting in the public sector are clearly not completely divorced from those in the private sector. More attention and effort is typically required on the 'softer' aspects of change – enabling leadership, engaging staff and managing change continuously.

Having coaching leaders at multiple levels who lead change and embed it successfully is more important when dealing with hierarchical public sector organisations. But more effort is required in communicating. Communicating is not just telling, but really engaging with staff to get their input as to the best solutions and listen to their, usually legitimate, concerns about proposed changes. Resistance to change does not mean that something is wrong. It is more likely a sign of the importance of the issues. There are many models and much research on the best approach to change (Lewin, 1947; Kotter, 1979; Hides et al., 2000; Strebel and Lu, 2008). Experience suggests that the best solutions are those given by people doing the day-to-day work. These solutions are certainly the most likely to be wholeheartedly adopted, which is an often underrated component in the definition of 'best'. For projects looking at change to processes and ways of a working, a rule of thumb to spend 1/3 of project resources on 'change management' is not unreasonable.

*Overcoming the commercial constraints*

Currently, the contracting process appears to be an inflexible system that suits neither the government nor consultants. However, commercial arrangements and partnerships are not always focused on delivering real value. Consultants do not always demonstrate the value they bring. They are sometimes indistinguishable from contractors and temporary staff, and are drawn into roles better suited to government employees, contractors and temporary staff (Morse, 2016b). Whilst this can be at the request of the government client, even where the commercial returns are obvious – that is, long stable roles with high utilisation, requiring minimal management supervision, and the potential to identify and satisfy additional resourcing needs through more of their own consultants – it is not 'doing the right thing' for clients, as embedded in the professional code of practice (MCA, 2016a). All consultancies that are MCA members have signed on to its consulting excellence principles, which include not engaging in contracting/resource substitution. There are many opportunities for genuine capability development of government staff and upfront exit-planning of the consulting team. This would strengthen value-add to government as well as better develop consultants who are able to transform public services. To improve the value and reduce the cost of consulting, the MCA has proposed a number of changes to government procurement processes. These include:

- More pre-procurement dialogue to help shape project proposals to achieve the best outcomes,
- More sharing of risks and rewards to give government greater confidence in each project,
- More effective evaluation of all consulting assignments, with sharing of lessons learned,
- More access for government clients to a wider range of consulting firms, including many smaller, quality specialist firms,
- More efforts to reduce the costs of bidding, through a streamlined procurement and bidding process.

In particular, much more work is required to grow the use of SME consulting firms in the public sector. Some of the more practical steps include (CCS, 2015):

- Simplifying the bidding process, especially for broad frameworks, such as ConsultancyOne, for SMEs. The responses produced by the larger consultancies will almost invariably score better due to the scale of resource they can expend on such frameworks,
- Amending the commercial and contractual requirements for SMEs to avoid exclusion because they do not 'comply' with one of the many procurement requirements such as ISO 14001 and 18001 accreditation,
- Adapting some of the 'lot' arrangements to allow specialised SMEs to bid in their own right without the need to sub-contract to a larger consulting firm or to form an SME consortium.

*Establishing the right (commercial) delivery strategies for major capital programmes*

The largest public sector programmes (e.g. Crossrail, HS2, Astute and the Olympics) have some particular challenges – they are 'too big to fail', they are very expensive and they have inherent uncertainty and risk. There are very few examples of effective transfer of contractual responsibility for programmes of this size to the private sector, especially a single entity working in a 'prime' role. The private sector is often unwilling or unable to take on this risk, and even when it does the government may still hold the real risk, as when the military was needed to take over security for the London 2012 Olympics.

There is increasing recognition that alternative delivery models are required for the largest public sector programmes, and that they can also add value in other parts of government. They involve a more nuanced boundary between public and private sectors, with a bigger role for the public sector in creating the conditions under which the private sector can deliver successfully. There are good examples of this working for 'green field' projects such as Crossrail and (potentially) HS2, but these need extending into more standard departmental project delivery. Real clarity is imperative regarding roles, like 'client', systems integrator, funding provider and with whom technical delivery responsibility lies.

An important component of any new ways of working is the development of bespoke approval and financial frameworks. Where HM Treasury chooses to hold ultimate financial liability, they will need to have a much deeper understanding of the cost model and risks than is typically the case. In particular, a move away from fixed funding cycles (such as are used by Network Rail and Highways England), to a model where money can be moved between years and between capital and revenue expenditure as required by the project, is an important tool.

There is typically a need for a more sophisticated commercial and operating environment, requiring enhanced public sector capability – especially in the client function. The consulting industry has a key role in helping departments on this journey with their understating of the private sector and their experience in other industries with similar scale programmes, such as Oil & Gas and Defence.

## Notes

1  HM Revenue & Customs (HMRC); Department for Transport (DfT); Department for Work and Pensions (DWP); Ministry of Justice (MoJ); Department for Business Innovation and Skills (BIS); Department for Environment, Food and Rural Affairs (DEFRA); the Home Office.
2  The largest suppliers are Pricewaterhouse Coopers LLP, Deloitte LLP, KPMG LLP, Ernst &Young LLP, PA Consulting Services Ltd and McKinsey & Company.
3  Reforms to make public procurement more accessible to SMEs, 18th February 2015.
4  PRojects IN Controlled Environments.

## References

Alonso, J. M., Clifton, J., and Díaz-Fuentes, D. (2015). Did new public management matter? An empirical analysis of the outsourcing and decentralization effects on public sector size. *Public Management Review*, 17(5), 643–660.

Andrews, R. (2014). *Performance management and public service improvement*. Wales: P. P. I. F. HMSO, (3).

Arnaboldi, M., Lapsley, I., and Steccolini, I. (2015). Performance management in the public sector: The ultimate challenge. *Financial Accountability & Management*, 31(1), 1–22.

Ashley, G. (2016). Rethinking risk. In *Chartered quality institute conference*, April 13, 2016, London, pp. 1–19.

Ayres, S., and Pearce, G. (2013). A Whitehall perspective on decentralisation in England's emerging territories. *Local Economy*, 28(7–8), 801–816.

Beuster, P. (2011). DWP lean journey – improving customer service delivering efficiency. *Management Services*, 55(4), 8–9.

Bowman, A., Erturk, I., Folkman, P., Froud, J., Haslam, C., Johal, S., Leaver, A., Moran, M., Tsitsianis, N., and Karel, W. (2015). *What a waste: Outsourcing and how it goes wrong.* Manchester: (Manchester Capitalism) Manchester University Press.

Brock, D. M., and Saks, M. (2016). Professions and organizations: A European perspective. *European Management Journal*, 34(1), 1–6.

Bryson, J. M., Crosby, B. C., and Bloomberg, L. (2015). *Creating public value in practice: Advancing the common good in a multi-sector, shared-power, no-one-wholly-in-charge world.* Washington, D.C.: Georgetown University Press.

Cabinet Office (2012). *Government digital strategy: November 2012.* London: HMSO.

Carr-Saunders, A. M., and Wilson, P. A. (1964). *The professions*, 1st ed. Cass. London: Frank Cass & Co.

Carter, B., Danford, A., Howcroft, D., Richardson, H., Smith, A., and Taylor, P. (2011). Lean and mean in the civil service: The case of processing in HMRC. *Public Money & Management*, 31(2), 115–122.

Carter, B., Danford, A., Howcroft, D., Richardson, H., Smith, A., and Taylor, P. (2013). 'Stressed out of my box': Employee experience of lean working and occupational ill-health in clerical work in the UK public sector. *Work, Employment & Society*. 27(5), 747–767.

CCS (2015). *Procurement policy note – reforms to make public procurement more accessible to SMES.* London: Crown Commercial Service.

Chynoweth, C. (2015). *The public sector faces terrifying challenges.* London: CIPD. Available from www.cipd.co.uk/pm/peoplemanagement/b/weblog/archive/2015/09/23/the-public-sector-faces-terrifying-challenges.aspx [Accessed 29/09/2016].

Clark, G. (2012). *Decentralisation: An assessment of progress.* London: Department for Communities and Local Government.

Cramer, S. (2015). *Creating stronger relationships between managers and clinicians.* London: Institute of Healthcare Management.

Crosson, F. J. (2003). Kaiser Permanente: A propensity for partnership. *BMJ*, 326(7390), 654.

Froud, J., and Leaver, A. (2015). What a waste! The process and outcome of outsourcing. In *Inequality in the 21st century*, July 2–4, London. Society for the Advancement of Socio-Economics. Available from https://sase.confex.com/sase/2015am/webprogram/Paper3455.html

Helfat, C. E., Finkelstein, S., Mitchell, W., Peteraf, M. A., Singh, H., Teece, D. J., and Winter, S. G. (2007). *Dynamic capabilities: Understanding strategic change in organizations.* Oxford: Blackwell.

Hendy, P. (2016). *Network Rail's investment programme – the Hendy report consultation.* London: Department for Transport.

Hides, M. T., Irani, Z., Polychronakis, I., and Sharp, J. M. (2000). Facilitating total quality through effective project management. *International Journal of Quality and Reliability Management*, 17(4/5), 407–422.

Hood, C. (1991). A public management for all seasons? *Public Administration*, 69(1), 3–19.

Hood, C., and Dixon, R. (2013). A model of cost-cutting in government? The great management revolution in UK central government reconsidered. *Public Administration*, 91(1), 114–134.

Kerslake, B. (2012). *The civil service reform plan.* London: HM Government.

King, A., and Crewe, I. (2014). *The blunders of our governments.* London: One World Publications.

Knight, F. H. (1921). *Risk, uncertainty and profit.* New York: Houghton Mifflin.

Kotter, J. P. (1979). Managing external dependence. *The Academy of Management Review*, 4(1), 87.

Kyratsis, Y., Atun, R., Phillips, N., Tracey, P., and George, G. (2017). Health systems in transition: Professional identity work in the context of shifting institutional logics. *Academy of Management Journal*. 60(2), 610–641.

Laffin, M., Mawson, J., and Ormston, C. (2014). Public services in a 'Postdemocratic Age': An alternative framework to network governance. *Environment and Planning C: Government and Policy*, 32(4), 762–776.

Lewin, K. (1947). Frontiers in group dynamics: Concept, method and reality in social science; social equilibria and social change. *Human Relations*, 1(1), 5–41.

Martin, J. (2010). Increasing public sector productivity could lean six sigma help improve services? *Accountancy Ireland*, 42(5), 58–59.

Matthias, O., and Brown, S. (2016). Implementing operations strategy through lean processes within health care – the example of NHS in the UK. *International Journal of Operations & Production Management*, 36(11), 1435–1457.

Matthias, O., and Buckle, M. (2016). Accidental lean – performance improvement in an NHS hospital and reflections on the role of operations strategy. In Z. Radnor, N. Bateman, A. Esain, M. Kumar, S. Williams and D. Upton (eds.), *Public services operations management: A research companion*. Abingdon, Oxford: Routledge, pp. 52–73.

MCA (2016a). *The consulting industry.* Management Consultancies Association: Online. Available from www.mca.org.uk/about-us/the-consulting-industry [Accessed July 1, 2016].

MCA (2016b). *The definitive guide to UK consulting industry statistics 2016.* London: MCA.

Mintzberg, H. (1983). *Structure in fives: Designing effective organizations.* Prentice-Hall International Editions. Englewood Cliffs, NJ; London: Prentice-Hall International.

Moore, M. H. (1995). *Creating public value: Strategic management in government.* Cambridge, MA; London Harvard University Press.

Morse, A. (2015). Delivering major projects in government: A briefing for the committee of public accounts. HC 713. London: National Audit Office.

Morse, A. (2016a). *Spending review 2015.* HC 571. London: National Audit Office.

Morse, A. (2016b). *Use of consultants and temporary staff.* London: National Audit Office.

Muzio, D., Brock, D. M., and Suddaby, R. (2013). Professions and institutional change: Towards an institutionalist sociology of the professions. *Journal of Management Studies*, 50(5), 699–721.

Nash, D. B., Malcolm, L., Wright, L., Barnett, P., Hendry, C., Crosson, F. J., Atun, R. A., and Thomas, H. (2003). Improving the doctor-manager relationship. *BMJ*, 326(7390), 652–653.

Office for Budget Responsibility (2015). *Fiscal sustainability report.* 02061511 06/15 49753 19585 London: HMSO.

Osborne, S. P., and Brown, K. H. (2005). *Managing change and innovation in public service organizations.* London: Routledge.

PRINCE2. (n.d.) PRINCE2 definition. ILX Group: Online. Available from www.prince2.com/usa/what-is-prince2#prince2-definition [Accessed June 6, 2017].

Procter, S., and Radnor, Z. (2014). Teamworking under Lean in UK public services: Lean teams and team targets in Her Majesty's Revenue & Customs (HMRC). *The International Journal of Human Resource Management*, 25(21), 2978–2995.

Radnor, Z., and Johnston, R. (2012). Lean in UK government: Internal efficiency or customer service? *Production Planning & Control*, 24(10–11), 903–915.

Radnor, Z., and Osborne, S. P. (2013). Lean: A failed theory for public services? *Public Management Review*, 15(2), 265–287.

Schmenner, R. W., and Swink, M. L. (1998). On theory in operations management. *Journal of Operations Management*, 17(1), 97–113.

Strebel, P., and Lu, H. (2008). Who gets the rewards? Promote value creation by rewarding the right stakeholders. *Perspectives for Managers*, 161, 1.

Wallace, J. (2016). Freedom of information statistics: Implementation in central government. Cabinet Office. Office of National Statistics.

Winter, S. G. (2012). Capabilities: Their origins and ancestry. *Journal of Management Studies*, 49(8), 1402–1406.

# 7 Applying research methods in strategy consulting

*Graham Manville and Chand Chudasama*

## Abstract

This chapter examines the symbiotic relationship between the client, the management skills of the consultant and the application and relevance of robust research methods to solve client problems in a value adding way. The chapter begins by discussing the importance of deploying rigorous research techniques in concert with effective client management in order to ask the important, correct research questions. This involves working more closely with the client than a conventional academic researcher would and is more rigorous than a typical consultancy engagement. It requires an action learning approach (Revans, 1983) whereby mutual symbiosis (Dayasindhu, 2002) of shared knowledge acquisition is achieved through a deep, affective and trusting relationship. The principles of applied research are discussed followed by a discussion of the client–consultant relationship using the 7 Cs of consulting (Cope, 2010). An application of research is subsequently discussed using two case studies from a critical realist, ontological standpoint (Bhaskar, 1975).

## Introduction

Advising organisations on business strategy can be perceived as the ultimate intersection between theory and practice. Strategy consulting is a competitive environment with many small and large firms competing in the space as sector generalists and specialists. The purpose of all consultancy practices and independent consultants is to provide objective advice relating to the strategy, structure, management and operations of an organisation. They achieve this by solving problems and bringing an outside perspective to enhance business capability (Management Consultancies Association, 2016). A definition of management consulting provided by one of the leading UK trade and certification bodies, the Institute of Consulting (IC, 2016), is reproduced below:

> The provision to businesses of objective advice and assistance relating to the strategy, structure, management and operations of an organisation in pursuit of its long-term purposes and objectives. Such assistance may include the identification of options with recommendations, the provision of additional resources and/or the implementation of solutions.

Anecdotal experience from many consultants has shown that the mechanisms used to solve client problems are often distorted by three factors. Firstly, an over-reliance by consultants on 'things' (such as spreadsheets, processes, financial statements, intellectual property and data) not 'people' (specifically themselves and their clients).

| Research Attribute | Continuum | |
| --- | --- | --- |
| **Ontology – Beliefs about Reality** | Realism/Single Reality discovered by objective measurements and generalizable. | Multiple Realities/ Relativism (Socially Constructed by context individual perception) Truth created by meanings and experiences |
| **Epistemology – How you acquire the knowledge** | Positivism (A Natural Scientist) i.e. observable/ objective and measurable | Interpret Reality – Interact with people to find out what truth means |
| **Methodology – Research Strategy** | Deductive – Start with the theory – Data is collected and analysed to prove or disprove the theory | Inductive – Generally starts with data collection and relates it back to theory |
| **Research Strategy** | Surveys, larger sample sizes | Semi-Structured interviews, Focus Groups, smaller sample sizes. |
| **Timescale** | Cross Sectional – Research taken at a single moment in time | Longitudinal – Research carried out at multiple times in the project |
| **Sample** | Entire Population Sample | Single Sample (Case Study) |

*Figure 7.1* A continuum of research philosophies and strategies

Source: Adapted from Saunders et al. (2015), Killam (2013) and Badewi (2013).

When observing many junior consultants, it is common to see them start with a clear scope and to-do-list and, over the course of a few weeks, the contents of the list generates greater agency than the critical and creative thinking capabilities of the individual – this often manifests with the mismanagement of client expectations.

Secondly, consultants often rely heavily on 'tools' – such as SWOTs, 2x2 matrices, statistics, net present values and other metrics – without really understanding how specifically these tools contribute (or do not contribute) to answering the client's problems they have been hired to resolve. Both of these limitations are common and symptomatic of a weak understanding of applied research methods.

Finally, and potentially of most concern, is the client's expectations of what a consultant will deliver, which range from cynicism to a magic bullet. The emotional and psychological state of a client's leaders are driven by a multitude of personal and professional factors, and understanding and managing these are key to being able to deliver consulting services that add value.

The premise of this chapter is that applying research methods requires a core set of characteristics from the consultant. Crucially however, the effectiveness of the consultant's approach, and therefore subsequent findings, is relative to the client's readiness to seek answers to difficult questions. For example, the initial questions that the brief is asking may only be treating the symptom and not the cause. Preparing client readiness is a prerequisite function of client management and is the first part of the 7 Cs of consulting (Cope, 2010).

Broadly, this sounds straightforward, yet experience reveals that consultants often struggle to possess all of the required traits and clients' expectations can often be mismanaged. However, addressing these issues can lead to higher quality engagements that add value to the client and also provide opportunities for future engagement (ibid).

## Literature review

Management research may seem like a straightforward activity but the interpretation of the academic research community and the business community is often different, largely due to different motivations. For example, in academia, research is governed by the isomorphic behaviours (the tendency to be similar) (DiMaggio and Powell, 1983) of legitimation because the quality of management research in higher education institutions (HEIs) is, for want of a better word, regulated by academic work being accepted for publication in leading academic journals. Normative isomorphic behaviours are also present within the consultancy profession as consultancy practices and their consultants seek practice membership to demonstrate their legitimacy (Institute of Consulting, 2016; Management Consultancies Association, 2016). In addition, the larger organisations behave in a similar way by leveraging the power of their respective brands (e.g. the big four of PwC, KPMG, Deloitte and EY). But how does an academic know what makes a journal high quality and leading? There are several management journal lists which rank journals in four to five categories of respective quality based upon the judgement of committees of academics from leading business schools. For example, in the United Kingdom, it is the Association of Business Schools (ABS) journal ranking (ABS, 2015), in Australasia, it is the Australian Business Deans Council ranking (ABDC, 2013). In addition, the *Financial Times* list, the FT45, lists of the top forty-five highly rated business journals, which influences the global ranking of university business schools (Harzing, 2016). Such rankings can determine the career trajectory of academics and, as a result, perceived high quality research becomes concentrated in those particular outlets. This provides a challenge for leading business schools to produce quality research that is useful to the business community without compromising the reputation of the university. The tensions of the research community and the business community have been discussed in the academic literature by MacDonald and Simpson (2001). They argued that academic research is more transactional in approach, and that lessons could be learned from the management consultancy profession. In 2002, an academic think tank, the Advanced Institute of Management (AIM), began a ten-year project to make management research more accessible and relevant to the business community. In 2015, MacDonald et al. were still highly critical of the success of the AIM project in addressing problems related to relevance of management research and the awarding process of projects including the selection of academic staff. The former AIM directors provided a response to the claims in a position piece in the *Financial Times* (2016), which addressed the claims about the objectivity of the selection process and the awarding of projects. However, the response did not extend to the relevance of management research in the business community.

For many consultancy projects, the extent of research in academic terms has a relatively light touch, and is not always tested in terms of the validity and reliability that would be expected in an academic paper. For example, survey data and associated quantitative data will be presented in graphic and tabular formats but will seldom include reliability and validity testing. In addition, management consultants produce a report for the client organization, whereas an academic produces a research report for the world (MacDonald and Simpson, 2001). This view may be a little simplistic in that academic institutions need to ensure that their research is objective, rigorous, repeatable, valid and reliable (Saunders et al., 2015). If those protocols are not rigorously enforced, the danger is that the research of an academic from a HEI could be perceived as, at best, lacking in objectivity and, at worst, a lobbying document for the client, which could undermine the reputation of a HEI. This leads to the conclusion that the issues raised by MacDonald and Simpson (2001) and MacDonald et al. (2015), relating to the utility and effectiveness of management research, is not an easily solvable problem. For a start, the term 'management research' paints the issue in very broad strokes which can conceal the fact that research is multi-faceted and business operates in many contexts and among multiple stakeholders.

Academics consider research in terms of ontology and epistemology which are well understood by research-active academics, but when mentioned to a practitioner or a teaching academic it is less clear. This lack of understanding could be attributed to the lack of clarity in the definition of such terms within the research literature. Ontology and epistemology have been defined in simple terms by useful videos and books, such as Killam (2013), to support early career researchers. In order to provide a clearer understanding of management research, the research onion model devised by Saunders et al. (2015) provides a nomenclature of the classifications of different research philosophies used in the academic community. The research onion model illustrates the relationship between the layers of research philosophies, approaches and designs. Within each layer it can be considered to be more of a continuum with multiple options. Figure 7.1 provides further explanation of each 'onion layer'.

Conducting research-led consultancy differs from academic research as it is dependent upon the relationship between the client and the consultant. It can be a relationship based upon transactional trust, or it can be a relationship based more on affective trust (Akrout et al., 2016). Transactional trust is where the scope of work is objectively communicated and a set of deliverables is clearly set out in the proposal. Affective trust, on the other hand, is based upon a relationship. This requires a degree of emotional investment and can lead to a richer consultancy engagement. With the latter, much of the consultancy discussion

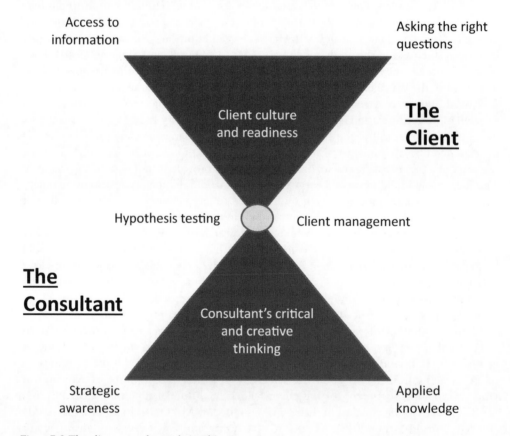

*Figure 7.2* The client-consultant relationship

may take place in liminal space, such as dinner engagements and/or more social contexts (Sturdy et al., 2006; Matthias, 2013).

There are two series of key questions that need to be asked. The first set of questions is generic and is not related to the topic area of the brief. According to Saunders et al. (2015), they include: What information does the client expect? What is the purpose of the report? How will the findings be used? Who is the intended readership of the report? The more specific questions relate to the brief itself and this where the relationship of the client and consultant is important. For example, a client may start with a particular project brief, but with skilful questioning in the early stages of the engagement the original question may only be addressing the symptom and not the cause, and so a more appropriate set of questions may be asked which may differ from the original brief. Care must be taken with the client as the organization may not be ready to confront more deep-seated issues. Cliff Bowman from Cranfield University has developed a process for navigating difficult decisions (Bowman, 1995). He refers to it as the zone of uncomfortable debate (ZOUD), and broaching those deep-seated issues requires a deft political touch and high credibility. Bailey (2011) adds that the ZOUD (i.e. the unspoken process that prevents us from questioning too closely the things that are held dear in business can be fraught with danger) can lead to a range of behaviours as benign as ridicule, escapism and delaying tactics to more serious behaviours like political power plays and downright hostility. The brief itself is only an initial discussion document and the consultant will likely develop a contractual proposal that will include the scope of work, the access to information and people and the deliverables. Occasionally, consultancy may be more open-ended and may take the form of a monthly retainer, but this kind of engagement will not be discussed in this chapter.

Access to information or people is critical to completing a successful research consultancy project. This can take the form of people; for example, key stakeholders such as employees, suppliers, customers and regulatory bodies. With larger organisations, access will be subject to confidentiality, and even consultancy that is based upon affective trust will require a more formalised negotiated contract. These are commonly referred to as non-disclosure agreements, which protect the reputation, client base, human capital and intellectual property rights of the organisation.

## The consultant

A consultant possesses not only tacit and explicit knowledge (Nonaka and Takeuchi, 1995) but also a vast array of models, frameworks and approaches at their disposal. They also possess a high degree of subject matter expertise in their specialised field of work. In addition, the consultant provides a big picture perspective, mastery of detail and the requisite project management skills to execute the project. Research into business practice by Harvard Business School refers to these attributes as 'deep smarts' (Leonard and Swap, 2005). A summary of deep smarts is shown in Figure 7.3. The consultancy relationship should also be an opportunity for the consultant to learn from the project although this should be a welcome by-product of the consultancy intervention. This learning is achieved through formal and informal knowledge exchange via a process of open innovation (Dayasindhu, 2002). So long as this knowledge exchange does not breech the terms of the NDA, then this opportunity for synergistic and symbiotic learning should be encouraged.

## The client relationship

The client-consultant relationship is vital for managing the successful completion of the consultancy project and the continuing relationship with the client. Many consultancy

- adaptive
- quick to learn
- quick to identify trends
- quick to identify anomalies
- hold an extensive repertoire of experience
- know rules of thumb
- know when rules of thumb do not apply
- good with teams, groups and personalities
- can apply systems thinking
- demonstrate managerial/technical intuition
- can modify actions responsively
- can cope with unusual situations
- have perspective beyond generalisations
- remain emotionally intelligent
- understand consequences of actions
- understand the big picture
- can focus on the details
- do not understand their own thinking process
- sometimes surprise themselves with their own thoughts

*Figure 7.3* Attributes of deep smarts

Source: Adapted from Leonard and Swap (2005).

practices follow the principles of the 7 Cs of consulting (Cope, 2010). These principles relate to: client, clarification, creation, confirm, change, continue and closure, as summarised below.

*Client:* This aspect of the 7 Cs relates to building affective and cognitive trust with the client and seeking to understand the world as the client interprets it. An idealistic state is to build symbiotic benefits that can benefit both parties. This stage will seek to identify the critical questions that require answering within the project.

*Clarify:* This process enables the client to plot and subsequently navigate the political terrain of the organization. This is where issues relating to ZOUD issues may be revealed. Alternatively, it may clarify the Terms of Reference where such issues are expressly not to be discussed. Also, it provides opportunities and timings for periodic check-ins with the client to ensure that the project is effectively stage gated to ensure that all stakeholders are clear with respect to the project management of the project.

*Create:* Within this phase, the consultant will conduct initial literature research, secondary research and then deploy appropriate models, frameworks and research methodologies to tackle the project brief.

*Change:* This relates to the extent of management change required in order to successfully implement the consultancy project. Research by Hailey and Balogun (2002) into managing change within organizations, has identified four types of change: incremental change v. step change, and realignment v. transformation. The latter dichotomy relates to whether or not a culture change is required. Realignment is within the existing paradigm of the organization and a transformational change requires a cultural change programme. From this research, they developed the change kaleidoscope model, which recognizes that change is context specific and includes the client's readiness for change, the power structures, the timing of the change, the scope of the change, what elements of the existing organization need to be preserved and the level of diversity of opinion within the organization that can relate to the capacity to question the status quo. Finally, change refers to the capacity and capability of the organization, which may determine or identify that the organization requires external capability to deliver the change (Hailey and Balogun, 2002).

*Confirm.* This is a function of good project management techniques and performance measurement of the consultancy project. It involves recognizing the change blockers and taking appropriate action to counteract any potential resistance to change. It also relates to the periodic check-in points with the client as well as confirming acceptance with appropriate stakeholders. At the conclusion of these confirmation points, the stage gates and milestones of the project can be signed off.

*Continue:* This requires effective knowledge transfer from the consultant to the client in order to make the change stick and to embed it within the routines and rituals within the organization. Without putting this process in place, there is a risk that the change would not become routinized and that things may revert to the existing state once the consultant has departed. This is an important part of creating a legacy of change.

*Close:* This an important and often overlooked part of the consultancy process as it not only signals the end of the consultancy project but can pave the way for future consultancy engagements.

## Reflective practice

The purpose of the following reflective practices is to provide tangible examples of research methods that have been deployed in consultancy projects to address two separate issues. These examples apply methodological techniques and explore the interplay between theory and practice. These reflections are written with an understanding that the reader has a good grounding in research methods. Both case studies adopt a critical realist stance (Bhaskar, 1975; Rutjes, 2016), which means that the researcher (management consultant) adopts the ontological stance that takes elements of positivism (i.e. a single reality that is affected by environmental factors). The first reflective practice uses quantitative analysis based upon the use of data derived from the Beta coefficient (Accounting Explained, 2016). In addition, inductive research is also applied to shape the coefficient by interpreting the data from demolition and asbestos disposal. For the second reflective practice, the ontological stance is also critical realism, which uses quantitative analysis of customer usage and then underpins it with a mixed-method research strategy using surveys, interviews and diaries. The two reflective practice case studies will contextualized and explained in more detail.

### Reflective practice 1: Clean-technology project

#### Situation

In late 2013, a fast growing, innovative, family waste management business was seeking to grow their new clean-technology product globally. However, the major driver of group profitability was a more traditional waste transportation business specialising in moving asbestos from demolition sites to landfill.

*Task*

A strategy and corporate finance consulting team was hired to work out how to take the new product to the global market. It was quickly identified that private equity would be the right source of funds to help facilitate growth. However, the impact of the global recession of 2008 was still being understood, and it was vital to be able to accurately forecast group turnover and profitability with a level of accuracy that went beyond the norm of typical management information.

*Action*

The team recognised that, given the macro trends impacting the industry, an inductive leading indicator that could forecast demand was required. Bodies of knowledge from both corporate finance and statistical analysis were evaluated to develop a simple solution that would give the client the right information to time decisions around dilution, and the new investor's confidence in the group and the sector.

The consultants concluded that a bespoke version of the investment statistic of 'Beta' was required (Accounting Explained, 2016). Beta is a simple number, derived from a standardised formula that tracks whether an investment is more or less volatile than the market.

$$\beta_p = \frac{Cov\left(r_a, r_b\right)}{Var\left(r_b\right)}$$

*Figure 7.4* The Beta coefficient equation

Where $r_a$ is the return of the asset (for example, share price), and $r_b$ is the return of the benchmark (for example, the S&P 500).

It is traditionally used to measure investment risk, but it is also used as a component part of some valuation methods, such as the capital asset pricing model (CAPM) (Finance Formulas, 2016). There is, however, a valid debate amongst practitioners about the relevance of Beta in analysing businesses that are not publicly traded. It is also worth noting that Beta is not a predictive coefficient, but rather an analysis of history. Notwithstanding, when you really look at the constituent parts, the formula has value beyond being a somewhat arbitrary statistic.

Variance, in simple terms, shows how 'spread' a series of data is from the arithmetic mean. Financiers and strategists use this to see what the spread of returns could be and therefore use the concept (and standard deviation) as measures of volatility and risk. Covariance essentially tells us how much two variables change together. The output of dividing one by the other is a measure of change relative to a benchmark. This is expressed as a coefficient. For example, any stock with a Beta higher than 1.00 is considered more volatile than the market, and therefore riskier to hold, whereas a stock with a Beta lower than 1.00 is expected to rise or fall more slowly than the market.

For example, the five-year Beta of Unilever plc (ULVR) against the S&P 500, as reported by Reuters (2016), is 0.78, whereas the five-year Beta for Thomas Cook Group plc (TGC) is 2.06. This means that, over the last sixty months, if the S&P 500 rose by 10%, ULVR share price would only rise by 7.8%, whereas TGC would rise by 20.6%. However, when the market fell by 8%, ULVR would have historically only fallen by 6.24%, whereas TGC would have fallen by 16.48%. Therefore, Beta provides a useful contribution to valuing a company, planning strategy and M&A activity, or designing portfolios.

The consulting team on this engagement recognised this value, but asked: if we ignore the need to compare Beta between assets and instead focus on the sector (asbestos disposal) rather than individual company or 'asset' and see Beta for its intuitive value rather than pushing for the statistic, then why can we not:

- Define the 'asset' as something more real than share price – for example, a non-financial driver expression of the varying size of the total asbestos market; and
- Define the 'benchmark', more specifically by refining it down to movement in share price of the firms that dictate the size of the market. In our case, this involved looking at UK quoted companies in construction and demolition as these firms create a had a major impact on revenue in our client's sub-sector.

Following the new definitions, the data that was collected and re-analysed showed:

1 A 95% correlation between asset and benchmark movement, thus allowing the team to advise both the client and future investors on risk correlation;
2 More importantly, a six-month lag between movements in the benchmark to movements in the size of the market, thus allowing the team to advise both the client and future investors on the timing of risk, capital requirements and the need for agility throughout the business.

There was no need to create coefficient statistics to prove the point, given the strength of the correlation, which was a more inductive-generalised conclusion.

In this case, the goal was not to create a simple deductive statistic, but rather to use the same principles to create an inductive guide to address the task.

Following an extensive data gathering and modelling process, time-series covariance and variance analysis was conducted on both series a and b above.

## Result

The team was able to develop a general theory – later proven by deductive tests to be 95% accurate – that forecasts how the total available market of asbestos disposal in the UK (or, in Beta terms, 'the asset') varied according to movements in the financial data of UK construction and demolition plcs (or, in Beta terms, 'the benchmark'). Not only did the test validate consistent demand despite the troubled post-recession environment, but the conclusions also accurately showed the business when they could expect demand to increase. This insight meant that they could compete better by timing sales and marketing activity and, crucially, time new investment better by making informed choices on dilution.

## Learning

The key pieces of learning from this example are centred on the need for making sure the right question is being asked and answered. This required a good understanding of corporate finance, operations and statistics. Creativity was also needed to be able to totally deconstruct a traditional formula and instead take guiding principles. This consultancy project benefitted from an understanding of when to be inductive in the research process.

This is often a more 'scary' choice for a financially orientated consultant as you do not know what you will find and may struggle to make promises about outputs. The ability to think critically about what drives financial performance in your client's sector was of key ingredient. In total, thirteen drivers were considered and eventually whittled down to series a and b. Knowing what to ignore can be challenging. The management of the client relationship was important, but was one small piece of a very large project. It would have been easy to drift into other issues and forget the simple reason this question needed to be asked. Gaining access to the right information is normally easier than consultants think, the hard part is being confident enough to not go looking for information until you know you are seeking the right data to answer the right question. With respect to value and pace, this piece of the engagement, whilst very important, was not the source of value. For the client, the important thing is the advice on what decisions to make as a result of this analysis and other information that is relevant. It was therefore important to get through this phase quickly and not overestimate the value the client placed on the phase. The task took a team of three people four days to complete.

### Reflective practice 2: Global consumer media engagement

#### Situation

A team of consultants were engaged by a large broadcaster to increase equity value prior to a series of large acquisitions. The engagement was split between projects focused on increasing profitability and those increasing sentiment and prospects (expressed in strategy and corporate finance terms as the price-earnings ratio). The business' leaders already knew that they needed a much better digital presence to allow them to be closer to the consumer. However, what they had lacked in the past was advice that was genuinely strategic in facilitating their ability to grow both organically and by M&A.

#### Task

The client wanted to create synergies from a series of large acquisitions but lacked the underlying consumer engagement to ensure this possibility. In particular, it was clear that the client wanted to be preeminent in news and sport. Therefore, the task was to find a way to get closer to consumers around the world to facilitate a more commercial M&A strategy.

#### Action

The team started with by using macro analysis to identify a portfolio of global cities selected to provide a balance of mature and emerging markets. If successful, commercial penetration into mature cities would provide 'wallet steal', or market share from competitors from mature markets, whereas gaining market share from the growth of an emerging market could help ensure the development of a loyal presence in high value territories. Combined, success across the portfolio could be positive for all stakeholders including M&A targets looking for international synergy, investors looking for differentiated assets and advertisers looking for the right communication channels to select consumers.

The team then created a template set of demographic traditional criteria such as age, education, gender and income, as well as more innovative sentiment criteria around aspiration and views on well-known global socio-economic issues. These 'boxes' would be used to allow the team to analyse differences in international markets. Standard deviation and covariance were used to ensure that banded data within each category of analysis was broadly similar, which meant that the boxes were constantly measured to make sure they were appropriate structures to define groups of consumers.

A global mixed-methodology consumer engagement exercise was then conducted to ascertain how different groups consumed news and sport throughout a twelve-week period. Focus groups, interviews and surveys were used, but were not as powerful as ethnography, analysing social media, analysing app engagement and usage and running consumer rapid prototyping workshops to develop new digital media concepts.

### Result

The key finding was identifying, for each market, who 'makes the weather' (the most influential group), who 'reports on the weather' (the fastest public opinions) and who 'dressed for the weather' (followers). The team was able to draw counterintuitive conclusions on which markets were similar/different and see how strong messaging (like news and advertising) spread amongst strategic markets.

The team was able to create an international market entry plan that: prioritised market entry across the portfolio; dictated the pace and content of product development and used audience analysis to be more confident in pricing and valuing advertising channels. The market entry plan thus provided a powerful growth narrative to investors which clearly showed future M&A targets and how they could achieve scale internationally by joining forces.

### Learning

The client had to believe that the methodology would be powerful enough to generate the required insight and answers. The gravity of the project's impact on M&A activity had put pressure on the team to cut corners. This required confident pushback and client management from the whole team. Securing access to information was challenging as secondary information was of limited value once it informed which cities to research. In order to gain empirical evidence, primary research was key. Asking the right questions was challenging as local differences mattered.

Having a robust methodological process of data collection was an important part of the empirics, and sorting, analysis and triangulation acted as control mechanisms to ensure quality and comparability.

Using a mixed-methods approach created an innovative context for hypothesis testing, but it increased the complexity in managing the process of transforming data into

| Time and motion study of competitor app usage |
| --- |
| Focus groups |
| Interviews |
| Survey |
| Ethnography – consumer diaries via an app |

*Figure 7.5* Summary of research methods used to analyse consumer behaviours

information. Having confidence to be innovative about the method of data collection, sorting and analysis were key ingredients to the success of the project. Having strategic awareness to recognise what different stakeholders (i.e. the board, marketing and product teams, advertisers, investors and M&A targets) want from a growth story is a challenge. The timescale of twelve weeks was considered too short for some stakeholders and too long for others. The information itself was not the point of value per se, but what really mattered was the advice about what decisions to make and why, when, how and with what budget.

## Conclusion

This chapter has discussed the importance of the client-consultant relationship in deploying appropriate research methods to solve client problems in two different contexts. This chapter has shown how research methods learned in a university business school context can be applied in innovative ways to solve client problems in a rigorous and robust systematic manner. The rich empirical case studies provide worked examples of how research methods can be applied in a business context. In both case studies, an ontological stance of a critical realist was adopted, although this is not the only paradigm available to management consultancy. A consultancy brief requiring a more socially constructed paradigm may require qualitative study as the research instrument. This is the preferred method when using a facilitative approach and when dealing with 'heart and minds' issues such as the ZOUD. Alternatively, another consultancy brief (such as merger and acquisition appraisal) may choose purely quantitative data that will have more robust reliability and validity testing than simply presenting data in graphs and tables. This chapter has intended to shine a light on the value of research methods within management consulting. The hope is that this chapter promotes further study into empirical research on the applied use of research methods within a business context beyond simply presenting tables and graphs.

## References

ABDC (2013). *Master journal list*. Available from www.abdc.edu.au/master-journal-list.php [Accessed October 14, 2016].

ABS (2016). *Academic journal guide*. Available from https://charteredabs.org/academic-journal-guide-2015/ [Accessed October 10, 2016].

Accounting Explained (2016). *Beta coefficient*. Available from http://accountingexplained.com/misc/corporate-finance/beta-coefficient [Accessed October 14, 2016].

Akrout, H., Diallo, M. F., Akrout, W., and Chandon, J. L. (2016). Affective trust in buyer-seller relationships: A two-dimensional scale. *Journal of Business & Industrial Marketing*, 31(2), 260–273.

Badewi, A. (2013). *How could your ontology and epistemology affect your research report structure?* Available from www.youtube.com/watch?v=BHArrSe9wz8 [Accessed October 10, 2016].

Bailey, C. (2011). Available from www.som.cranfield.ac.uk/som/dinamic-content/media/General%20Management%20Programmes/Working%20through%20the%20ZOUD.pdf [Accessed October 10, 2016].

Bhaskar, R. (1975). *A realist theory of science*. Leeds: Leeds Books.

Bowman, C. (1995). Strategy workshops and top-team commitment to strategic change. *Journal of Managerial Psychology*, 10(8), 4–12.

Cope, M. (2010). *The seven Cs of consulting: The definitive guide to the consulting process*, 3rd ed. Harlow: Pearson Education.

Dayasindhu, N. (2002). Embeddedness, knowledge transfer, industry clusters and global competitiveness: A case study of the Indian software industry. *Technovation*, 22(9), 551–560.

DiMaggio, P. J., and Powell, W. W. (1983). The iron cage revisited: Institutional isomorphism and collective rationality in organisational fields. *American Sociological Review*, 48, 147–160.

Finance Formulas (2016). *The capital asset pricing model.* Available from www.financeformulas.net/Capital-Asset-Pricing-Model.html [Accessed October 10, 2016].

*Financial Times* (2016). *Misleading messages on management research.* Available from www.ft.com/content/048090d4-b5f6-11e5-8358-9a82b43f6b2f?siteedition=intl [Accessed October 10, 2016].

Hailey, V. H., and Balogun, J. (2002). Devising context sensitive approaches to change: The example of Glaxo Wellcome. *Long Range Planning*, 35(2), 153–178.

Harzing (2016). *Journal quality list.* Available from www.harzing.com/download/jql_subject.pdf [Accessed October 10, 2016].

Institute of Consulting (2016). Available from www.iconsulting.org.uk/about_us [Accessed October 12, 2016].

Killam, L. (2013). *Research terminology simplified: Paradigms, axiology, ontology, epistemology and methodology.* Sudbury, ON: Author.

Leonard, D., and Swap, W. (2005). Deep smarts. *Harvard Business Review*, 30(2), 157–169.

MacDonald, S., and Simpson, M. (2001). Learning from management consultants: The lesson for management researchers. *Prometheus*, 19(2), 117–133.

Macdonald, S., Steen, J., and Shazi, R. (2015). Aiming for excellence: Reflections on the advanced institute of management research and its elite. *British Journal of Management*, 27, 438–454.

Management Consultancies Association (2016). Available from www.mca.org.uk/about-us/the-consulting-industry/ [Accessed October 14, 2016].

Matthias, O. (2013). Developing a customisation blueprint for management consultancies to better serve their clients. DBA, University of Bradford School of Management.

Nonaka, I. and Takeuchi, H. (1995). *The knowledge creation company: How Japanese companies create the dynamics of innovation.* New York: Oxford University Press.

Reuters (2016). *Reuters stock overview.* Available from www.reuters.com/finance/stocks/overview?symbol=ULVR.L [Accessed October 10, 2016].

Revans, R. W. (1983). Action learning: Its terms and character. *Management Decision*, 21(1), 39–50.

Rutjes, H. (2016). *Critical realism.* Available from www.youtube.com/watch?v=0UvjDMpYfrQ [Accessed October 16, 2016].

Saunders, M., Lewis, P., and Thornhill, A. (2016). *Research methods for business students*, 7th ed. Harlow: Pearson Education.

Sturdy, A., Schwarz, M., and Spicer, A. (2006). Guess who's coming to dinner? Structures and uses of liminality in strategic management consultancy. *Human Relations*, 59(7), 929–960.

# 8 Consultancy in management education

*Olga Matthias and Julian Campbell*

## Abstract

This chapter interrogates the teaching and application of management consultancy as part of a master's degree in business administration (MBA) and examines its relevance in management education. Mature and experienced students, many with impressive CVs and multiple career successes, demand that the core experience of their MBA programmes provide opportunities to apply theoretical knowledge in real-life situations. Opportunities to work with blue-chip clients on some of their projects of strategic importance offers further opportunities for students to test management thinking and consultancy practise in a robust and challenging manner. Students often have previous experience working with consultants, but most have little experience managing and delivering projects for clients within a consultancy framework. The pedagogical challenge is to teach students the true value proposition of consultancy beyond the transactional relationship inherent in answering a work-based learning challenge set by the client. The basic process approach moves students from considering consultancy as a phenomenon that 'happens' to a client, with a solution magically appearing upon project conclusion, to a position where students recognise consultants as a true 'change agent', unfreezing clients from previous positions and realising new capabilities (Lewin, 1951). There is an examination of ensuring the *relevance* of the management consultancy approach to students as part of their MBA journey as well as *relevance* to the client companies in engaging with the university. There is discussion on how teaching a *rigorous* approach to management consultancy project management and research-orientated methodology retains the focus on the *impact* to the client organisation (Appelbaum and Steed, 2005). There is consideration of how true *impact* on client companies is achieved by ensuring that legacy forms part of expectation management (Kirk, 2000) with client companies keen to reengage with future MBA student teams. The chapter concludes with a reflection on the future development of consultancy within management education, and how that embeds theoretical learning with individual context.

## Introduction – designing a new MBA

For many years, business schools have incorporated aspects of management consultancy into their MBA programmes, either through specific consultancy modules or through offering consultancy projects. Many of the modules in management consultancy are accredited by the Chartered Management Institute (CMI) for the Level 7 diploma in professional consulting. Given that MBA graduates tend to gravitate towards consultancy as the career of choice following their qualification, many students choose the module because of its content and the additional qualification they receive. Those schools that have chosen to go down the path of offering consultancy projects have found both difficulties and rewards arising from their choice.

This chapter uses a specific example of the experience of one business school and how its programme has evolved with regard to management consultancy projects during the course of MBA study. The initial driver, a little over 10 years ago in mid-2006, for considering such an approach was the decision to launch a full-time MBA program. The University of East Anglia contemplated the fact that the MBA market was already crowded and realised that if their new programme were to succeed, they had to offer something different to aspiring management professionals who were keen on investing in MBA study as the catalyst to helping them secure more advanced leadership positions. Prospective candidates consistently stated that beyond the standard syllabus covering the key areas of business and management strategy, they wanted an experience that allowed them to put theory into practice. This needed to be academically robust, beyond the 'interesting project' experience, demonstrating how MBA-level thinking could be applied and implemented to effect real change in organisations.

Fortunately, an element to their already-established Executive MBA program invited students to work with blue-chip companies in the Czech Republic. This had been developed by an emeritus professor who had been a member of the faculty delivering that programme. There was therefore a degree of organisational competence in the mechanics of working with large companies at a senior level and a number of senior relationships in that regard. In addition, they recruited other colleagues to the MBA team who had a number of years' experience as independent management consultants.

Together, this experienced team further developed this aspect of the full-time and Executive MBA programmes. The innovation at the time was to offer students the opportunity to complete management consultancy projects in organisations willing to open themselves up to this kind of exposure. The objective was to deliver strategic and practical recommendations to a range of client organisations.

The management consultancy project element in the MBA program is now the substantive element to the course, carrying 40 of the 180 credits required for the qualification, which replaces the more usual dissertation component. Through close cooperation with the Institute of Consulting (now part of the Chartered Management Institute) regarding syllabus development, MBA graduands are dual qualified, with both their master's degree and the diploma in professional consulting. The University of East Anglia have the distinction of being the first MBA course in the UK to offer this combination.

## The challenge of recruiting clients and demonstrating relevance

Although companies were willing to collaborate and work in partnership with business schools on events, research collaborations or employability-themed initiatives that helped them recruit new talent, offering projects for students to work on was not something they were willing to embark upon. Despite pre-existing working relationships, recruiting clients for this aspect was a struggle. Companies stated they were reluctant to undergo the potential discomfort of having a group of experienced managers, who were studying for an MBA, accessing and then commenting on important elements of the operations of their business.

Serious consideration had to be given to how this could be changed. If the programme were to succeed, this innovative aspect had to be implemented. Much as the theory of client-consulting relationships advocates, the University of East Anglia had to engage with the businesses they already were working with in a new way. If they could not succeed in existing relationships, it was felt that expanding this idea to new businesses might be irrevocably compromised. The approach adopted was one advocated by Cialdini (1993).

The first step was persuading clients that there was real commercial value (for which they would not have to pay!) in the work the students would carry out for them. Success was slow and based on carefully targeting which businesses with existing relationships would be approached. In selectively choosing the clients they were prepared to work with, and emphasising the selective nature of recruitment of candidates to the MBA programme (not quite the 'best of the best' but a sufficient statement of quality to create a desire in prospective clients to want to work with the students), there came a shift in demand from 'push' to 'pull' in classic consultancy client management terms (Cope, 2003). Reciprocity and scarcity were key influencing factors and helped build trust in a structured way for what became an unwritten contract about working together institutionally.

Success in this regard then created a different challenge – to ensure the module was designed in such a way that it enabled students to deliver on the inherent promise under-pinning the company: university contract. Much like the client-consultant relationship itself, in which the firm's brand provides a kind of corporate banner associated with a track record of successful collaboration (Matthias, 2013), so the students are associated with this relationship between organisation and university. As such, this creates an expectation by the company which the student, as representative of the university must fulfil. Thus, the basis of the framework for the student project is formed from a relationship standpoint.

To ensure that the university maintains its reputation, from both a current and future student perspective and in terms of continuing successful engagement with business, the first step had to be to engage the students and create an appetite for success in a structured yet flexible way. Thoroughness and creativity, sometimes seen as opposing traits, had to be built into the programme and needed to be a student-learning outcome.

## Methodology and focussing on performance

Undoubtedly, many people are prejudiced against the consulting industry as a result of consistently negative media exposure and coverage of high-profile project failures (BBC, 2013; McDonald, 2013). Despite this, consultancy draws in many people. As well as being inherently interesting in and of itself, the skills and techniques learnt for management consultancy are easily transferable to any management role because of the results-driven focus, which is achieved through the deployment of quantitative, research and problem-solving skills, which are then seamlessly married to the so-called 'soft' interpersonal skills of negotiation, facilitation, coaching and communication.

The first step to generate success for the programme, the clients and the students them-selves (even for students who had worked with consultants in their own organisations previously) had to be to open up students' minds to considering management consultancy in a new light. This process began with a little humour. Lectures begin with light-hearted references to pictures of J K Rowling's *Harry Potter* characters and Charles Darwin. In this way, students are challenged to reject the myth that effective consultancy is a smoke-and-mirrors parlour game where solutions emerge at the end of the project through the 'wizard' or 'guru' mode (Clark and Greatbatch, 2002; Clegg et al., 2004; Johansson, 2004). The assertion is that good consultancy remains true to the definition:

> A contracted service delivered by specially qualified individuals who assist and sup-port in an objective and independent manner. Management consultants identify

management problems, analyse the cause of such problems, recommend solutions and help – where requested – in the implementation of solutions.

(Greiner and Metzger, 1983)

This definition is a consistent theme throughout the module, and principles such as objectivity and the need to work towards practical solutions are paramount throughout. Also emphasized throughout the programme is value, as understood in the recognised definition of consultancy published by the Management Consultancy Association: "The creation of value for organisations, through the application of knowledge, techniques and assets, to improve business performance" (MCA, 2016).

The core structure of the syllabus provides an outline of the core features of consulting work:

- *A process approach.* The first challenge is to encourage students to understand consulting from a process-driven approach, rather than a phenomenon in action, using a simple, five-step approach: engagement and contracting, research and diagnosis, recommendation, implementation and exit (Block, 2000). There is also a need to define the roles that effective consultants can play in the process (Lippitt and Lippitt, 1986), such as problem solver, advocate and trainer.
- *Business research.* MBA students are often familiar with the output of market and business research, and may have been involved in conducting commercial research themselves. Rarely, however, do they possess traditional academic research skills. The requirement in this part of the syllabus is to emphasise the importance of offering credible recommendations to a client, based on empirical research, from market trends to industry best practice to competitor analysis. This is the consultancy as objective expert, where the expertise is directly informed by the research commissioned specifically for the project. In teaching students to conduct research associated with their projects, core concepts such as correlation and causality, validity and reliability are taught, in addition to the most common research methodologies such as the survey, focus groups and interviews.
- *Client management.* From the early doctor-patient models to client management (Schein, 1999) to Cope's 7 Cs of consulting (Cope, 2003), understanding and building professional relationships with the client is critical to navigating the challenges of consulting. In some respects, this is the feature of consulting work that MBA students are instinctively the most comfortable with because most are already seasoned professionals used to handling clients and demonstrating a mature understanding that relationship management is key to success (Palmatier et al., 2006).
- *Project management.* MBA students are in another comfort zone when considering the importance of project management in the execution of a successful consultancy project. Straightforward project management skills and frameworks form this part of the syllabus, informed by the PMBOK guide (PMI, 2013), but the emphasis is on the effective use of these project management skills in the subtly different arena of management consulting and, notably, their additional importance within the client relationship (Handley et al., 2006).
- *Recommendations and implementation.* High-level clients will see through the gloss of the beautifully presented report or well-rehearsed presentations that have superficial impact, and the pressure to perform well in delivery is an experiential element to the MBA that students reflect on for further personal development. The projects cannot

therefore be artificial. In making recommendations, the focus has to be on improving the client's business performance (Kubr, 2002) and the application of MBA-level thinking to solve problems (Merron, 2005).

Essentially, these features are about the ability to address high-level problems, whether as an employee or a consultant. From the perspective of an MBA programme, these aspects, incorporated into this module, provide the opportunity to draw upon and integrate the knowledge base from the other MBA units within a taught framework of management consultancy skills. This module offers opportunities to apply previously taught tools and techniques and reflection on personal development. Reflective practice and personal reflection have been found to enhance individual and organisational performance (Schön, 1991; Moon, 1999). Although in the high-pressured world of consulting where there is not always the time for this kind of personal development, the firm, the individual and clients see the benefit in the longer term (Adams and Zanzi, 2005; Bradley et al., 2011; Brivot, 2011).

Another feature is a focus on effective performance in a team environment. This is different to the ubiquitous 'team working' frequently incorporated into many programmes. The difference is that the former utilises individuals' contributions in group processes, which then jointly contribute to the overall outcome rather than seeking to create a false perception that everything must be done as a group. Team selection, delegation, development and management of each feature are important aspects. A particular example came to light in the Czech Republic with the university's longstanding collaborating organization, Unilever. The pressure was such that the project launch and the team gelling was described by a number of participants as "Tuckman on steroids", based on the long-established work on teams carried out by Tuckman (1965). Well-functioning teams are often taken for granted so it is an aspect of the taught element of this module that is emphasised (Nelson and McFadzean, 1998).

In the classroom sessions, it is also pointed out that there is something often forgotten by scholars and practitioners alike: an additional stage to working in a team, and one which a management consultant may not be overly familiar with but has experienced multiple times. This is 'mourning' (Tuckman and Jensen, 1977). It happens at the end of every project, and also even when just one member is removed or changed, thus impacting performance, however inadvertently. Raising awareness of team theory links strongly to the personal reflective learning component, and students are particularly asked to give consideration to the activity within teams so that they can reflect on their associated learning from that. It is highlighted that they can learn from positive and negative experiences. 'How not to' is sometimes better embedded as a learning experience than 'how to'.

Students apply this theoretical learning to scenarios and discussions during the in-class work, and then have the opportunity to explore the application further during the two real live consultancy projects they undertake. All contributors to the programme, companies and students alike, emphasise the absolute necessity of practical recommendations and the requirement for the absence of superficiality and soundbites.

Together, these aspects build to a significant individual piece of reflective assessment over the year, and thus justifiably comprise a large component of the MBA degree.

## Ensuring legacy and impact

One important element of successful consultancy interventions is remaining focused on improving the performance of the client organisation (Appelbaum and Steed, 2005).

This is especially challenging for projects where the students are operating not as paid consultants under any kind of transactional contract, but almost as 'expert volunteers' working for a benevolent client. The potential jeopardy of non-payment or contractual sanction does not exist (although the students may fail their MBA if they fail to deliver adequately!).

Achieving any kind of legacy for these projects has to start with the nature of the question asked of the students. The university works with the client to undertake projects that require clear recommendations for action, or not – such as, a route map for implementation of a marketing strategy; a go/no-go recommendation for investment; or a new way of organising an international operational or HR process.

A number of good examples have arisen over the years. A new strategy for Unilever in the Czech Republic to help the company retain more female managerial talent after maternity leave. Co-design of a new risk management tool to help Marsh Insurance launch a new product to help companies dealing with historical asbestos-related claims. Analysing Lego's packaging process to identify operational efficiencies.

Perhaps the most dramatic was advice for Kodak in 2014. The company had been investing a number of new technologies developed by the company's own researchers and scientists that may have commercial potential for market innovation. The MBA team was tasked with analysing the potential for one particular invention with potential applications in the medical, sports and defence industries. The details remain commercially sensitive but, in essence, the technology was concerned with inserting a certain inorganic compound into various fabrics to give additional capabilities. The company's own Innovation and Business Development managers were certain of the potential and expected the students to identify and quantify the commercial potential. However, the students were working directly with senior managers at Kodak and decided they were being asked a more fundamental question: 'Should we do this?'

Upon project completion, the students recommended that Kodak walk away from any of the potential uses for this technology, but keep the IP until such a time in the future where the sums added up. The MBA team felt that although new products could be launched, there would be no first-mover advantage in the markets identified and that the costs to entry would mean no real return for in excess of 10 years. It was a bold set of recommendations (in effect it was one simple recommendation!), but the analysis and treatment of the financial investment requirements demonstrated the robust nature of the work carried out and ultimately the validity of the answer. Kodak accepted the recommendation and put all of the relevant projects on hold for the foreseeable future. One vice president commented: 'You have just saved us a very large amount of money'.

The essence of the success and legacy here (Kodak has asked successive student teams to return and work on other projects) was good recommendations based upon a process managed using effective consultancy skills. The students could have kept matters very transactional and given a 'positive' answer, but with maturity and a recognition that the client wanted 'value', they identified value in this context as though an understanding of the *real* question they were being asked.

## Where are we now and where do we go from here?

As with all service businesses, delivering good quality service and creating client satisfaction is critical to establishing long-term relationships and gaining repeat business. Typically, clients are keen on working with the university again to generate 'repeat business'. This demonstrates a satisfaction with the service, the outcomes and the relationships, in keeping with good consulting practice (Patterson, 2000; Armbruster, 2006). It also extends beyond the annual project phenomenon. In many of the client companies, there is a curiosity arising. Questions are triggered, prompting a proactive search for ways of engaging, both further and differently. Questions such as: What can we do with this next time around? Can we use the students to challenge our internal cultural boundaries? Can the MBA consultancy team address the unspoken shibboleth that nobody who works here can take the risk to address? It is almost as if an adventurism has been awakened within these clients that would not perhaps be present in a commercial consultancy arrangement. Perhaps also it is the kind of 'nice to have' thinking that is rarely, if ever, part of a commercial agreement. As much as reflection is a part of studying this module before the client-facing work begins, so it would appear that it buys time in the client organisation. It is another manifestation of the 'bricolage' Bradley et al. (2011) referred to when discussing the need for creating the time to think and reflect – this time from the perspective of the firm, so it is organisational rather than personal development but on a gentle rather than transformational scale.

As we work with certain clients on a 'repeat basis', we see an interest beyond having another good experience with our MBA students and the delivery of more valued recommendations. We now see clients wanting to understand the mechanics of how we are teaching these students in advance of project engagement. What toolkits are we giving them? What processes underpin the way they work? What competencies are you building? This general level of interest and interrogation is leading to another set of questions and observations. How can we help in this endeavour? Can we be involved and give an active client perspective? Why don't you do X to make them better consultants from our perspective as clients? Their motivations seem to stem from genuine interest rather than any commercial perspective.

It does appear, however, to be consistent with principles of true co-design (Edvardsson et al., 2006) as opposed to merely being 'helpful', and it is a development of the relationship between the university and these client companies. Perhaps because it is a unique relationship between large companies and a leading university, focussed upon the education of students. Perhaps because it is also an outlet for the creativity and innovation of those senior managers within these firms (Kristensson, 2006).

Whatever the cause, it will continue to shape the delivery of this part of our MBA.

## Conclusion

The University of East Anglia never sought to develop an MBA which would be the MBA for management consultants, although many of its MBA alumni gravitate towards careers in the consulting sector (anecdotally, more so than from many other MBA courses in the UK). What alumni have found, however, is that it is the consultancy education and experience that has proven to be the foundation of the future success for those who have experienced the course.

Good management consultancy is about client management, effective project discipline and productive teamwork when under pressure. It is about building a case for change based on credible research and robust diagnostic analysis that includes the capability to identify assumptions, evaluate statements in terms of evidence, detect false logic or reasoning, identify implicit values, define terms adequately and generalise appropriately. Other core skills are critical thinking and creativity, managing creative processes in one's self and others, organising thoughts, analysis, synthesis and critical appraisal. These days, good management is about every one of these skills too. Little wonder, then, that these are invaluable skills that MBA students are looking to develop.

The vehicle for this learning at the University of East Anglia is the management consultancy projects module within the MBA. The extra value in a strict consultancy sense is the application of recognised consultancy methodologies and an emphasis on value through practical solutions. As already stated, there are design elements to this management education experience that are incredibly portable in a career and career progression sense. The pedagogical framework developed for this module offers academic veracity and rigour, but its value goes beyond merely teaching and testing management consultancy projects. Management education is necessarily broad: students are from diverse sectors and professional backgrounds and have a variety of aspirations, like promotion, career change and self-employment. Consultancy, as a broad discipline, offers the scope to achieve this goal.

Plans to further develop the programme are underway. Reflection on the need to ensure the resonance created and identified in the value proposition of the MBA course is continuous. For support and input, developments in the profession are looked to and sought out. However, the team looks for true inspiration to the body of clients who have worked with the university over the last 10 years. The clients have observed that working with students in this consultancy capacity has revealed things about their organisations that were unexpected. The invocation of the law of unintended consequences has not really revealed operational 'unknowns' (although that has happened), but a new light has been shed on the cultural and social nature of professional relationships.

This has led to more companies expressing a desire to work as engaged clients, beyond just the 'commercial' aspect of the MBA project. Recent developments have been in regard to engaging with social enterprise activity with senior managers, to offering ideas and suggestions for new ventures and to mentoring staff and previous client-consultant contacts. What began as a transactional collaboration between the university and an external company has resulted in the wholly unexpected outcome of collaboration amongst a constantly changing team of equals coming together formally and informally to the rhythm of the academic year for mutual benefit. A key challenge for the future design of the course is to maintain that momentum and continue reaping the benefits of academic rigour with commercial need for value-added outcome for both business and university.

## References

Adams, S. M., and Zanzi, A. (2005). The consulting career in transition: From partnership to corporate. *Career Development International*, 10(4), 325–338.

Appelbaum, S. H., and Steed, A. J. (2005). The critical success factors in the client-consulting relationship. *The Journal of Management Development*, 24(1/2), 68–93.

Armbruster, T. (2006). *The economics and sociology of management consulting*. Cambridge: Cambridge University Press.

BBC (2013). *NHS IT system one of 'worst fiascos ever'*. London: BBC. Available from www.bbc.co.uk/news/uk-politics-24130684 [Accessed September 23, 2012].

Block, P. (2000). *Flawless consulting*. San Francisco, CA: Jossey-Bass, Pfeiffer.

Bradley, S. W., Shepherd, D. A., and Wiklund, J. (2011). The importance of slack for new organizations facing 'tough' environments. *Journal of Management Studies*, 48(5), 1071–1097.

Brivot, M. (2011). Controls of knowledge production, sharing and use in bureaucratized professional service firms. *Organization Studies*, 32(4), 489–508.

Cialdini, R. B. (1993). *Influence: The psychology of persuasion*, revised ed. New York: Morrow.

Clark, T., and Greatbatch, D. (2002). Knowledge legitimation and audience affiliation through storytelling: The example of management gurus. In T. Clark and R. Fincham (eds.), *Critical consulting: New perspectives on the management advice industry*. Oxford: Blackwells, pp. 152–171.

Clegg, S. R., Kornberger, M., and Rhodes, C. (2004). Noise, parasites and translation: Theory and practice in management consulting. *Management Learning*, 35(1), 31–44.

Cope, M. (2003). *The seven Cs of consulting: The definitive guide to the consulting process*, 2nd ed. London: FT Prentice Hall.

Edvardsson, B., Gustafsson, A., Kristensson, P., Magnusson, P., and Matthing, J. (eds.). (2006). *Involving customers in new service development*. London: Imperial College Press.

Greiner, L. E., and Metzger, R. O. (1983). *Consulting to management*. Englewood Cliffs, NJ; London: Prentice-Hall.

Handley, K., Sturdy, A., Clark, T., and Fincham, R. (2006). The type of relationship clients really want with their consultancies. *People Management*, 12(10), 52.

Johansson, A. W. (2004). Consulting as story-making. *Journal of Management Development*, 23(4), 339–354.

Kirk, D. (2000) *Managing Expectations*. Project Management Institute, Pennsylvania, USA .

Kristensson, P. (2006). Managing ideas that are unthinkable in advance: A matter of how and where you ask. In B. Edvardsson, A. Gustafsson, P. Kristensson, P. Magnusson and J. Matthing (eds.), *Involving customers in new service development*. London: Imperial College Press, pp. 127–142.

Kristensson, P., Magnusson, P., and Matthing, J. (2002). Users as a hidden resource for creativity: Findings from an experimental study on user involvement. *Creativity and Innovation Management*, 11(1), 55–61.

Kubr, M. (2002). *Management consulting: A guide to the profession*. Geneva: International Labour Office.

Lewin, K. (1951) Field theory in social science; selected theoretical papers. D. Cartwright (ed.). New York: Harper & Row.

Lippitt, G., and Lippitt, R. (1986). *The consulting process in action*. San Diego, CA: Pfeiffer & Company.

Matthias, O. (2013). Developing a customisation blueprint for management consultancies to better serve their clients. DBA. University of Bradford School of Management.

MCA (2016). *The consulting industry*. Management Consultancies Association: Online. Available from www.mca.org.uk/about-us/the-consulting-industry [Accessed July 1, 2016].

MCA (2017). *The UK Consulting Industry*. Available from https://www.mca.org.uk/about-us/the-consulting-industry/ [Accessed June 5, 2017].

McDonald, D. (2013). *The firm: The inside story of McKinsey: The world's most controversial management consultancy*. New York: Simon & Schuster.

Merron, K. (2005). Masterful consulting. *Consulting to Management*, 16(2), 5–8.

Moon, J. A. (1999). *Learning journals: A handbook for academics, students and professional development*. London: Kogan Page.

Nelson, T., and McFadzean, E. (1998). Facilitating problem-solving groups: Facilitator competences. *Leadership & Organization Development Journal*, 19(2), 72–82.

Palmatier, R. W., Dant, R. P., Grewal, R. P., and Evans, K. (2006). Factors influencing the effectiveness of relationship marketing: A meta-analysis. *Journal of Marketing*, 70(4), 136–153.

Patterson, P. G. (2000). A contingency approach to modeling satisfaction with management consulting services. *Journal of Service Research*, 3(2), 138–153.

Project Management Institute (2013). *Project Management Body of Knowledge (PMBOK Guide)*. Newtown Square, PA: PMI.

Schein, E. H. (1999). *Process consultation revisited – building the helping relationship*. Boston, MA: Addison-Wesley.

Schön, D. A. (1991). *The reflective practitioner: How professionals think in action*. Aldershot: Ashgate.

Tuckman, B. W. (1965). Developmental sequence in small groups. *Psychological Bulletin*, 63(6), 384–399.

Tuckman, B. W., and Jensen, M. A. C. (1977). Stages of small-group development revisited. *Group & Organization Management*, 2(4), 419–427.

# Part II

# Practical implementation

Case studies in management consulting

## Introduction to Part II

Part I provided a scholarly perspective on management consultancy and reflected on some of the challenges, potential approaches and theoretical considerations that may help the professional practice and future researchers. The following chapters offer contributions from management consultants worldwide. Part II includes nine chapters, which present case studies from Europe, Africa, Asia, Australasia and America. Each one presents a different industry, the consulting situation and the difficulties therein, and then takes the reader through the reality of day-to-day consulting and how satisfactory solutions are reached in what can best be described as a messy world.

As previously discussed in Part I, management consultancy has become a global phenomenon in the 100 or so years of its existence. To some, it feels as if organisations are dependent on them. It is fair to assume that clients know the value consultants add, otherwise they would not continue to buy those services. The cases in this section demonstrate the breadth of problems with which consultants are presented. Consultants tend to use tried and tested methodologies to solve their clients' issues to help them gain or maintain competitive advantage. Each chapter in Part II presents an approach to a particular issue in a particular set of circumstances and describes how it was dealt with.

Warren and Allen discuss, in Chapter 9, how capacity was developed for farm consultancy in New Zealand. This is an economically important sector and therefore an issue not just for individual businesses but also for the country's prosperity. Hine and Lynas provide another example of capacity building in Chapter 10, this time demonstrating it with work carried out in the UK National Health Service (NHS). In Chapter 11, Farrow discusses the challenge of getting people to buy into any need for change and how hearts and minds are never accounted for, yet without successfully converting staff to any new ideas or ways of working, profitability and success proves elusive. Further to changing ways of thinking and embedded behaviours, Lewis, Bairatchnyi and Lewis, in Chapter 12, present a story of competency development in cross-cultural management and describe how global organisations can be moved from a state of 'cultural awareness' to one of 'global competence'. Continuing the theme of developing individual and corporate competency, in Chapter 13, Rodway and Manville recount the development of a talent management programme of Generation Y/Millennial employees in a global investment bank. Chapter 14, written by Cordier and Hameed, presents a case demonstrating client-consultant knowledge applied to enable corporate growth, while Kariuki, in Chapter 15, presents that in regard to a whole continent. Mika, in Chapter 16, takes a look at the importance of ethnicity in the world of consulting. Finally, Knowles and Manville, in

Chapter 17, expound that consultants are custodians of best practice, based on consultants' position as possessors of inter-organisational knowledge derived from a network of heterogeneous firms that provide inspiration from different social systems and are then adapted judiciously. It is perhaps this latter point that goes some way to explaining the continued growth and increasing interest in this industry, which appears to have transitioned from a dispensable service to an institutionalised one, embedded in client business cycles and operating procedures.

# 9 Developing capacity for farm consultancy in New Zealand

*Lorraine Warren and Peter Allen*

## Executive summary

Agriculture is New Zealand's biggest sector (NZTE, 2016), creating a demand for basic business advice in accountancy and law, but also for the softer, more systemic aspects of farm life, such as governance and family succession. Nationally, there is a strategic need to develop consulting capacity to support the industry overall. This chapter is based on reflections following a 12-week teaching experience of 15 farm consultants in New Zealand in 2015, which was designed to meet a national shortage of trainers and was based on the expertise and experiences of one of the authors (PA). The course consisted of distance learning with a two-day teaching block shared with an experienced consultant. We discuss the variety of teaching approaches used and evaluate their effectiveness in a context where client farmers seek solution-based outcomes. We conclude by making recommendations for future practice.

## Introduction

Farming is big business in New Zealand, particularly dairy, and it dominates the national economy. With annual exports in excess of NZ$13.7 billion, the dairy industry is New Zealand's biggest export earner, accounting for more than 29% by value of the country's merchandise exports and employing 37,000 people. Around 95% of New Zealand's milk is exported (NZTE, 2016). Dairy has struggled in recent years as products such as milk powder have fallen in price on the world commodity markets (for example, RNZ, 2016). Therefore, there are strategic pressures on the sector overall, giving rise to the need to innovate away from commodities to higher added value milk products, or alternatively, to innovate to realise greater economies of scale. Troubles in the sector place economic pressure on farmers in some obvious ways, such as making ends meet day-to-day, but also in regard to longer term issues, for example, they create uncertainty around the imperative of succession management. Multiple heirs, splitting the farm, or buying another farm are difficult and risky challenges in the current economic climate. Another challenge is the possibility that there may be no heir-in-waiting. If farming is unattractive, then sons and daughters may want to take up other professions, perhaps away from the land.

Not surprisingly, rural consultancy is important in New Zealand, to advise farmers on developing the farm as a business, keeping it in profit and within the law. There are many independent consultants, consultancy agencies and networks (for example, AgFirst, 2016) and specialist staff in organisations, such as banks and accountancy practices. However, one of the main motivations for the creation of the advisory course discussed in this chapter was the paucity of consultants nationally who were able to advise on governance matters generally, and fewer still in the rural context. Governance of a farm business spans a wide range of functions, including financial, legal, strategic and leadership matters relating to the business of farming (Allen, 2016):

1   Clarity and agreement by the owners of the values, purpose and objectives for the business.
2   Agreement on the objectives and specific actions of strategic plans looking out three to five years ahead.
3   Agreement on annual business objectives, targets and operational plans.
4   Clarity of organisational leadership with clear roles and responsibilities, and with proper delegation of the authority to fulfil that role.
5   Transparent and timely systems of accountability, reporting and benchmarking that are then used to improve the performance of the business.
6   Business risks are identified and an appropriate response made.

There is little training available in the marketplace in New Zealand concerning governance that might apply to SMEs. There is even less specialist expertise geared to the needs of family-owned businesses. For example, a popular course is the Institute of Directors (IoD) five-day course on governance, but it, like others, is geared for the largest of organisations. Thus, accountants and others in the sector were seeing the need to advise clients about governance, as many of them were operating in an *ad hoc* manner and did not yet have any models to put forward that were appropriate for the identified need. Further, the IoD course is geared more towards learning *about* governance than learning to implement governance. Sound implementation of governance principles requires farm businesses to have an effective board of directors to oversee the necessary functions, alongside the family members who typically own the farm. As many farms have evolved from small family concerns, they may only have embryonic understandings of governance (little beyond compliance with the law), and often lack the means to develop their governance on an ongoing basis. By 2011–2013, 'governance' had become a trendy topic, but alongside that emergent need there was a growing, misguided view that it could be the next 'answer' to all business problems, even a 'cure-all'. For governance to succeed, the sector needs to encourage farmers to undertake and make progress along a 'governance learning journey', and further make sure that the right training is in place for aspirant directors who are still in short supply.

The need to equip consultants to address governance issues throughout the sector has been recognised nationally with the establishment of initiatives such as OneFarm, a university-led partnership (Massey and Lincoln University) supported by the government (Ministry for Primary Industries) and industry bodies (DairyNZ, Red Meat Profit Partnership). OneFarm is dedicated to increasing farm business management capability through research and education, including professional development courses for consultants in governance and family succession that are informed by research and industry professionals. The institutional support for the programme reflects the course being seen as a nationally initiated response to solve a problem that was impacting the economy, particularly as no other provider was aiming at the same target in quite the same way.

To respond to the need, they drew on the experience of one of the authors (PA) and another experienced consultant in the field, JT. Both PA and JT were driven by the need to develop long-term solutions for families, rather than deliver piecemeal quick fixes that did not address underlying issues particularly around family relationships. Part of that ethos was that families needed to 'learn to learn', take ownership of their own problems and become more proficient in setting their own strategies and problem solving. Inherent in the provision, therefore, is the principle that processual, systemic approaches to farm consultancy, which focus on participants learning from each other and taking ownership of problems, are beneficial in the long term. This was based predominantly on the long-established traditions of Schein (1997), but also Senge (1990) and Checkland (1981) who championed the softer, more subjective side of change management (particularly consultancy practice) against the prevailing, rational, mechanistic norms of the post-war era.

The expectation, then, is that consultants need to instil this way of thinking into client businesses and, in doing so, learn to learn themselves. Thus, building on Kolb's Experiential Learning Cycle (Figure 9.1), course facilitators must enable aspirant farm consultants to act as the hub of a reflexive learning cycle (Allen, 2016, Figure 9.2).

# The Experiential Learning Cycle

Kolb's experiential learning style theory is typically represented by a four stage learning cycle in which the learner 'touches all the bases':

## Concrete Experience
(doing / having an experience)

## Active Experimentation
(planning / trying out what you have learned)

## Reflective Observation
(reviewing / reflecting on the experience)

## Abstract Conceptualisation
(concluding / learning from the experience)

*Figure 9.1* Kolb's experiential learning cycle

Source: Kolb (1984).

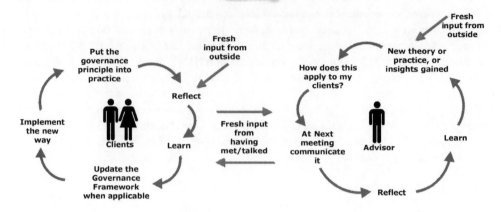

*Figure 9.2* Reflexive learning cycle for governance

Source: Allen (2016).

This is the challenge for the course facilitators, who must address the necessary range of functional areas that comprise governance in a holistic way, and also change thinking about how the process of consultancy itself should be carried out. Thus, in the following sections, we set out the brief for the course, the details of the approach and how we tried to meet that brief. In the final sections, we critically reflect on our own practice, concluding with recommendations.

## The brief

The course was marketed and delivered under the auspices of OneFarm and had evolved from previous provision and feedback from participants. In the previous year, a lot of new material derived from PA and JT's experience had been tested in the classroom context, so there was some sense of what worked well, and also what formats for delivery best matched participants' needs. Responsive tailoring of the learning package overall was important as the participants (15) not only had very different levels of experience, with new entrants mixing with old hands, but also diverse practitioner backgrounds, including lawyers, bankers and chartered accountants. All had been involved in dispensing advice to farm business clients at some point, but this was often based around specific functional areas rather than the longer-term strategy outside that. Additionally, the clients had many calls on their time, and were spread out across New Zealand.

To deal with the distance aspect, we were able to make use of Massey's distance learning platform, Stream, throughout the course, which enables discussions, content management and online assessment. It also allows for tutors to interact directly with participants by video. To support face-to-face discussions and, over time, build new networks, a two-day intensive block compulsory for all participants was placed at the heart of the schedule, which allowed for preparation time and reflective debriefing afterwards. The course was led by PA and was aided by the other author of this chapter (LW) who is a staff member from the university's management school with systems consultancy (but not farming) experience. There was also input from JT, via video, during one of the block sessions, and an experienced learning advisor from Massey (AJ) who aided with Stream and some general teaching and learning guidelines during the block.

The challenge for facilitators, as stated earlier, is to effect changes in thinking and attitudes, rather than transfer a ready-made knowledge base. Yet many aspiring governance consultants arrive primarily to get answers, solutions, quick fixes and toolsets that they can apply immediately with clients. Typically, they do not come to learn the processual approach *per se*, although they discover all too often that it is needed. This attitude is perhaps not surprising given their client-farmers are under economic pressure and may resist taking the necessary consultancy time, which costs money, to develop long-term solutions, which tends to quickly hasten 'the answer'. Thus, all this puts pressure on consultants to develop short-term fixes, as they need to keep their clients generating repeat business and also developing new business usually through word of mouth.

## Our approach

Our plan took advantage of the teaching structure afforded by the available learning platform (online/block) to develop a blended approach where conversations could be developed around materials in the online environment, in preparation for a two-day block in the middle of the course (compulsory for all participants), and finally a debriefing period for assessment and reflection (Table 9.1).

During Phase 1, participants were asked to reflect on their own practice and that of others in the group, following a set of prompts designated as Task 1:

- What does a 'typical' working day look like? Is it what you expected when you became a consultant?
- Can you tell me a bit about yourself?
- Can you tell me something that you think is really important to you in your consulting relationships?
- Can you tell me a bit about your own experience of working with your clients, and your experience of farm businesses?
- What do you understand by consultancy?
- What do you understand your role to be as an advisor?
- What do you understand your role to be as a professional intermediary?

*Table 9.1* Phases of the course

| Phase | Activity | Purpose |
|---|---|---|
| 1 – Online | Pre-reading, discussion groups | 1 Participants get to know each other and staff, learn through interaction<br>2 Get the conversation started around process |
| 2 – Block, face-to-face | Group activities, mini-lectures, videos | 1 Revise process thinking<br>2 Introduce governance model and principles<br>3 Connect governance principles to process thinking |
| 3 – Assessment and reflection | Case study | 1 Summative assessment<br>2 Feedback from tutors<br>3 Student feedback |

During this phase, the ice was broken, at least online, as participants got to know each other through discussion and shared experiences. Participants were then provided with readings that framed the course around process consultancy. This was achieved by introducing the idea of process consultancy and distinguishing it from 'doctor–patient' approaches and 'purchase of information' approaches, which were probably more in line with the

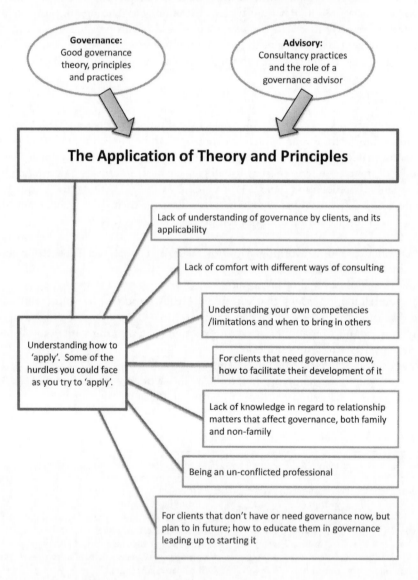

*Figure 9.3* Connecting governance and consultancy

Source: Allen (2016).

experience and practice of many in the group. A mixture of readings were then provided, including some of Schein's original work (from the academic world) and other readings in which experienced consultants discussed the distinctions between, and issues concerning, the different types of consultancy. In this way, the origins of the material could be followed up by those who might want to get more deeply into it, while others could enjoy the translation of the ideas into readily accessible and familiar vocabulary. Task 2, questions about the readings, was like Task 1 as it was carried out on the public discussion board to further encourage interaction.

The class was also introduced to the 'fit' of the governance knowledge base with consultancy practices at the outset, to highlight that the overall course was about more than providing 'the answer' to participants and, eventually, clients. They were asked to discuss Figure 9.2, and were also introduced to Figure 9.3:

This diagram connects the application of theory and principles to the practical context, and additionally highlights the challenges to practice that might occur at an early stage in the course. This gives participants the chance to think about the ideas while they are working in the field prior to the block.

In weeks 3 and 4, the attention turned to the topic of governance where, following more directed readings, participants were asked to reflect upon and discuss what they meant by governance in their own practice. In week 5, they had to complete their first assessment. This required them to analyse a governance situation with which they were involved personally, but from a process point of review, considering aspects such as the mode of consultancy being used, its appropriateness and if there was a need for different kinds of consultancy during different phases in the intervention. They were also asked to reflect upon what they considered to be a 'success', both from their own point of view and from that of the client. In this assessment, although it appeared quite simple on the surface, it actually presented quite a subtle and challenging demand, in that participants were now being asked to discuss governance *per se*; that is, the need for governance and a specific advisory setting in relation to their own consulting process. During these weeks, a number of structured discussions took place around perceptions of both governance and process, structured through the PMI tool (pluses, minuses, interesting) to keep the focus.

In weeks 6 and 7, the central model of the course, designed by PA, was introduced (Figures 9.4 and Table 9.2).

*Figure 9.4* Governance capability development model

Source: Allen (2016).

Table 9.2 The 'hardware and software' of governance practice

Table 9.2a

Governance 'hardware' and 'software'

| Governance practice | A governance framework could include (i.e. examples of governance 'hardware'): | What makes governance 'good' (i.e. examples of governance 'software'): | Personal skills that help |
|---|---|---|---|
| 1 Acting with a purpose in mind | A recorded purpose, vision<br>Business values recorded<br>Business plan, strategic plans<br>Legal structure | Making sure the purpose is clear for everyone<br>Articulating the purpose regularly<br>Explaining it as the reason why certain decisions are made<br>Annually deciding on which parts of the long-term strategic plan will be accomplished next year<br>Reviewing purpose with respect to the other shareholders to ensure we are aligned | The ability to lead others by inspiring them |
| 2 Planning effective governance meetings | Annual governance work plan<br>Annual governance meeting calendar<br>Governance meeting agendas<br>Minutes of meetings<br>Governance meeting papers guideline<br>Guideline for how we run effective and time-efficient meetings<br>Recorded expectations of directors between meetings | Meeting agendas are followed<br>Governance meetings are time-efficient<br>Governors know the difference between governance and management, and can instruct others in this<br>Governance papers are prepared and delivered well in advance of a governance meeting<br>Management topics are not discussed at governance meetings<br>Governors are preparing well for governance meetings | Planning ability |
| 3 Working with other people effectively | The values that describe how the board behaves<br>Description of board roles and responsibilities<br>Strengths map and possible future talent requirements<br>Board member succession policy<br>Consensus-gaining policy<br>Board gender composition<br>Board size | Governance is happening in a 'safe zone'<br>There is thoughtful challenging and debating, which does not become personal. Disagreement is viewed positively in the knowledge that the best and most robust decisions are being made.<br>Differences of opinion are used as a way of gathering more information, clarifying issues, and allowing those governing to seek better alternatives<br>Courage<br>Consensus is being achieved without groupthink<br>The role of the chairman is being performed well<br>There is a virtuous cycle of respect, trust, and candour<br>Leadership without self-interest<br>Morality and ethics | Understanding yourself<br>Understanding others<br>Servant leadership |

*Table 9.2b*

| | | | |
|---|---|---|---|
| 4 Making right decisions | Guideline on how to create policies and parameters within which decisions are made<br>Financial decision-making and treasury policy<br>Capital expenditure policy<br>Investment policy<br>Borrowing policy<br>Dividend policy<br>Interests Register<br>Family decision-making policy<br>Prudent decision-making checklist<br>Process for getting board approval<br>Delegations of authorities table | There is careful evaluation of alternatives and the risks involved with each<br>The governors' decisions stay within the decision-making parameters they have set for themselves<br>Governors are known for their good stewardship<br>Governors are getting the perspective of other stakeholders | Understanding budgets and how to set financial parameters |
| 5 Maintaining a learning orientation | Learning policy: how the plan-do-review cycle is used Board performance review policy<br>Policy on how we review past decisions<br>Recording learnings that build and demonstrate progress in governance | Governors reflect on the outcome of all major decisions, good or bad<br>Governors evaluate their performance each meeting<br>Seeking feedback in order to learn<br>A culture of learning<br>Critical reflection | A willingness to learn through humility and open-mindedness<br>An ability to inspire others to learn |
| 6 Knowing what's going on and what to do about it | Reporting policy, including reporting calendar<br>KPIs policy<br>Financial forecasts and budget creation policy<br>Recorded critical success factors<br>Accurate and timely reports, budget versus actual<br>Reports showing financial performance<br>Reports showing financial health<br>Reports on progress against the strategic plan<br>Reports showing trends<br>Reports showing financial parameters and 'early warning' alert levels<br>Financial and non-financial KPIs | The governors ask a lot of probing questions about performance<br>The annual budget is produced on time, and after careful consideration of the strategic plan<br>Only when governors take personal and collective responsibility do they hold management and others to account appropriately | Understanding financial statements and KPIs. An ability to interpret those reports |
| 7 Managing risks effectively | Risk Identification, prioritisation, & management<br>Policy Ethics policy<br>Folder for the living<br>Sustainability policy | Governors are taking a collaborative approach to risk-taking (risk appetite) by involving stakeholders in their risk management planning<br>Governors meet all compliance requirements honestly and fairly, on time and in full | Proactive planning and management |

Figure 9.4 shows how the 'Four Pillars' of governance, as defined by the New Zealand Institute of Directors, aligns with the Seven Governance Practices that had been developed by PA.

Table 9.2 shows how the seven practices can be applied, using the metaphor of 'hardware and software'. Here, the activities (reflections, discussions, learning) that governors should be carrying out (software) are distinguished from the documentation, policies and reports (hardware) necessary for complying with the law and also for clarifying and achieving consensus around strategy.

So going into Phase 2, the block part of the course, the participants had reached the stage of:

- Knowing each other and the staff facilitating the course. Much of this interaction had been online, though quite a few people had met each other in person too, either before or after the course had started.
- Understanding that the course was about the practice of consultancy as much as the knowledge of governance itself.
- Recognising the '7-stage model' as a key construct and 'take away' for the course overall.

It was now vital to ensure that attending a course for two full days provided value for money and was seen as a good use of time by a group of very busy people. While a detailed

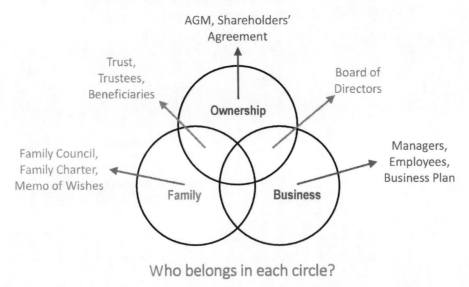

*Figure 9.5* Governance forms

Source: Allen (2016).

agenda for the two days was supplied, essentially there were five main components to the block:

1  A refresher on all the materials and the discussions that had been presented thus far
2  Toolsets to support the application of the '7 practices'
3  Further development of the '7 practices' in relation to the governance journey
4  Connection of the '7 practices' to the reflexive learning cycle
5  Introduction to the case study that was to form the heart of the final summative assessment

In the list above, 1, 2 and 5 are perhaps the most straightforward. An example of a tool to support application is shown in Figure 9.5 (based on Aronoff and Ward, 1996), which shows how the '7 practices' can be related to the specifics of a farm business:

A more subtle point was connecting the '7 practices' to the 'governance learning journey' that farmers face. Many farmers are in the very early stages of governance, with no board of directors outside the family. Others have evolved dysfunctional 'kitchen table' practices over time where dominant family members rule the roost and others, who may

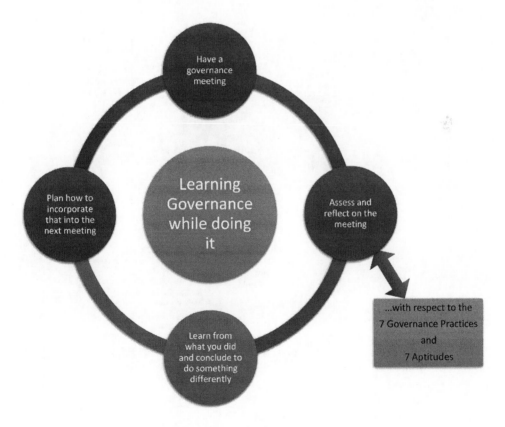

*Figure 9.6* Learning governance while doing it – families

Source: Allen (2016).

well have a valuable contribution to make, are shut out from the discussion. This is often the case where sensitive generational issues are present, such as an ageing farmer who does not want to either modernise or give up control, or both, to the frustration of younger family members. Or there are difficult succession issues compounded by gendered expectations of children. Or there are difficult relationships with spouses from, obviously, outside the family. Persuading such families of the need to move to systems of appropriate governance with boards is a considerable challenge, given that these meetings would take

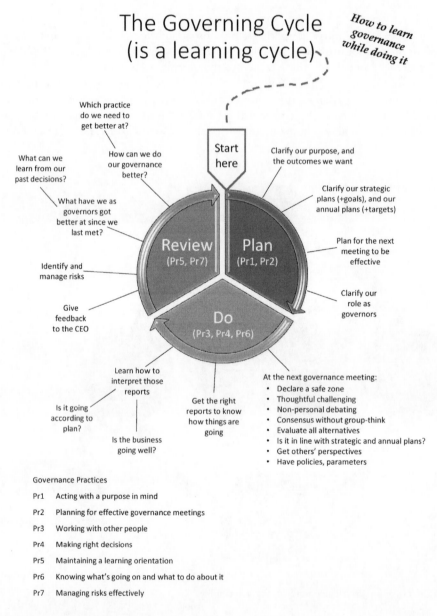

*Figure 9.7* The governing cycle is a learning cycle

Source Source: Allen (2016).

place outside the family home and with 'safe zones' for discussion in which family members are not excluded.

This was addressed in the classroom through the use of role play, where students acted out discussion scenarios, and also through a very powerful demonstration of the 'journey' metaphor by PA who enacted the 'steps' that a family might need to take, and how they might be persuaded to do so, not just by consultants but by environmental pressures. This particular section of the block really highlighted the value of the face-to-face element.

Finally, to make the circle complete, the group was asked to reflect on and review the connection of the '7 practices' to the learning cycle for families using the schemas shown in Figures 9.6 and 9.7.

## Reflections and conclusions

It was rewarding to see that of the 15 participants who started the course, 13 completed it. The two who did not complete the course had personal reasons as to why they failed to engage. In general, the marks were good, with the three background professions (bankers, lawyers, accountants) performing equally well. Generally, the feedback was positive, though of course there were many suggestions as to how we could organise the material differently, such as better orderings and different emphases. That is neither surprising, nor concerning. We had an articulate and responsive group that was very positive in terms of wanting us to improve the course for next year. As experienced tutors, we respect and value such feedback and can readily respond. Of course, as for any programme, we had to overcome the challenges that chance threw at us. The very week that the course commenced, there was a significant update for Stream, which lead, unexpectedly, to considerable disruption of communication and interaction during the first two weeks. Such an update would not have taken place during the main semesters of the university due to the risk for large numbers of students. Of course, we were a small group working outside term time. We managed to get over the difficulty and respond, but it did not help the overall mission, as the hiccups impacted the foundational segment of the course that was focussing on the need to think differently. While that disruption was unfortunate, rather than worrying about water under the bridge, it is more useful now to address the more strategic questions about the overall course in this section.

First, is the content right? The 'heart' of the course is the '7 practices' model and its application. The final assessment, the case study, showed that participants had clearly understood those principles. Further, the feedback and classroom response showed this to be a very well received part of the course. Participants were also able to apply the model appropriately in the case study. It was not surprising that a well-developed, tested model that provided a clear, tangible takeaway was popular. It is grounded in the principles of governance set out within the sector, and connects the learning of governance to a process view, as well as the documents and procedures with which clients will already be familiar. In itself, the dissemination of the model must be seen as a valuable contribution to the sector.

Second, did participants understand the process consultancy view? The final assessment showed a mixed picture. Some had clearly absorbed the point of aspiring to move beyond doctor-patient models and were able to discuss the value of the approach and where it was suitable. Others were avoiding that part of the case study, and were still seeming to tell us, as tutors, 'the answer' rather than reflecting on their own process. Third, were the participants developing a 'learning to learn' ethos? This will take time to evaluate. Some participants were definitely showing an ability to reflect on and critique their own practice. We do not know, of course, whether they were able to do this before the course, or whether it will last afterwards. Follow up studies and pre-course testing would help answer these questions. Fourth, will the participants be able to instil a learning ethos in their clients? This cannot be assessed at this point as it is too early to say, but it would be a useful follow-up study.

The more subtle aspects of process and the reflexive learning cycle are inevitably more difficult to assess and evaluate. They are also the aspects that are the hardest to explain to participants in terms of ongoing value. We had introduced the 'content' of the course in the online sessions prior to the block, to enable us to focus on these key aspects face-to-face. This was undoubtedly the right thing to do, but as facilitators, we are left with that nagging feeling as to whether we did enough. One might consider having two face-to-face sessions: one to hit home the model, and then one at a later date to follow up on process and learning. However, logistics, practicalities and busy schedules militate against that. Another possibility would be to enable some form of post-course networking, particularly where different cohorts were able to mix with each other to share experiences. OneFarm certainly has the resources to support this, and such a mechanism would facilitate the harvesting of anecdotes and case studies that would contribute to demonstrating the value of the approach to new students.

Finally, has it helped the sector? As facilitators, we have to ask ourselves, what would success look like? We can obviously infer incremental success from what we have seen, and what our students have said during the course. But what about the longer term? From our point of view, we would like to see an emergent grouping of process consultants who provide long-term value to their clients and who recognise the value of the approach that we have enabled them to develop in whatever way is appropriate to their own practice. We would also like to see the OneFarm team gain further recognition as promoters of excellence in this field.

## References

AgFirst Consultants NZ Ltd. (2016). *Sound unbiased advice*. Available from www.agfirst.co.nz/about/ [Accessed June 20, 2016].

Allen, P. (2016). *Rural governance development programme 2016*. Available from www.businesstorque.co.nz/ [Accessed June 20, 2016].

Aronoff, C. E., and Ward, J. L. (1996). *Family business governance: Maximizing family and business potential (No. 8)*. New Zealand: Family Enterprise Publisher.

Checkland, P. (1981). *Systems thinking, systems practice*. New York: Wiley.

Kolb, D. (1984). Experiential learning: Experience as the source of learning and development. Englewood Cliffs, NJ: Prentice Hall.

New Zealand Trade and Enterprise (2016). *Agribusiness*. Available from www.nzte.govt.nz/en/buy/our-sectors/agribusiness/ [Accessed June 20, 2016].

Radio New Zealand (2016). *Global dairy prices drop overnight*. Available from www.radionz.co.nz/news/business/299027/global-dairy-prices-drop-overnight [Accessed June 20, 2016].

Schein, E. H. (1997). The concept of 'client' from a process consultation perspective: A guide for change agents. *Journal of Organizational Change Management*, 10(3), 202–216.

Senge, P. M. (1990). *The art and practice of the learning organization*. New York: Doubleday.

# 10 A collaboration for better healthcare

*Andrew Hine and Karen Lynas*

## Executive summary

In 2013, a public inquiry raised concerns about the quality of leadership in England's National Health Service (NHS). The Francis Inquiry considered serious care failings at Mid Staffordshire NHS Foundation Trust, where hundreds of patients had died unnecessarily. Sir Robert Francis QC's report suggested that a lack of consistent leadership development in the NHS had contributed to a situation in which patients had suffered unnecessarily.

The NHS Leadership Academy was central to the health service's response to these findings. A new body, it was charged with creating leaders in the English National Health Service, as well as supporting and inspiring existing ones. Its ultimate purpose was to improve patient care.

An urgent initial priority for the body was the creation of new learning programmes for healthcare leaders. These needed to reflect a very different healthcare landscape, and they were the result of a major reorganization of the English NHS and the aftermath of the Mid Staffordshire scandal.

There was a need to move at real pace – courses needed to be up and running by September 2013 – as well as at significant scale.

The challenge was such that staff at NHS Leadership Academy concluded there was a need to engage an external delivery partner. Rather than entirely handing over all responsibility for the project, however, the Academy wanted to adopt a co-design approach to the work.

The bid chosen was from a consortium created and led by KPMG. By offering a deep understanding of the domestic and international healthcare sector, strong connections with an array of partners; superior project management abilities; and a willingness to embrace the innovative, the firm significantly contributed to the project's success. This case study is thus an excellent example of the breadth of support that management consultancies can offer clients.

## Introduction

### The sector

There are arguably few sectors as complex, pressurized, and busy as healthcare. The business of those running hospitals and other health facilities – and of the clinicians who care for patients – is literally one of life and death. Its customers are every single one of us, and the ageing population and a growth in long-term conditions means an exponential growth in need as funding becomes more constrained. In England, the National Health Service (NHS) now cares for more than one million patients every 36 hours (NHS Confederation, 2016).

The complexities of the English NHS are increased by its fragmented nature. Although citizens tend to see the service as a cohesive whole, it is in fact made up of a patchwork of organizations and providers. As of September 2016, there were 209 clinical commissioning groups (responsible for planning and commissioning healthcare services in local areas); 137 hospital trusts; 56 mental health trusts; 35 community providers; 10 ambulance trusts; and over 7,800 GP practices (ibid).

Delivering a cohesive approach across this wealth of organizations, and ensuring a consistent standard for all users of health services, represents a significant challenge. When staff at the NHS Leadership Academy were charged with establishing large-scale learning programmes for health service leaders, they engaged the support of KPMG.

### The context of the project

The NHS Leadership Academy[1] was formally founded in April 2012. Its mandate was to create new leaders in the English National Health Service, as well as to support and inspire existing ones (NHS Leadership Academy, 2012). The challenge was a significant and pressing one. Two inquiries by Sir Robert Francis QC had thrown into stark relief the urgent need to develop stronger leadership skills at all levels of the health service.

A noted barrister with extensive experience of clinical negligence claims, Francis had been asked to investigate serious failings of care which took place at Mid Staffordshire NHS Foundation Trust between January 2005 and March 2009. "Appalling" standards had been uncovered at the trust, with significantly higher than expected mortality rates and real patient suffering (Smith, 2009).

In his first independent inquiry, Francis explored the failings of the hospital trust itself (Francis, 2010). The resulting reports frequently referenced problems with leadership across the organization, and cited a highly negative culture. Both argued that weak leadership contributed to the serious failures in patient care, and so to avoidable suffering.

A second inquiry followed, this one public and focused on the problems in the wider healthcare system that had contributed to the situation at Mid Staffordshire. Francis's final report once again had leadership as a central theme. He raised concerns about the lack of consistent development of healthcare leaders, and the absence of agreed national standards. His conclusion: the health service needed to "enhance the recruitment, education, training and support of all the key contributors to the provision of healthcare, but in particular those in nursing and leadership positions" (Francis, 2013).

Francis also recommended that "a leadership staff college should be created to provide common professional training in management and leadership to potential senior staff" (ibid).

His concerns about the standards of NHS leadership, and the need to make significant improvements, were echoed and reinforced by other reports. The prominent healthcare think tank The King's Fund launched a commission on leadership and management in 2011 (The Kings Fund, 2011), for instance, and *Health Service Journal*'s inquiry into the future of NHS leadership from 2013 to 2015 (HSJ, 2015).

Both pointed out the need for a new type of leadership in healthcare. They also highlighted that a complete reorganization of the health service meant many leaders were finding themselves with entirely new responsibilities.

The Health and Social Care Act, which came into force on 1 April 2013, fundamentally – not to mention controversially – altered the structure of the English National Health Service (NHS England, 2014). The Act abolished primary care trusts and strategic health authorities. Clinical commissioning groups (CCGs) took on the role of planning healthcare in local areas, with general practitioners (GPs) intended to lead such decisions – a role in which few had any significant experience. NHS England, an entirely new national body, was created to authorize CCGs and allocate resources.

New collaborative health and wellbeing boards were also established. The intention of these local bodies was to unite commissioners and providers of NHS services with the local authorities who plan and provide social care. These two groups had often worked in isolation, and the new boards represented a general push for greater levels of integration in the care system, which encouraged separate organizations to work together and reduced the number of citizens falling 'between the cracks' of fragmented provision. The heroic leadership, which might traditionally have characterized the NHS, felt increasingly outdated. Instead, the desire was for collaboration, dispersed leadership, and a cadre of emotionally intelligent individuals focused on patient experience as much as the bottom line.

It was in this context that the NHS Leadership Academy was launched. It was tasked with nothing less than establishing an entirely new, national approach to healthcare leadership; creating consistent standards where none previously existed; and addressing the concerns raised by two inquiries into high-profile care failings that had threatened public confidence in the NHS and those working within it.

## The consultancy brief

### The decision to seek external support

One of the most urgent priorities for the newly created Leadership Academy was the creation of entirely new, high quality leadership development programmes. There was a need to quickly train several hundred healthcare leaders and to bolster their leadership skills so as to ultimately improve the care offered by England's National Health Service.

Equally crucial, however, was to ensure that any new programmes were useful and academically rigorous. There had been no shortage of healthcare leadership courses on offer in the period prior to the Mid Staffordshire scandal. The natural conclusion, therefore, was that the programmes that did exist had not been meeting the needs of the health service and its leaders.

The scale of the task, its unprecedented nature, and the speed with which the courses needed to be established – at a time when the Academy also had numerous other urgent responsibilities to meet – meant the need for an external delivery partner was quickly established.

### The invitation to tender

The content of the invitation to tender was perhaps somewhat unconventional, in as much as staff at the Academy were very clear in their desire to co-design the leadership programmes. They were definitely not seeking to engage an insular organization which would work entirely in isolation, instead wanting senior leaders across the NHS to be involved in creating the programmes. They were also clear that the courses would need to be innovative and engage learning methods that had not previously been used at scale in the NHS. In addition, the programmes would have to be designed entirely from scratch.

It was believed to be unlikely that any one organization could meet all of these complex needs, and KPMG's bid – which was based on a consortium in which the firm was the lead partner – was therefore of immediate interest.

In February 2013, the firm was formally engaged to help deliver two programmes:

- Elizabeth Garrett Anderson: A two-year master's degree course for those at the middle management level of the NHS, whether clinical or non-clinical.[2]
- Nye Bevan: A one-year programme for those who aspire to become executive directors within the English NHS.[3]

### The decision to engage a management consultancy

KPMG's bid was selected because it embodied the qualities associated with the best management consultancies:

- Strong relationship management

Creating the courses necessitated input from academics, patients, and from cutting edge learning technology organizations. Senior staff at the Academy knew that managing these relationships and personalities would be complex. There was a particular sense that engaging academia in a very different way of working could be challenging and time consuming.

That KPMG Healthcare Practice[4] would assemble the consortium and manage all connections – and do so with aplomb given the firm's extensive day-to-day work of managing complex relationships – made the bid particularly appealing. Staff at the Academy were convinced KPMG would be able to bring together a range of partners, create a cohesive consortium, and make the whole greater than the sum of its parts.

- Connections with multiple sources of expertise

A frequent criticism of the English NHS is that it operates in a 'siloed' manner. The day-to-day pressures are such that it can be difficult for organizations to move their focus beyond their own boundaries. Management consultancies, in contrast, harvest relationships across sectors and nations. KPMG has been a regular partner in healthcare across the UK, but also operates internationally. Its consultants are familiar with how hospitals work in South East Asia, or in the United States of America, or in Europe, which is an in-depth familiarity that NHS leaders may not be able to gain in the same way.

That familiarity is borne out of an extensive 'black book' of international contacts. This meant KPMG staff could call on a range of partners to be part of the consortium and contribute expertise. While the lead academic partners, for instance, were UK-based – the Universities of Birmingham and Manchester – the consortium also included the Harvard T. H. Chan School of Public Health in the United States; the University of Pretoria in South Africa; and the Erasmus University, Rotterdam, in Holland. Staff at the NHS Leadership Academy considered the strength, depth, and variety of these relationships to be particularly valuable.

- Superior project management abilities, and an ability to move at speed

Speed was a key consideration in this project. Both the Elizabeth Garrett Anderson and Nye Bevan programmes had to be up and running in time for the academic year beginning September 2013. Work began in February 2013. That meant there were just seven months in which to create two, high-quality academic programmes completely from scratch using innovative learning methods and via a multi-partner consortium.

The tightness of those timelines is made clear when one considers the creation of a master's degree programme at a Russell Group university typically takes two years from start of design to final accreditation. It is perhaps little wonder, then, that many of the academic institutions that considered bidding for the project argued that the timelines were impossible to meet. While staff at the Academy were under no illusions about the tightness of the deadlines, there was also a firm belief that the right partner would in fact be able to help deliver successful programmes in seven months.

That KPMG was a management consultancy – and thus had extensive project management experience and familiarity with what it takes to meet tight deadlines – was key in its selection for the project.

- Willingness to embrace innovation

The traditional obstacle to large-scale training programmes in the NHS has been the difficulty of taking large numbers of staff away from care settings for large periods of time. This is a particular difficulty when it comes to developing the skills of clinicians; clearly, it is not possible to cease the business of healthcare so that staff can receive training.

With both the Elizabeth Garrett Anderson and Nye Bevan programmes, there was therefore a strong desire to minimize the amount of 'talk and chalk' learning. Staff at the Academy were keen to embrace more cutting-edge learning techniques, with a particular interest in using online methods to deliver the majority of content. This would allow learners to access material from wherever they were, at whatever time suited them.

While no interested party questioned the rationale for such a plan, there were concerns about the practicalities. Conventional wisdom is that the often-outdated technology used within NHS organizations makes it risky to deliver learning which requires high spec devices. KPMG, however, quickly embraced the vision and committed to delivering a programme which utilized the very best and most online e-learning opportunities. They shared a belief that the programmes represented an opportunity to showcase how the NHS might better use technology, engaging individuals who had previously been sceptical about the possibilities it offers to transform healthcare.

This willingness to embrace innovation, to challenge conventional wisdom, and to make the impossible a reality are unique assets of management consultancy and were not necessarily mirrored by other potential partners for the project.

- Willingness to learn

While staff at KPMG demonstrated a clear willingness to embrace innovation, consultants from the firm were ruthlessly honest about the areas in which they were expert and those with which they were less familiar. The courses were designed to include educational techniques that were relatively new even to staff at the NHS Leadership Academy, but completely new to many of those at KPMG.

Yet, Academy staff were instantly impressed by the consultants' desire to gain knowledge and their lack of resistance to and scepticism about the new. It made the partnership and co-design approach possible, and was perhaps a quality that would not have been present in more traditional, more closed-minded, and less agile organizations.

•    Knowing practice as well as theory

Good management consultants are imbued with a unique understanding of the sector in which they operate – one which, ironically, those who directly work in the sector can struggle to gain. KPMG's healthcare management consultancy business has a constant presence across the English NHS. Its staff spend time in NHS organizations across the country, observing and helping address problems. They do the same in other healthcare systems in other countries.

What this means is that staff have an understanding of the true heartbeat of the NHS as an entire system. Their knowledge is not insular or parochial. That KPMG were able to bring this perspective of the day-to-day realities of a diverse range of health organizations was hugely beneficial to the project with the Leadership Academy. It was, in fact, just as valuable as the technical knowledge of processes which a management consultant brings to any project.

•    An ability to free up clients to do what they do best

The bold and exciting nature of this project meant that much creative work was needed. Some of the online learning, for instance, was based on complex imaginary healthcare scenarios. Through the adoption of a co-design approach, the client was closely involved in the development of these case studies.

However, there was also a great deal of 'nuts and bolts' work to be done to take two learning courses from conception to implementation in seven months. Creating and checking storyboards for the e-learning, for instance, was a crucial but time-consuming process that necessitated a meticulous approach. Having KPMG carry out this sort of work freed the client up for work in which they could add the most value – whether on this project or other tasks. The heavy lifting of making two programmes a reality was carried out by the consultancy.

## The methodology

### Project management

The speed and scale of this project necessitated an extremely thorough and comprehensive project management plan. As would be expected, staff from KPMG created a detailed breakdown of each step of the process needed to take the courses from design to implementation. The plan made absolutely clear what would be needed to design, create, and finalize each and every individual module of both courses.

This helped ensure that, from the very outset of the project, both parties were thoroughly clear on the timeframes for the work – including the mini deadlines that would need to be hit to meet the major deadline of a September 2013 launch. There was also a shared understanding that the schedule was one from which there could be absolutely no deviation. In addition, KPMG made absolutely clear to its consortium partners which deadlines would have to be met and by when.

As a client, the NHS Leadership Academy made very clear it was expecting KPMG to do what they said they were going to do, when they said they were going to do it. But senior Academy staff appreciated they had the same responsibility. The need to be a good customer was clearly communicated to those working on the project: the client would not miss a deadline and then expect its partner to turn around work far more speedily than initially discussed.

### Just in time delivery

The sheer quantity of work and the need for students to begin the courses within seven months meant a just in time delivery model was employed. When the Elizabeth Garrett Anderson programme launched, for instance, only the first module of the programme was entirely complete. Proposals and concepts for the other eight modules were with the consortium universities for approval, but content had not been prepared.

### Strong client/consultancy connection

Central to the methodology of the project, and to its ultimate success, was the strength of the relationship between client and consultancy. The authors, as the two leaders of the work, were in frequent communication in order to review progress and troubleshoot issues as appropriate.

The strength of relationship was made possible by an entirely shared vision. From the very outset of the work, the senior leaders at the NHS Leadership Academy spoke repeatedly about the purpose of the organization and the project. Part of the reason KPMG was selected as partner was because there was a sense that colleagues there fully understood the nature of the challenge and the *raison d'être* of the Academy.

## The output

### A blended approach, with multiple contributors

A major aim of the Academy was to develop courses which felt genuinely innovative to NHS leaders, using entirely up-to-date learning techniques. The result is that both courses combine online, residential, and face-to-face learning.

Around one third of the content is delivered via traditional lectures. Another third is delivered via 'learning sets'; that is, groups of seven or eight course participants. A tutor works with the group to discuss how members are applying the learning from their lectures to their workplace, and how their leadership style is changing as a result. The final third of the content is delivered via sophisticated e-learning techniques.

Both courses enable regular interaction with tutors, academics, other course participants and – notably – patients. One of the major findings of the Francis inquiry was that leaders at Mid Staffordshire had lost sight of their duty of care to patients. Instead, they became focused on financial performance at the expense of patient experience.

Addressing this issue was a key responsibility for the Academy as its ultimate purpose is to improve the care offered to those using the health service in England. That KPMG was able to include National Voices as a partner in the consortium was key to supporting the fulfilment of this purpose. A coalition of health and social care charities, the involvement of National Voices ensured that programmes tackle issues that matter to patients. Service users have helped design and deliver the programme, but also assess the learning of students.

## Use of technology

The presence of technology companies in the consortium enabled the creation of a 'Virtual Campus'. Accessible via computers, tablets, and smartphones, the campus allows the flexible access to learning required by those responsible for the day-to-day provision of healthcare. It also helps create a sense of community among learners working in different organizations across the country as ideas can be shared and debated via social networking, and relevant academic papers and news items discussed.

The strength of KPMG's connections and breadth of its experience meant it was able to bring LEO Learning Ltd, an advanced e-learning company, into the consortium. The organization had previously designed modules for pre-deployment learning in the military, as it prepared members of the armed forces for complex, emotional, and highly charged situations.

For the NHS leadership programmes, the firm created complex 'choose your own adventure'-style scenarios. Participants are shown an opening video that closely reflects a common health service leadership challenge. Having watched the video, they are asked to choose what they feel is the most appropriate response to the situation. The subsequent videos depend entirely on the choices made by the individual. At the end of the scenario, a final film is shown with existing senior NHS leaders commenting on the implications of the decisions taken. Each filmed segment lasts no more than five minutes, which is a bite-sized approach that again addressed the 'time poor' challenge of those working in healthcare.

For the Nye Bevan programme, the consortium created an entire virtual health and social care system based around a fictitious county. The challenges of its hospitals, social services, GP practices, and political environment closely mirrored the reality of many health economies. This was a very deliberate way of tying the course content to the realities of modern healthcare leadership and, again, a way in which the approach of a management consultant to the project might differ from an academic institution working in isolation.

One scenario was directly based on the challenging environment of an overstretched accident and emergency department. The most successful choices in this situation were ones based on an approach that looked beyond the boundaries of an individual organization. Instead, participants were encouraged to embrace collaborations across a local health and care economy – a message that strongly embodies current understandings of the best form of healthcare leadership.

## KPMG's influence on course content

Staff at the Academy largely expected KPMG to simply help deliver content. An unexpected benefit of the partnership, however, was the extent to which KPMG consultants were actually able to valuably shape that content. The client has concluded that the course curricula were much richer by virtue of having worked with a management consultancy, and with KPMG in particular.

Contributions included:

- **Reflections on how to best build relationships with a diverse range of partners.** This is an inherent part of management consultancy, but arguably it had been less central in healthcare leadership in the period preceding the Mid Staffordshire scandal. The changing nature of the NHS landscape made it crucial that the new courses reflected the need to bolster collaborative, relationship building skills. It was important that course participants gained an ability to understand the diverse needs, interests, and values of organizations and individuals operating in healthcare, and to form coalitions with them. KPMG were ideally placed to offer input and insight in this respect.
- **An insight into change.** Each programme features a session on megatrends; that is, the transformative global movements which will quickly force changes across business and society. KPMG had vast experience in supporting a variety of clients in a variety of sectors to understand how quickly the world can change, and to appreciate that the specific nature of a megatrend is difficult to predict. They were therefore able to immediately offer content for this section of the course.

It is notable that consultants from the firm serve as part of the faculty for both programmes, sharing their experience of leading change in healthcare systems across the world. It has also been possible for course participants to study leadership practice at some of KPMG's largest corporate clients.

### Outcomes

By the end of the 2015/2016 academic year, 3,000 people had been through the Elizabeth Garrett Anderson and Nye Bevan courses. That is sufficient to make Garrett Anderson the largest master's degree awarding programme in Europe by repute.

The quality of the courses has been recognized with multiple awards. In 2014, the virtual campus system won the best use of blended learning category at the Brandon Hall Group Excellence Awards. These celebrate excellence in learning and development, workforce management, and technology.

Some 35% of Nye Bevan graduates have been promoted since starting the programme. Both this course and the Elizabeth Garrett Anderson master's programme are regularly oversubscribed.

### Key lessons

- Management consultancy can offer much more than merely technical support to its clients

The frequent perception is that a client would only ever hire a consultancy to take cost out of its organization, perhaps by introducing six sigma or other lean methodology. This project, however, proves that professional services firms can offer far more. In this instance, the client benefited from a partner that offered a truly collaborative approach; which could bring multiple parties to the table and ensure they worked cohesively; which offered a wealth of knowledge derived from a daily presence at the frontline of the sector; and which could move at pace thanks to project management abilities.

- A shared vision and strong relationship is essential

The client must have the sense he or she can work with the consultant – and vice versa. This applies to all projects but is particularly crucial in a situation where the stakes are high and time and external pressures extreme. Forming this relationship is greatly helped by ensuring that the consultant who would ultimately be managing the project is present in initial pitches. The authors feel that their own collaboration was considerably aided by having had the opportunity to meet and converse during the procurement process.

- Clients do not necessarily have to know the solution, but they do need to know the problem

The NHS Leadership Academy put out an invitation to tender that explained it was seeking a partner to develop and deliver two entirely new leadership programmes. At this point, staff did not know exactly what the content of those programmes would look like but they absolutely knew what they had to do – provide outstanding, consistent leadership training, which had perhaps not previously existed at a national level in healthcare. Being able to explain this clearly to KPMG, and to detail why the courses were needed, meant it was possible to quickly establish a shared vision and together come to a solution.

## Conclusion

By working with KPMG, the NHS Leadership Academy successfully created a fundamentally different type of leadership course for those working within healthcare. The two programmes on which the organizations collaborated, met the significant challenge of creating and supporting a new type of leader for a new type of health service – one that was stabilizing after a complete reorganization and reeling after a significant failing.

The project is a particularly strong example of the breadth of contribution which can be made by a management consultancy. Professional services firms are not just helpful for improving processes or the bottom line. They can also support the introduction of truly bold, innovative ideas in sectors as complicated and important as healthcare.

## Notes

1 NHS Leadership Academy: www.leadershipacademy.nhs.uk
2 The Elizabeth Garrett Anderson programme: www.leadershipacademy.nhs.uk/programmes/elizabeth-garrett-anderson-programme/
3 The Nye Bevan programme: www.leadershipacademy.nhs.uk/programmes/nye-bevan-programme/
4 KPMG healthcare practice: https://home.kpmg.com/xx/en/home/industries/healthcare.html

## References

Francis, R. (2010). *Independent inquiry into care provided by Mid Staffordshire NHS Foundation Trust January 2001 to March 2009*, volumes 1 and 2. Available from www.gov.uk/government/publications/independent-inquiry-into-care-provided-by-mid-staffordshire-nhs-foundation-trust-january-2001-to-march-2009 [Accessed October 24, 2016].

Francis, R. (2013). *Report of the Mid Staffordshire NHS Foundation Trust public inquiry: Executive summary.* Available from http://webarchive.nationalarchives.gov.uk/20150407084003/www.midstaffspublicin quiry.com/sites/default/files/report/Executive%20summary.pdf [Accessed October 24, 2016].

HSJ (2015). *Ending the crisis in NHS leadership: A plan for renewal.* Available from www.hsj.co.uk/Journals/2015/06/12/y/m/e/HSJ-Future-of-NHS-Leadership-inquiry-report-June-2015.pdf [Accessed October 24, 2016].

The King's Fund (2011). *The future of leadership and management in the NHS: No more heroes.* Available from www.kingsfund.org.uk/sites/files/kf/future-of-leadership-and-management-nhs-may-2011-kings-fund.pdf [Accessed October 24, 2016].

NHS Confederation (2016, September). *Key statistics on the NHS.* Available from www.nhsconfed.org/resources/key-statistics-on-the-nhs [Accessed October 21, 2016].

NHS England (2014). *Understanding the new NHS.* Available from www.england.nhs.uk/wp-content/uploads/2014/06/simple-nhs-guide.pdf [Accessed October 24, 2016].

NHS Leadership Academy (2012). *National centre of excellence for NHS leaders opens.* Available from www.leadershipacademy.nhs.uk/news/national-centre-of-excellence-for-nhs-leaders-opens/ [Accessed October 24, 2016].

Smith, R. (2009). *Patients died due to 'appalling care' at Staffordshire hospitals – Healthcare Commission.* Available from www.telegraph.co.uk/news/health/news/5006037/Patients-died-due-to-appalling-care-at-Staffordshire-hospitals-Healthcare-Commission.html [Accessed October 24, 2016].

# 11 An organisational transition

## A case of preparation, persistence and person centredness

*Elissa Farrow*

### Executive summary

Our environment is changing. The pressure to do more with less puts challenges on organisational capacity to meet performance targets and also not to 'break the business' in the process. Working as a high-impact change strategist is incredibly rewarding work. Balanced with the challenges of structure and process, is shifting the hearts and minds of people who may not necessarily want to be shifted. Connecting with those people who do not necessarily want to be reached. When an opportunity emerged in a large financial institution to provide change consultancy to support the larger organisational change process, which was moving from design into the deployment phases, I seized the chance to be involved.

The design phase had not gone well. It had been delayed by an overly complex functional analysis, with no plan and consultants who had not completed this work before from a person-centred philosophy but had nonetheless won the job. I was operating on another change capability development assignment in the business, coaching a project manager into a change manager. I was asked to come on board to 'fix' the organisational change and restructuring process as it was nearing the transition phase. The project needed some structure and a clear set of objectives. I was able to quickly mobilise an internal diverse team of resources, including the coachee (as a learning opportunity to embed change capabilities). The restructure deployment was able to be recovered and a process created that would be used as a blueprint for future change processes – one that was supported by the senior leadership and many of the staff of the organisation to be successful.

### Introduction to the case context

The organisation that is the focus of this case study is from the financial services industry. The organisation manages over \$145 billion in assets, with 600 staff of mainly financial and accounting specialisms supported by a shared corporate services office. At the time of the change, there were approximately 100 people employed within a blended business change and information technology function including permanent and contracted project resources.

The main products and services offered relate to integrated financial services, including funds management, debt funding and management, cash management, financial risk management advisory services and financial education and capability development. The organisation operates in Australia in the markets of government, commercial and individual investors. The major competitors to this organisation are other major banks and investment companies operating across the Asia–Pacific region.

The initial contact with the financial institution was through a young man who wanted to move from being a professional project manager to a change manager. As is often the way with consulting assignments, the client and consultant met at a networking function and clicked around all things change. A meeting was arranged with his manager and a request for proposal followed to work as his change coach on a large $20 million information technology enabled project. It was the first time this organisation had ever committed resources for a dedicated change role, and they knew professional and skilled change expertise was needed to support them to deliver the project successfully. The project was impacting the core front office operating mechanisms that underpinned the organisation's whole service offering. At the same time as this change was occurring, the organisation was also slowly working through structural change process that would impact the team and the project.

The other organisational restructuring project had been in progress for some time, and to me (at this stage on the periphery of the project), there seemed to be no clear plan, no change strategy and the leaders were caught in a vortex of design and redesign using overly complication analysis processes. The end result of this project was going to impact 100 people delivering IT services, with the intention of dividing this group into two.

The view of a consultant in best practice needs to be 'unblinkered and unbiased' by the day-to-day operations of a business that sometime blinds leaders from the obvious. The broader restructure project, outside of the scope of my remit, was at risk of failure as there was no obvious plan, and the dissatisfaction of staff and the leadership was audible within the current process. Due to the delays of the restructure project and lack of involvement in the design by the majority of staff, rumour about the pending impact was high and many staff were worried there would be job losses.

In the end, 20 redundancies were made which, for an organisation that had been mostly stable and steadily growing for 25 years with no redundancies ever, was a huge cultural shift.

## Consultancy brief

Stephen Covey suggests, in *The 7 Habits of Highly Effective People* (2011), that one should 'begin with the end in mind'.

The received consultancy brief was clear: we have not gone well on this restructuring project to date and we need a defined approach to managing the actual transition into the new structures. The steering committee had only come to this realisation after the risk of having 'failure due to the lack of organisational change management' constantly raised by the two main leaders involved in the change process. It was a credit to their influence on their senior executives, with my support, that this assignment was created.

The original organisational restructure project was driven by the need to solve a number of key issues stemming from a very expensive 'mistake' in project execution 18 months previously. The key issues identified were:

- lack of visibility of the strategy and strategy-related functions;
- system-centred approach to business process design, information management and workflow rather than business-change or benefit-led approach;
- no unified business process model for changing the organisation;

- workflow was predominantly manual and dependant on people and knowledge to make it work;
- lack of an overall business-led system strategy and solution design;
- limited evidence of ICT areas informing strategic business directions and product development but being more tool focussed and reactive in nature; and
- low maturity in project delivery and portfolio management and no approach to organisational change management.

When I arrived, the organisational restructure project was in trouble, and issues needed to be solved, including:

- Resistance and impatience amongst staff in relation to the restructure project was high.
- The steering committee were quite risk adverse, so the legal department was involved in every decision. Therefore, considerable delays were occurring due to rework and redesign.
- No overall project plan for the restructure. Over the past six months, activity occurred to three high-level milestones only, which were constantly not met.
- The restructure design process was not inclusive of current people leaders.
- The vision had been lost along the way as to the 'why are we doing this?'
- Overly complicated design processes, not tailored to the core customer's requirements or using an approach that had a co-design or person-centred process.
- Transactional rather than empowering leadership and design was the main approach.
- Not benefit-led but more activity-led, which resulted in a lack of focus and staff disengagement.

As mentioned previously, this was the first time this organisation had done an organisational change of this nature. There had been pressure from the board of directors to not have any other 'mistakes' like the major project failure of the past, so scrutiny was tight over the design process. A risk-averse nature of steering committees in my experience is very common in organisations with lower maturity in delivery change, in financial or heavy compliance based industries or those that have a legacy of inability to deliver successful projects.

My primary objectives of the transition and embedding piece built on documented lessons learned from *About Your Transition* tested approaches (Farrow, 2011–16). These objectives were to:

- finalise the project and successfully transition staff into a new functionally aligned structure;
- position the team's relevance and alignment to the organisation's strategy and demonstrate its value;
- show what effective person-centred change management processes were like and the benefits they could bring;
- help leaders build a cohesive and consistent team culture that fosters open communication in a supportive environment; and
- communicate 'wins' to the broader organisation, translating technical content using audience-tailored messaging while showcasing its innovation.

Given the lack of a project plan dating from? the commencement of the change six months prior, I needed to fulfil the role of both change and project manager. A tactical plan was required quickly to guide the work of the delivery team. Key deliverables I co-created with the delivery team included:

- change strategy including governance Terms of Reference;
- tactical change plan (with a project plan overlay);
- stakeholder engagement and communication materials and products (including a restricted intranet site);
- resilience training and coaching materials and products;
- 'expression of interest' documented process and materials;
- team process models;
- team integration charters;
- impact and readiness assessment surveys;
- access to an employee assistance service;
- 'lessons learned' report with detailed process outlined to inform future processes; and
- project control documents, e.g. risk register, issues register, quality logs and change control processes.

The change strategy and the tactical plan ended up being seen by the steering committee as what gave the process focus and agility. The decision was made to have change, capability and communication activities all in the same document, which was agreed as a low documentation and agile based application that I preferred. The tactical plan, in particular, was updated weekly and was used as the single source of truth about delivery tasks as well as status, which provided the steering committee and the project team with focus in weekly meetings and daily stand-up processes.

## Resources and timescales

At the time of my engagement, there had been a team of external consultants working on a design that had taken what had seemed like an overly long duration. Six months into the project, there was still no agreement on the final structure or key functional role descriptions. There had been limited engagement with leaders or staff in the two impacted areas, with the main determination around structure and function being done by the two most senior leaders and a steering committee of executives under what seemed to be overly strict confidentiality codes.

Once I was in place, I broadened the core consultancy group to focus on what would be required to agree and deploy the structure successfully, and to re-engage a relatively unhappy, impatient and shifting workgroup. I was able to negotiate with the provision of good evidence, the time for re-litigating concepts and re-tuning the design was over. The time for deployment was here, with the view that the soon-to-be confirmed leadership teams of the two new branches could do any minor tweaks to the structure once the majority of roles and workflows were in place.

Given there had been no project plan directing the design work to date, a right-sized change team to get on with delivery was agreed with the steering committee as one of the immediate tasks. The change team roles and responsibilities are shown in Table 11.1.

Timescales for the transition and embed phase was four months before business-as-usual processes would begin, with some monitoring to ensure the anticipated value was being created. The approach also included reviews by the broader business about enhanced levels of services as a direct result of the structure.

*Table 11.1* Project change management team roles and responsibilities

| Role | Responsibility in managing the change |
| --- | --- |
| Project steering committee | • Overall direction of the change<br>• Overall accountability for successful transition<br>• Make funding available for agreed change deliverables<br>• Future leadership of the new structures (so a vested interest in a smooth outcome) |
| Project change consultant (the author) | • Change complexity and effort assessments<br>• Situational and impact assessments<br>• Change capacity and capability assessments<br>• Production of change management deliverables<br>• Resilience and change leadership capability development<br>• Define the change strategy<br>• Develop and manage the change plan for the transition based on lessons learned from pre-transition design activities<br>• Manage project scope, including change-related scope elements<br>• Ensure change team is informed of changes to scope, schedule, risks or issues<br>• Responsible for overall progress (including change) and use of resources<br>• Handover embed and sustain activities to operations during closing the project |
| Leaders of teams (nine in total – two primary executives) | • Ensure team commitment to change<br>• Lead operational team change cycle (as they were formally confirmed into positions)<br>• Responsible for embedding new working practices and processes<br>• Work to an agreed set of team integration principles |
| Project administration/ Support officer | • Configuration management of change management products<br>• Scheduling of meetings and minute taking<br>• Support EOI process under direction of the human resource officer |
| Human resources officer/s (one lead and one support) | • Involvement in designing the recruitment strategy for the change in line with HR policy<br>• Manage the EOI process and associated redundancy processes for impacted staff<br>• Manage the capability plan development piece linked to updated individual performance agreements |
| Legal officer (one part-time, with direction from head of legal) | • Advise on the industrial relations legal aspects were appropriately covered<br>• Ensure that employment and redundancy policy was upheld<br>• Review team-facing communication materials for legal risk |
| Change agents (nine – one in each impacted sub-team) | • Team members who have an interest in change and a willingness to fulfil a role of being a channel for issues up and messages out<br>• Facilitate team Impact assessment workshops<br>• Provide feedback to project team to guide direction of the approach |
| Communications officer (one lead with support for some technical publisher/video editing skills) | • Quality assure change communication products<br>• Create change communication products under the direction of the project change manager<br>• Be responsible for intranet site for project<br>• Contribute to change strategy and plan |

## Key stakeholders

From my experience, stakeholders in a project context are anyone who has an impact, interest or influence on a project's objectives. In deploying change from person-centred and co-designed processes, stakeholder segmentation and customised engagement approaches are key.

In this restructure program, the stakeholders fell mainly into seven primary groupings as seen in Figure 11.1.

- Senior leadership and line managers of the various groups were re-invigorated. When commencing the assignment, the ruling from the steering committee was to not liaise with all leaders and managers, just the two most senior. This was a risk-based approach and also demonstrated a lack of trust between leadership and management levels. From previous engagements, the evidence was clear that this would not bring success, and therefore advice, guidance and careful framing made the governance group aware of what was considered good practice.
- The two primary leaders who had been 'the meat in the middle of the sandwich' also provided their perspectives of the restricted approach not being ideal, given that it put tremendous pressure on two individuals who needed to manage all staff concerns, BAU and change processes. One manager had 60 staff in his area while the other had 40.
- Coaching was a key strategy to support local leaders in change and in channelling their concerns, which was a good practice of involving managers in messaging being the most effective method to the steering committee and they shifted their approach.

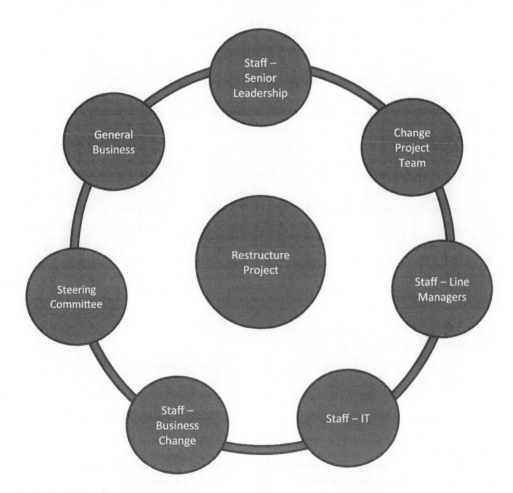

*Figure 11.1* Stakeholders

- The steering committee had general managers for corporate, legal, human resources and the two leads of information technology and business change. The culture of leadership in this organisation was more formal than informal. They had been operating for six months without a clear agenda or strategic focus. One of the first things I undertook was to create Terms of Reference and bring structure into the weekly steering committee meetings. At the peak of transition, while expression of interest and selection processes were occurring, the steering committee had twice-weekly meetings.
- I led the Change Project Team and instigated daily 15 to 30-minute stand-up meetings to keep focus on work packages delivery. This team was all internal staff who had never done a project of this nature in this organisation and had limited experience even from previous organisational contexts. The main concern was how to do the work required within limited resources. Working with human resources and communication officers, I was able to plan a week-by-week tactical plan of activities that took the information about tasks out of their heads and put it onto paper. This was shared, in particular, with the general manager of human resources, and I recommended a bolstering of resources, particularly during the EOI and appointment process to the HR officer, which was accepted. The daily stand-ups were also very effective for team cohesion and problem-solving.
- Staff of strategic delivery, who had not been involved with the previous design piece, were a key group. It was important to not see this group as general staff, but to see the sub-groups within these groups. Doing stakeholder analysis at too high a level is a common mistake in change processes. The staff cohort had been neglected with some involvement since six months prior, but the group were clearly fatigued, confused by the lack of progress or a clear plan and many were 'over' the process. When the structure was released, just before I came on the project, it was met with shock and with some staff being quite emotional when they saw no role for them on the chart. Managers had not been prepared. The new defined change approach had leaders and staff-care at the centre.

I worked closely with line managers to work with staff, but had an open policy and met with key staff to check in. Change agents were also identified who were positive about the change but also key to calming the group, in particular, the administration officer who I met with regularly to get a pulse of feeling and issues. Often, it is not the manager who has the finger on the pulse of the team. I find that executive assistants and administration officers are exceptionally good at knowing what is going on, and I deliberately factor them in to the change strategy (even confidentially).

## Methodology approach employed

Stanford (2007) defines organisational design as 'the outcome of shaping and aligning all the components of an enterprise towards the achievement of an agreed mission'.

The design phase had been progressing for some months, but the general feeling was not positive and staff and leaders were tired of waiting for the senior leadership to make a decision. Therefore, speed and agility was paramount to finalise design, implement and embed. This change methodology was designed and influenced by models referenced from the Change Management Institute, The Effective Change Manager: Change Management Body of Knowledge (CMBoK) (2013).

The methodology varied based on the primary deliverables expected and covered:

1   Vision, gap and impact analysis
2   Project control framework
3   Coaching and change leadership
4   Communication
5   Selection and appointment
6   Redundancy and adjourning
7   Team reformation and performance

### 1. Vision, gap and impact analysis

Kotter (2012) describes a vision 'as a picture of the future with some implicit or explicit commentary on why people should strive to create that future'.

At the heart of the methodology a reconfirmation of the vision and plan was needed, which seemed to have been lost in the preceding six months, during the discovery phase, and had not been reinforced through communication. Key members of the existing management team and the steering committee were involved. There needed to be a common set of definitions put in place to ensure there were no areas of uncertainty. The vision then became the focal point in all key messages about the future state of the group and the why.

A vision re-confirmation workshop created an impact and gap analysis to determine the best starting place. This impact and gap analysis workshop, involving the previous consultancy team, leadership team and steering committee, was conducted using world café style method in a stand-up approach, with a 'change room' established with the key aspects of the past posted on the walls with a clean flip chart for the impact and gap analysis information and feedback. The gap and impact analysis used McKinsey 7-S model developed by Peters and Waterman (1982). The McKinsey 7-S model focuses on seven internal aspects of an organisation that need to be aligned and reinforced if it is to be successful:

*   Strategy
*   Structure
*   Systems
*   Shared Values
*   Style
*   Staff
*   Skills

I often use the McKinsey 7-S model as one approach to set the current state-future state across the seven aspects and then the gap analysis falls from that analysis. This was also a good engagement approach for leaders and key staff with the 'change room' being a focus point to re-group, clarify and communicate.

### 2. Project control framework

The organisation had been embedding PRINCE2™ (2009) as their project management methodology over the past 12 months. A tailored PRINCE2™ (2009) project management method was used to cover issues and change control processes, product-based planning, risk and issues management, lessons learned and benefits realisation. The tailoring came through omitting a full start up and initiation phase, given that the project had been in duration but a forced managing stage boundary was conducted to ensure the viability, achievability and desirability of the model was re-settled.

A document and controls review process was also conducted, which determined that a tailored project management approach with an embedded change model was the requirement. Managing change risk and issue resolution was instrumental and therefore a risk and issue analysis of the process was conducted immediately and then appropriate mitigations put in place. The change risks were affecting the business as usual operations given the duration of the discovery phase and no effective change communication or engagement activities.

The high-profile risks and issues were responded to immediately by the steering committee with the assistance of the legal officer to ensure actions were in line with employee contracts, awards, recruitment and retention policy. The risk profile showed a number of events that required immediate intervention from the CEO (beyond the project steering committee).

I used product-based planning technique from PRINCE2™ (2009) to scope up core change products and then the PRINCE2™ (2009) planning technique to populate a plan. I also used a facilitatory approach, which strengthened the permanent leaders of the team to do the communication and change interventions with other team members, at times taking more of a guidance and advisory role. Given the project had no formalised project management structure at the time I came on board to manage the change component, I also fulfilled a quasi-project/change management function to bring some control back to the process.

### 3. Coaching and change leadership

For the coaching model, the International Institute of Project Coaching methodology was used (Figure 11.3). I always pride myself on being a consultant who not only knows how to walk the talk but also to be certified and evidence-based in my approach. Therefore, I am a Master Certified Project Coach. This is an ideal model which includes coaching and facilitation methods, such as the GROW model, to ensure leader and staff conversations were structured from a competency-based perspective.

There are several reasons why a coaching engagement with a leader was established. Sometimes, a leader has identified the need to improve certain areas of their own performance as a result of self-reflection, whilst other times, coaching is recommended due to a competency (in this case, change leadership competency) not being strong in a leader so therefore a key lever to drive but also sustain the change in the longer term.

Coaching sessions were established with each leader to assess their sponsorship capability and then a process of reinforcing and supporting them in the challenge areas was activated. The coaching approach was one of the powerful options that in lessons learned was agreed by leaders to be useful to the immediate process as well as their leadership competency moving forward.

Leadership coaching pushed the change process along and was supplemented with staff and leadership resilience workshops. Ideally, if I had been engaged six months earlier, these workshops would have occurred earlier than right at the point of change. This approach would have readied the staff, leaders and business rather than a just in time approach due to a previously poorly managed process that had been set up broadly by other consultants prior to the engagement.

| Risk Level | Corporate Responses Required |
| --- | --- |
| Extreme | Immediate executive intervention and board involvement required. CEO accountability |
| High | Executive team management with nominated executive accountability |
| Moderate | Nominated manager accountability with regular reporting to executive team |
| Low | Periodically assess for escalation with management via routine procedures |

**Risk Likelihood Table**

| Likelihood Descriptor | Description |
| --- | --- |
| 5 – Almost Certain | The event is expected to occur in most circumstances |
| 4 – Likely | The event will probably occur in most circumstances |
| 3 – Possible | The event should occur at some time |
| 2 – Unlikely | The event could occur at some time |
| 1 – Rare | The event may occur in exceptional circumstances |

**Risk Matrix**

Consequence →
Likelihood ↓

| Likelihood | 1 Insignificant | 2 Minor | 3 Moderate | 4 Major | 5 Catastrophic |
| --- | --- | --- | --- | --- | --- |
| 5 Almost Certain | | | | | |
| 4 Likely | | | 6 | 2 | |
| 3 Possible | | | 1, 3 | 4, 5 | |
| 2 Unlikely | | | | | |
| 1 Rare | | | | | |

Figure 11.2 Key risk profile

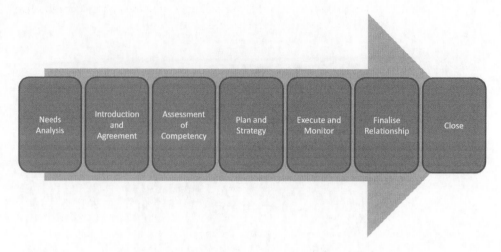

*Figure 11.3* The International Institute of Project Coaching methodology

Source: Used with permission from the International Institute of Project Coaching methodology 2012©.

## 4. Communication

Communication was designed to match internal communication policy and procedural platforms and utilise existing intranet, town hall and team meeting structures in the main for the dissemination of group messages. Individual messages were prepared in advanced, checked for consistency and leaders were coached to ensure conversations occurred with the primary messages being delivered. The approach was to provide as much 'rich' information as possible and to utilise interactive models with multiple cues (visual, kinaesthetic, auditory).

With any change, staff need to be orientated to the reasons behind the change and the new environment they are moving to, and this change needs to be reinforced by a manager using effective communication. The change team had a fantastic internal communication specialist who not only knew the players, but knew the business and could work the internal communication channels to their best effect. Our approach focussed on getting the right information out to people in the right time, which enabled push and pull mechanisms to allow people to be self-sustaining in the change. Change messages communicated verbally or in writing needed to follow a few basic principles:

- Key messages need to be repeated five to seven times.
- The 'what's in it for me' question needs to be answered.
- Do not rely just on project team or change manager communication – the most effective messages come from the line manager who has the relationship.
- Answer the questions about why the change is happening.
- Be visible and listen to staff questions and concerns.
- Ensure multiple channels exist and ensure two-way communication opportunities are created and face-to-face opportunities, including accessibility for those staff with large text or visuals.
- Consider the cultural needs to staff: are interpreters required or do culturally sensitive language and protocol need to be considered?

- Assess the effectiveness of communication and do not assume the communication has been effective until you have tested understanding.

### 5. Selection and appointment

The selection and appointment process was carefully considered as there had been no other internal examples of this nature, yet the human resources business partner working on the core change team and lead of human resources had previous experience of a full scale 'spill and fill' process.

In the case study organisation, there was a strong requirement to ensure the legal obligations were met. The steering committee were reasonably risk-averse and therefore did not want a 'bad' appointment and selection process coming back in the form of litigation. So, therefore, all communication and the process itself was verified by legal internally and with an external legal assurance. This seemed overly bureaucratic and additional time had to be added to the change schedule, but matched the risk appetite of the steering committee and the chief executive. The process approved is shown in Figure 11.4.

What also assisted were the following support processes:

- Resilience workshops covering stress, change curve, what we can influence.
- How to fill out an Expression of Interest (EOI) and resume update workshop.
- Guidance and EOI forms.
- Top down recruitment with leaders being appointed first, and then those leaders being involved in the decisions for lower-level team leaders and staff members.
- One-on-one sessions with managers answering questions on expectations.
- A secure intranet with all new job descriptions and the structure.
- Contested roles only having a formal interview process.
- Daily 15-minute stand ups of the change team to assess progress on appointment activities.
- Speed in the process and quick adjourning of staff once redundancy was the only option left for them.

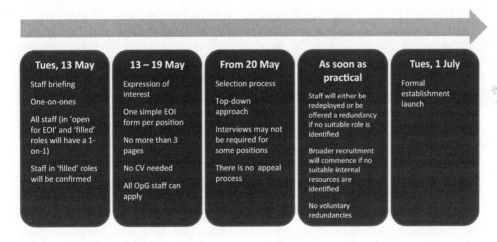

*Figure 11.4* Selection and appointment process

## 6. Redundancy and adjourning

Tuckman and Jensen (1977) expanded on the team development model by adding in the concept of adjourning. Change strategists need to ensure that any change process that affects people's position in an organisation is handled with sensitivity. There was no legacy of redundancy processes in this organisation, so there was a unique opportunity to design a process that was as 'kind' as possible to the staff involved.

Once the impacted staff posted the EOI and the appointment phase was known, given there were no voluntary redundancies on offer, staff were provided with a one-on-two meeting with a human resource representative and their relevant senior manager. A script was prepared by HR and verified by legal to ensure appropriateness, and a meeting held with the details of the redundancy offer available to staff, a pack of six (optional) career and psychological appointments with employee placement services and a transport voucher if the staff member wanted to leave immediately due to the emotion around the final decision.

Staff were also given the option if they wanted the news of their redundancy made public to the rest of the organisation. Interestingly, no one took up this offer and preferred to manage their own farewells privately. In this case, staff were not given access back to their computers due to the nature of the company and access to finance and IT systems, but they did have access back to their desks to pick up their belongings.

## 7. Team reformation and performance

A focus on forming and integration post the staff departures was a major consideration, given there were a number of projects that needed to be delivered and business as usual service desk and other service security functions needed to continue. This time had been sad for not only the staff leaving but for those who were left behind. Often in change situations, the person who stays often feels a range of mixed emotions that can be confusing, so involvement in the future focus is a key to moving forward. The two divisions now needed to work together to deliver the overall change portfolio for the organisation.

It was critical that some protocols were put in place early to ensure engagement. I facilitated a joint workshop where they agreed on principles that would cover the next three months of reformation and performance – some of the process and system entanglement issues would still be required to be rectified though the structure and team process was complete. The created protocols were placed on posters around the walls, and special communications to other areas highlighting the process and team reformation process were also shared in order to ask for patience during this period. In fact, leaders had this set within their performance agreement with their new general managers.

The team decided in their words: We will all:

1  Be approachable and be positive about the change internally and externally.
2  Be open and transparent about concerns, without fear of retribution (challenging professionally).
3  Collaborate on decisions and then support that decision in its implementation.
4  Go direct to the right person to call out an inconsistency or when we are not following these principles – even if we feel more comfortable taking someone with us.
5  Commit to no surprises and ensure all necessary key change milestones are known well in advance, and what we need from each other (not just rely on formal meetings but also have informal meetings.

6   Take individual ownership of all requests and get back within x amount of time – e.g. 'I don't know but will take ownership to find out who the best person is'.
7   Not get frustrated or blame others when there is uncertainty – acknowledge that sometimes things are just going to be hard and we are doing the best we can.
8   Not assume things are happening in the way we asked them to so will process check if we need to.
9   Ensure where there is ambiguity we will clarify it as best we can and work together to do this.
10  Create a habit of clear communication, collaborative practice and active engagement – this practice will not be the rarity but the common practice.

These principles were used as the basis for team reviews over the three-month period. Performance was assessed and an active approach to issues management was employed with a weekly joint leadership team stand-up to identify issues and solve them quickly.

## Business management tools and techniques employed

I checked in through a regular stand-up meeting and HR Senior Leader briefings and also, once complete, was able to tick off weekly tasks and iteratively review the schedule moving forward. I formalised status reporting and risk and issues management, which was a core part of the formal agenda for these meetings and to ensure that client issues were being actively covered. At the end of the process, I facilitated a formal 'lessons learned' workshop and documented the results with the core delivery team and the steering committee. I received positive commentary for the approach, including one comment saying that I had changed the mind of a senior manager about the benefit of change management. I thought this was a great win.

All staff were given positive feedback on their individual performance and the team felt a strong sense of cohesion, which meant problem-solving was smooth. They agreed a change/project manager was needed much earlier in the process and had noted the improvement in process and speed when I came and played that dual role.

It was also learning for the HR team to ensure that the HR advisor needed to be fully offline on the project rather than still carry her BAU. I ensured that she described the change approach in some detail to the HR team, who would be seen as the key group moving forward to maintain some of the organisational development elements in collaboration with the EPMO and delivery areas. This was identified through the process, but only after I raised it up and the advisor had pulled some heavy hours before the HR team took her BAU off her so she could focus. The team agreed that sizing the change and planning needed to occur much earlier in the process for next time thanks to the reinforcement and value add.

Note, this was the first time the team had experienced a change of this nature in this organisation, so there was no legacy apart from experience the team may have had individually in other organisations. So, I documented the approach so that it could be used as a blueprint for future redundancies, which was considered by the leadership team as good practice.

Consulting tools and techniques used:

•   Personal resilience – which I believe is important for all change consultants.
•   Project management – creating plans and managing and controlling delivery.

- Change management – applying change psychological and behavioural theory to individuals and groups (a mixture of models from the CMBoK (CMI, 2013).
- Risk Management – applying project and transition risk analysis, tools and process.
- Contract negotiation and assignment confirmation and follow on.
- Risk and issue management.
- Ethical decision making – based on some decisions not being seen as favourable by staff but being the most appropriate thing.
- Leadership – leading a team of staff and new change agents.
- Governance – assisted the steering committee in governance and formed a Terms of Reference to guide this group.
- Negotiation and conflict resolution – through staff upset by the change and feeling frustration with the length of time; e.g. nine months from beginning to end.

Overall this added a great base of learnings that could be shared as part of my broader mission to increase organisational maturity in change leadership and use these learnings to value add to the client experience.

## Conclusions and key recommendations

William Bridges (2009) makes a distinction between change and transition: 'Change: the actual events, activities and steps that can be put into a diary or project plan. Transition: the human, psychological process of letting go of one patter and engaging with a new one'. The case study presented here offered some unique insights into typical challenges that occur in organisations where their change maturity is low. This project, which took nine months from start to conclusion, had not considered the change impact on staff and leaders and had meandered with no compelling sense of urgency and no clear change purpose for five months before I came on board and provided change and project management expertise to produce a positive finish. The steering committee and staff felt that the actual transition piece led by me occurred in a way that was truly respectful of their requirements and controlled enough to build confidence.

It has been a great exercise to reflect on this project. Even now, a few years later, even those who were made redundant refer consultancy assignments to me, which is one demonstration that they respected the approach and the way I formed the change strategy. As the teams were working on stabilisation activities, it was the right time to examine the transition from discovery phase through to deployment with a formal lessons learned process. The process involved a number of facilitated workshops, including feedback, the project governance, project delivery team and from impacted staff and management.

Overall, the steering committee was positive of the outcome of the change and noted that many of the learnings from the process would be of benefit to the organisation into the future.

Key recommendations for future change processes in other contexts:

1 Early preparation and the establishment of a dedicated project team and change network drives the success.
2 Appointment of a change manager gave the project the coordination and proactive planning that was required; ideally being appointed at the beginning of the project to guide the approach.

3   Ensure appropriate governance is in place at steering committee level, and working party level taking an agile approach.

4   Ensure there is a sense of urgency that is followed up in a plan; nine months was too long a process with no clear plan of when the process would be finalised.

5   Have a clear Terms of Reference and an on-boarding process for steering committee members, including being clear on expectations of time to be committed.

6   Where redundancies will occur, include representatives from the business, human resources, communications and legal in review of documents; though more time consuming, meant messages were consistent and risks mitigated.

7   Key constraints, such as budget or headcount, should be identified prior to preparing new organisational structures.

8   Make the change process that actually affects staff's feeling of safety as short term as possible; long-term change where uncertainty is rife will impact performance and morale.

9   Staff need help through the process; use briefings, employee assistance services, FAQs and other sessions to provide practical information.

10  Treat all staff equally and respectfully, with visibility to available roles up for change.

11  Delays create uncertainty and dissatisfaction; set up the process to enable decisions to be made quickly, with a clear understanding of approval processes.

12  Much of the process was dictated by internal policy documents; ensure they reflect the needs of the business and do not stifle the process.

13  Communications to the whole organisation about process and impact were essential.

Since the time of this assignment, the organisation has gone through further change. The direction of the organisation changed and a decision was made to outsource all ICT and project delivery services to a panel of providers. The future state was to procure these resources as a service through a portfolio management office when project needs arose. This process saw another 25 people made redundant. It is unclear if this move has brought the benefits for the business, given that over 20 years of knowledge left the business when this team exited and some of the panel providers have not been able to access the now limited subject matter experts. However, it is also worth saying in closing that this second round of changes, which I was not part of, did take into account the lessons learned from the previous change process I had been part of. This is a positive thing for any consultant to hear: that your brief time in an organisation and a generous approach to capably building internal resources has made a tangible difference in an organisation, and lifted the maturity of change management consultancy and the difficult task of making people redundant.

## References

Bridges, W. (2009). *Managing transitions: Making most of change*. Cambridge, MA: Da Capo Press.

Change Management Institute (CMI) (2013). *The effective change manager: The change management body of knowledge (CMBoK)*. Sydney: Change Management Institute.

Covey, S. R. (2011). *The 7 habits of highly effective people*. New York: Simon & Schuster.

Farrow, E. (2011–2016). Your transition. Available from http://aboutyourtransition.com.au – authored blog posts and articles, Brisbane, Australia.

International Institute of Project Coaching (2012). *Project coaching lifecycle, Australia*. Available from http://iiprojectcoaching.com

Kotter, J. P. (2012). *Leading change with a new preface*. Boston, MA: Harvard Business Review Press.

Peters, T., and Waterman, R. (1982). *In search of excellence: Lessons from America's best-run companies*. New York: Harper and Row.

OGC (Office of Government Commerce) (2009). *Managing Successful Projects with PRINCE2*. London: TSO (The Stationary Office).

Stanford, N. (2007). *Guide to organisation design: Creating, high performing and adaptable enterprises*. London: Profile Books Ltd.

Tuckman, B. W., and Jensen, M. A. (1977). Stages of small-group development revisited. *Group and Organisational Studies*, 2(4), 419–427.

# 12 Richard Lewis Communications – cross-cultural management consulting

## From cultural awareness to global competence

*Richard D. Lewis, Iouri P. Bairatchnyi and Caroline M. Lewis*

### Executive summary

The purpose of this chapter is threefold: (1) to present cross-cultural challenges that increasingly affect organizational behavior and performance, especially in the case of mergers and acquisitions; (2) to describe the proprietary theoretical framework for cross-cultural interventions based on the Lewis Model and how it is used at Richard Lewis Communications (RLC); and (3) to demonstrate the effectiveness of the RLC approach to cross-cultural consulting through three case studies.

The failure rate of mergers and acquisitions has been historically high (70–90%). Bringing two companies under one corporate roof naturally provides numerous logistical challenges. However, the main problems emerge when different cultures collide, therefore most failures are due to inadequate attention to cultural alignment and behavioral adjustments from both cultural perspectives – national and organizational.

The theoretical underpinning of the RLC approach is based on a belief that any cultural learning is sequential and largely moves from awareness to practical knowledge, to skills development, and, ultimately, to the formation of cultural competence. Additionally, learning occurs in three domains (very often simultaneously): self, others, self and others. The Lewis Model of culture and the web-based tool CultureActive provide a holistic framework for cultural and cross-cultural learning and organizational interventions.

The RLC consultancy cycle consists of four stages: cultural assessment, awareness and knowledge development, alignments and adjustments, and re-assessment. Three case studies were selected for this paper to demonstrate the conditions for success and failure.

### History of RLC engagements

The Management Consulting Division of RLC benefits from its 45-year experience and expertise in successfully addressing *cultural* and *cross-cultural* problems that have been increasingly affecting the organizational behaviour and performance of various organizations.

RLC involvement in cross-border transitions and mergers and acquisitions began in the early 1970s, as RLC consulted for ambitious European companies like NOKIA, KONE, and FIAT, which were growing through international mergers and acquisitions. In the following years, RLC carried out large-scale transformational training projects at SAP (Germany), Abu Dhabi National Oil Company (ADNOC), Lufthansa – LSG catering merger, NOKIA Data – ILC (UK), KONE – Westinghouse (lifts and cranes), Pfizer (Swedish acquisition), the Stockholm and Helsinki stock exchanges merger, Statoil – Total, Shell (M&A division), Deutsche Bank – Bankers Trust (merger), Finnish Government Ministries (entry to the EU), and One World (consolidation project).

RLC's success led to long-term consultancy with multinational institutions (the World Bank Group, several UN agencies) and joint research projects and activities in a large number of academic bodies in Europe, Asia, and the US.

## Why we do what we do

While the influence of a national culture on organizations is hardly questionable, it is surprising how far apart cultural studies and organizational theory have been positioned academically. Anthropology has never left the humanities, and organizational theory (organizational culture, in particular) is still chained to business schools. Real life, however – mainly in its commercial domain – draws its own borders, especially today, when national borders are being crossed seamlessly.

There is a basic, though not completely obvious, "excuse" for the distance between cultural understanding in general and depictions of organizational behavior. A "monocultural" environment (in either a national or organizational sense) does not demand an immediate explanation: we rarely have to define our culture for ourselves. Basic assumptions and values are largely shared intuitively, behavioral norms are largely accepted, and communication and interaction patterns usually do not raise any eyebrows or cause major misunderstandings. Real problems – the problems without easily predictable solutions – emerge when "others" join the game or when different cultures chart a collision course, no matter whether the differences are seemingly insignificant (e.g., between the Nordic countries) or starkly contrasting (e.g., between Asian and Anglo-Saxon cultures). A *cross-cultural environment* generates enough complexity in social settings. In a business context though, it is not only more intricate but also more urgent and increasingly more consequential.

It is widely known that the failure rate of mergers and acquisitions has been historically high. According to collated research and a recent *Harvard Business Review* report (Martin, 2016), it is in the astonishing range of 70-90%. It is understandable that bringing two companies under one corporate mission entails steep challenges in strategic planning, stakeholder engagement, and systems alignment. The main challenge, however, emerges from bringing together large groups of people with their inevitably different personalities, aspirations, behavioural traits, and ways of working. We believe that in cases where strategic and logistical work is done properly, yet a merger fails anyway, it is largely due to inadequate attention being paid to the cultural alignment and behavioural adjustments from both cultural perspectives: national and organizational.

There have been several significant attempts to bridge national culture and organizational behaviour (Adler and Gundersen, 2008); Hofstede, 2001; Trompenaars and Hampden-Turner, 2012), but the transition from academically sound (descriptive) concepts to practical (prescriptive) frameworks still remains a challenge. We believe that the Lewis L-M-R Model (Lewis, 2006) of culture, applied through the cultural profiling instrument CultureActive (cultureactive.com) and RLC's methodological approach (crossculture.com), offers a proven and practical solution to cultural challenges.

### *Methodological approach*

#### *Cultural learning*

The main premise of the RLC methodology is the conscious and deliberate development of *behavioural intelligence* in general and *cultural competence* in particular, which essentially comes down to *the capability of an individual or a group to function effectively in situations characterized by cultural diversity in both social and professional settings.*

It is a complex and gradual process that requires: (1) a good understanding of what cultural learning is and how it happens, and (2) a holistic conceptual framework for country-specific and cross-cultural learning.

Figure 12.1 shows the flow and dynamics of cultural learning in general.

Cultural learning begins with raised awareness: what needs to be learned and why. Acquiring relevant knowledge is the next natural step. Here, it is critical to use the same concepts for learning about self and others. The following step is much harder, as we all know, because it requires deliberate practising, evaluation, and adjustments. Having acquired the necessary knowledge and desired skills, it is important to transition to the state of mind where no reminders are necessary and communicating effectively and interacting appropriately becomes one's second nature.

Figure 12.2 presents the conceptual framework for country-specific and cross-cultural learning at RLC, which is based on the Lewis L-M-R Model of culture.

Richard D. Lewis suggested a triangle of interconnected dominating points representing basic cultural types:

**Linear-active** types generally are cool, factual, and decisive planners.
**Multi-active** types are warm, emotional, loquacious, and impulsive interrelators.
**Reactive** types are courteous, amiable, accommodating compromisers, and good listeners.

In very general terms, each type (in a pure form) has its own "anchors", which "ground" those belonging to their particular values and beliefs (Table 12.1). The cultural anchors of

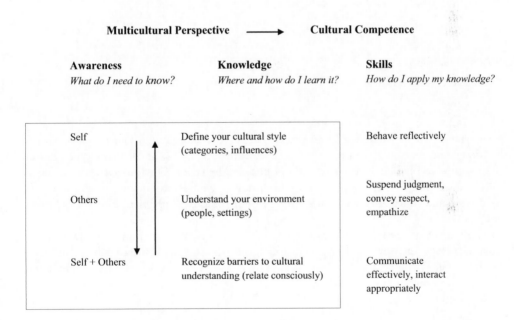

*Figure 12.1* The process of developing cultural competence within a culture in the context of diversity, and when crossing borders

Source: Bairatchnyi (2013).

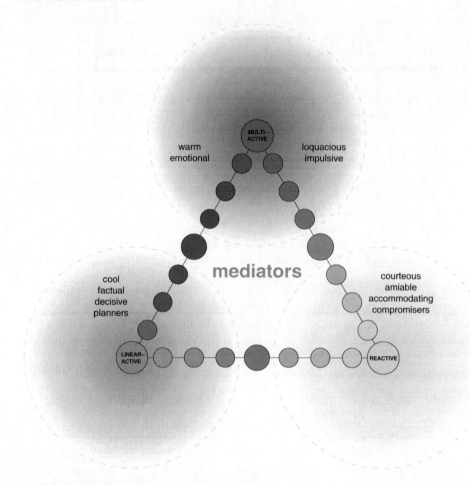

*Figure 12.2* The Lewis L-M-R Model

Source: Lewis (2006).

each type are further extended into fifteen behavioural alternatives that provide choices for describing personal, group, or national cultures (Table 12.2). All three types reflect their values and beliefs in their social and business behavior. Obviously, there are rarely fully "monochrome" people, most of us are hybrid – we possess qualities of all three cultural types and attain our own "colouring", which could be somewhat different in different settings.

The benefit of having such a model is two-fold. It serves as one frame of reference for learning about one's own cultural style and about others. Also, it is rather harmonious – neither type is beneficial on its own because there might be one or even two dominating points that complement each other.

We need each other:

– we need **linear–active** types to . . . organize, plan and see problems, analyze consequences, hold consistent policies, access rational thought, generate data, challenge us objectively;

*Table 12.1* Behavioural "anchors" of the Lewis L-M-R Model

| Linear-active | Multi-active | Reactive |
| --- | --- | --- |
| **Facts** – pragmatism | **Family** – showing warmth and compassion | **Intuition** – instinctive reaction to attitudes of others |
| **Planning** – ahead step by step | **Hierarchy** – obedience | **Courtesy** – ultra-polite, indirect |
| **Products** – job-orientation | **Relationships** – people orientation | **Networking** – cooperative spirit |
| **Timeliness** – punctuality | **Emotions** – displays feelings | **Common obligations** – statements are promises |
| **Word-deed correlation** – reliability | **Eloquence** – love and art of talking | **Collective harmony** – avoidance of confrontation |
| **Institutions** – love of clubs and associations | **Persuasion** – flexibility of truth | **Face** – diplomacy before truth |
| **Law** – high legal consciousness | **Loyalty** – close ties | |

*Table 12.2* Behavioural alternatives of the Lewis L-M-R Model

| | Linear-active | Multi-active | Reactive |
| --- | --- | --- | --- |
| *Listening and speaking* | Talks half the time | Talks most of the time | Listens most of the time |
| *Planning* | Plans ahead step by step | Plans grand outline only | Looks at general principles |
| *Directness* | Polite but direct | Emotional | Polite, indirect |
| *Connections* | Uses official channels | Seeks out top or key person | Uses connections |
| *Feelings* | Partly conceals feelings | Displays feelings | Hides feelings |
| *Tasks and action* | Does one thing at a time | Does several things at once | Reacts to partner's action |
| *"Face"* | Dislikes losing face | Has good excuses | Must not lose face |
| *Job/people orientation* | Job-oriented | People-oriented | Very people-oriented |
| *Expressing disagreement* | Confronts with logic | Confronts emotionally | Never confronts |
| *Interruptions* | Rarely interrupts | Often interrupts | Does not interrupt |
| *Truth* | Truth before diplomacy | Flexible truth | Diplomacy over truth |
| *Patience* | Sometimes impatient | Impatient | Patient |
| *Body language* | Limited body language | Unlimited body language | Subtle body language |
| *Facts* | Uses mainly facts | Puts feelings before facts | Statements are promises |
| *Social/professional* | Separates social and professional | Mixes social and professional | Connects social and professional |

- we need **multi-active** types to . . . generate enthusiasm, motivate, persuade, create positive social atmosphere, access emotions, generate dialogue, challenge us personally;
- we need **reactive** types to . . . harmonize, act intuitively, be patient and see a big picture, think and act long-term, access feelings, listen, empathize . . . and not to challenge directly.

After taking an assessment at cultureactive.com and identifying your personal cultural preferences, you can compare them with those of others (family, friends, colleagues, or business partners). The resulting diagram will indicate which affinities you (and those

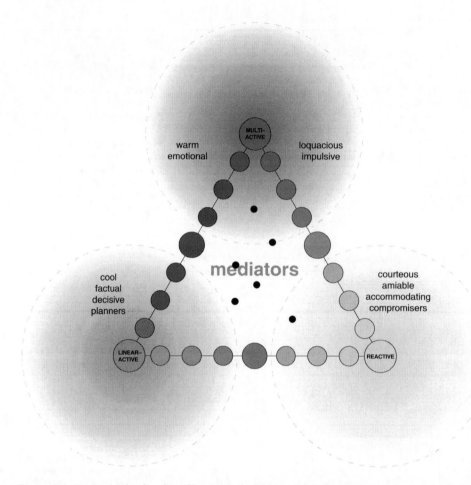

*Figure 12.3* Categorized cultural profiling with the Lewis L-M-R Model (anonymous group sample)

around you) have with other cultures. It could also be a clue to which social or working environment you find sympathetic. Figure 12.3 displays a generic group profile, and Figure 12.4 shows a profile with a relative placement of countries/cultures along the sides of the triangle.

In addition to L-M-R profiling, CultureActive-generated reports provide descriptive and comparative depictions of particular countries/cultures in both general and business contexts, including *values* and *beliefs, communication and interaction* patterns (speech patterns, audience expectations and listening habits, presentation styles, meeting patterns, conflict resolution, negotiations, etc.), use of *space* and *time, language of management, motivation* and *empathy, trust, gender* factors, etc.

Another extremely useful feature is that the software offers the possibility to retake the assessment and to map the distance in differences between the current and the desired states. This is a *cultural gap*, which is critical for action planning to achieve desired change.

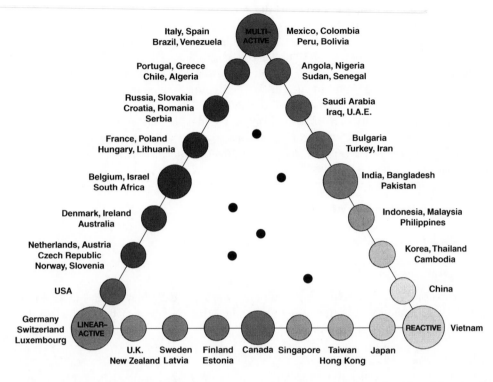

*Figure 12.4* L–M–R group sample related to country/culture positioning along the sides of the triangle (anonymous group sample)

## RLC consultancy cycle

In an organizational context, where the focus is on a comparative analysis of the national cultures involved and the synthesis of the resulting corporate/organizational culture, RLC uses a four-phase approach:

(a) assessing culture and its strengths and weaknesses (values, beliefs, norms),
(b) defining objectives of prospective changes (cultural gaps – what, why, and how to change),
(c) developing an actionable plan for alignment/adjustments over a certain period of time, and
(d) checking on "narrowing the gap" during an established timeframe (re-assessment).

Cultural assessments are limited to metadata. Besides the "label" of an organization, we have self-reported and relatively quantified (but not qualified!) data about certain aspects of organizational behavior; e.g., whether we communicate or work in teams well enough, etc. It is possible, but not easy, to turn this type of data into information and knowledge electronically in order to make informed decisions and develop action plans for further development. The data must be validated through accounts of concrete behaviours and procedures. This stage of cultural analysis is done through interviews, focus groups, and workshops to identify the gap between "the current" and "the preferred" status, followed by the development of an action plan. Repeating the assessment over time is the final step of the cycle that measures the progress expected in the action plans.

Measuring and aligning cultures "under one corporate roof" is a delicate part of the sequence, especially when change is needed. Culture is vast and not entirely measurable. It is more practical and useful to measure certain cultural elements, depending on your overall target. Some consultancies carry out cultural assessments to link organizational behaviour to productivity, performance, adaptability, etc. RLC targets the *internal dynamics* in organizations, which are the most important attributes of interpersonal communication and interaction: *leadership, decision making, communication, teamwork,* and *people/task management.*

### Case studies (Hammerich and Lewis, 2013)

#### 1. Pharmaceutical giants Upjohn (USA) and Pharmacia (Sweden)

LOOKING FOR COMMON GROUND

These two companies had an unhappy union for over a decade. When Pfizer took Upjohn's place, it determined to avoid the numerous conflicts that had arisen between the partners, particularly in the area of decision-making.

*Pfizer – Upjohn – Pharmacia*
In the 1990s, it was well-known that the union of the two pharmaceutical companies – Upjohn (US) and Pharmacia (Sweden) – was an uneasy one. We gave several seminars in Helsingborg to mixed Swedish-US teams without feeling we were achieving very much. The "us and them" atmosphere was readily apparent. The workshops had in fact been arranged a few years too late: the damage had already been done in terms of working relationships and reputations. The remedial programme was sporadic, actually spread out over three to four years.

In early 2003, the giant American pharmaceutical company, Pfizer, bought out Upjohn and took over Pharmacia. They were well aware of the cultural and operating difficulties that Upjohn had experienced and were anxious to avoid similar complications. They started out with the premise that Upjohn, operating in Sweden, had failed to come to terms with the Swedish cultural environment and had committed a series of gaffes not uncommon for an American company making new forays into European and Asian territory.

In the Pfizer HQ in Morris Plains, New Jersey, there happened to be a rather sophisticated and multinational team concerned in the takeover, led by Richard d'Souza and including members from Italy, South Africa, French Canada, and the United Kingdom. Richard d'Souza, aware of my knowledge of the Swedish operation, asked us to hold a two-day seminar in Morris Plains to give his team (of 25) a full briefing on the Swedish business environment. It was clearly quite different from the American, not only because of wildly diverging national psychologies, but also due to dissimilar legislation and structures imposed by the Swedish state.

We were aided in my task by rather copious notes that the Swedish half of the Upjohn-Pharmacia teams had made in the months when the Upjohn exit was foreseen. Swedes, though generally non-confrontational with partners and conscientious in listening to others' points of view, nevertheless do not abandon their own attitudes easily and like to have recourse to self-justification if their suggestions are set aside.

Frustration had been felt by both sides, though the list of Swedish complaints was the longer of the two. As I related to Pfizer, they were as follows:

- In general, they objected to the American managers' "hard-charging" style. Upjohn's "commanding captains" did not mesh well with the Swedish system of working in autonomous small groups.
- US managers were seen as "brutally" frank and direct. American frankness is almost unique. Only Germans and Finns accept it readily. Swedes certainly do not.
- The American managers often overruled Swedish top executives in public, causing them to lose face. Neither did they seem to realise they had done it.
- Upjohn required frequent reporting: monthly research reports, budgets, staffing updates, etc. This type of monthly monitoring created extra process in Swedish eyes.
- Typically, American quarterly rolling forecasts also annoyed the Swedes, who are traditionally uncomfortable with most forms of speculation.
- Monthly staffing updates seemed outright idiotic to Swedes. There is much less mobility in Swedish companies. Employees usually maintain a "steady performance".
- Upjohn banned smoking and wine on company premises. Swedes felt this interfered with personal liberty. They were further upset by, and subsequently opposed, alcohol and drug testing of workers.
- The US emphasis on personal accountability shocked the Swedes, who often take refuge in "group responsibility".
- The Americans created an extra layer of management by setting up a London "regional HQ". Swedes complained of having two bosses.

The American managers also found cause for complaint. Swedes normally take all July off. US executives scheduling meetings in July got them called off, as their partners were on the beach. American employees do not take time off when a major project is underway or in time of business crisis. Swedes are sensitive about infringements on their leisure time. In American eyes, they are quick to insist on their rights and often fail to focus on their corresponding duties. The power of the Swedish workers' unions irritated the Americans.

The blame for some problems lay at the feet of both sides. Often, one side's computers did not relate to the other's. Product launches were delayed because of lack of communication between the teams. Nationalist overtones were observable on both sides.

The Swedes noted that Upjohn met with tough resistance in the Italian subsidiary. Problems concerned the banning of wine and cigarettes, questions of hierarchy, impenetrable fiscal controls (Italian), and the struggles between company loyalty and family loyalty.

The Pfizer team discussed at length the sources of irritation between Upjohn and Pharmacia. It was a valuable learning experience. I stressed the key factors in motivating Swedish staff:

- ask for everybody's opinion
- attend meetings patiently (there are many of them)
- wait for them to reach decisions by consensus
- be part of this consensus
- discuss technical points at length and in detail

- see business as beneficial to society rather than primarily profit-oriented
- always be consultative and understanding
- never bulldoze them.

I pointed out that while Swedes like to be considered internationally minded and impartial, they are not the easiest of people to deal with in multinational teams. Not only Americans, but other nationalities such as British, Finns, and Norwegians are often exasperated by Swedish complacency, slow-decision making and conviction that the Swedish way must be best.

Swedish business people have undoubted strengths in the international arena. They have a high level of education, technical competence, upstream industry based on science and technology, sound investment in research, absence of corruption, Lutheran ethics, and excellent linguistic skills. Their different political groups cooperate readily in promoting national business. This is the good news.

The bad news includes too many meetings (going round in circles), managers afraid of staff, over-cosseted employees who absent themselves at the slightest excuse (backed up legally), woolly directives given by low-key managers, obsessive admiration for the welfare state, and a tendency to over-analyze and to require too much context before acting. Some of these weaknesses do not sit easily with Americans.

The Pfizer executives digested this information. It was hard for them to visualize a twenty-first century business person who did not share their driving work ethic, zest for results and attachment to numbers and statistics. D'Souza saw clearly that they would have to adapt quickly to Swedish psychology if they were to make a success of their new venture. Compared to Upjohn, Pfizer would be low-key, laid back (at least for a while), and demonstrate some humility in a new set of circumstances.

To a considerable degree, that is how it turned out. New teams worked quietly and well. It was largely the Americans who adapted. They gave their Swedish colleagues what they considered to be an inordinate amount of time to reach decisions. They played to the welfare state and "green" mentalities, and paid respects to the formal aspects of Swedish business, where correctness and harmony seem more important than results. Profit is one of the goals, but a distant last. Swedes are happy "travelling hopefully".

Referring back to Figure 12.5, Pfizer had, in fact, by adopting a new, relaxed approach, completed Phase One of the alignment process. By sidestepping contentious issues and showing respect for the somewhat idiosyncratic Swedish views of rights, privacy, and liberty, they started business with their new partner in an atmosphere of cooperation and understanding. Thus, an organizational culture based both on American drive and Swedish restraint developed in an equable manner over a lengthy period.

### 2. KONE: Cultural agility

AGILITY AND HUMILITY

KONE is a Finnish manufacturer of lifts and cranes – the third largest in the world in its cluster. As in the case of Nokia, many eyebrows were raised at the prospect of a modest-sized company from a nation of five million inhabitants securing a dominant position in a major world industry. How did they achieve this feat in a rapid surge in development between the years 1967 and 2010? What was their business strategy? How were they able

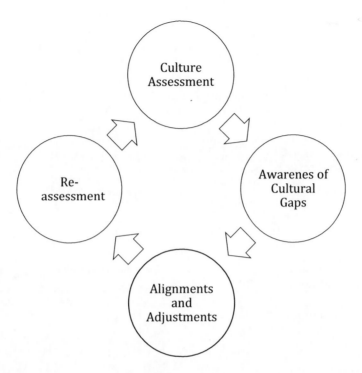

*Figure 12.5* High-level view of the RLC cultural consultancy cycle

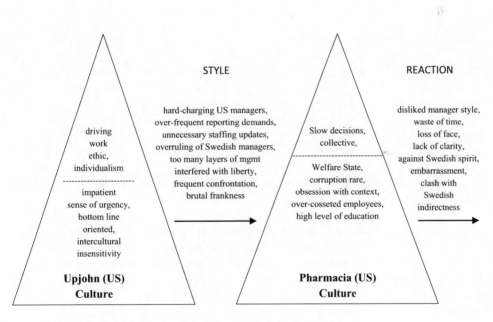

*Figure 12.6* Upjohn model: ignoring Swedish national characteristics

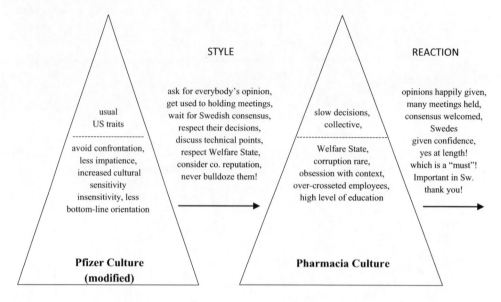

*Figure 12.7* Pfizer model: giving primacy to Swedish national traits

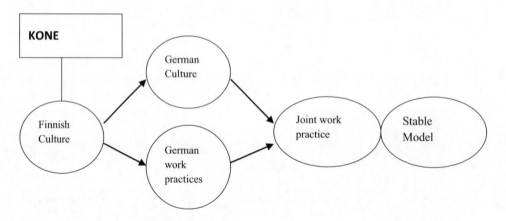

*Figure 12.8* KONE model: agility and humility

to change their corporate image (surely Finnish culture is relatively unknown to many) in order to synchronize rapid change and cultural imperatives?

KONE's business strategy from 1966 was international growth through acquisitions. American companies beat all comers making acquisitions mainly through financial muscle. What was remarkable about KONE's purchases was that they started acquiring rivals considerably larger than themselves and in major manufacturing countries such as France, Germany, Italy, Spain, Belgium, and the US. How did they get away with this, and why were good relations quickly developed with the French, German, American, and other managers?

I was based in Finland in the early '70s and got to know the KONE management just when they embarked on their ambitious expansion. As I became involved with their cultural and linguistic training, I realised that their board consisted not only of more than a dozen exceptionally forward-looking individuals, led by the legendary Pekka Herlin, but also that it was one of the most diversified groups I had worked with and consequently was admirably equipped to combine world views and perspectives. It was an agile, multicultural team in itself with Germans, French, British, and Australian members who added spice to some outstanding Finns and Finn-Swedes whom Herlin had assembled.

KONE's acquisition programme was extremely ambitious. They devoured big names such as Westinghouse Europe, Montgomery USA, UK Lift Company, Fuji Elevator, Havemeier & Sander, and Asea-Graham in rapid succession, acquiring not only manufacturing units, but entire staff and management systems steeped in the national cultural traits of France, Germany, the US, etc. The business strategy was clear: rapid growth, integration and consolidation, economies of scale, and satisfactory profits. The cultural clashes, nearly a dozen different ones, loomed ominously.

Pekka Herlin, though renowned for his strong will and resilience, declared as early as 1972: "There is no way that problems spread all over the world can be solved from Helsinki" (Hammerich and Lewis, 2013, p.155). The far-seeing chairman made it a principle from the first acquisitions that Finnish teams moving in should give considerable leeway to local management. Finns, known for their common sense and humility, had a healthy respect for the positions and achievements of companies belonging to bigger countries than Finland. This respectful approach maintained much of the touch and feel of the best cultural features of acquired companies and consequently minimized customer flight. "Local excellence backed by global resources" became KONE's slogan. The KONE corporate culture during the 33-year period of acquiring 26 companies changed from being stubbornly Finnish (small-but-good, rural values are best) to truly international (multifaceted, adaptable, tolerant). The cultural change preceded the implantation of strategic imperatives, or at the very least took place in tandem with them. Finnish humility and relaxed management traits obviated the multiple conflicts, misunderstandings, tension, and gaffes that occurred because of a lack of preparation in the cases of Walmart and Daimler-Chrysler. Matti Alahuhta, KONE's former CEO, himself a relaxed and genial senior executive, presided over the KONE far-sighted philosophy (in its service and maintenance division), "CARE FOR LIFE".

Changing corporate culture in time requires nimbleness and agility, which is often easier to find in small nations such as the Netherlands and the four Nordic countries than in bigger ones with cumbersome structures and more complex cultural baggage.

In the Pfizer-Upjohn-Pharmacia and KONE case studies, we have had good examples of how two companies succeeded in approaching M&A situations correctly. Before beginning to specify the organizational culture, they paid meticulous attention to the national characteristics of the entities being acquired. Pfizer took into consideration the inclinations of the inherently Swedish pharmaceutical giant Pharmacia. In the case of KONE, their management displayed admirable humility during various foreign acquisitions, and looked at the respective national traits in order to align with them. Before they entered into negotiations for a joint venture with mighty Toshiba, they again showed great insight in familiarising themselves with Japanese company practices prior to engaging them face to face. Both Pfizer and KONE respected the requirement of completing Phase One in the acquisition process before commencing the "heavy lifting" that Phase Two inevitably required.

Next, we examine a case study where a much larger enterprise failed in paying enough attention to the cultural alignment required in Phase One and, consequently, was never able to plan adequately for Phase Two.

## 3. Daimler-Chrysler

In May 1998, when the impending merger of Daimler-Benz and Chrysler was announced, it heralded the biggest cross-border industrial merger ever. The rationale was obvious. Chrysler was perennially third in the Detroit Big Three and, despite heroic efforts by Lee Iacocca to revitalize the company, it struggled to maintain its productivity and world ranking. Daimler-Benz – more prestigious and dynamic – was essentially a specialist producer of premium saloons and had made few efforts to widen its product range and customer base.

The amalgamation of the two companies produced an industrial giant with global sales of more than $150 billion, making it fifth among the world's car manufacturers. It was to be a shining example of what globalization could achieve for an adventurous group combining two well established brand names. A smooth integration of the two famous corporations would enable the group to meet the demands of nearly all segments of the car market, and sales could be expected to increase exponentially.

The phrase "smooth integration", was a key challenge to Daimler-Chrysler as well as the route to success.

Certain elements of the Daimler-Benz management were sensitive to the problems likely to arise when German and American executives and workforces were to be united at various levels of activity and responsibility: German and American mindsets and world views differ sharply. There are worse cross-cultural mismatches, but there are also better ones. Wisely, Daimler-Benz appointed a senior executive, Andreas Renschler, to supervise the integration. He had worked for several years in the United States and was sufficiently well-versed in both cultures to foresee and hopefully circumvent cultural difficulties which would undoubtedly present themselves.

We had worked with Mercedes executives and teams in the years between 1975 and 1995. Andreas Renschler contacted Richard Lewis Communications and arranged an initial meeting in Stuttgart to discuss training programmes for executives who would be involved in the early stages of cross-border activity. We sent a three-man team to the headquarters in Sindelfingen – two of our English consultants who had lived in Germany and one German–American who flew in from New York. We spent the whole day with Renschler, an experienced and mature individual with a good grasp of cross-cultural issues and a keen insight into American and German behavioural patterns. We were joined during the day with a German HR team, assembled specially to facilitate the merger.

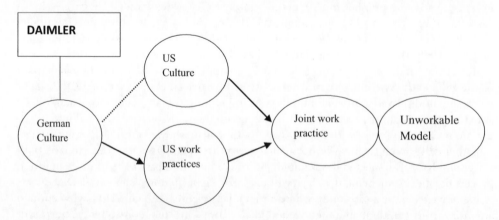

*Figure 12.9* Daimler-Chrysler model

## Communication styles

We made a presentation predicting the likely obstacles in the way of quick understanding. In the early stages of the merger, differences in communication styles would be the first major hurdles to be surmounted. In Germany, the primary purpose of speech is to give and receive information. Americans are also factual, but use speech emphatically to give opinions and are more persuasive than Germans. In this respect they often use hyperbole, which Germans instinctively react against. Americans tend to evince optimism and put forward best scenarios. Germans are more comfortable with a cautious, somewhat pessimistic, view that envisages worst scenarios. They want a lot of context before approaching any important decision. The let us get-on-with-it approach of the Americans often increases German caution. "Yes, but what happens if . . ."? is a typically German attitude. Americans are anxious to expound the grand strategy and mop up the details later. They seek simplification of issues to clarify their route to action. Germans have a tendency to complicate discussion (life is not simple, you know).

German formality is evident in their style of communication. When meeting strangers, they usually enter a room with a serious look on their face, contrasting with the broad Hollywood smiles of the Americans. Germans at this stage may seem stiff and distant to Americans. Surnames are used for years and full titles are expected. Americans go for first names from the start and have an informal way of conducting a discussion, using slang, irony, and kidding, which disconcerts most Germans, especially senior ones. Germans are used to asking serious questions to which they expect serious answers. Americans, fond of humour, often reply in a rather flippant or casual manner. Germans fail to appreciate jokes, wisecracks, or sarcasm during a business discussion. Germans are not fond of small talk and often find Americans chatty. Charismatic Americans find Germans lacking in charisma and perhaps dull. Germans, in fact, distrust charisma and instant smiles. As they generally think in silence, they are not quite sure how to react when Americans think aloud. Are they making statements, suggestions, or are they trying to make up their own mind? Brainstorming is popular with Americans but less so with Germans, who would be reluctant to speak out in front of a superior. German ideas are expressed guardedly with considerable caution. American speech is quick, mobile, opportunistic. Germans seldom argue with a colleague's remarks. Americans prefer a free-for-all discussion. Their speech is loaded with clichés (e.g., "Let's get this show on the road" or "I can't fly this by the seat of my pants") or tough talk (e.g., "I tell you I can walk away from this deal"). Both are absent from German speech. American agreements are usually reached by persistent persuasion in open discussion; Germans find agreement through thorough analysis of details, leading to clarification and justification.

Listening habits, too, are part of the communication process. How would Germans and Americans listen to each other? The American (audience) demands initial entertainment and tends to listen in snatches if not amused. The next phase is "What is new"? Time is money so get on with it. Do not complicate issues – tell it like it is! Slogans and catch phrases are readily absorbed by Americans. Germans do not use them.

The German listener does not yet wish to know about the present as the past must come first. Consequently, all the context leading up to the deal must be gone into. When this need has been satisfied, then one can describe the present situation before edging cautiously forward. Questions in the mind of the German listener are: "Does this sound too simple?"; "What happens if . . .?"; "Am I getting the hard sell?"; "Aren't we rushing into things?"; and "Can I have more (technical) information, please?"

## Other differences

Diversity in communication styles would lead to early misunderstandings, but later procedural and structural differences would appear. US corporations usually have strictly centralized reporting. Large German companies often feature decentralisation and compartmentalisation. Each department reports vertically to its department head. Horizontal communication across departments at different levels is practically taboo. Departmental rivalry is much more acute than in the US. In this area, German managers tend to be extremely touchy. Americans are more thick-skinned. Americans go from office to office in their gregarious manner. German offices are strongholds of privacy, usually with doors shut. American managers chase their staff around the building exchanging views ("Say, Jack I've just had a great idea"). Germans, by contrast, like to do the job on their own ("No monitoring, please, until the end of the day"). American managers like to shower good executives with praise ("You're doing a heckuva job!"). German staff expect no praise from the boss. They are paid to do the job efficiently.

Germans are class conscious. Senior managers are usually intellectuals. In classless America, intellectuals are often called "eggheads". American managers speak out loud. Senior Germans command in a low voice. Americans prize spontaneity, flexibility, and adaptability in reaching their goals. Germans give pride of place to well-tested procedures and processes. If these structures have brought the company so far, why change things?

Renschler and the Mercedes training officers concurred with the points made in our presentation. What should be done in terms of training to facilitate the merger? Our basic reply was that many mergers fail because both sides are not sufficiently versed in the historical values, core beliefs, communication patterns, behavioural habits, and world views of the other. Training would address these issues systematically according to the model we would put forward. An important target in such training is to make one side like the other. This transcends simple knowledge of the other culture.

It was agreed that we would refine our training model to fit the proposed merger of the two companies and would return to Stuttgart one month later with a detailed programme.

## The training model

When we returned the following month, Renschler had assembled a somewhat larger HR team (six or seven people), including one professor from DaimlerChrysler University. They had formed various executive teams that would tackle various projects in the merger. In Stuttgart, the teams consisted largely of Germans with a sprinkling of Americans and British. Other teams, with more American members, were being formed in Detroit.

Our model envisaged a six-month training period in which teams would be exposed to full-day seminars, workshops, special briefings, and a home study programme. We have formalized cross-cultural studies under the following sub-headings:

**Culture – general:** Religion, cultural classification, languages, values and core beliefs, cultural black holes, concept of space, concepts of time, self-image.

**Culture – communication:** Communication patterns and use of language, listening habits, audience expectations, body language and non-verbal communication.

**Culture – interaction:** Concept of status, the position of women, leadership style, language of management, motivation factors, general behaviour at meetings, negotiating characteristics, contracts and commitments, manners and taboos, how to empathize with them.

Renschler and his "committee" were sufficiently pleased with the programme. It was agreed that 50-60% of the activity would be carried out in Stuttgart with the aim of familiarizing the largely German teams with American mindsets and business culture, and similar "mirror" seminars would be held in Detroit to help Americans understand Germans. The emphasis throughout would be the fostering of a favourable view of the foreign partner.

As we all agreed on general principles, we discussed a starting date with Renschler. In view of the urgency of the consummation of the merger, he was anxious to start as soon as possible. There was only one obstacle: the programme would first have to be approved by DaimlerChrysler University. The professor on our committee promised to submit the programme to the university the following week. Soon after, Renschler changed jobs. We never heard from DaimlerChrysler again.

## Five years later

Five years later, after addressing the annual conference of the G100 group in New York, I attended a cocktail party hosted by Jack Welch and Raymond Gilmartin. At this function, I met a German DaimlerChrysler board member who had been one of the first Germans to be sent to the United States where he had worked from 1998–2003. He gave me an account of the unfolding of events after the merger was consummated. The time taken by DaimlerChrysler University in considering the content of a cross-cultural training programme resulted in most executive teams being sent from Stuttgart to the United States with no training at all. The cultural clashes we had forecast in 1998 took place in the first few months of joint operations. Differing behavioural habits and attitudes irritated both sides. This situation was exacerbated by the maintenance of the fiction that the amalgamation was a merger of equals. It was nothing of the sort. Daimler could not afford a merger formula with a jointly owned company based in the Netherlands, since this would have triggered a huge tax charge. This meant that Chrysler had to become part of a German *Aktiengesellschaft*. It was in fact a quiet takeover, in compensation of which the Chrysler shareholders were paid a 28% premium over the then market price. Managers maintained the "merger" fiction for some time, which was relatively harmless in itself except that American staff continued to believe that there would be "joint control". It took years to achieve any measure of integration of two different ways of working. Neither side had been given time or training to study the other's mindset.

It is true that the Germans learnt to be less formal and to cut down on paper work. The Americans, for their part, learnt more discipline in their meetings and decision-making. German and American commonalities such as work ethic, bluntness, lack of tact, a linear approach to tasks and time, punctuality, following agendas, results-orientation, and emphasis on competitive prices and reliable delivery dates created a potential modus operandi, but two different mindsets led to irritation and misunderstanding on both sides. The German board member listed dozens of incidents. He opined that the Americans he was working with showed a complete lack of understanding of German values, methods, and working culture. They found that Germans shook hands too much, were often too intense and followed rigid manuals and rule books which deflated American spontaneity. German meetings were boring, American meetings were exciting; the German drive towards conformity clashed with American invention, innovation, and opportunism. Germans adhered to old traditions and well-tried procedures; Americans preferred a DIY ambience. Germans who stayed on sought deep friendships, not segmented ones like the Americans (tennis friend, bridge friend, drinking friend, etc.). Americans got annoyed by the German habit of offering constructive criticism. Half the time, Germans and Americans just talked past each other. Germans took long holidays, unthinkable in American eyes, especially when there was a crisis, but when difficulties arose, who was in control? For one year, the group had two chairmen, Mr Schrempp from Daimler and Bob Eaton, who had been boss of Chrysler. Within one year, Eaton was fired and his American successor lasted less than 12 months. DaimlerChrysler's share price fell from $108 in January 1999, to $38 in November 2000. Nobody was quite sure how the combined companies should be run. Cultural differences led to differences of opinion and methods at all levels. In German eyes, Chrysler was a company with problems in every department, not least productivity. Each vehicle took Chrysler 40 hours to make. Honda and Toyota produce a car every 20 hours. The Germans, with their emphasis on quality, found Chrysler quality control way out of line. Even worse there was no plan in place to improve it. Chrysler swung from a profit of $2.5 billion in the first half of the merger year to a loss of $2 billion in the second.

The German solution was to import a crack German executive, Dieter Zetsche, to apply German principles to the problem: He set a target of 30 hours per vehicle in 2007; he slashed spending from $42 billion (five-year plan) to $28 billion; he brought new models forward six months faster; and he shut six factories and cut 45,000 jobs – one third of the total.

Under Zetsche's efficient control, Chrysler was, in 2006, perhaps the healthiest car company in Detroit. However, a second important factor emerged from the troublesome acquisition of the American company. An initial mistake of the Germans had been that, in order not to be seen as heavy-handed, they had "stayed away" from Detroit. For this reason, it took them two years to come to grips with the American company's fragility. Then when Zetsche concentrated on rescuing his ailing colleague, Mercedes itself slipped badly. Neglect led to its reputation for quality being dented by unfavourable consumer reports and the company's move down-market into Smart cars piled up huge losses.

Ironically, Zetsche himself was moved back to Germany to assume control of the whole group. It was then the turn of the German end of the DaimlerChrysler group to undergo painful restructuring similar to that which had taken place in the previous four to five years in Detroit. Zetsche joked that since a Chrysler boss (himself) was now running the show in Stuttgart, everyone could at last see clearly that it was a takeover.

## Conclusion

In view of the incredibly high failure rate of mergers and acquisitions where a mix of nationalities is involved, it is clearly imperative that companies with the intention of setting up such alliances should consult with cross-cultural experts before taking the very first steps. It is common sense to do this, for neglect of cultural issues can lead to early and huge losses running into millions. Yet, it is our experience that many firms only belatedly look into cultural compatibility after the basic deal has been signed and established. Training officers are seen to scramble when the problems quickly become apparent. Only too often, measures taken typify the "too little too late" syndrome (disastrous in the military sphere but equally damaging in commerce). Top cultural experts' fees amount to thousands or tens of thousands of dollars or pounds. First year losses for failing M&As can run into one thousand times that. Not only should cultural alignment be attended to initially, but it takes experienced cultural experts to know what steps to take. Few HR managers have adequate training to deal with the complex intricacies involved, even when only two national cultures are concerned. With a truly international conglomerate, the "lifting is much heavier". There may be no more than a dozen consultancy companies in this field in the world who can advise on and help to manage cultural alignment on such a scale.

## References

Adler, N., and Gundersen, A. (2008). *International dimensions of organizational behavior*, 5th ed. Mason, OH: Thomson South-Western.

Bairatchnyi, I. (2013). Cultural identity and a global mindset: Awareness to knowledge, skills to competence. In A. Green (eds.), *Making it real: Sustaining knowledge management*. Reading: ACPI, pp. 55–85.

Hammerich, K., and Lewis, R. D. (2013). *Fish can't see water*. Chichester: Wiley.

Hofstede, G. (2001). *Culture's consequences*, 2nd ed. London: Sage.

Lewis, R. D. (2006). *When cultures collide: Leading across cultures*, 3rd ed. Boston, MA; London: Nicholas Brealy International.

Martin, R. (2016). *M&A: The one thing you need to get right*. Available from https://hbr.org/2016/06/ma-the-one-thing-you-need-to-get-right.

Trompenaars, F., and Hampden-Turner, C. (2012). *Riding the waves of culture*, 3rd ed. New York: McGraw-Hill.

# 13 Talent management within XYZ global investment bank

*Oliver Rodway and Graham Manville*

## Executive summary

Investment banking is a global, fast-moving, 24/7 business, and technology is a key enabler for maintaining a competitive edge and the continued improved performance of organisations within this sector. Annual spending on technology runs into the billions of dollars and the front and back office functions of the banking sector are dependent on the support of technology. During the last decade, this has been brought into sharp focus as organisations reeled from the shockwaves of the global financial crisis (GFC). The GFC began in 2007, following the collapse in subprime lending in the USA, and came to a head in 2008. The GFC was caused by overleveraging in the banking industry, which resulted in the collapse in confidence and seizing up of inter-bank lending. This resulted in the collapse of a major global investment bank and other global banks that were vulnerable due to insufficient capital reserves. Following the GFC of 2008, investment banks experienced a period of consolidation through merger and acquisition, which required affected banks to re-engineer their business processes. Due to the continuous nature of global banking, front, middle and back office functions need to be optimised as time is literally money and as technology is a key enabler for trades and back office reconciliation. As a result, the role of the technologist has gained greater importance, especially after the GFC. XYZ investment bank has recognised that this was an opportune time to reinvigorate its technology graduate training in order to rise to the challenge by instigating a consulting project. Investment banking has a youthful demographic relative to other industries, and the consulting team needed to devise a solution with Generation Y at its heart. The bank recognised that employee retention was a challenge across the sector and, as a consequence, the graduate training scheme was revitalised to promote talent management and employee retention. The project took place between late-2007 and mid-2008 in the run up to the seismic events in the autumn of 2008.

## Introduction to the case context

The corporation is a top tier-global investment bank with multibillion-dollar annual revenues. The bank is composed of five sublines of business: investment banking, commercial banking, asset and wealth management, retail banking and treasury and securities services – each with their own technology organisations. Competing against similar banks headquartered in New York, London and Hong Kong, this bank had gone through the global financial crisis facing many of the same external forces as its competitors, like: an ever-growing focus on regulatory oversight and control, and an ongoing compression of earnings due to constricting global markets. There were also continuing pressures on cost reduction and this resulted in reduced staff. The fallout from the GFC has manifested a laser focus from governments on the organisational culture throughout the financial services industry. Internal pressures resulted from the complexity of products, technology and an enterprise that stretches across all regions and time zones.

The bank has a rich history, having been formed over decades through growth and acquisition. The prevailing ethos and mission focuses on building a robust bank that can service clients with all their banking needs throughout the world, whether they are high net worth individuals or a first-time buyer looking to finance their first home.

The investment bank offers a full spectrum of products to all client groups. From advisory services, such as merger and acquisition, to supporting clients who trade in complex derivative products. The bank supports clients from investment funds and governments to sovereign wealth funds with their corporate banking needs. As a top-tier bank, the organisation services clients in all major financial markets with predominance in the US and European markets. Like all its major competitors, there is a determined focus to grow in the Asia-Pacific region.

Major competitors include both universal full-service banks based in the US and Asia, and those banks that focus on corporate banking only. With competitors based in all the same key financial locations (i.e. New York, City of London and Hong Kong), a talent attraction phenomenon is created with all key competitors offering many similar roles to a pool of highly mobile, highly aspirational and often young talent. This 'war for talent' is fuelled by a vibrant recruitment consultant industry based in the same financial centres. Banks differentiate through opportunities for career growth, the prestige of firm, location (in many major financial centres being on the 'right island' or metro line is seen as a key differentiator) and ultimately financial package. This competitive approach for talent and skills, whilst not unique to financial services, is heightened by the co-location of so many major banks in so few global locations. A similar clustering phenomenon has been witnessed in other industries such as technology in the Silicon Valley in California, the M4 corridor in England, offshore oil and gas in Aberdeen, Scotland, etc.

Developing high-quality training and development programmes, especially those targeted at graduates, can accelerate talent development and make an attractive marketing proposition at campus recruitment events.

## Consultancy brief

XYZ Investment Bank is a multi-national bank holding company and one of the largest public companies in the world. They are able to recruit the very best graduates from leading universities in both technological and operational roles. They employ more than 230,000 employees and have a turnover in excess of $96 billion. The company has pursued an acquisition strategy that gathered pace following the global financial crisis of 2008. This has resulted in a number of legacy systems and processes. The issue of inconsistency across the various lines of business prompted a rethink into graduate training with a particular focus on the Technology Graduate Training Programme. The brief focused on the UK arm of the business, but the intention was for the solution to be scalable to other parts of the organisation.

A team of three external consultants, along with an internal consultant, were assembled to conduct a needs analysis followed by a reconfiguration of the Technology Training Programme. The brief was to benchmark performance against not only their peers within the sector but also best practice from outside of the sector. At the launch of the project, the consultancy team comprised an MBA programme leader from a university business school, two independent consultants and an internal consultant employed by the bank. The team benefited from an internal champion at Chief Technology Officer (CTO) level who could facilitate budget and access to meet with managers and graduates. The internal consultant was also a vice president within XYZ and was effectively the project team leader.

## The issue

Within the area of technology graduate training at XYZ, there was no structured corporate technology programme. The graduates had a degree of semi-structure in that they were provided with a number of work rotations lasting between three and six months during their training, and their final rotation was usually the destination of their first position of responsibility. The lack of structure had led to issues of consistency across the organization and lack of guidance from the Lines of Business (LoB) managers who supervised the graduates during their departmental rotation. There was also no visibility or understanding of how competitors trained their technology graduates, so it was unclear as to whether this was an organisational problem or a sector-specific problem. This lack of formalised training correlated to an above average staff turnover as graduates were leaving to join rival organisations.

## Deliverables

The project deliverables included the following:

- A structured training programme with the flexibility for graduates to tailor their training subject to the needs of the Line of Business manager
- To promote the importance of hybrid technologist roles, which combine subject matter expertise in the technical sphere as well as demonstrating excellent business acumen
- The structured training programme would benefit from some form of assessment and/or external accreditation
- To recognise and satisfy the needs and challenges of a Generation Y workforce and their assimilation within the rest of the organisation
- To deliver a template for a training programme that is among the best in the industry, and that can appeal not only to existing XYZ graduates but could also serve as a recruiting tool for future cohorts.

## Training needs to training solution – existing state

The challenges faced by creating bespoke training solutions for individual graduates by locally sourced training needs are demonstrated in the visual below. Whilst the focus was undoubtedly to support the legitimate training needs for a distinct cohort of graduates in one location, it did not support: the scaling of solutions (one training solution supports multiple sites at potentially lower cost), mobility (learners learn consistent content so that knowledge can be more easily transferable) and record keeping and metrics (records were often kept locally on spreadsheets, for easy maintenance, without being added to the enterprise-wide learning management system).

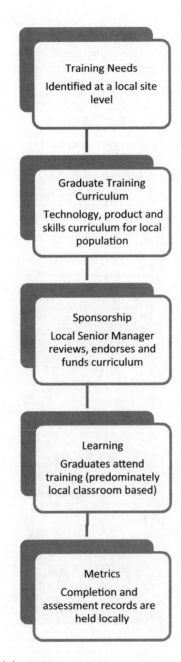

*Figure 13.1* Training needs – existing state

## Training needs – desired state

In the desired/future state, training needs would be captured centrally at a national or global level. These needs would also be benchmarked to external learning frameworks (e.g. British computer society learning framework) to ensure the relevance and integrity of any curriculum that is created. The final curriculum would then be validated and centrally funded with an overarching goal to create scalability and efficiency through using e-learning and on-demand options as much as possible (for pure knowledge requirements), and consistent classroom-based learning where application of knowledge and development of

*Figure 13.2* Training needs – desired state

skill is required. Standardising learning at a national level would offer greater leverage with training vendors to drive down unit cost and would support mobility as learners could complete a standardised curriculum regardless of the location they undertook their learning. Finally, metrics would be consistent and readily available as they would all be recorded on the prime record in the enterprise-wide learning management system.

## Contextual factors of the workforce

In the workplace, there has always been the challenge of managing different generations. Previous generations had experienced recessions. Following the recession in 1993, the UK economy experienced an unprecedented continuous growth period that lasted more than fifteen years. The latest generation to enter the workforce had experienced this golden period of growth as well as the rise of the Internet. This new generation of employees that now forms a considerable part of the workforce has the opportunity to shape organisational culture. Generation Y is a polarised generation as it comprises rising stars as well as problem children who can be challenging because of their extended adolescence, which extends beyond graduation, their demanding needs and their sense of entitlement (Manville and Sheil, 2008). This workforce phenomenon is being faced by all sectors, but is more acute in investment banking. The reasons for this are: IB is a youthful sector and generation Y has a larger percentage of the workforce than in other sectors.

Generation Y workers have both positive and negative traits. With respect to their positive attributes, they are technologically savvy, confident, ambitious and can work independently and collaboratively. Conversely, they expect rapid promotion, which is sometimes out of kilter with their capabilities (Manville and Schiel, 2008; Ng et al., 2010). Although they do not require direct supervision, they do prefer regular check-ins, and that provides a challenge for managers, especially when managing multi-generational workforces. A summary of the workplace values of multiple generations is shown in Table 13.1 below.

From an investment banking perspective, they are a good fit for this sector as the banking sector is global and therefore operates in a 24/7 working environment. Members of Generation Y tend to be more loyal to their network rather than their organization, which was common in earlier generations. According to Martin (2005), both Generation X and

*Table 13.1* Intergenerational summaries of the workforce

| Generation | Year of Birth | Entered Workforce | Work Values | Work is . . . |
|---|---|---|---|---|
| Silent Generation | 1920–1944 | 1940s – 1950s | Hardworking, conservative, organisational loyalty | An inevitable obligation |
| Baby Boomers | 1945–1963 | 1960s – 1970s | Quality of life, ambitious, organisational loyalty | An exciting adventure |
| Generation X | 1964–1979 | 1980s – 1990s | Flexibility, job-satisfaction, loyal to self, work life balance | A difficult challenge |
| Generation Y | 1979–1995 | 2000s – 2010s | Value diversity, sociability, global mindset, technology savvy | A means to an end. Work to live |

Source: Adapted from Meredith et al. (2002), Clurman (1997), Zemke et al. (2001) and Sayers (2007).

Generation Y have experienced the end of the 'job for life' paradigm, which was the norm with both the 'silent generation' and the 'baby-boomer generation'. The global recessions of the 1980s and 1990s have changed recruitment and retention to focus on the needs of the business, and this brought challenges for both the organisation and the workforce. The organisation began to focus on re-balanced workforces using core workers supplemented by temporary workers and self-employed sub-contract staff. This was based on an organisational structure referred to as the shamrock organisation (Handy, 1989).

From 1992 until the global financial crisis, there was continued economic growth and the shamrock approach fell out of favour. As a result, the number of the full-time employee (FTE) constituency increased dramatically as a result of the stability brought about by continued economic growth. Generation Y grew up in a context of continuing economic growth and this shaped their behaviours. In addition, they also developed a more global outlook than previous generations. The rising stars of this generation no longer wanted a job for life and exhibited a greater sense of self-efficacy and self-reliance than the previous generations. To add to the challenges facing organisations, the potential of working remotely or at home was made possible by fast broadband technology. The more talented members of this generation were beginning to negotiate deals in ways that the older generation would never have conceived, let alone attempted (Martin, 2005).

The result is that they have become more career-agile, which makes employee retention a pressing issue for their employers. It is not uncommon for a Generation Y worker to have several employers in a five-year period on their CV. With past generations, this would have been a black mark on their job prospects. This fits with the profile of an employee in an investment bank, and therefore this project was timely as XYZ had forecasted that Generation Y would constitute approximately 40% of the workforce by 2014.

## Project execution

As the group were not previously acquainted, it was important that the team dynamics started off on the right foot. A combined icebreaker and stakeholder management exercise initiated the project. The exercise was called a 'Hopes and Fears' statement, which was originally developed by the leadership consultant Eddie Obeng, and it aimed to capture both the hopes and aspirations of the project as well as the concerns and risks to the project (Obeng, 1994). Obeng's 'Hopes and Fears' tool is simple in nature and execution and relies on straight-forward brainstorming from the group. Its value and uniqueness come from the use of the words 'Hopes' and 'Fears' as these words are rich, emotive words that elicit gut responses based more on emotion than intellectual thought. Airing the project team's emotive, gut feel, 'in the bones' responses early on in the project allowed for 'elephants in the room' to be addressed and for a positive expression of drive and ambition to be shared.

The fears that were identified followed many standard concerns faced at the initiation of a project. For example, funding, timescales and the availability of resources were all noted. However, what did stand out, and was a great example of the emotive output of this 'Hopes and Fears' process, was the fear that 'academics and investment bankers' were not a natural fit in terms of style, pace and perspective for a cohesive consultancy team. This fear was then turned into a set of risk factors (communication, expectation management, use of technical language, etc.) to be addressed in the project plan through mitigating actions/ milestones.

The 'hopes' points that were identified included the ability to 'make a difference to young people starting out in their career' and 'to learn from external experts'. Both of these statements became hard and soft success criteria for the resultant project. The mapping exercise identified a number of criteria for these hopes and fears. For example, with respect to the 'hopes' section, project success, innovation of the project and working styles were identified and populated. For the 'fears' part, scope management, clarity of deliverables and time management were identified.

## Benchmarking of competitors

At the start of the project, there was little understanding of how the graduate technology training at XYZ bank compared with other banks in the sector or best practice technology graduate training outside of the sector. The best in class was thought to be IBM as their graduate training was approved by the British Computer Society (BCS) and the Project Management Institute, and included a structured career path to achieve either Chartered Information Technology Professional (CITP) status or a professional project management award.

The technology graduates' roles at XYZ fall into three categories: technology generalists, software and infrastructure engineers and business technologists. A summary of the three generic roles is shown in Table 13.2.

At XYZ, there was no structured graduate training programme for graduate trainees in technology. Their training comprised a number of courses based on business skills, soft skills and banking skills but lacked any tailored technology training. What was also surprising was that there was no central recording of the training, which was invariably organised locally.

The average number of recorded structured training days for technology graduates was 1.15 days per annum against an average of 19.6 days by their competitors, which was highlighted by a 2007 benchmarking analysis. This study not only looked at key competitors within banking but also best practice within technology graduates in other

*Table 13.2* Generic roles for technology graduates in XYZ

|  | Technology Generalists | Software and Infrastructure Engineers | Business Technologists |
|---|---|---|---|
| **Summary** | Technology grads we recruit today – some technology experience but strong communication, teamwork and leadership potential | Stronger on technology than business/ leadership (with relevant degree in software or infrastructure engineering) | Strong technical, mathematical ad/or financials knowledge – targeted for very integrated business-aligned development (e.g. RAD) |
| **Entry Roles** | **Plan/Operate/Control roles** | **Build & Infrastructure roles** | **Business Technologists (RAD/BA areas)** |
| **General Career Direction** | Any leadership roles in technology | Senior Developer, Application Design, Infrastructure Design, Expert Engineer | Any leadership roles in technology and possibly in business |

industries. The training days recorded by XYZ could not be taken at face value on account of the localised reporting of training and the lack of consistent reporting in a centralised repository.

The graduates were on a two-year 'programme' that involved a series of rotations (i.e. placements within key parts of the organisation), which lasted between six and nine months. The work allocation for the technology graduates was provided by the LoB managers.

## Focus groups

In order to gain greater insight into technology training within XYZ UK, a series of focus groups was initiated in three of the UK locations, London and two regional offices. At each location, two separate focus groups would take place: one with the LoBs and one with the graduates. The focus groups were segregated to elicit a more honest insight into the key issues for both stakeholders. The focus groups were conducted using the following principles espoused by Krueger and Casey (2014):

- Insight not Rules
- Social not Individual
- Homogenous not Diverse
- Flexible not Standardised
- Warm not Hot (or Cold!)
- Words not Numbers.

A semi-structured briefing sheet was used in order to maintain consistency. However, there was sufficient flexibility in the design of the focus to group to allow for discussion in areas not in the brief but which were important to the business and within the scope of the project. In total, six focus groups were held in the three locations where there was a significant technology back office function. At each location, there were focus groups for both the LOBS and the technology graduates.

## Initial results

A summary of the emergent themes from each of the LOBs and technology graduates was collated and it revealed some interesting insight. For example, the LOB managers wanted graduates to hit the ground running within their departments and have an understanding of the basics of technology such as networks. They wanted the training to be tailored to the needs of their business and they recognised that the training should be blended to include the softer people skills which Generation Y lacked from both the perspectives of the published research and the personal experience of the LOB manager. Another important requirement was that there, ideally, should be a tool to facilitate the creation of a personalised training path.

From the perspective of the technology graduates, they wanted to be able to apply the training that they had learned in order to maintain their competence. They also wanted to understand how their technology training linked to the bigger picture of the XYZ technology architecture. They wanted accredited training, ideally with an industry standard. They wanted travel opportunities as well as the opportunity of blended learning, which would include both face-to-face as well as online learning. More importantly, they wanted their training to be linked to a promotion pathway to their first position of associate.

An important insight from the results of the focus groups was that there were some common areas of shared thinking between the graduates and the managers. By triangulating the feedback from the stakeholder groups, four common themes emerged: practical application, business knowledge, training plan and progress tracker and finally career ownership. Practical application meant identifying the appropriate training and the appropriate time to receive the training. The training should translate theory into practice within the context of end to end services. More importantly, the business needed to be focused on the needs of the business.

The business knowledge theme meant that it should build subject matter expertise and reciprocal learning for both graduate and manager. It should also combine business acumen and soft skills as well as core technology skills. Moreover, as XYZ operates throughout the world in multiple sites and time zones, virtual and remote management skills would need to be developed, including cultural awareness of the locations of the LOBs. A summary of the focus group findings is found in Figure 13.3.

The training plan would entail a menu of training courses that the graduate could select, subject to the approval of his/her manager. A set of generic competencies would need to be developed for each generic graduate role that would be easy to view online. At the moment, the training is ad hoc and self-selected by the graduate, which both stakeholders believe is not an ideal solution.

The final theme was for the graduate to have both ownership and accountability for their careers. The graduates relished the ownership aspect and the LOB manager wanted

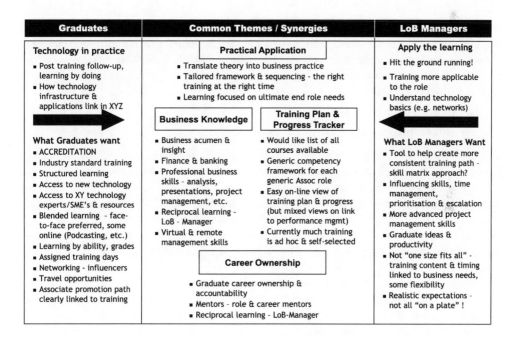

*Figure 13.3* A summary of the focus groups held in London and two regional offices

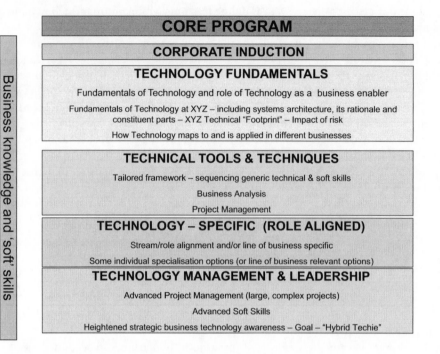

*Figure 13.4* Schematic of technology graduate training at XYZ

the accountability. There was a consensus that there should be mentors to advise the graduate in their current role as well as their career. The mentor would not necessarily be their LoB. An interesting insight was that there should be reciprocal learning opportunities between the graduate and their manager. An indicative sample of a structured training course is shown in Figure 13.4.

## Career development beyond graduate training

Having benchmarked the competition, both within the sector and outside of the sector, it became evident that XYZ needed to have a novel training programme that was not only competitive relative to the sector but also satisfied the needs of the lines of business managers and the needs of a bright but demanding Generation Y workforce. The research into Generation Y found that this section of the workforce values accreditations and qualifications. Therefore, it was important to ensure that the structured training programme satisfied the requirements of the premier professional IT institution within the United Kingdom, the British Computer Society (BCS).

Someone who completed the two-year training course developed by XYZ for its graduates could become a member of the BCS after two years. This was an encouraging development for XYZ, but it appears to be a threshold level for any leading investment bank or FTSE 100 organisation that has a graduate training scheme for IT roles. Further research revealed that there was an industry standard known as Skills Framework for the

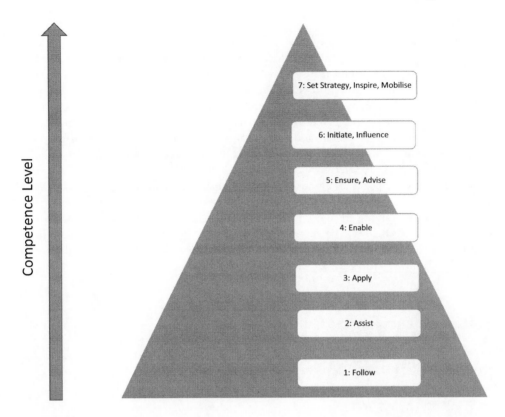

*Figure 13.5* The seven competencies of the SFIA

Source: Vanharen (2016).

Information Age (SFIA), which was created by a consortium of organisations including professional bodies, such as the BCS, and multi-nationals including IBM (Skills Framework for the Information Age, 2014). The framework provides a model for defining and managing competencies within the ICT profession beyond graduate training and spanning promotion into senior management roles. The competencies have seven stratifications ranging from 'follow' (which requires IT staff to be able to organise and follow under close supervision) to the more advanced level of seven (which requires the IT person to be able to 'set strategy, inspire and mobilise'). From level five to seven, IT professionals can apply to become a Chartered Information Technology Professional (CITP). This process can take as long as seven years and it was chosen by XYZ to improve both recruitment and retention within the bank (CITP, 2013). The SFIA programme provides a formalised structural training programming of competencies that would appeal to a LoB manager whilst at the same time providing a degree of tailoring and customisation for the IT professional as it empowers them to build their own capabilities through a 'career building map'. This dovetailed with the corporate volunteering programme run by XYZ, which allowed employees two days paid leave per annum to participate in volunteering roles. If the volunteering opportunities were IT related, it could also be recognised as part of the SFIA mapping criteria and be centrally recorded on their training record.

## Central recording

A key requirement for the solution was for the structured training programme to be centrally recorded. In the past, training was locally recorded and this did not provide a facility for comparison or curriculum management. All training carried out by LoB managers is now centrally recorded, which provides a number of benefits to the bank. For example, there is a more accurate and globally accessible view of training across its lines of business. In addition, there is improved data integrity regarding the extent of training, which makes training and development and succession planning decisions for graduates more appropriate to the needs of the business and the career aspirations of its technology graduates. Training courses are selected via an online menu platform that is user friendly and provides a readily accessible and indexed view of internal and external training, which can be either classroom-based or online, accredited or assessed. This allows technology graduates to map their training in line with the objectives of their respective LoB managers. Any training undertaken will be centrally recorded in a repository with a personal profile accessible by each graduate. An illustration of the centrally recorded and personally accessible profile is shown in Figure 13.6 below.

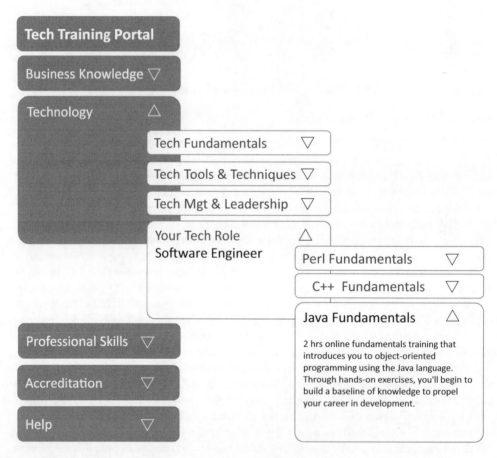

*Figure 13.6* An indicative structure of a centrally recorded database profile

## Conclusion

The project concluded in mid-2008 and was subsequently adapted by the XYZ training staff and piloted in India. Upon successful completion of the pilot project, it was rolled out in other regions throughout the world ensuring that it was tailored to the context of the chosen region. The issues addressed in this consultancy project are more important within the banking sector as the profile of the workforce is young relative to other sectors and the opportunities and challenges will be discussed in more depth in the lessons learnt and legacy section below. XYZ now has a centralised training repository and all of their UK graduates now receive membership in the BCS on completion of their training. The SFIA career mapping has not been adopted as part of the training programme. However, it is optional and aspiring technology managers can use it to manage their own training and development plans. Another benefit from this project is that the importance of the hybrid technologist has been embraced and it is now an intrinsic part of the graduate training programme within XYZ UK. The subject of talent management of Generation Y within the investment banking sector continues to be a hot topic in 2016 as practitioners such as Hall (2016) have raised it in the professional press.

## Lessons learnt and legacy

*Technology industry trends.* In 2008, the drivers for the financial services industry were apparent and clear, even if the response was not. The response to the seismic shift in regulatory requirements ensured that time, energy, effort and finances would be directed towards meeting the requirements raised by the regulators across the major European and US markets. What has also become apparent since 2008 is the ever accelerating changes in technology. The need to stay on top of changes in the technology area is even more relevant today than it was in 2008. Considering that the iPhone was only one year old in 2008, personal technology has developed at an exponential rate. In financial services, the rate of change has not been as pronounced but we are now in an age of robotics (Deloitte, 2016) and cloud computing – areas that will require a new skills set from graduate entrants. The need for consultants to be cognizant of macro-level trends is essential for any future project in financial services.

*Power of external and internal benchmarking.* In any large, corporate organization, there is a risk of looking inwards to seek solutions to challenges. The power of looking to peers in the industry or similar industries is pronounced when the challenge is as strategic as looking at how to improve talent pipelines. Benchmarking is now part of any large or mid-scale project.

*Value of targeted use consultancy support in large organisations.* Along with benchmarking, high-quality consultancy can offer greater reflection and investigation capabilities to a project in a corporate setting. Using management consultants enables new research, and project and analytical data approaches to be used and incorporated into future projects.

*Dynamic/accelerating nature of graduate needs/expectations.* In tandem with the changes in technology during the last 10 years, the expectations and needs of young people (i.e. Generation Y) has changed significantly relative to previous generations. This project highlighted those changes and ensured that the bank is fully engaging Generation Y in innovation and social learning as these are skills that Generation Y has inherent capability. Since the completion of the original project, the graduate program has scaled globally in several iterations and now provides training that firmly meets the technology needs of the firm and the needs of Generation Y learners. The technology graduate programme recruits some of the brightest and most diverse talent from across the major financial hubs in Europe, US, India and Asia.

## References

CITP (2013). Available from www.bcs.org/category/10977 [Accessed June 17, 2016].

Clurman, A. (1997). *Rocking the ages: The Yankelovich report on generational marketing*. New York: Harper Business.

Deloitte (2016). *The robots are coming*. Available from http://www2.deloitte.com/uk/en/pages/finance/articles/robots-coming-global-business-services.html [Accessed October 16, 2016].

Hall (2016). Available from http://thefinancialbrand.com/57998/winning-talent-wars-banking/ [Accessed July 21, 2016].

Handy, C. (1989). *The age of unreason*. London: Century Business.

Krueger, R. A., and Casey, M. A. (2014). *Focus groups: A practical guide for applied research*. Thousand Oaks, CA: Sage Publications.

Manville, G., and Sheil, G. (2008). Generation Y is wired up and ready for action so what is the problem. *Times Higher Education*.

Martin, C. A. (2005). From high maintenance to high productivity: What managers need to know about Generation Y. *Industrial and Commercial Training*, 37(1), 39–44.

Meredith, G. E., Schewe, C. D., and Karlovich, J. (2002). *Defining markets, defining moments: America's 7 generational cohorts, their shared experiences, and why businesses should care*. Hoboken, NJ: Wiley.

Ng, E. S., Schweitzer, L., and Lyons, S. T. (2010). New generation, great expectations: A field study of the millennial generation. *Journal of Business and Psychology*, 25(2), 281–292.

Obeng, E. (1994). *All change: The project leader as secret handbook*. London: FT Prentice Hall.

Sayers, R. (2007). The right staff from X to Y: Generational change and professional development in future academic libraries. *Library Management*, 28(8/9), 474–487.

Skills Framework for the Information Age (2014). Available from www.sfia-online.org/en [Accessed May 26, 2016].

Vanharen (2016). *SFIA in three minutes*. Available from www.vanharen.net/blog/it-management/sfia-version-6-in-3-minutes/ [Accessed June 17, 2016].

Zemke, R. (2001). Here come the millennials. *Training*, 38(7), 44–49.

# 14 Making lemonade from lemons

## The role of client-consultant knowledge as the Limoneira company goes global

*Jason Cordier*[1] *and Tahir Hameed*

## Executive summary

At the onset of the global economic crisis in 2008, the Limoneira Company was considering an aggressive international expansion as a means to realize a quantum leap in sales. Already the largest lemon producer in the United States, pursuing such a goal would require significant organizational reconfiguration. To do so, Limoneira would also need to leave the powerful citrus grower cooperative, Sunkist. Since the early 1900s, Sunkist had been responsible for almost all of Limoneira's market access, and accordingly the vast majority of its revenue. To assist with evaluating Limoneira's reconfiguration, the executive management of the lemon giant looked outward for help. MTI Consulting, a management consulting firm headquartered in Bahrain, was selected. MTI worked closely with Limoneira to assess the viability of leaving Sunkist, as well as establishing a global expansion plan from which the board of directors could weigh the risks of leaving their lifelong partner Sunkist. This case study reflects the client-consultant interactions of this consulting assignment. It focuses on the daily situated activities that constitute reality for the client and project consultants, and how frameworks for knowledge sharing emerged within this dynamic. It pays particular attention to how close, personal relationships developed over the course of the project, and how such personal interactions facilitated client and consultant knowledge pools alike. This case illustrates that social capital and strong personal skills positively influenced consultant and client learning, and accordingly an array of project outcomes.

Hilmy Cader, MTI Consulting's CEO glanced out the window across the Persian Gulf as he put down the phone. It was the summer of 2008 and he had just completed a call with Harold Edwards, the CEO and President of the Limoneira Company, a soon to be NASDAQ[2] listed corporation and the largest lemon producer in the United States. After several months of discussion he had been given formal approval to commence a significant strategic consulting project in which Limoneira wanted to ascertain if it was in a position to restructure itself to become a 365-day-a-year global lemon supplier, and if so how? At the heart of the project was a politically sensitive issue of investigating if Limoneira would be best served by remaining part of the large growers cooperative Sunkist, or depart Sunkist and conduct business independently. The cooperative boasted over 6,000 growers in California at the time, and held strong brand recognition with an extensive array of value-added licenced products such as fruit juices, as well as a globally extensive and substantial marketing capability.

Hilmy's mind turned towards the more immediate and practical matters at hand. A project of this nature required significant resource allocation. A diverse mix of internal consulting expertise would be required to address the anticipated strategic, marketing, supply chain and financial elements that a project of this nature entailed. MTI Consulting was experiencing a busy year with 35 projects occurring across the markets MTI operated. The issue with knowledge work, however, was that it involved a strong reliance on human capital. Capacity was limited, especially amongst senior consultants who had more experience in dealing with ambiguity. In Pakistan, a large government project was fully underway, and already consumed significant resources from multiple markets. Prevailing political instability meant times were uncertain. More resources would be required to deal with the inevitable scope of changes. Optimally using MTI's consultants would be essential for the Limoneira project given the tight capacity issues. This would involve using individual and collective resources from each of MTI's operations at different times throughout the project, often with individuals from different country operations working together remotely to carry out various elements of the project; all while dealing with a client in a country where MTI had no physical presence. Furthermore, the project scope required looking at Limoneira optimally operating across a great portion of the world, and accordingly entering new markets. This would entail time on the ground in markets where MTI had no presence, dealing with a product category that MTI had no previous experience with and accordingly possessing no market contacts. In short, there was considerable uncertainty as to how to approach this project.

## The consulting firm – MTI Consulting

MTI Consulting was founded in 1997 by Hilmy Cader. Starting under the name Marketing Technologies International, the consultancy quickly expanded its capabilities beyond marketing to focus on management consultancy. This expansion of scope meant that at the turn of the millennium it was referred to simply as MTI Consulting. By 2008, MTI had gone from Hilmy Cader solely operating out of his house in Bahrain, to having consulting offices in Sri Lanka, Pakistan, Bahrain, Dubai, Bangladesh and the United Kingdom. In addition to its consulting operations, MTI also had a Business Process Outsourcing (BPO) office in Bangalore, India. This dealt exclusively in finding codified explicit knowledge (Internet, databases and reports) as a means to support consulting projects through analysing critical market data.

Being competitive in the international consulting arena was no easy task with significant competition existing across markets. While MTI was regularly competing with 'Big Four' consulting firms in its respective markets, the name of the game was capabilities and reputation. Lacking the scale and scope of larger firms, MTI had to be flat, nimble and responsive.

Changing market dynamics had begun to present challenges within the management consulting industry. As *Fortune* magazine noted, the 'long running love affair between big companies and traditional management consultants ha[d] come to an abrupt end' (Warner, 2003). Information technology consulting (ITC) firms had started to enter explorative consulting spaces, putting pressure on traditional management consulting firms, while the explorative management consulting industry reacted to industry change with many firms also moving into exploitative practices that were formally dominated by ITC firms (Van den Bosch et al., 2005).

*Exploitative consulting practices* are where knowledge already exists in codified formats and template-based routines, or where domains and solutions are familiar (Van den Bosch et al., 2005). ITC activities largely draw from repetitive solutions and help firms with technology implementation and management. *Explorative practices* require moving beyond what is known to develop new knowledge (Levinthal and March, 1993; Lavie et al., 2010).

MTI positioned itself to be competitive by developing an *ambidextrous* configuration, using both *exploratory* and *exploitative* knowledge. While it operated in the domains of corporate finance, technology and market research, its bread and butter was strategic consulting, working very closely with the client. It had conducted over 400 projects across 40 countries going into 2008, having increased its exposure and capabilities by being willing to step into unchartered waters while successfully delivering value to its clients. It had a total of 40 staff internationally in the analyst and consultant categories. This relatively small number of staff, given its geographic presence, required that consultants regularly interact with each other across markets, with resources in Bahrain for example helping deliver projects in Sri Lanka.

## The client – Limoneira

Located in Ventura County, just up the coast from Los Angles, the Limoneira Company established itself in the cultivation of lemons, oranges and walnuts in 1893. The name Limoneira means 'lemon lands' in Portuguese. The company expanded rapidly heading into the 1920s, quadrupling its production. Sound management decisions meant that the company was able to weather the great depression of the 1930s. Limoneira continued to perform throughout the remainder of the 1900s to steadily increase its market share and position. By 2007, it had become a leading producer of lemons, oranges and avocados throughout the world, having also taken the position of the largest lemon producer in the United States. In addition to its agricultural interest, the company held substantive residential and commercial real estate holdings as well as water rights across its 11,000 acres. The company had most recently configured as a dedicated sustainability company and had also moved into solar farming. Figure 14.1 illustrates key events leading up to the Limoneira consulting project.

## Client's distribution network – Sunkist

Sunkist is responsible for the marketing and distribution operations of its 6,000 members (Kim, 2013) who grow and sell citrus products across 12 US states and three Canadian provinces. It was established in 1893 (Eversull, 2014) as the Southern California Fruit Exchange and changed its name to Sunkist in 1952 (Sunkist, 2016a). The cooperative emerged with the objective of diluting the risk to its members while increasing collective profitability amongst Californian citrus growers (FundingUniverse, 2016). The Sunkist cooperative grew its revenue base to just under one billion dollars a year by 2007 (Sunkist, 2012), with nearly half of its revenue coming from outside the United States (Plunkett, 2008). It stood as the largest fresh produce shipper in the US, while commanding the position of the most diversified citrus processing and marketing cooperative in the world (Sunkist, 2016c). Sunkist's well-managed brand (Kim, 2013) greatly increased its earnings through diversified value addition, having entered into licensing agreements of its trademark with a multitude of companies across the globe, including General Mills and Snapple (Sunkist, 2016b). This entailed the marketing of more than 600 citrus-flavoured products such as soft drinks and juices (Sunkist, 2016b).

Sunkist developed an extensive array of market subsidiaries and channel partners throughout the world that marketed and sold the growers' products on their behalf. The

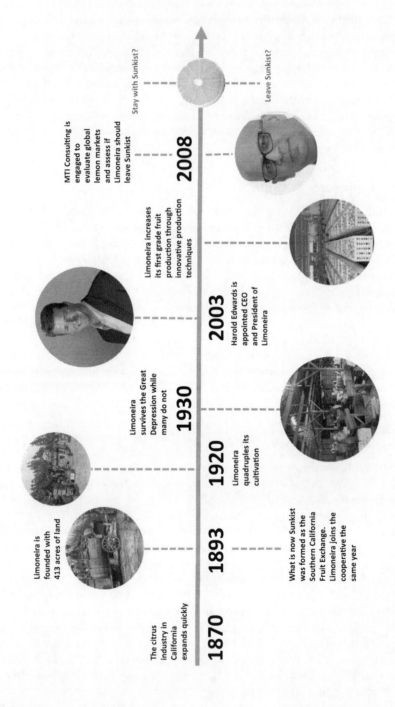

1870 — The citrus industry in California expands quickly

1893 — Limoneira is founded with 413 acres of land

What is now Sunkist was formed as the Southern California Fruit Exchange. Limoneira joins the cooperative the same year

1920 — Limoneira quadruples its cultivation

1930 — Limoneira survives the Great Depression while many do not

2003 — Harold Edwards is appointed CEO and President of Limoneira

Limoneira increases its first grade fruit production through innovative production techniques

2008 — MTI Consulting is engaged to evaluate global lemon markets and assess if Limoneira should leave Sunkist

Stay with Sunkist?

Leave Sunkist?

*Figure 14.1* Limoneira timeline

cooperative maintained four offices outside North America and 31 across the United States and Canada (Burden, 2014). For growers – particularly medium sized and small producers – these economies of scale and scope offered access to markets that would not be viable otherwise. The Sunkist brand offered:

- Recognition from buyers globally
- Access to extensive markets both within the US and internationally
- Marketing and branding expertise allowing growers to focus on the core business of cultivation.

## Sunkist-Limoneira relationship

Limoneira was a founding member of Sunkist, and recently had become its largest lemon producer. Significant parts of Sunkist's produce from Limoneira were exported to foreign markets in the Pacific Rim including Hong Kong, Taiwan, Korea, Malaysia and Singapore, with Japan always receiving premium grades of lemon (MacGregor, 1997).

Major competitors of Sunkist/Limoneira included a diversified group of countries. Due to the seasonality of lemons, demand was met alternatively between northern and southern hemisphere growers. Table 14.1 shows the major producers, within the global lemon

*Table 14.1* Major producers in the global lemon market

| Company | Country | Production | Export countries |
|---|---|---|---|
| San Miguel | Argentina | 5,000 hectares of lemon tree plantation<br>1,200 lemon pallets/day produced<br>15% of world lemon concentrate | Major clients are mostly located in the European community and Russia. The remaining production is exported to Asia, Canada and the Middle and Far East. |
| Vicente Trapani | Argentina | 150,000 tons of lemons produced each year<br>2,100 hectares of lemon trees | USA, Canada, Germany, Switzerland, the United Kingdom, France, Denmark, Japan and Israel. |
| Paramount Citrus | USA | Farm approximately 30,000 acres of Navel oranges, lemons, Valencia oranges, Clementine mandarins, and other citrus varieties throughout California | Paramount Citrus is a member of California and Arizona Lemon Growers Association (CALGA) and California Citrus Growers Association (CCGA). |
| Sierra Foods | Mexico | Lemon groves span over 7,100 acres<br>Production is estimated to be in excess of 2 million cartons. | United States, Europe, Japan and Hong Kong under the Sierra Citrus brand. |
| Capespan | South Africa | Data not available to author | Data not available to author |
| Cal Citrus | USA | 4,000 hectares of Citrus<br>2.5 million cartons of fresh Citrus | Data not available to author |
| Aksun | Turkey | Data not available to author | Export to Europe and Russia |
| A.L.G. Estates, Citrusdal | South Africa | Data not available to author | USA, EU, Middle East, Japan, Russia and Southern Africa. |

Source: Dutt (2008b).

*Table 14.2* Major associations and cooperatives in the citrus market

| Association/Cooperatives | Country | Members | Export countries |
| --- | --- | --- | --- |
| Sunkist | USA | • 6,000 members and a billion dollar association | China, Japan, Hong Kong and Korean markets |
| Corona-College Heights Orange and Lemon Association | USA | • Represents about 14% of the California lemon market | Far East and North America |
| Saticoy Lemon Association (affiliated with Sunkist Growers) | USA | • 12,000 plus acres of lemons<br>• 11 million cartons of lemons a year marketed through Sunkist | China, Japan, Hong Kong and Korean markets |
| Guimarra | USA | • Growers from California, Chile and New Zealand<br>• Lisbon and Eureka lemon varieties with 365-day supply | Global |
| Australian Citrus Growers (ACG) | Australia | • Nine grower organizations<br>• Three State Statutory Citrus Authorities, which in turn represent approximately 2,500 commercial citrus growers. | USA, Hong Kong and Malaysia |
| Aneecop | Spain | • Represents 98 co-operatives located in Spain | Europe |
| Jaffa | Israel | • Israeli exports of citrus fruit are sold under the recognized 'Jaffa' trade name, which helps to promote the sales of Israeli fruit overseas | Europe, Russia and North America |

Source: Dutt (2008a).

market, while Table 14.2 shows other associations and cooperatives operating throughout the world in the citrus market.

## Analysis of US and global lemon/citrus markets

The global market size for lemons was around 6.9 million metric tons (MT) in 2007. Top producers included Argentina, Spain, Turkey, Chile and the United States. Western European countries were the largest consumers and importers of lemons followed by Russia and Japan. The United States held a solid position in medium-sized markets like Japan and Canada, while Spain, Turkey and Argentina were key suppliers to the EU markets where Sunkist had little presence. Around 2007, another group of importers emerged from the Ukraine, Saudi Arabia, China and Serbia, which looked to offer significant market potential (see Figure 14.2).

The United States (US) produced around 637,800 metric tons (MT) of fresh lemon, with around 116,000 MT exported globally. The remainder was consumed by the US domestic market with an additional 35,000 MT of special varieties of lemon imported into the US from Mexico, Brazil and Argentina.

Lemons are sold in cartons, and branded lemons like Sunkist command a premium price for their superior quality. Japanese customers were willing to pay a premium for the best quality lemons while countries like Russia, Korea and the Middle East were

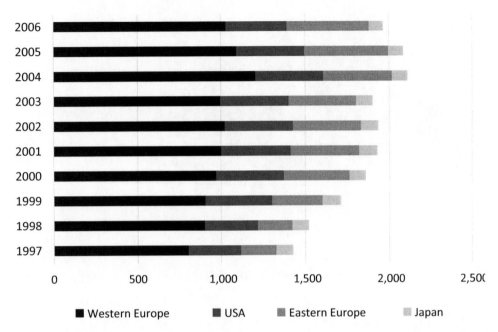

*Figure 14.2* Global fresh lemon consumption

Source: Adapted from Imbert (2008).

also willing to pay some form of premium. While Limoneira had established significant product recognition across Asian markets, a number of substitute products – most notably limes – had begun to emerge in large volumes across world markets. This particularly created difficulties for lemon producers wishing to access emerging markets where considerable growth opportunities had emerged for other premium and mid-tier agriculture and non-agricultural goods.

Importers, distributors, wholesalers, retailers/suppliers and before end-users constitute the lemon supply chain (Figure 14.5). The three consumer segments in the lemon industry are: industrial users, hotels, restaurants and institutional (HRI) customers and home users. Lower grade lemons go to industrial usage, while almost 70% of high-quality lemon consumption were channelled through the chef's table (HRI category), and the remaining 30% of direct sales went to home users via retailers.

## Challenge for Limoneira

When Harold Edwards was appointed CEO and President of Limoneira in 2003, he brought back Alex Teague who shared a long history with Limoneira. Alex had worked there before, and his great grandfather, C.C. Teague, was the first General Manager of Limoneira over a century before. With Alex moving to Senior Vice President, the two swiftly worked towards developing new and innovative approaches to the conservative agricultural sector by creating a performance-based business that cared for its employees.

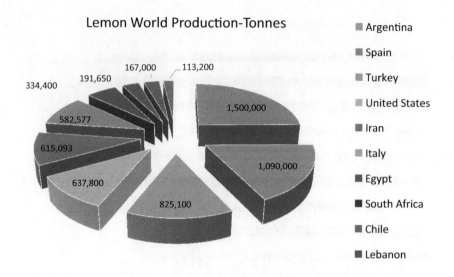

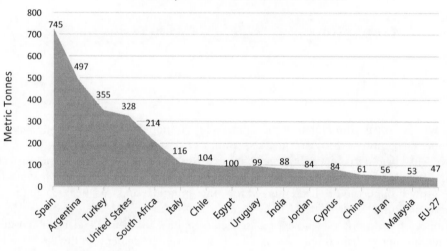

*Figure 14.3* World lemon production and exports in 2007

Source: Adapted from Imbert (2008).

Alex noted that this focused around cultural issues. They addressed the top-heavy structure of the company by downsizing 29 management and supervisory positions without
any lawsuits, and 'over a three-year period we went and we took what was deemed an
entitlement process by the hourly employees – meaning they pretty much dictated what
went on – and we changed to a performance-based incentives model.'

Subsequently, over the course of the next five years Limoneira developed a lean and
closely knit team as well as an exceedingly efficient production operation that resulted
in high-quality fruit that became sought after both nationally and internationally. For

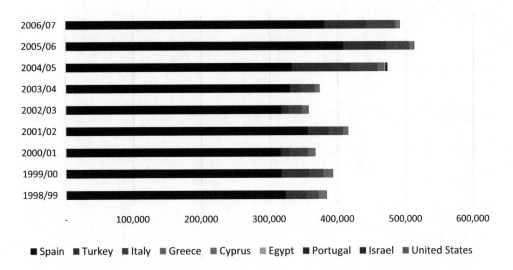

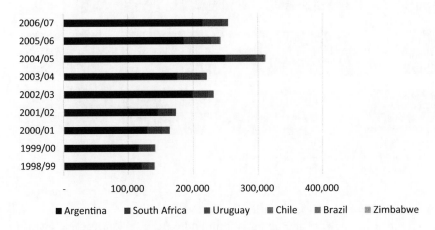

*Figure 14.4* Seasonal (winter and summer) lemon supplies to EU-27

Source: Adapted from Imbert (2008).

instance, Japanese buyers had developed a strong preference for Limoneira's products and recognized Limoneira lemons as superior. The four Japanese importers that controlled the Japanese market would offer access to Limoneira products through a ratio system. Buyers would be rewarded with Limoneira products on their purchase volumes as a whole.

At this point, Harold and Alex started to look at the future direction of the lemon industry and began to see their relationship with Sunkist as a double-edged sword. In one respect, Sunkist offered stability. The marketing cooperative's channel access was extensive, and their relationship with Sunkist meant Limoneira could focus on the business

*Table 14.3* Lemon substitute products overview

| Alternate product | Market Size | Producing Countries | Usage |
|---|---|---|---|
| Lime | ~ 6,000–7,000 mt/year | Mexico, India, China, Brazil | Cooking, beverages, perfumes, cleaning products, and aromatherapy |
| Lemongrass | 1,300 mt/year (2006) | India, China, Brazil, Africa and smaller countries like Thailand and Vietnam | Cooking, herbal teas, and baked goods. Oil from lemon grass for fragrance in perfumes and cosmetics |
| Lemon Balm | | Europe, Asia and Africa | Most of the production goes into processing (lemon balm essential oil is very popular in aromatherapy) |
| Lemon Myrtle | | Australia | Most of the production goes into processing (oil is a popular ingredient in health care and cleaning products) |

Source: Dutt and Krishna (2008).

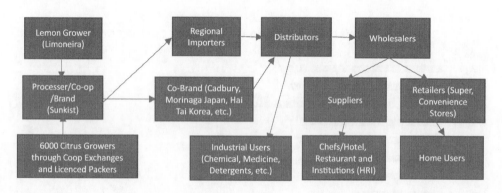

*Figure 14.5* Sunkist and Limoneira's lemon supply chain

of growing lemons – something it knew a lot about. However, this position came with an opportunity cost of having the sales potential limited by the cooperatives framework, which restrained Limoneira's future growth prospects. Being a California-based grower's cooperative, it became politically untenable to have a 365-day supply chain – something that would be a strong strategic advantage – as this would require producing fruit in locations outside of North America – something the cooperative could not accept. The global lemon market was largely commodity driven, resulting in prices being determined mostly from a supply perspective. The more lemons produced in a season from the industry as a whole, the lower the price on the commodity markets, while the fewer lemons grown, the greater the price (MailOnline, 2008). The way the cooperative worked, resulted in the number of fresh fruit lemons that could be sold by Limoneira being limited by a quota system, even if their fruit quality exceeded other growers, or if buyers specifically requested more of Limoneira's product. For an organization like Limoneira that had developed significant dynamic capabilities around efficiency and quality, the Sunkist system, to a large degree, levelled the playing field and stripped the advantages gained from Limoneira's capabilities of producing higher volumes of quality first grade fruit. Alex explains:

> A supply side controlled group [Sunkist] was taking a piece of the pie and dividing it up; and in a cooperative you have to be 'fair.' Here you are saying a person who puts out a poor quality [lemon] box – both in terms of aesthetic quality and holding quality – are going to get the same percentage share as us; that is not an incentive! That discouraged us and other large quality players . . . essentially, the Sunkist system only teaches the class up to the level of the lowest level kid in the class.

The preference for Limoneira's fruit by domestic and international buyers – such as the case in Japan – started to signal to Limoneira's management team that perhaps they could go it alone and expand market share from competency sets unique to Limoneira that other growers did not have. However, while Limoneira held an excellent base of knowledge regarding the dynamics of producing lemons, it knew little about accessing alternative channels outside of where its fruit was currently sold, the value of these channels and what markets and product categories to optimally position itself towards. Essentially, for all Limoneira's strengths, it had not been required to address external environment issues – the 'business as usual' activities that most business deal with daily. Rather, the Sunkist system resulted in Limoneira focusing on production and lemon growing, with its dynamic capabilities centred squarely on production. In essence, all Limoneira's distribution, marketing and sales had been conducted by Sunkist for almost a century, which did not require Limoneira to learn or develop capabilities for such functions. Yet, Limoneira's strategic intent was to make a quantum leap in its production and sales from its current production level of 1.5 million cartons to 12.5 million cartons. Such a global expansion would require:

- A rationale for Limoneira's strategic intent to expand globally
- Confirmation that by leaving Sunkist there would be increased profitability, not just increased market share without profitability
- A board of directors go-no-go decision on leaving Sunkist
- A comprehensive strategic plan that provided a detailed road map, clearly directing strategies into executable steps related to marketing, sales and distribution on a global scale
- Employees culturally shifting to a global mindset.

Alex Teague remarks on what Limoneira sought from MTI Consulting:

> For us, as we spoke and we could all agree, from a general knowledge position across all the growing areas and sectors in lemons, from timing, from the intricacies of the industry, we were very knowledgeable. However, when you make a strategic move to have third-party verification on the strategy is essential, not only to check your own ego – which is always a good thing to do – but also politically with your ownership and your board of directors. It is very worthwhile to verify and critique the plan as you are always missing something.

## MTI's approach

The extensive number of markets involved in the project, the nature of the project, and limited codified market data availability brought complexity to the project. Historical factors, such as the way MTI had conducted previous projects and MTI's relationship with Limoneira's CEO Harold Edwards – extending back to the days when Harold worked at Agribrands, running their offices in the Philippines – resulted in a strong desire and need for both Limoneira and MTI to draw knowledge from one another. This was enabled through a very strong consultant–client relationship where MTI was granted deep access from the top of the organization. This was further facilitated by the consultants and the clients warming to each other quickly at a personal level. Alex discusses the importance of the project from Limoneira's perspective:

> You give two people a good [drink] and they will learn a lot . . . MTI is trying to get information, human nature for us is to hold back. By the same token, when MTI is telling us something, we could be thinking 'yeah, but what are they really missing?' [A strong personal relationship] that is social breaks down those unwritten rules.

From experience, Hilmy Cader from MTI had come to believe that the most successful projects were ones that were highly integrated between the client and the consultant. This factored into the approach MTI used on this project and the consultants MTI deployed. A strong relationship with the client leverages the client's knowledge, which can be viewed as a critical success factor of consulting projects in general, but particularly so in larger international strategic projects where unknown variables can compound quickly. Hilmy notes that:

> There can be a belief that consultants are fountains of knowledge that ride in and magically have intelligence that the client does not. . . . We resist the urge to imply we know more than the client in their domain as a means to justify our value and fee, as we don't. They know their business! We deliver our value by working side by side with the client.

An MTI consultant discusses the Limoneira project specifically:

> There is always this nagging thought in the back of your mind that you are going to ask a stupid question, and this is going to impact the way the client views you . . . with Limoneira, however, there was no such problem. We were partners in a great adventure and we all had a part to play. No ego existed on either side of the fence and we all drew from each other's knowledge sets in social and formal settings.

## Business intelligence and knowledge management in consulting projects

The business intelligence (BI) collected in a consulting project includes knowledge about professional know-how or product and market characteristics. It also includes managerial know-how regarding the management practices of the business, and tactical and strategic responses to markets and competitors. However, such knowledge or BI can be categorized to be either explicit or tacit. Explicit knowledge refers to the coded knowledge easily accessible in the form of documents, images, recordings, emails, etc., by the consultant or client from past projects or operations. Tacit knowledge on the other hand represents the expertise and understanding that consultants or clients have, but this exists in one's head and may not have been documented. Both explicit and tacit knowledge bases do not only

Table 14.4 A simple view of knowledge management activities in management consulting projects

| | Explicit to Tacit INTERNALIZATION | Explicit to Explicit COMBINATION | Tacit to Explicit EXTERNALIZATION | Tacit to Tacit SOCIALIZATION |
|---|---|---|---|---|
| INTERNAL KNOWLEDGE BASES – Knowledge available within consultant-client organization (Needs exploitation) | • Contract<br>• Project scope<br>• Project plan<br>• Consultant's knowledge from similar past projects<br>• Client's knowledge from past projects and operations | • Knowledge about:<br>  Client's product<br>  Client's partners<br>  Client's customers<br>  Client's competitors<br>• Consultant's partners in similar industries<br>• Client's knowledge from past projects | • Client's managerial know-how and relationships through: interviews, focus groups and workshops<br>• Consultant's professional and managerial know-how through: trainings and workshops | • Consultant's team interactions<br>• Consultant-Client project team meetings |
| EXTERNAL KNOWLEDGE BASES – Knowledge available in supply chain, industry associations, regulators and other consultants (Needs exploration) | • Key competitors/ markets analysis<br>• Industry scan<br>• Trends: industry, technology, global/social | • Industry research reports<br>• Data from industry associations<br>• Desk research | • Business/ Innovation opportunities<br>• Business solutions/ strategic options in the project context | • Interactions with industry players to explore information embedded in supply chains and organizations, e.g. hedonic value, hidden costs, social networks, trusted channels |

Source: Based on Nonaka (1994) and Nonaka and Takeuchi (1995).

exist inside an organization but also outside the consultant-client nexus. Industry data and research reports are good examples of external explicit knowledge, while good examples of tacit knowledge embedded in organizations and supply chains would be hedonic value, business culture, social networks and trusted channels or connections.

Based on the explicit and tacit knowledge dimension, Nonaka (1994) organized knowledge management activities and interactions into the following four categories commonly known as the SECI model of knowledge management:

1   Socialization. Tacit to Tacit, e.g. transfer of know-how between individuals, interviews, information about relationships
2   Externalization. Tacit to Explicit, e.g. articulating known or new observations, writing a process
3   Combination. Explicit to Explicit, e.g. aggregating data from reports, desk research
4   Internalization. Explicit to Tacit, e.g. making sense of aggregated data, review and assessments, strategic recommendations.

Nonaka (1994) explained how organizations learn by managing the above knowledge activities iteratively over time. While externalization, combination and internalization activities are already adopted by organizations, he argued further that socialization is relatively less understood despite it being an important source of new knowledge creation, innovation and competitiveness. Morris and Empson (1998) emphasized that the appropriation of different types of knowledge – particularly tacit knowledge created by employees when facing client or market problems – could be critical for professional service firm's (PSF) innovativeness. Knowledge codification, as it is called, mainly involves activities that access and convert people's experiences and techniques into ideas for new revenue streams, standardized group procedures or organizational norms. Although the objectives of management consulting projects are slightly different from operations, and idiosyncratic between themselves, they also draw partly on existing knowledge bases – internal or external – and partly on new knowledge (Hislop, 2003).

While, consultants confront not only the challenges of exploring and exploiting different types of internal and external knowledge bases, they should also choose apt knowledge management strategies that enable them to create valuable solutions for the client's current project while learning for their own future projects. Therefore, it is imperative that consultant teams need the ability to recognize and adapt knowledge management activities (typically Nonaka's (1994) SECI and knowledge codification or personalization activities) to balance between various knowledge needs of their own organization and the client's (Sturdy et al., 2008).

## MTI's consulting project plan and implementation

The project required the following knowledge-based activities to occur.

*   Searching, collecting, analysing and synthesizing explicit and tacit knowledge available within the consultant's own team, client, client's partners, customers, competitors, and industry and global supply chain
*   Focusing only on that information that supports the project objectives.

MTI used their in-house eight-step strategic planning process called '8S PlanScape' for the Limoneira project (Figure 14.6). It rests on established business theories and industry

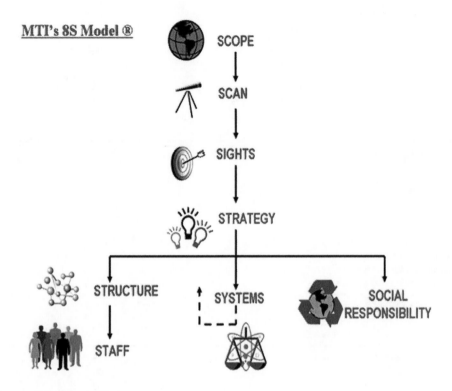

*Figure 14.6* MTI Consulting project model

experience with practices made up of external and internal environment scanning, forecasting, planning, organizational design, control systems and social responsibilities.

For the project, each of the PlanScape tasks were then broken down into sub-tasks and mapped onto nucleus modules. The nucleus is another proprietary scoping tool developed by MTI that helps their project teams identify specific elements of knowledge (sometimes also referred to as business intelligence in the management discipline) for the task or project. It also identifies the sources of business intelligence (BI) and how they could be acquired. In sum, the nucleus's role is to help the project team define the BI activity, gather a sense of the required knowledge management technique (i.e. explorative or exploitative) and develop methods and strategies to acquire the BI. Such strategies could be: interviews (INT), desk research (DR), field visits (FV), expert opinion (EO), secondary research (SR), focus group discussions (FGD), observations (OBS) and/or client workshops (CW). These focus around capturing both explicit and tacit knowledge to leverage exploitative and explorative pathways. Accordingly, the BI required by each nucleus could be captured by disparate methods; for example interviews, focus group discussions (FGD), observations (OBS) and consultants' previous experience (EXP). Table 14.5 illustrates an example taken from the MTI–Limoneira project that shows how the nucleus is broken down at the broader levels of planning. Here, the deliverable being sought (DIVs) to a first-tier project question is listed with the intelligence gathering methods outlined in support of this.

As the nucleus moves down into more specific subunits, broader questions are replaced with more detailed project questions, and these are also accompanied by the likely method

*Table 14.5* MTI project nucleus

| Nucleus 3: DIVs & SOIs | | |
|---|---|---|
| *Sub-Module* | *DIVs* | *Source of Intelligence (PS/CS/PR/DR/SR/EO/LC/CW)* |
| SCOPE | 1.1 PRODUCT OVERVIEW What are the types of fresh lemon yellow (FLY) produced? | DR >PR, CW |

Source: Cordier et al. (2008a).

*Table 14.6* Primary research conducted on the client

| Nucleus 4.3b – Primary Research Client | | | | | |
|---|---|---|---|---|---|
| *λ Module: (List down all the Modules, irrespective of whether there is a DIV or NOT)* | *λ DIV – # Question* | *λ Method λ (INT/FGD / OBS/EXP)* | *λ If INT:F2F/ Location, TEL or EMAIL* | *λ Respondent* | *λ Specification* |
| • **3.1 STRATEGY** | • What are the strategies adopted? | • INT | • TEL>F2F | | |

Source: Cordier et al. (2008b).

of intelligence gathering. As the nucleus is only a project plan, it often evolves considerably as phases of the project are implemented. While knowledge is not static, a solid basis that outlines what needs to be asked is required at the planning stages of a project. Outlining BI methods acts as a foundation to allocate resources, identify areas where knowledge exists and map out where knowledge does not exist.

Table 14.6 offers an overview of a primary research module of the project where explicit knowledge was deemed unlikely to yield the knowledge sought at this subunit of knowledge gathering. Accordingly, interviews (INT), using both telephone (TEL) and face-to-face (F2F) methods, have been identified as suitable. In the case of MTI Consulting and many other consulting firms, such plans often work on lean documentation that attempts to remove unnecessary text from internal documents.

## Project key success factors

The nature of the knowledge sought and utilized in the project is discussed in Table 14.7. This is additional to seeking operational business intelligence, which is an ongoing part of routine activities.

What was of considerable significance for this project was not only the value created by varied forms of BI, but how they resulted in strategy formulation, and particularly the creation of new knowledge. The matrix of BI was employed to deliver a business solution that the client not only bought into, but held a strong role in the developmental process and the final solution.

The exploration of knowledge for MTI was first based on client domain knowledge. The acknowledgement that MTI were not lemon specialists, had not worked in the lemon

*Table 14.7* Summary of project

| Project Planning Facts | |
|---|---|
| **Project characteristics** | Nature of the project was a strategic plan for building a global brand and underlying global distribution and marketing networks |
| **Deliverables** | • Extensive PowerPoint presentation<br>• Board presentation<br>• Implementation plan |
| **Project consultants** | • Five Consultants<br>• Three nationalities (New Zealand, Sri Lanka and Bangladesh)<br>• Five markets |
| **Analysts** | • Four rotating analysts (India, Sri Lanka and Bahrain) |
| **Project duration** | Five months |
| **Time with client** | 14 days |
| **Activities with client** | Workshops, formal interviews, site visits |
| **Market visits** | EU Countries, USA, trade show visit |
| **Availability of external explicit BI** | Low |
| **Access to client tacit knowledge** | Extremely high |
| **Access to client explicit knowledge** | Extremely high |
| **Lead generation through client** | High |
| **Top management buy-in** | Extremely high |
| **Middle management buy-in** | Extremely high |
| **Employee buy-in** | Extremely high |
| **Need for consultant to be seen as legitimate** | Low. Up front and honest discourse placed the consultants in a position where their value was clearly articulated, with consultants not being seen as domain specialists. |
| **Success of knowledge sharing between consultants** | Moderate. Multiple markets and different consultants assigned to differing deliverables made connecting the dots difficult, especially with considerable ambiguity surrounding market situations |

market or even citrus market before, acted as a pillar for inquiry – although they had worked in the agricultural sector before. This explicit and open position helped form the dynamics that would follow. On the consultant's part, not having to justify their history with lemons meant they approached seeking knowledge openly and freely, acknowledging they needed to learn the lemon business from the client before they could offer value. MTI often used the concept of a 'clean slate,' where consultants would initially resist the urge to draw from previous experiences to develop a solution. Rather, listening and learning dominated the initial stages of the project, essentially working on the principle that prior experiences and knowledge on the consultants' part can act as baggage that inhibits or constrains thought.

Strong client executive management support enabled the consultants to successfully employ a 'clean slate' approach to the project. Through Limoneira's CEO and Senior Vice President communicating this position across the organization, coupled with knowledge sharing being considerably enhanced by interpersonal dynamics based on strong social connections, the consultants were able to quickly undertake explorative knowledge practices.

Limoneira's performance culture also strongly supported learning and explorative knowledge positioning, in which a senior executive of Limoneira credit 75% of this culture to Harold Edwards's leadership approach when becoming the CEO, and the other 25% to the legacy of how Limoneira had operated in an open and inclusive manner. An MTI consultant on the project comments on knowledge sharing and learning:

> We knew almost nothing about lemons . . . we leveraged Limoneira's good relationships to [develop] open forums . . . from here we applied our cross-market learnings and we came up with a means to address the complexity. None of this could be done without the client's interaction and their knowledge.

While MTI itself faced knowledge transference issues with its project team working across multiple markets, a strong and supportive culture within MTI resulted in any knowledge that needed to be shared being done so. The firm's culture challenged its consultants never to think of themselves as experts on a position, as that inhibits looking at new and different avenues. If the firm were to be configured purely towards an exploitative structure, this culture may have in fact been detrimental to project profitability and success. In such instances where you are looking to reproduce what is already known, not drastically challenging knowledge is beneficial. To do so decreases efficiencies such as requiring time spent trying to develop new thought when a perfectly satisfactory solution or knowledge set exists already that needs little modification.

## May 2010

MTI Consulting's CEO Hilmy Cader woke up early as usual and started to scan the news. An article entitled "Limoneira to sever its Sunkist ties" (Hoops, 2010) immediately jumped out. The article talked about how Limoneira's CEO, Harold Edwards, had rang the opening bell of the NASDAQ as Limoneira listed on the exchange while also announcing that it would be leaving Sunkist as of November that year. The market would react favourably over the coming days with a 19% increase in the value of Limoneira's shares. As he had done those years before, Hilmy leaned backed and cast his eyes towards the Persian Gulf. He reflected on the project recommendations in which it had been agreed that a quantum leap in sales was untenable within the Sunkist system. War gaming, market analysis and channel strategies had been presented to the executive management and board. The board – while largely excited about growth prospects beyond a Sunkist relationship – had been uneasy about leaving the cooperative given the business climate created by the global financial crisis. The executive management, however, having worked very closely with MTI, were more bullish in their position. The final MTI-client solution that was presented to the board shared the position of the executive management. Arguably, MTI's status as outsiders, coupled with the client's strong industry knowledge, made the initial unease of leaving Sunkist more palatable to the board of directors. A close partnership between Limoneira executives and consultants – in which areas of strategic concern had been worked through and challenged from differing positions – resulted in a strong yet balanced position being presented to the board.

Two years on, Limoneira's project implementation was now complete and clearly successful. Yet, Hilmy could not help but think how this project could have been different if he did not have a strong relationship with Harold, or if the team he had picked had not been able to develop strong social ties with the client? If Limoneira's culture was not open, and rather had individuals who treated knowledge as a resource of power, how would his team have dealt with that? How would his consultants have accessed core tacit information existing within the client's mind had their relationship not been strong? Would it have been even possible for MTI to have undertaken the project given the complexities and explorative knowledge setting this project entailed? Finally, he could not help but wonder if the recommendation would have been different had the process of accessing knowledge had also been different?

## Notes

1  The first author was one of MTI Consulting's senior consultants assigned to the Limoneira project.
2  Limoneira common stock started trading on the NASDAQ Global market on May 27, 2010.

## References

Burden, D. (2014). *Aquaculture cooperative established and management guide.* Ames, IA: Agriculture Marketing Research Center. Available from www.agmrc.org/media/cms/aquaculturecooperativemanagement_6701B325513F1.pdf [Accessed May 21, 2016].

Cordier, J., Dean, S., Krishna, N., Dutt, P., and Reddy, S. (2008a). *Nucleus 3: DIVs & SOIs* [Unpublished internal report]. Sri Lanka: MTI Consulting [Accessed March 2, 2016].

Cordier, J., Dean, S., Krishna, N., Dutt, P., and Reddy, S. (2008b). *Nucleus 4.3b – primary research client* [Unpublished internal report]. Sri Lanka: MTI Consulting. [Accessed March 5, 2016].

Dutt, P. (2008a). *Major associations and cooperatives in the citrus market* [Unpublished internal report]. India: MTI Consulting.

Dutt, P. (2008b). *Major producers in the global lemon market* [Unpublished internal report]. India: MTI Consulting.

Dutt, P., and Krishna, N. (2008). *Market for world lemons* [Unpublished internal report]. India: MTI Consulting.

Eversull, E. E. (2014). The long run. *Rural Cooperatives*, 81, 18.

FundingUniverse. (2016). *Sunkist Growers Inc. history* [Online]. Available from www.fundinguniverse.com/company-histories/sunkist-growers-inc-history/ [Accessed June 14, 2016].

Hislop, D. (2003). Knowledge integration processes and the appropriation of innovations. *European Journal of Innovation Management*, 6, 159–172.

Hoops, S. (2010). Limoneira to sever its Sunkist ties. *Venture County Star*, August 3. Available from www.vcstar.com/business/limoneira-to-sever-its-sunkist-ties-ep-368044408-348556711.html [Accessed June 4, 2016].

Imbert, E. (2008). Close-up. In D. Loeillet and E. Imbert (eds.), *Fruitrop*. Montpellier, France: French Agricultural Research Centre for International Development.

Kim, J.-Y. (2013). Development of the agricultural cooperatives for revitalization of the rural community-focusing on the case study of 'Sunkist'. *International Journal of Smart Home*, 7, 293–300.

Lavie, D., Stettner, U., and Tushman, M. L. (2010). Exploration and exploitation within and across organizations. *The Academy of Management Annals*, 4, 109–155.

Levinthal, D. A., and March, J. G. (1993). The myopia of learning. *Strategic Management Journal*, 14, 95–112.

MacGregor, H. (1997). No 'Lemons' allowed: The pick of Ventura county's crop satisfies Japanese taste for flawless citrus. *Los Angeles Times*. Available from http://articles.latimes.com/1997-01-06/news/mn-15893_1_ventura-county [Accessed April 15, 2016].

MailOnline. (2008). Lemons shortage will leave the UK feeling bitter. *MailOnline*, June 10. Available from www.dailymail.co.uk/news/article-1025486/Lemons-shortage-leave-UK-feeling-bitter.html [Accessed May 4, 2016].

Morris, T., and Empson, L. (1998). Organisation and expertise: An exploration of knowledge bases and the management of accounting and consulting firms. *Accounting, Organizations and Society*, 23, 609–624.

Nonaka, I. (1994). A dynamic theory of organizational knowledge creation. *Organization Science*, 5, 14–37.

Nonaka, I., and Takeuchi, H. (1995). *The knowledge-creating company: How Japanese companies create the dynamics of innovation*. Oxford: Oxford University Press.

Plunkett, J. W. (2008). *Plunkett's Food Industry Almanac 2007: Food industries market research, statistics, trends & leading companies*. Houston, TX: Plunkett Research, Ltd.

Sturdy, A., Handley, K., Clark, T., and Fincham, R. (2008). Rethinking the role of management consultants as disseminators of business knowledge: Knowledge flows, directions, and conditions in consulting projects. In H. Scarbrough (ed.), *The evolution of business knowledge*. Oxford: Oxford University Press.

Sunkist. (2012). Sunkist passes 118-year mark riding very strong. *Western Farm Press*, p. 8. Available from http://ezproxy.massey.ac.nz/login?url=http://search.ebscohost.com/login.aspx?direct=true&db=bth&AN=74444288&site=eds-live&scope=site.

Sunkist. (2016a). *About us* [Online]. Available from www.sunkist.com/about-us/#cooperative-history [Accessed June 25, 2016].

Sunkist. (2016b). *Licensed products* [Online]. Available from www.sunkist.com/licensed-products/?doing_wp_cron=1466833412.9649150371551513671875 [Accessed June 23, 2016].

Sunkist. (2016c). *Sunkist quality* [Online]. Available from http://ca.sunkist.com/tabid/350/Default.aspx [Accessed June 25, 2016].

Van den Bosch, F. A., Baaij, M. G., and Volberda, H. W. (2005). How knowledge accumulation has changed strategy consulting: Strategic options for established strategy consulting firms. *Strategic Change*, 14, 25–34.

Warner, M. (2003). The incredible shrinking consultant to survive, the big three strategy firms – McKinsey, Bain, and BCG – need to make big changes. *Fortune Magazine*. Available from http://archive.fortune.com/magazines/fortune/fortune_archive/2003/05/26/343083/index.htm [Accessed June 23, 2016].

# 15 Case study

## Public sector management consulting in Sub-Saharan Africa

*Elizabeth Kariuki*

## Executive summary

In Sub-Saharan Africa, the demand for management consulting services is unique as management skills are in short supply and governments continually strive to develop their countries through the pursuit of constant change. In the more politically stable countries, public sector management issues in the main revolve around poor governance. Such countries therefore seek consultants' support in five broad areas: policy and strategy; public financial management; human resource management; modernisation of the public administration; and management and evaluation of programmes, projects and reform initiatives.

The immediate priorities in countries coming out of conflict are different. An imperative is for post-conflict governments to establish the foundations for an efficient and effective public service to frame and implement economic and fiscal policies and to deliver services. Building capacity in the public service is an area in which consultants can provide the needed technical expertise. In addition, consultants provide backstopping support in areas such as fiscal management, accounting and audit services, project delivery and management, and monitoring and evaluation.

Suppliers of public sector consulting services mostly secure assignments through a competitive bidding process. Suppliers are categorised into four main groups: dedicated public sector management consulting firms; development and policy research institutes of leading think tanks and western universities; local policy research institutes; and local boutique consulting firms and individuals.

Public sector management consulting in a low-income and post-conflict country setting can be rewarding. The results can make a significant difference. However, in order to take consultant-supported reform initiatives forward, it is necessary to: align national political agendas with reforms; promote skills transfer; ensure that civil servants are adequately paid and incentivised; mobilise more domestic revenue; and curb unethical and corrupt practices.

## Demand for public sector management consulting services in Sub-Saharan Africa

The public sector in virtually every country has some demand for management consulting services. Indeed, even in developed countries, whenever a major programme for changes in organisation, management and systems arise, the need for the governments and other state organs to seek external consulting services has been inescapable.

The public sectors of Sub-Saharan Africa (SSA) have a unique demand for management consulting services for two main reasons. First, comparatively, there is a dearth of management skills in the region's public sector organisations. Second, given its current state of underdevelopment, the pursuit of change is constant in the public sector. In other words, over the past several decades, the demand for management consulting services has been comparatively high in SSA.

However, even with the SSA region, there is variance in both the demand and nature of public sector management consulting among countries. The region consists of around 50 countries. Some of these countries – particularly, Botswana, Ghana, Malawi, South Africa, Tanzania and Zambia – have enjoyed relatively stable political environments since independence. In contrast, countries such as Burundi, the Central African Republic, Ivory Coast, Liberia, South Sudan and Somalia have experienced violent conflicts.

In the more politically stable countries, public sector management issues in the main revolve around poor governance. The five most common issues have to do with: (1) the rule of law; (2) a bureaucratic regulatory environment that hampers the growth and vibrancy of the private sector; (3) rampant corruption (Mbaku, 2010); (4) limited voice by and accountability to non-state actors; and (5) government ineffectiveness. Enhancing the quality of life of disadvantaged and vulnerable groups by financing initiatives in social services and infrastructure is an imperative in SSA countries, many of which are low income – thus explaining why government effectiveness has received a great deal of attention in recent years. Against this backdrop, this case study will focus on typical consultancy assignments aimed at improving government effectiveness.

Countries coming out of conflict are confronted with both the challenge of securing resources for development as well as legitimacy. Governments have the huge task of reconstructing their nations' infrastructure and political and social systems. This feat is particularly problematic given that their civil services and public administration systems no longer, or barely, function. Moreover, in post-conflict environments the public resources needed to finance reconstruction are in short supply. Therefore, a recurring trend is for the governments of post-conflict countries to collaboratively prioritise medium- and long-term reconstruction needs, and secure funding from international development partners. As capacity to administer funding and projects is weak, governments and international development partners engage consultants primarily to support implementation and build capacity in the public service.

## Consulting for relatively stable governments

Most SSA countries falling within this relatively stable category are still developing and classified as low or lower-middle income. Revenue from tax collections is insufficient to meet public expenditure needs, which results in high fiscal deficits and/or a reliance on external funding from international development partners. The key challenges, therefore, have to do with raising domestic revenue, and delivering services more efficiently and effectively by instituting a variety of reforms.

In the context of the above, the five broad areas in which stable governments in SSA commonly seek consultants' support in strengthening government effectiveness are: policy and strategy; public financial management (PFM); human resource management (HRM); modernisation of the public administration; and management and evaluation of programmes, projects and reform initiatives. With respect to strategy, governments do contract consultants to facilitate internal and external stakeholders in the development of long-term (20–30 years) national development visions, which subsequently feed into medium-term (5 years) national development plans (NDPs); fiscal strategies; sector strategies; and ministry, department or agency (MDA) strategic plans that are costed and incorporated into Medium Term Expenditure Frameworks (MTEFs) and annual budgets.

The framework in Figure 15.1 displays the characteristics of causal logic where given certain necessary external conditions; at the top of the hierarchy, the national development vision and NDP outcomes result from achieving MDA strategic objectives (intermediate outcomes), and MDA strategic objectives are achieved through the production of programme outputs by undertaking prescribed activities that are costed in annual budgets at the bottom of the hierarchy. In other words, the figure seeks to illustrate that inputs specify resources expended against a budget, but say nothing about results. Outputs are indicators of workload (implementing specified activities), but they do not explain the quality or impact or the work that is done. Outcomes focus on results – the impact or the quality of the intervention.

In order to measure progress towards the achievement of results, key performance indicators are assigned to each outcome, intermediate outcome and output. So, for example,

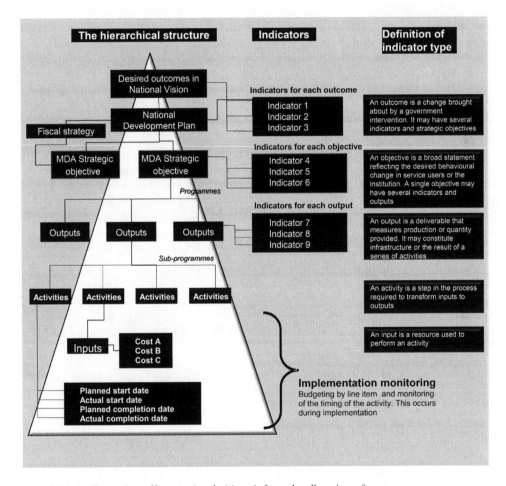

*Figure 15.1* An illustration of how national visions inform the allocation of resources

progress towards achieving a national outcome to increase literacy in education, would use an indicator such as primary school enrolment rate. An increased enrolment rate is likely to be dependent on building and equipping new schools as well as recruiting more teachers, all of which require resources.

In Tanzania, for example, since 2005, the government has been implementing the National Strategy for Growth and Reduction of Poverty (NSGRP), which is underpinned by Development Vision 2025. The vision outlines the country's long-term targets for poverty eradication, human development, good governance and stability. A main feature of NSGRP is that it has an outcome orientation (goals) which fall under three clusters: (1) growth and reduction of income poverty; (2) improvement of quality of life and social well-being; and (3) governance and accountability.

PFM spans a wide range of components which ideally aim to ensure that objectives contained in the fiscal strategy are met. A government's fiscal strategy specifies plans for managing finances and achieving vital socio-economic objectives defined in the NDP by setting clear targets for the level of taxation, public expenditure and public debt. A fiscal strategy informs planning and budgeting in MDAs – in other words, the preparation of strategic plans and MTEFs/budgets.

The MTEF/budget provides for consultants to advise MDAs during implementation of revenue enhancing measures, and initiatives aimed at cost reduction and realising efficiencies. This includes, for example, guiding revenue collection agencies on ways to increase the level of tax and non-tax revenue collected. This was the case for a study commissioned by the African Tax Administrative Forum in 2013. The consultants' recommended measures are illustrated in Table 15.1. The five stages indicated in the table represent a sequence of steps to be implemented over a 15-year period, starting with getting the basics right, and progressing until the point where a revenue administration has attained world class status.

It is noteworthy that the table above includes both HRM and modernisation initiatives, which often require inputs from consultants. Other HRM interventions not specified above include organisation design and staff appraisal. With respect to modernisation, many public sector organisations are taking advantage of ICT to realise efficiencies in administration and improve service offerings. For example: an integrated financial management information system aims to enhance the efficiency and effectiveness of government budget and accounting processes; an integrated human resource management information system enables MDAs to interact with their employees; and electronic services provided on the World Wide Web seek to increase access to services at affordable costs.

On the expenditure side, improving controls over the payroll and strengthening procurement practices are priorities as both of these elements take up almost all of the expenditure budget. The problem of ghost and duplicate workers, and errors on the payroll, can be pervasive. As a consequence, governments hire consultants to undertake physical verification exercises in which civil servants must appear at a prescribed venue with supporting documentation such as letters of appointment/promotion, payroll slips and national identification cards. Unauthenticated civil servants are removed from the payroll. Such exercises can be bolstered by initiatives such as audits of the payroll using computer assisted audit techniques.

Procurement is strategically important to public sector organisations. MDAs procure medium-value items, such as equipment, to high-value and complex works such as rehabilitation of trunk roads. Goods, works and services need to be procured when needed and also be of the right quality, be cost effective and be available in the most economic

*Table 15.1* Summary of measures to improve tax administration over the long-term

| Stage | Examples of measures |
|---|---|
| 1 Get the basics right | • Qualified staff recruited into the approved establishment<br>• Tax education programme designed and launched<br>• A medium-term strategic plan developed<br>• Taxpayers segmented<br>• Taxpayer database developed |
| 2 Attain an enabling socio-political institutional environment[1] | • Staff capacity built through learning and education<br>• Adequate staff compensation system in place<br>• Taxpayers' views solicited and internalised<br>• A website to inform and educate the public about the tax administration's plans and achievements, tax laws and so forth launched |
| 3 Design and implement comprehensive reforms | • A comprehensive culture change programme developed and launched<br>• Proposals developed which contribute to comprehensive and harmonised tax policies and legislative framework<br>• Medium-term strategic plan revamped<br>• A compliance programme designed and launched<br>• An Information, Communication and Technology (ICT) strategy developed |
| 4 Modernise the tax system | • Culture change programme consolidated<br>• Innovations made to service and enforcement functions<br>• ICT infrastructure enhanced |
| 5 Attain and sustain world class status | • Strong contacts with taxpayers maintained<br>• Medium-term strategic plan revamped<br>• Continuous innovations introduced to realise improvements in service access and quality |

Source: Kariuki (2013).

quantities. To this end, governments hire consultants to assist in strengthening its procurement arrangements. Consulting services include, but are not limited to: the review of the regulatory framework, development of procurement plans, delivery of training to civil servants on procurement and contract management and procurement audits.

Reporting is a vital tool for accountability. However, many governments in SSA do not prepare reports on a timely basis and/or are not compliant with international standards. In this respect, governments are working with consultants to meet the basic standard issued by the International Public Sector Accounting Standards Board. The aim is for governments to prepare financial statements and disclosures in formats that are consistent, and facilitate informed evaluations of decisions made with respect to resource allocation.

It is also common for governments and international development partners to engage consultants to undertake independent evaluations of their operations. In the area of PFM, the Public Expenditure and Financial Accountability (PEFA) Review and Tax Administration Diagnostic Assessment Tool (TADAT), are two universal evaluation tools developed by the World Bank and the International Monetary Fund, respectively. On the one hand, PEFA uses evidence to assess indicators falling under seven pillars of PFM performance: (1) budget reliability; (2) transparency of public finances; (3) management of assets and liabilities; (4) policy-based fiscal strategy and budgeting; (5) predictability and control of budget execution; (6) accounting and reporting; and (7) external scrutiny and audit.[2] Figure 15.2 summarises the results of PEFA reviews in Kenya.

In 2006 the government of Kenya (GoK) was subject to a PEFA. Areas in which GoK performed poorly evolved around: (1) the credibility of the budget (score C for 'aggregate revenue/expenditure outturn compared to original approved budget'); (2) comprehensiveness and transparency (score D+ for 'extent of unreported government operations'); (3) budget cycle (score D+ for 'effectiveness in the collection of tax payments' and 'effectiveness of payroll controls'); (4) accounting, recording and reporting (score D+ for 'quality and timeliness of annual reports'); (5) external scrutiny and audit (score D+ for all three indicators falling under this dimension); and (6) donor practices (score D for all three indicators included in this dimension).

In the context of the above, from 2006, GoK launched a strategy to revitalise PFM and thereby promote efficiency and effectiveness in public service and enhance service delivery. The strategy was implemented through the Public Financial Management Reform Programme (PFMRP), which received funding from GoK and development partners through a joint pooling arrangement. A PFMR Coordinating Unit (PFMR-CU) had responsibility for the coordination and monitoring of the programme.

A subsequent PEFA undertaken in 2009, reported considerable improvements particularly with respect to: (1) the credibility of the budget (score A for 'aggregate revenue outturn compared to the original approved budget'); (2) budget cycle (score B for 'effectiveness of measures for taxpayer registration and assessment'); and (3) external scrutiny and audit (score C+ for 'scope, nature and follow-up of external audit').

The third PEFA of 2012 reported that, in general, GoK's performance remained unchanged. However, there were some exceptions. For instance, the government's scores improved in some dimensions including: the budget cycle (orderliness and participation in the annual budget process – from C+ to B); internal controls (effectiveness of payroll controls – from C+ to B+); and external scrutiny and audit (legislative scrutiny of external audit reports – from D+ to C+). In contrast, PFM is assessed to have deteriorated in some respects such as: budget credibility (stock and monitoring of expenditure payment arrears – from B to C+); and budget cycle (timeliness and regularity of accounts reconciliation – from C+ to D).

*Figure 15.2* PEFA in Kenya

Source: European Union (2009, 2012).

On the other hand, TADAT focuses on assessing a country's tax administration systems, processes, and institutions. Each evaluation is evidence based, and assesses performance using a set of indicators linked to nine performance outcome areas: (1) integrity of the registered taxpayer base; (2) management of risks to the tax system; (3) support given to taxpayers to help them comply; (4) on-time filing of tax returns; (5) on-time payment of taxes; (6) accuracy of information reported in tax returns; (7) adequacy of dispute resolution processes; (8) efficiency and effectiveness of operations; and (9) accountability and transparency.[3]

Evaluations are also carried out at a programme, project and reform initiative level, usually halfway during implementation or soon after completion. A mid-term evaluation reviews implementation progress and bottlenecks, and recommends corrective actions to ensure that a programme, project and reform initiative achieves its intended results within the timeframe set for completion. An end-term evaluation: verifies and assesses the implementation results; identifies lessons learnt and successes for replication; recommends design modifications; and proposes measures needed to consolidate and sustain achievements.

## Consulting in a post-conflict environment

The array of consulting assignments described thus far, are also pertinent for post-conflict country governments. However, many of them, such as supporting the development of long-term plans, MTEFs and electronic services, are only likely to be pursued in the medium to long-term. There are normally three immediate priorities in a post-conflict environment. First, to restore security in the country:

> There may be different degrees of security in different parts of the country. This may limit geographic reach of [programmes] and policies during the immediate post-conflict period. It is important to increase steadily the degree and scope of security, not only through policing and the visible presence of armed authorities, but also through political and economic means.
>
> (USAID, 2009)

Second, rebuilding the economy by restoring macro-economic and fiscal stability (as a means of reducing inflation, stabilising the exchange rate and reducing the fiscal deficit through raising domestic revenues), delivering social services and spurring private sector growth are fundamentals. To these ends, an imperative is for post-conflict governments to establish the foundations for an efficient and effective public service, to frame and implement economic and fiscal policies and to deliver services. Establishing a public service entails: revising legislative and regulatory frameworks for new institutions and in areas such as economic and financial management, procurement and audit; setting up new institutions; building capacity in MDAs through induction and refresher training, and retooling; enhancing information management through use of email and the establishment of basic systems; and improving capacity to communicate within the public service and with external parties. These are largely areas in which consultants can provide the needed technical expertise.

Third, in tandem, during the period that the public service is being rebuilt, a post-conflict country can expect increased flows of aid for reconstruction. Yet its capacity to absorb these resources is limited. Therefore, it is common for governments and international development partners to adopt, as an interim measure, alternative modalities (e.g. trust funds, programmes, projects) for channelling funding, which are outside the government system. Trust funds, programmes and projects hire consultants to provide backstopping support in areas such as fiscal management, accounting and audit services in accordance with international standards, project delivery and management, and monitoring and evaluation.

Coordination of external assistance from international development partners, promotes collaboration through sharing of funding modalities (common mechanisms for disbursing and managing financial resources – e.g. pooling), systems (such as joint arrangements for procurement, accounting and reporting outside government systems) and information (for example through periodic meetings of a donor forum). It is key to ensuring that aid in the form of financial, technical and in-kind (humanitarian) assistance meets country priorities, is sequenced, not duplicated and can be sustained. Pooling of funds helps to reduce transaction costs by applying common institutional, administrative and financial management arrangements. An example of a country that used pooling is South Sudan.

The effects of the civil war in Sudan caused devastation. Apart from an 11-year period from 1972–1983, Sudan was at war continuously since it gained independence in 1956. In 2005, South and North Sudan signed a comprehensive peace agreement committing to a permanent ceasefire and to implement the peace deal. Following a joint assessment of needs by government and international development partners, a multi-donor trust fund (MDTF) was set up to finance capacity building, institutional development, the delivery of basic services, private sector development and building of infrastructure (see Figure 15.3). In July 2011, South Sudan became a republic.[4]

Between 11 and 12 April 2005, in Oslo, donor nations came together to welcome peace in Sudan through pledges for reconstruction. As a result of weak capacity, a multi-donor trust fund (MDTF) was selected as the preferred aid instrument for this post-conflict environment in which the donors pooled their financial contributions. The overall implementation period of the MDTF was eight years (2005–2013), during which time a total of US $712 million was spent on 21 projects. International development partners and government financed 75% and 25% of this total, respectively.

Responsibility for accounting, procurement and auditing was contracted to international firms, under a Core Fiduciary Systems Support project funded by the MDTF. With respect to accounting, a Project Financial Management Unit (supported by KPMG), was set up within the government treasury to prepare bank reconciliations and reports. The procurement adviser from Crown Agents supported the government by drafting a procurement bill, preparing procurement plans and delivering training on institutionalising public procurement. The audit firm assisted the newly established National Audit Chamber to build audit capacity. It also audited MDTF projects and the government's annual accounts.

The MDTF contracted a Monitoring Agent (PwC) to: document procedures in an operations manual; assess financial management capacity of potential grant/sub-grant recipients and support the closing of any gaps identified; monitor the procurement of goods, works and services; screen and recommend for approval fund disbursement applications; monitor expenditures out of the MDTF; and report progress. Consultants were also hired to develop a medium-term framework for capacity building and to support functional reviews within government. Furthermore, the MDTF hired consultants to provide technical expertise in fields such as civil engineering, education, health and sanitation.

When the MDTF was closed, a consultant (Fafo) was hired to undertake an independent final evaluation to assess its performance and propose future development interventions. The consultants' overall assessment was positive – in particular, the portfolio of projects delivered the intended results, especially those to do with capacity building. However, they did flag concerns about the sustainability of outcomes.

*Figure 15.3* South Sudan's reconstruction and development arrangements

Sources: Fafo (2013) and World Bank (2013).

## Suppliers of public sector management consulting services

Suppliers of public sector consulting services mostly secure assignments through a competitive bidding process, and therefore a substantial amount of effort goes into putting together high-quality submissions. The process normally entails consultants expressing interest in a procurement notice issued to the media and/or posted on the World Wide Web by an MDA/international development partner. The MDA/international development partner shortlists consultants on the basis of the strongest expressions of interest, and issues them with a request for proposal (RFP). The RFP contains the information needed by consultants to prepare technical and financial proposals – such as evaluation criteria (see Table 15.2), Terms of Reference, submission date and any templates to be used. The MDA/international development partner evaluates proposals usually on the basis of quality and cost, and thereafter contracts the preferred bidder.

There are four major groups of suppliers of public sector management consulting services. The first group are dedicated public sector management consulting firms – including the big four accountancy firms,[5] who typically provide some of the PFM, HRM and ICT services described earlier. India-based firms, such as Tata Consulting Services, have created a niche in the delivery of ICT systems across SSA governments, particularly in revenue administrations that are pursuing a service transformation agenda.

*Table 15.2* Indicative evaluation criteria for the selection of consultants

| Criterion | Percentage points |
| --- | --- |
| Consultant's specific experience | 0 to 10 |
| Methodology | 20 to 50 |
| Key experts | 30 to 60 |
| Transfer of knowledge | 0 to 10 |
| Participation by national experts | 0 to 10 |
| Total | 100 |

Source: The World Bank (2011).

It is also noteworthy that in a number of countries in the region, programme and fund management has become an important service offering especially for the locally based offices of the big four accountancy firms. In addition to pooled funds mentioned earlier, there are special funds targeted at strengthening civil society (such as the media) and/ or providing access to finance to businesses that plan to introduce innovations like the Africa Enterprise Challenge Fund, which receives funding from the International Fund for Agricultural Development and the governments of Austria, Denmark, the Netherlands, Sweden and the United Kingdom.[6] This work entails a wide range of administrative responsibilities, from appraising applicants, making funding recommendations and monitoring and reporting on implementation and advocacy.

The second group of suppliers are development and policy research institutes of leading think tanks and western universities. The Overseas Development Institute (ODI) is one well known supplier in this area. One of ODI's flagship projects is the Budget Strengthening Initiative, which seeks 'to build more effective, transparent and accountable budget systems' in countries such as the Democratic Republic of Congo, Liberia and South Sudan (ODI, 2015). ODI also seconds fellows to SSA governments to fill any capacity gaps in disciplines such as planning, economics and statistics. Examples of other well known institutions providing services include the University of Sussex's Institute of Development Studies and the Brookings Institution in the United States.

The third group of suppliers include local policy research institutes. Some are funded by their country's governments (such as the Kenya Institute for Public Policy Research and Analysis (KIPPRA)), and others funded directly or indirectly by development partners (e.g. Research on Poverty Alleviation in Tanzania). Such institutions also focus on a handful of areas. For instance, KIPPRA's research programmes centre on: macroeconomics; productive sector; social sector; infrastructure and economic services; private sector development; trade and foreign policy; and governance.

The fourth group consists of local boutique consulting firms and individuals. This group of suppliers provide a range of services including policy analysis, strategic planning, PFM and capacity building. Some of these firms are owned and run by previous employees of the big four firms. Both firms and individuals in this group commonly partner with the other groups described above on particular consulting assignments.

## Common challenges in taking consultant-supported reform initiatives forward

Public sector management consulting in a low-income and post-conflict country setting can be rewarding. The results can make a significant difference – particularly initiatives that lead to expanded access to services, the delivery of critical infrastructure, strengthened human capacity, PFM systems and so forth. However, consulting in such environments does present some challenges, which mean that even the best consultants' deliverables (report recommendations, the introduction of new ICT enabled systems and skills transfer through formal and on the job training) are not carried forward, and/or the most qualified consultants are not selected and/or there is resistance or even hostility to the consultants' presence. Some common challenges are expounded here, although note that while ameliorating measures are largely internally driven, it is important for consultants to be aware of them and, where possible, cater for them.

First, lessons of experience abound that the state of national politics determines the feasibility of policies and strategies for change. If democratisation in a developing country is not well managed, it can result in political tensions that are inimical to consistent implementation of reforms. In other words, continued commitment to sustaining and, where necessary, expanding reforms by a country's present and future political leadership is vital. This commitment is probably best secured by promoting clarity of vision among all the country's leaders, and aligning reform targets and implementation strategies to the vision and ambitions of the political leadership.

Second, severe skills gaps in the public service and private sector of many SSA countries as a whole have significantly hampered the pace and effectiveness of the implementation of reform initiatives. Programme management and coordination is one area where the dearth of capacity is most obvious and pervasive. In addition, limited strategic, PFM, HRM and technology skills continue to considerably constrain the roll out of policy changes, modifications to strategy based on lessons of experience and new human resource management and financial management information systems. Whilst this problem is alleviated through the hire of consultants, initiatives cannot be sustained without effective skills transfer and retention of public servants. With respect to retention, the challenge is for governments to formulate and implement policies that adequately pay and incentivise public servants.

Third, SSA governments are severely resource constrained. Given this constraint, in the absence of concerted efforts to raise domestic revenues, there is a risk that allocations made to reform initiatives remain low. Where international development partners finance reforms, there are also the dangers of low local ownership and commitment to the reform agenda, and/or leaders being sceptical and dismissive of the reforms as a foreign agenda.

Fourth, corrupt and unethical practices in all forms have serious repercussions, and contribute to misprocurement, loss of public resources from theft and wastage, delayed service provision and poor quality services. According to Transparency International's 2015 Corruption Index, with the exception of Botswana (ranked the 28th most corrupt country out of 167 countries), 27 SSA countries were low scorers ranking in the bottom 100s.[7] The challenge is for SSA governments to take a more visible action against unethical and corrupt practices, and raise awareness of rights among stakeholders/general public.

## Concluding remarks

This case study sought to illustrate the variety of public sector management consulting assignments in demand in both relatively stable and post-conflict SSA countries. It also contrasts the two settings: stable countries with a long-term development agenda, and the range of consulting services required vis-à-vis post-conflict countries with the immediate need to reconstruct the public service and at the same time quickly restore basic services and infrastructure.

The case study also acknowledges that consultants can make a real contribution to development, but their work is often undertaken within a country context that is turbulent. Specifically, results can be undermined by a country's political leadership, capacity constraints, corruption and financial resources. The challenge for SSA countries is to mitigate the associated risks by aligning political agendas with reforms, skills transfer, putting in place adequate incentives and pay, increasing domestic revenue collections and taking visible action against unethical and corrupt practices. Consultants can be more effective in delivering services by taking into account these issues as they provide their services.

## Notes

1  Both social and political factors are taken into account. In this case, political leaders would be expected to support an efficient and effective tax system. Furthermore, the tax administration would promote voluntary compliance by simplifying the tax system.
2  PEFA. (n.d.) The PEFA Framework. Online. Available from https://pefa.org/content/pefa-framework [Accessed on 30 June 2016].
3  www.tadat.org [Accessed on 30 June 2016].
4  In 2011, the people of South Sudan voted to secede from the Republic of Sudan.
5  The big four are PwC, Deloitte, Ernst & Young and KPMG.
6  Africa Enterprise Challenge Fund. (n.d.) Online. Available from www.aecfafrica.org [Accessed 23 July 2016].
7  Transparency International. (n.d.) Online. Available from www.transparency.org/cpi2015 [Accessed 1 July 2016].

## References

European Union (2009). *PEFA public financial management performance assessment report for Kenya.* A project implemented by LINPICO009, March 25. Project No. 9 FED.
European Union (2012). *PEFA public expenditure and financial accountability assessment.* A project implemented by Ace and Ecorys. August 8. EU Framework contract Project No. 2011/281098/1 and GIZ contract No. 81142463 Project No. 10.2038.7-001.00.
Fafo (2013). *Independent evaluation of the multi-donor trust fund – South Sudan (MDTF-SS).* Oslo: Fafo Institute for Applied International Studies.
Kariuki, E. (2013) *Building Blocks of a Modern African Tax Administration.* Pretoria: African Tax Administration Forum.
Mbaku, J. M. (2010). Corruption in Africa: Causes, consequences, and cleanups. Plymouth: Lexington Books.
ODI (2015). *Annual report 2014–2015.* London: Overseas Development Institute.
USAID (2009). *A guide to economic growth in post-conflict countries.* Washington, DC: United States Agency for International Development.
The World Bank (2011). *Guidelines: Selection and employment of consultants under IBRD loans and IDA credits & grants by World Bank borrowers.* Washington, DC: The International Bank for Reconstruction and Development / The World Bank.
The World Bank (2013). *Implementation completion and results report on grants in the amount of US$ 16.4 million to government of South Sudan for core fiduciary systems support project.* Washington, DC: The World Bank.

# 16 Indigeneity and management consulting in Aotearoa New Zealand

*Jason Paul Mika*

## Executive summary

This chapter is about what it means to be an indigenous management consultant and practice management consulting from an indigenous perspective within Aotearoa New Zealand. The chapter draws on the experience of Māori management consultants as self-employed contractors, owner-operators of management consulting firms and as management consultants in 'mainstream' firms. The chapter focuses on the role of culture and identity in management consulting for indigenous management consultants and discusses implications of this for non-indigenous management consultants. The chapter concludes with case studies of how Māori management consultants are assisting Māori enterprises with transformative organisational and economic developments in a post-treaty settlement environment.

## Of indigenous peoples and their economies

Like most real world phenomena, there are two sides to every story, and the story of indigenous peoples is a case in point. On the one hand, the narrative speaks of the desperate plight of some 370 million indigenous peoples worldwide, recovering from 500 years of Western colonisation, subjugation, exploitation and expropriation of indigenous lands, language, culture and economies (Battiste and Henderson, 2000; Smith, 1999). On the other hand, the narrative speaks of renewed hope on the back of internationally recognised indigenous human rights, self-determination and self-governance, language and cultural revitalisation and economic self-sufficiency within tribal (collective) and nontribal (individual) enterprises (Cornell and Kalt, 1993; Foley, 2004; Henry, 2007; Spiller, 2010). This dichotomy of circumstance and perspective reflects the archetypal battle between strengths ('glass half full') versus deficit ('glass half empty') thinking routinely applied to analyses of indigenous problems (Ford and Grantham, 2003; Ford et al., 2002; Winiata, 1998). Undoubtedly, the comparatively dire circumstances and ongoing struggle for recognition within one's own state characterises life for many indigenous folk around the world. Yet, even among them, indigenous organisations and enterprises are emerging as constructive change agents and emancipatory entrepreneurs and exemplars, both social and economic (Collins et al., 2014; Foley, 2007; Henry, 2012; Hindle and Moroz, 2009; Seton, 1999).

Indigenous social disadvantage and indigenous economic advantage are providing impetus for indigenous and non-indigenous organisations to actively intervene with social and economic policy and institutions designed to improve both indigenous peoples' lives and livelihoods. It is this activity within indigenous and non-indigenous organisations that has given rise to the indigenous management consultant and marks out a large part of their market. There are, thus, two sides to the market for indigenous management consulting expertise. The first is helping indigenous organisations to realise their aspirations for self-determination and to be effective in delivering services to their own and other people. And the second is aiding non-indigenous (mainstream) organisations to be responsive to indigenous peoples in ways that make a difference to indigenous peoples' lives.

The present case relates to Aotearoa ('land of the long white cloud'), which is the Māori name for New Zealand, referred to hereafter as Aotearoa New Zealand (King, 2003). As a country, Aotearoa New Zealand is relatively small, comprising some 271,000 square kilometres. We are a little larger in land size than the United Kingdom, but with far fewer people – 4,711,824 to be precise, according to the country's official 'population clock' as at 2 September 2016 (Statistics New Zealand, 2005, 2016b). With our nearest neighbours being Australia (about a three-hour flight west across the Tasman Sea) and the Pacific Islands of Tonga, Samoa and Fiji (another three-hour or so flight northward), Aotearoa New Zealand is variously regarded as an Australasian, South Pacific or Oceanic country, as allegiances vary depending on whether one is talking football, politics or economics.

Aotearoa New Zealand comprises two main islands, conveniently named the North Island (*Te Ika-a-Māui*, the fish of Māui) and the South Island (*Te Waipounamu*, the waters of greenstone) (LINZ, 2013). Aotearoa New Zealand has existed as a parliamentary democracy since 1854, but operated under British rule from the signing of the Treaty of Waitangi in 1840 (King, 2003; Orange, 1987). While parts of the Pacific were settled by the great Polynesian seafarers around 3,000 years ago (Crocombe, 2008; R. Smith, 2008), Aotearoa New Zealand, has a much more recent human history, with the early ancestors of the New Zealand Māori arriving sometime around 1350 AD; though traditional accounts suggest an earlier discovery by *Kupe* around 925 AD (Best, 1996; Buck, 1987; King, 2003; Walker, 2004). Prior to Captain Cook's arrival in Aotearoa New Zealand, in 1769, the Māori people had lived undisturbed by outside European influence for around 400 years, notwithstanding an earlier skirmish between the Dutch explorer Able Janszoon Tasman and local Māori in December, 1642 (Mika and O'Sullivan, 2014; Wilson, 2016).

Today, 712,300 people identify as Māori (around 15 percent of New Zealand's total resident population) (Statistics New Zealand, 2016a). Māori identity is closely tied to tribal affiliation, of which there are at least 116 distinct *iwi* (tribes) and many more *hapū* (subtribes) (Statistics New Zealand, 2013a, 2013b). In terms of culture and identity, 125,352 Māori (21.3 percent) can converse in *te reo* Māori (the Māori language) about everyday things (Statistics New Zealand, 2013b). Moreover, Māori are a relatively youthful population, with the median age being 23.9 years, compared with 41.0 years for *Pākehā* (New Zealanders of European descent) (Statistics New Zealand, 2013b, 2013c). The vast majority of Māori (86 percent) live in the North Island, with 23.8 percent of all Māori living in the Auckland region (Statistics New Zealand, 2013b).

## On the indigenous management consultant

Mainstream public and private sector organisations have significant contact with Māori in Aotearoa New Zealand as customers, employees and increasingly as business partners, suppliers and investors. An important distinction is that public sector organisations have a constitutional and legal duty to recognise Māori as *tangata whenua* (indigenous people), with such obligations flowing from the Treaty of Waitangi of 1840 signed by Māori tribal chiefs and representatives of the British Crown (Hancock and Grover, 2001; Walker, 2004). Public sector organisations are, therefore, obliged to provide for Māori cultural preferences, use of the Māori language, active support for Māori development and to involve Māori in the design and delivery of policies that affect them (Mika, 2003). While regarded as a founding document of Aotearoa New Zealand, treaty-based protections have historically been denied by successive governments with disasterous consequences for Māori (Walker, 2004). Treaty settlements for past breaches of the Crown obligations to Māori are, however, helping restore, to the extent possible, some semblance of what was lost (J. Gardiner, 2010; Harmsworth, 2009; Office of Treaty Settlements, 2002).

Responsiveness to Māori within mainstream organisations presents scope for indigenous management consultants to be involved for two main reasons: first, because of improving goodwill toward Māori under the treaty; and second, because of nonpartisan political disdain for persistent policy failures in respect of Māori. Given that government activity accounts for around 40 percent (NZ$96 billion) of Aotearoa New Zealand's Gross Domestic Product (GDP) (NZ$240 billion in 2015), the public sector represents a substantial market for indigenous and non-indigenous management consultants alike (Statistics New Zealand, 2015). With renewed recognition of the treaty and indigenous rights, public sector organisations appear to be changing how they engage with Māori and deliver on Māori outcomes (Office of the Auditor General, 1998). Constant vigilance is, however, required as the treaty is not affixed as an immovable instrument of our constitutional arrangements. As such, treaty cognizance tends to wax and wane within mainstream consciousness, sometimes directed by divisive political rhetoric or uncomfortable revelations of past prejudice (Brash, 2004; Burrows et al., 2013; Tuckey, 2016).

Indigenous management consultants are sought after for their advice, capability and services in helping mainstream public sector organisations to be responsive to the needs, priorities and aspirations of Māori people as *tangata whenua*, as clients of public services, and as citizens of Aotearoa New Zealand. Indigenous management consultants may be called on to provide advice on departmental strategy, public policy, programme design, delivery, and evaluation or as representatives on governmental committees (Henare et al., 1991; Māori Economic Taskforce, 2010). They may be engaged to facilitate governmental consultation with Māori on policies and reforms that may affect Māori, including highly controversial policies (W. Gardiner, 1996). They may be sought after because of their *mana* (standing) among Māori and Pākehā or because of their industry or sector position, or both (Mika, 2016a).

The private sector, which accounts for the other 60 percent of the nation's economy (GDP of NZ$144 billion in 2015), represents an even larger market for management consultants than the public sector. One of the differences is that the private sector has no corresponding obligation to Māori under the treaty or indigenous rights. Instead, Māori may be viewed as consumers, employees, producers and suppliers who are uniformly subject to the same legal, moral and practical obligations that enterprises owe to people of any culture and ethnicity. Any imperative for responsiveness toward Māori in the private sector has, hitherto, been on the basis that diversity and cultural empathy are good for business, despite these being relatively novel management theories (Crane et al., 2008; Spiller et al., 2006). One might contend that goodwill toward Māori in the private sector is significant because Māori happen to constitute a sizeable portion of the local populace (for example, Māori make up 50 percent of the Gisborne population) or workforce (where, for example, 53 percent of Māori are employed in manufacturing) (Parker, 2000; Statistics New Zealand, 2014). History shows, however, that goodwill toward Māori is easily vaporised amidst economic decline, as Māori predominate in labouring jobs, which are usually among the first to go as industries and enterprises shed labour in order to survive (Dalziel, 1991; Te Puni Kōkiri, 1999).

A discernible development is that the private sector is rethinking its view of Māori as a more favourable section of the economy in which to invest (Dickson, 2010; Sapere Research Group, 2011; Solomon, 2010). Again, treaty settlements are likely to have much to do with this change of heart. While often controversial and a comparatively minor part of the Māori economy (comprising around one percent of the NZ$42 billion Māori asset base), treaty settlements are nonetheless increasingly accepted by the public as important for social cohesion, peace and security – things we here in Aotearoa New Zealand may take too easily for granted, but not so those who live in more unsettled zones (Nana, 2013; Te Puni Kōkiri, 2012). Yet, it is the financial redress of treaty settlements that is likely to be garnering much of the private sector zeal in the Māori economy given that most treaty settlements consist mainly of cash.

Financial institutions have become particularly responsive to Māori. Competition for 'Māori money' seems to be driving this as Māori banking units, Māori banking managers, Māori financial products and services and commentaries on the Māori economy have all become positively 'mainstream' among our trading banks (ANZ, 2015; Dickson, 2010; Mika, 2010; New Zealand Council for Sustainable Development and Westpac New Zealand, 2005; Norman, 2016). A reappraisal of the Māori market provides scope for indigenous management consultants to work with mainstream private sector institutions, like the banks, to better engage with Māori, and to improve Māori participation and outcomes in commerce, entrepreneurship and innovation.

Whether in the private or public sector, the work of indigenous management consultants is premised upon the notion that they possess unique knowledge, skills and attributes that non-indigenous management consultants may not. Moreover, the indigenous management consultant is likely to operate intuitively and explicitly from an indigenous world view. That is to say, a world view derived from being raised as Māori, socialised within, connected to and accepted by social, cultural and economic institutions of *te ao* Māori (Māori society) (Mika, 2015; Rangihau, 1992). In plain terms, one's world view conditions one's beliefs about what constitutes what is possible, reality and socially acceptable behaviour, helping one understand one's own ways and those of other people's (Heidegger and Grene, 1976; Sumner, 1959).

A traditional Māori world view is metaphysical, founded upon Māori cosmology, the essence of which is the union and separation of *Rangi* (sky-father) and *Papatūānuku* (earth-mother) and seeing humanity as descendants of these celestial beings (Harmsworth and Awatere, 2013; Henry and Pene, 2001; Marsden, 1992; Mika et al., 2016; Reedy, 2003; Royal, 2005). One of the important lessons from the Māori world view is that all things are interconnected, the human, natural and spiritual worlds. Achieving a sustainable existence with this view in mind requires one to understand one's place in this order of things. In pragmatic terms, Māori cosmology manifests in core beliefs, values and principles that shape Māori culture, including Māori organisational and enterprise culture; indicative of a Māori way of doing business (Durie, 2011; Knox, 2005; Mika, 2014, 2015; Mika et al., 2016; Tinirau and Gillies, 2010; Winiata, 2012; Yates, 2009).

When such a unique combination of attributes is matched with professional training, business acumen and technical ability, the indigenous management consultant's advantage is asserted through bicultural potency and bilingual proficiency (Mika et al., 2003; Scott and Guy, 2004). In this guise, an indigenous perspective is not an 'add-on' or a 'value-add,' it is an intrinsic component of the indigenous management consultant's being and core offering, evidenced by a propensity to operate with equal fluidity in the Māori and Pākehā worlds of commerce (Barber, 1993; Ernst and Young, 2014; Gibson, 2015a, 2015b, 2016; Hanita et al., 2016; Mika, 2016b).

## On the practice of indigenous management consulting

Two aspects of indigenous management consulting are discussed as case studies of practice within the context of Māori organisations: organisational development and enterprise development. In terms of Māori organisational development, strategy, structure and change, there are three common services for which indigenous management consultants are engaged to help. An immediate thought of the uninitiated person is: What could be so different about Māori organisations that might warrant an indigenous approach to strategy, structure and change? The retort has to do with understanding what a Māori organisation is and how differently one might manage within one. According to Mika and O'Sullivan (2014: 655), a Māori organisation is one 'where the identity, values and ownership of an organisation are predominantly Māori, and whose activities produce benefits for the organisation's members and others.' Moreover, they suggest that Māori organisations approach managerial activities like strategy, structure and change 'from a cultural lens peculiar to them, informed by cultural imperatives, stakeholder expectations, resource availability, and their [organisation's] particular needs and circumstances' (Mika and O'Sullivan, 2014: 655).

When an organisation identifies as a Māori organisation, it assumes and projects a Māori cultural identity, ethos and values derived from its Māori members, the *iwi* (tribe) to which its founders belong (e.g., Ngāi Tahu), the local area in which the organisation was established (e.g., Wellington District Māori Council), or its pan-tribal Māori community (e.g., urban Māori authority, Te Whānau o Waipareira Trust in West Auckland). While each tribe has its own history and traditions, Māori organisations commonly ascribe to a set of core values, with their number and expression varying according to locality (Knox, 2005). Examples of such commonly held values include: *rangatiratanga* (self-determination); *whanaungatanga* (relationships); *kaitiakitanga* (guardianship); *manaakitanga* (generosity); and *wairuatanga* (spirituality) (Mika and O'Sullivan, 2014; Morgan and Mulligan, 2006). Adherence to such values imbues Māori organisations with a cultural milieu that shapes strategy, structure and change. In this context, Māori organisations can expect to be self-determining (as an expression of *rangatiratanga*), to place great purchase on relationships (*whanaungatanga*), to take seriously the protection of their natural, phyiscal and intellectual resources (*kaitiakitanga*), to be generous hosts (*manaakitanga*) and to acknowledge that all of this takes place under the purview of one's ancestors (*wairuatanga*).

The job of the indigenous management consultant is to know and understand these values (i.e., how they are derived and manifested within a given Māori organisation), and to factor them into advice on strategy, structure and change. This is typically done in three main ways. The first strategy is to draw on one's own identity as Māori and the values this entails as an initial guide. The second strategy is to study the application of Māori values within multiple Māori organisations, which comes with experience and academic enquiry, and to extrapolate their application to a given Māori organisation. And the third strategy is to incorporate an element of preview into every consulting assignment as a way to readily grasp some sense of the organisation's identity, value-set and interpretation of itself and its business environment. Where a non-indigenous management consultant is working with a Māori organisation, deference to the second and third methods is typical. This procedure (the 'preview') is otherwise known as a discovery process, an organisational assessment, or simply a review. Even though the method may resemble an audit, one should refrain from calling a preview an audit because audits occur after the fact and carry a reductionist connotation rather than a developmental one (no offence to auditors intended).

The preview essentially involves perusing corporate documentation (especially the constitution, strategic and business plans, annual reports, organisational policies, evaluative studies, industry and sector policy and trend data). Next, a sample of organisational members who may be drawn from the board, management, employees, customers and suppliers is interviewed. Finally, some assessment of the state of the organisation's strategy, structure and operations and the exhibition of values characteristic of Māori organisations is made. Armed with these insights, the indigenous management consultant is equipped to go in any direction the client wishes to take the assignment: a refresh of strategy, an entirely novel strategy, a review of performance, a restructure, a merger or disestablishment. What makes the preview distinctive are the indigenous values and purposes, which influence decision-making, managerial style and methods, and the language and culture of Māori organisations.

By way of example, the author was engaged to facilitate the development of a strategic plan for a new Māori organisation, a charity that provides health and social services to Māori and non-Māori in and around its community. The organisation was formed from the merger of two separate Māori organisations that provided related services. The impetus for the merger was threefold: a belief by their common chair that it was the right thing to do; a trend toward integration in health services; and efficiency, administrative and operational advantages. The planning process involved extensive environmental scanning, facilitating planning meetings with the board and senior management and the production of a plan.

Being an organisation whose service history, methods and provision are underpinned by *kaupapa* Māori (Māori philosophy), the charity aspired to be world class in the services and outcomes it achieved for indigenous and non-indigenous people in its locality. Attaining such an outcome would be contingent upon effective integration and a focus on wellbeing, excellence, opportunities and leadership. The strategy provided a clear statement of intent for the organisation to focus on health and wellbeing for all, but from an indigenous perspective.

In an example of change, the author was engaged by a tribal organisation that had settled some of its treaty claims with the Crown. The organisation's structure is typical of post-settlement governance entities (PSGEs): an overarching tribal council providing representation, with two main subsidiaries, one a commercial company charged with administering settlement assets and generating income for the group, and the other, a charity for tribal development and distributional purposes (Harmsworth, 2009). Two important characteristics of PSGEs are that their structures are generally prescribed by settlement legislation and the earning potential of settlement assets varies markedly depending on the nature of the assets, strategy and capabilities of the organisation. This means designing organisations that conform with legislation and sustaining them with a basket of assets that may comprise a mix of inalienable, yet culturally significant, sites (e.g., mountain peaks), settlement assets which are difficult to divest (e.g., fish quota), and cash. In this case, the board wished to review its structure to ensure that it was 'fit-for-purpose' and operating as efficiently as possible.

Commencing with an organisational review, we studied the client's corporate documents, interviewed board members and employees and furnished a report detailing its strategy, structure and performance with recommendations for change. An imperative of the organisation is to preserve the tribe's culture, identity and language. One of the board members, a staunch advocate of *te reo* Māori (the Māori language), was interviewed entirely in Māori. The ability to consult in Māori is a distinctive feature of indigenous management consulting practice. The review had the potential to cause much dissension because of the suggested structural change and because most employees are themselves tribal members. Discord was staved by two main actions: first, regular communication with the board and employees about the unfolding review; and second, not being of the tribe, but indigenous nonetheless, gave the consultants an awareness of the tribe's values, structure and methods. The outcome was a resizing and refocusing of the organisation on priorities that included finalising outstanding claims, and environmental, cultural and enterprise developments.

## On becoming an indigenous management consultant

Becoming a management consultant is a curious affair. Unlike many other professional occupations, namely accountants, lawyers and financial advisors, there is no guild, no institute, no association and no bar to calling oneself a management consultant. All a person needs do is adopt the moniker 'management consultant,' buy a mobile phone and that person is instantly in the business of management consulting. The principal hurdle is to establish credibility in the marketplace, and then to keep it. This is usually achieved by gaining relevant experience and skills, which for indigenous management consultants in Aotearoa New Zealand are traditionally acquired after some years in the employ of the public service. A university degree also helps, but has not, hitherto, been essential. Now, the private sector is proving an effective training ground and more direct route for indigenous management consultants who present an outlook and capability sharpened by the disciplines of the marketplace. Moreover, a university degree, perhaps two, accelerates the learning process and draws in candidates more *au fait* with technology and global commerce. International experience is inherently desirable. Thus, the demographic of indigenous management consultants may be gradually changing from older ex-public servants with some qualifications, to younger private sector tyros with satchels full of qualifications and unbridled confidence (Brown, 2016).

Along with this changing demographic is the changing face of indigenous management consulting firms. Most indigenous management consultants in Aotearoa New Zealand operate as self-employed persons, consistent with the fact that 97 percent of all firms in Aotearoa New Zealand are small (having 19 or fewer employees) (Ministry of Business Innovation and Employment, 2014, 2016). While collaboration among indigenous management consultants is not uncommon because the nature of an assignment may demand a broader skill set or because the isolation of working on one's own makes group assignments desirable from time-to-time, establishing a firm of two or more is less common. In Aotearoa New Zealand, there have been a few indigenous management consulting firms over the years. Notable examples include: THS & Associates Limited of Hamilton, started by Traci Houpapa and Sharon Mariu in 2000; Pareārau, an all-female chartered accounting and management consulting firm started in Wellington in 1998 by Fiona Wilson; Richard Jefferies who operated his management consultancy, KCSM, from his Ōpōtiki base; HKM, founded by Alan Haronga, Arama Kukutai and Paul Morgan in 1998; Kahui

Tautoko, started in Wellington in 2000 by Mara Andrews and Marama Parore; and Tuia Group, established by Guy Royal, Toko Kapea and Mike Taitoko in 2006, in Wellington. The commonality these firms share is a desire to help Māori and other indigenous enterprises using indigenous insights, capabilities and networks, and they have each done this in their own way.

One firm of note is Glenn Hawkins & Associates Limited (GHA), a chartered accounting and management consultancy established in the Bay of Plenty city of Rotorua in 2005 by Glenn Hawkins, of Ngāti Whakaue and Ngāti Maniapoto descent. Like many small businesses, the company started from home, with Glenn initially providing management consulting services. Demand for accounting services has seen consulting play a lessor role until recently. Glenn's vision for the company has been to provide quality services to Māori organisations, both commercial and noncommercial, and to allow the reputation for good work and the hiring of good people to help realise the firm's growth potential. Two recent developments intimate the merit of this strategy. In 2013, a second partner joined GHA, Mere George, a chartered accountant with *whakapapa* (genealogical) connections to several *iwi* of the region within which GHA operates, including Ngāti Whare, Ngāti Manawa, Tūwharetoa, and Ngāti Porou. In 2015, the GHA Centre, a purpose-built office for the firm and its clients, was opened. By September 2016, GHA's staff numbered around 20, with 15 accountants and board secretaries, and five management consultants.

GHA's growth illustrates that there is sufficient scope within the Māori economy to sustain such a firm and others that operate in the indigenous market. The firm's survival and growth also suggests that the integration of Māori and Pākehā (Western) values, principles and practices of business is a plausible model of business practice and management consulting. Within GHA, kaupapa Māori values of *manaakitanga* (generosity), *pūkenga* (knowledge), *pono* (honesty) and *māhaki* (humility) find a way to coexist alongside the ethical code, accounting standards and procedures to which chartered accountants, in particular, must adhere.

For all that it has accomplished, GHA represents the exception rather than the rule (independent and growing), as many Māori management consultants tend to ply their trade within the global giants of the big four accounting firms (PriceWaterhouseCoopers, Ernst & Young, Deloitte and KPMG) and other 'second-tier' and specialist professional services firms. In Aotearoa New Zealand, all the big four, for instance, have established Māori management consulting teams; some loosely arranged, assembled as assignments dictate, others more permanently arranged as business units or subsidiary entities focused on serving the Māori economy (for example, EY Tahi) (Ernst and Young, 2014; Gibson, 2015a; Hanita et al., 2016). On one side of the ledger, the big four offer indigenous management consultants two irresistible advantages: exceptional training and exposure to global clients and networks. On the other side of the ledger, there is the potential for one's identity as an indigenous management consultant to be curtailed by conformity to the values and systems upon which such global firms are built. For the moment, there appears to be a willingness for a more inclusive view of indigeneity within large consulting firms, and for Māori consulting firms like GHA and others to hold their own in the market for management consulting from an indigenous perspective.

## Conclusion

This chapter set out to discuss what it means to be an indigenous management consultant and practice management consulting from an indigenous perspective within Aotearoa

New Zealand. The chapter discussed the experiences of Māori management consultants as self-employed contractors, owner-operators of management consulting firms and as management consultants in 'mainstream' firms. The central thesis of the chapter is that indigenous management consultants offer a distinctive proposition in the market for professional advisory services on the basis of their indigeneity. Indigenous management consultants approach their craft from an indigenous perspective, incorporating indigenous values, knowledge and methods, alongside technocratic knowledge and skills (such as accounting, finance and law, among others) to deliver customers advice that accords with indigenous peoples' needs, preferences, priorities, traditions and aspirations. Bicultural and bilingual competency (the ability to operate comfortably in two cultures and speak an indigenous and non-indigenous language) add an increasingly valued edge to indigenous management consultants, not as an added feature but as an integral part of who they are, what they are and how they perform their roles.

The demand for indigenous management consultants (consultants who self-identify as indigenous) and indigenous management consulting (the integration of indigenous and non-indigenous knowledge and practices in consulting), stems from two main sources. The first are indigenous organisations seeking management consultants with whom they share some cultural affinity. This transforms the consulting assignment beyond a mere professional exchange to one which is underpinned by mutual understanding of and concern for the history, context and challenges of indigenous development and indigenous enterprise. The second are non-indigenous (mainstream) organisations seeking to work with indigenous peoples, organisations and institutions in an effort to be more responsive to this market. Public sector responsiveness to Māori, for instance, is driven by legislation, policy and treaty obligations, whereas private sector responsiveness seems driven more by economic imperatives. While the nature, scale and scope of indigenous management consulting in each country that has an indigenous populace will differ, this chapter highlights the very real and distinctive contribution indigenous management consultants can and do make to management consulting. The challenge for our sector (management consulting) is to recognise and grow indigenous management consulting talent and use more deliberate, rather than emergent, strategies to cope with the growing need for this unique offering.

## References

ANZ. (2015). Te tirohanga whānui: The ANZ privately-owned business barometer: Māori business key insights 2015. Auckland, New Zealand: ANZ.

Barber, D. (1993). Maori the corporate warrior. *Management*, February, 37–41.

Battiste, M., and Henderson, J. S. Y. (2000). *Protecting indigenous knowledge and heritage: A global challenge*. Saskatoon, Canada: Purich.

Best, E. (1996). *Tuhoe, the children of the mist: A sketch of the origin, history, myths, and beliefs of the Tuhoe tribe of the Maori of New Zealand, with some account of other early tribes of the Bay of Plenty district*, 4th ed. Auckland, New Zealand: Reed.

Brash, D. (2004). Nationhood – Don Brash speech Orewa Rotary Club. *Scoop*, January 27. Available from www.scoop.co.nz/stories/PA0401/S00220.htm

Brown, H. (2016). Wright named on Forbes Asia list. *Māori Television*, March 1. Available from www.maoritelevision.com/news/sport/wright-named-on-forbes-asia-list

Buck, P. (1987). *The coming of the Maori*, 2nd ed. Wellington, New Zealand: Whitcoulls.

Burrows, J., O'Regan, T., Chin, P., Pihama, L., Coddington, D., Poutu, H., . . . Walker, R. (2013). *New Zealand's constitution: A report on a conversation: He kōtuinga kōrero mō te kaupapa ture o Aotearoa*. Wellington, New Zealand: Constitutional Advisory Panel – Te Ranga Kaupapa Ture, Department of the Prime Minister and Cabinet and Office of the Minister of Māori Affairs.

Collins, J., Morrison, M., Krivokapic-Skoko, B., and Butler, R. (2014). *Indigenous small businesses in the Australian indigenous economy.* Paper presented at the Engaging Indigenous Economies Conference, September 4–5, ANU Commons, Australian National University, Canberra, Australia.

Cornell, S., and Kalt, J. P. (eds.). (1993). *What can tribes do? Strategies and institutions in American Indian economic development.* Los Angles, CA: American Indian Studies Centre, University of California.

Crane, A., McWilliams, A., Matten, D., Moon, J., and Siegel, D. S. (eds.). (2008). *The Oxford handbook of corporate social responsibility,* 1st ed. Oxford: Oxford University Press.

Crocombe, R. (2008). *The South Pacific,* 7th ed. Suva, Fiji: IPS Publications.

Dalziel, P. (1991). Explaining ethnic differences in economic attainment: A survey. In J. Whitewell and M. A. Thompson (eds.), *Society and culture: Economic perspectives,* Vol. 1. Wellington, New Zealand: New Zealand Association of Economists Incorporated, pp. 23–38.

Dickson, I. (2010). Maori enterprise and the New Zealand capital market: Report 2a scoping report. Wellington, New Zealand: Māori Economic Taskforce.

Durie, M. (2011). *Ngā tini whetū: Navigating Māori futures.* Wellington, New Zealand: Huia.

Ernst & Young. (2014). *EY launches specialist Maori advisory firm* [Press release]. Available from www.ey.com/NZ/en/Newsroom/News-releases/EY-launches-specialist-maori-advisory-firm

Foley, D. (2004). *Understanding indigenous entrepreneurship: A case study analysis.* A paper submitted for the degree of Doctor of Philosophy, University of Queensland, Brisbane, Australia.

Foley, D. (2007). *Indigenous entrepreneurship: What, when, how and why?* Paper presented at the regional frontiers of entrepreneurship research conference: 4th international Australian Graduate School of Entrepreneurship (AGSE) entrepreneurship research exchange, February 6–9, Brisbane, Australia.

Ford, D.Y., and Grantham, T. C. (2003). Providing access for culturally diverse gifted students: From deficit to dynamic thinking. *Theory into Practice,* 42(3), 217–225.

Ford, D.Y., Harris, J. J., Tyson, C. A., and Trotman, M. A. (2002). Beyond deficit thinking: Providing access for gifted African American students. *Roeper Review Winter,* 24(2), 52–58.

Gardiner, J. (2010). Achieving enduring settlements. *PostTreatySettlements.org.nz,* 1(4). Available from http://posttreatysettlements.org.nz/achieving-enduring-settlements/

Gardiner, W. (1996). *Return to sender: What really happened at the fiscal envelope hui.* Auckland, New Zealand: Reed.

Gibson, A. (2015a). Mana and money – the Maori business evolution. *New Zealand Herald,* February 6. Available from www.nzherald.co.nz/business/news/article.cfm?c_id=3&objectid=11585325

Gibson, A. (2015b). Prospects appear even brighter for Maori economic renaissance. *New Zealand Herald,* February 6. Available from www.nzherald.co.nz/business/news/article.cfm?c_id=3&objectid=11397182

Gibson, A. (2016). Maori business leaders earn accolades for contributions. *New Zealand Herald,* May 14. Available from www.nzherald.c o.nz/business/news/article.cfm?c_id=3&objectid=11638979

Hancock, F., and Grover, K. (2001). *He tirohanga ō kawa ki te Tiriti o Waitangi: A guide to the principles of the Treaty of Waitangi as expressed by the courts and the Waitangi Tribunal.* Wellington, New Zealand: Te Puni Kōkiri.

Hanita, J., Te Kanawa, R., and Rihia, J. (2016). *Māui rau: Adapting in a changing world.* Auckland, New Zealand: KPMG.

Harmsworth, G. R. (2009). Sustainability and Māori business. In B. Frame, R. Gordon and C. Mortimer (eds.), *Hatched: The capacity for sustainable development.* Christchurch, New Zealand: Landcare Research (Manaaki Whenua), pp. 95–108.

Harmsworth, G. R., and Awatere, S. (2013). Indigenous Māori knowledge and perspectives of ecosystems. In J. R. Dymond (ed.), *Ecosystem services in New Zealand: Conditions and trends.* Lincoln, New Zealand: Manaaki Whenua Press, pp. 274–286.

Heidegger, M., and Grene, M. (1976). The age of the world view. *Boundary 2,* 4(2), 341–355. doi:10.2307/302139

Henare, D., Thompson, M. A., and Comer, L. (1991). *Ka awatea: A report of the Ministerial Planning Group, March 1991* (O. o. t. M. o. M. Affairs Ed.). Wellington, New Zealand: Office of the Minister of Māori Affairs.

Henry, E. (2007). Kaupapa Maori entrepreneurship. In L. P. Dana and R. B. Anderson (eds.), *International handbook of research on indigenous entrepreneurship.* Cheltenham: Edward Elgar, pp. 536–548.

Henry, E. (2012). *Te wairua auaha: Emancipatory Māori entrepreneurship in screen production.* A thesis submitted in partial fulfilment of the requirements for the degree of Doctor of Philosophy, Auckland University of Technology, Auckland, New Zealand.

Henry, E., and Pene, H. (2001). Kaupapa Māori: Locating indigenous ontology, epistemology and methodology in the academy. *Organization,* 8(2), 234–242. doi:10.1177/1350508401082009

Hindle, K., and Moroz, P. W. (2009). Indigenous entrepreneurship as a research field: developing a definitional framework from the emerging canon. *International Entrepreneurship and Management Journal,* 6, 357–385. doi:10.1007/s11365-009-0111-x

King, M. (2003). *The Penguin history of New Zealand.* Auckland, New Zealand: Penguin.

Knox, C. (2005). *Whakapūmau te mauri: Values-based Māori organisations.* A thesis presented in partial fulfilment of the requirements for the degree of Doctor of Philosophy in Māori Studies, Massey University, Palmerston North, New Zealand.

LINZ. (2013). *NZ Geographic Board welcomes Minister's decision on islands' names* [Press release]. Available from www.linz.govt.nz/news/2013-10/nz-geographic-board-welcomes-minister%E2%80%99s-decision-islands%E2%80%99-names

Māori Economic Taskforce. (2010). *Māori economic taskforce.* Wellington, New Zealand: Office of the Minister of Māori Affairs and Māori Economic Taskforce.

Marsden, M. (1992). God, man and universe: A Maori view. In M. King (ed.), *Te ao hurihuri: Aspects of Māoritanga,* 1st ed. Auckland, New Zealand: Reed, pp. 117–137.

Mika, J. P. (2003). Maori capacity-building: Shifting the policy settings toward Maori independence. *Public Sector,* 26(1), 13–18.

Mika, J. P. (2010). *Access to finance and banking services for Māori: A discussion paper.* Wellington, New Zealand: Te Puni Kōkiri.

Mika, J. P. (2014). Manaakitanga: Is generosity killing Māori enterprises? In P. Davidsson (ed.), *Proceedings of the Australian Centre for entrepreneurship research exchange conference,* February 4–7, UNSW, Sydney, Australia. Brisbane, Australia: Queensland University of Technology, pp. 815–829.

Mika, J. P. (2015). *The role of publicly funded enterprise assistance in Māori entrepreneurship in Aotearoa New Zealand.* A thesis submitted in partial fulfilment of the requirements for the degree of Doctor of Philosophy in Business, Massey University, Palmerston North, New Zealand.

Mika, J. P. (2016a). The role of elders in indigenous economic development: The case of kaumātua in Māori enterprises of Aotearoa New Zealand. In K. Iankova and A. Hassan (eds.), *Indigenous people and economic development: An international perspective.* London: Gower, pp. 151–176.

Mika, J. P. (2016b). What is Māori innovation? To snare the sun, and then some . . . *Idealog.* Available from http://idealog.co.nz/venture/2016/06/what-maori-innovation-snare-sun-and-then-some

Mika, J. P., Bensemann, J., and Fahey, N. (2016). *What is a Māori business: A study in the identity of indigenous enterprise.* Paper presented at the ANZAM Annual Conference, December 5–7, QUT, Brisbane, Australia.

Mika, J. P., and O'Sullivan, J. G. (2014). A Māori approach to management: Contrasting traditional and modern Māori management practices in Aotearoa New Zealand. *Journal of Management & Organization,* 20(5), 648–670. doi:10.1017/jmo.2014.48

Mika, J. P., Rangi, C., and Wilson, F. (2003). *Cluster export network delegation visit report, Suva, Fiji 23–26 June 2003.* Wellington, New Zealand: Positively Wellington Business.

Ministry of Business Innovation and Employment. (2014). *Māori in business: A report on Maori running their own business: December 2014.* Wellington, New Zealand: Author.

Ministry of Business Innovation and Employment. (2016). *Small businesses in New Zealand: How do they compare with larger firms?* Wellington, New Zealand: Author.

Morgan, P., and Mulligan, W. (2006). *Hei Whakamarama i ngā āhuatanga o te tūrua pō: Investigating key Māori business characteristics for future measures: Thinking paper.* Wellington, New Zealand: Te Puni Kōkiri.

Nana, G. (2013). *Estimates of Māori economy exports.* Wellington, New Zealand: Te Puni Kōkiri and BERL.

New Zealand Council for Sustainable Development, and Westpac New Zealand. (2005). *Let's settle this! Through settlement to sustainable Māori enterprise.* Auckland, New Zealand: Author.

Norman, D. (2016). *Industry insights: Māori in the New Zealand economy*, 1st ed. Auckland, New Zealand: Westpac.

Office of the Auditor General. (1998). *Third report for 1998: Part 4: Delivering effective outputs for Māori*. Wellington, New Zealand: Author.

Office of Treaty Settlements. (2002). *What is a treaty settlement? Treaty settlements*. Available from www.ots. govt.nz/

Orange, C. (1987). *The Treaty of Waitangi*. Wellington, New Zealand: Allen & Unwin.

Parker, B. (2000). *Māori in the New Zealand economy*, 2nd ed. Wellington, New Zealand: Te Puni Kōkiri.

Rangihau, J. T. R. A. (1992). Being Māori. In M. King (ed.), *Te ao hurihuri: Aspects of Māoritanga*, 1st ed. Auckland, New Zealand: Reed, pp. 183–190.

Reedy, A. (2003). *Te Maori mana rangatira: A programme specifically designed to motivate Maori into their own business*. Ruatoria, New Zealand: Nga Kete o te Matauranga Limited.

Royal, T. A. C. (2005). *An organic arising: An interpretation of tikanga based upon the Māori creation traditions*. Paper presented at the Tikanga Rangahau Mātauranga Tuku Iho: Traditional Knowledge and Research Ethics Conference, June 10–12, Te Papa Tongarewa, Wellington, New Zealand.

Sapere Research Group. (2011). *Māori enterprises and the capital markets: Phase two report*. Wellington, New Zealand: Māori Economic Taskforce.

Scott, H. M., and Guy, S. W. (2004). *The case of the Māori consultants cluster Wellington*. Paper presented at the 3rd Annual Hawaii International Conference on Social Sciences, June 16–19, Honolulu, Hawaii.

Seton, K. (1999). Fourth world nations in the era of globalisation: An introduction to contemporary theorizing posed by indigenous nations. Available from http://nointervention.com/archive/pubs/CWIS/fworld.html

Smith, L. T. (1999). *Decolonizing methodologies: Research and indigenous peoples*, 1st ed. London: Zed Books.

Smith, R. (2008). Beyond the blue horizon: How ancient voyages settled the far-flung islands of the Pacific. *Pioneers of the Pacific*. Available from http://ngm.nationalgeographic.com/print/2008/03/people-pacific/smith-text

Solomon, M. (2010). *Iwi infrastructure and investment*. Wellington, New Zealand: Māori Economic Taskforce.

Spiller, C. (2010). *How Māori tourism businesses create authentic and sustainable well-being*. A thesis submitted in partial fulfilment of the requirements for the degree of Doctor of Philosophy, University of Auckland, Auckland, New Zealand.

Spiller, C., Spiller, R. M., and Henare, M. (2006). *Making a difference: Why and how to employ and work effectively with Māori*. Auckland, New Zealand: EEO Trust.

Statistics New Zealand. (2005). *New Zealand in the OECD*. Wellington, New Zealand: Author.

Statistics New Zealand. (2013a). *2013 census QuickStats about Māori – tables*. Wellington, New Zealand: Author.

Statistics New Zealand. (2013b). *2013 QuickStats: About Māori*. Wellington, New Zealand: Author.

Statistics New Zealand. (2013c). *2013 QuickStats: About national highlights*. Wellington, New Zealand: Author

Statistics New Zealand. (2014). *Māori population estimates: At 30 June 2014 – tables*. Wellington, New Zealand: Author

Statistics New Zealand. (2015). *Gross domestic product: March 2015 quarter*. Wellington, New Zealand: Author.

Statistics New Zealand. (2016a). *Māori population estimates: Mean year ended 31 December 2015 – tables*. Wellington, New Zealand: Author.

Statistics New Zealand. (2016b). *Population clock*. Available from www.stats.govt.nz/tools_and_services/population_clock.aspx

Sumner, W. G. (1959). *Folkways: A study of the sociological importance of usages, manners, customs, mores, and morals*. New York, NY: Dover.

Te Puni Kōkiri. (1999). *Strategic response to Māori disparities*. Wellington, New Zealand: Author.

Te Puni Kōkiri. (2012). *The Māori economy*. Wellington, New Zealand: Author.

Tinirau, R. S., and Gillies, A. (2010). Turupoutia tō piki amokura: Distinguishing Māori values and practices in contemporary Māori businesses and organisations. In J. S. Te Rito and S. M. Healy (eds.),

*Proceedings of the 4th international traditional knowledge conference*, 6–9 June. Auckland, New Zealand: University of Auckland, pp. 357–364.

Tuckey, C. (2016). Massey racism provokes call for university name change. *Stuff*, September 29, pp. 1–3. Available from www.stuff.co.nz/national/84753337/massey-racism-provokes-call-for-university-name-change

Walker, R. (2004). *Ka whawhai tonu matou: Struggle without end*, 2nd ed. Auckland, New Zealand: Penguin.

Wilson, J. (2016). European discovery of New Zealand – Able Tasman. *Te Ara: The encyclopedia of New Zealand*, pp. 2–3. Available from www.teara.govt.nz/en/european-discovery-of-new-zealand/page-2

Winiata, P. (2012). *Guiding kaupapa of Te Wānanga-o-Raukawa*. Otaki, New Zealand: Te Wānanga o Raukawa.

Winiata, W. (1998). *Reducing the socio-economic disparities in housing, employment, health and education*. Wellington, New Zealand: TWM.

Yates, A. (2009). *Contemporary Māori business practices: A literature review*. Palmerston North, New Zealand: Massey University, School of Management, Te Au Rangahu Māori Business Research Centre.

# 17 Consultants

## The custodians of best practices

*Brett Knowles and Graham Manville*

## Executive summary

This chapter focuses on how the role of consultant has evolved over time from the birth of management consultancy at the end of the nineteenth century, through international expansion in the 1960s by major consulting houses using the model of "owner of proprietary intellectual property", to the business landscape of consulting in the present day. The chapter discusses the emancipation of tacit knowledge (previously the preserve of university business schools) and codified proprietary models of the larger consultancy practices via mass publication of consultancy authored books and how-to guides. Next, the chapter discusses the commoditization of models and the dangers of misinterpretation of techniques. Finally, the chapter explains the current context where the role of most consultants is the integration of these well published methodologies into a workable solution for each client situation. This may include employing multiple models and adapting them to the context of the specific organisation in partnership with the executives of that organisation. The chapter concludes by showcasing a case study of a balanced scorecard implementation using lean techniques and organisational development tools within a major organisation. The organization was the major telecommunications company AT&T Canada. The project was so well received that it has been featured in Kaplan and Norton's prestigious Hall of Fame.

## A brief history of strategic and business consulting

Consulting may not be the oldest profession (it runs a close second!), but it has an uncanny number of similarities to the oldest profession. For example, a cynic may argue this similarity as consultants work very odd hours; are paid a lot of money to keep their clients happy; charge by the hour but their time can be extended for the right price and creating fantasies for your clients is rewarded. The first "consultants" could be considered to be the traditional "wise men" and chiefs who became the custodians of "best practices" and it was their job to learn them and pass them on for the benefit of the community. It could be considered that some of the first management "how-to" books might, in fact, be our religious scrolls, testaments and psalms. They remind us of how we should behave in certain situations but were documented so as to ensure their continuity over generations. In management consultancy, the "best practices" that appear in contemporaneous publications are the interpretation through the prism of that period's culture and values.

The first recognised management consulting firm, Arthur D. Little (ADL), was formed in 1886, by Arthur D. Little, a chemistry graduate from MIT. The company initially specialised in technical research, and later built a specialization in what became to be known as "management engineering". ADL is still a multi-national organization today with over 1,000 employees (MIT Libraries, 2016).

Another pioneering consultant was Frederick Wilmslow Taylor who formed his consulting company in 1893, and his focus was the scientific management of work which effectively moved the planning of work from the craft worker to the management team (Taylor, 1914). (His field of study evolved into what became known as Time and Motion Studies popularized by Frank and Lillian Gilbreth (Price, 2003).) The management guru Peter Drucker (the man who developed the concept of management by objectives) paid tribute to the seminal work of Taylor in the 1970s stating that Taylor was:

> the first man in recorded history who deemed work deserving of systematic observation and study. On Taylor's "scientific management" rests, above all, the tremendous surge of affluence in the last seventy-five years which has lifted the working masses in the developed countries well above any level recorded before, even for the well-to-do. Taylor, though the Isaac Newton (or perhaps the Archimedes) of the science of work, laid only first foundations, however. Not much has been added to them since – even though he has been dead all of sixty years.
>
> (Drucker, 1974: 181)

Drucker was effectively a "pracademic", i.e. an academic that is able to successfully bridge the gap between academic theory and management practice. Drucker was a renowned university professor at the prestigious New York University (NYU), Stern Business School, a top 50 world-ranked university (ARWU, 2016; QS, 2016; THE, 2016) and top 20 world-ranked business school (FT.Com, 2016). During his tenure at NYU, he held a 20-year tenure as a columnist for the *Wall Street Journal* (Wall Street Journal, 1999) and he advised many Fortune 500 organisations. In 1969, he received the presidential citation award, the highest honour of NYU. He influenced many multi-national organisations, such as General Electric, IBM, Intel, Procter & Gamble, Girl Scouts of the USA, The Salvation Army, Red Cross, United Farm Workers and several US presidential administrations (Drucker Institute, 2016).

In the 1950s, he developed the concept of "Management by Objectives" (MBO) that seeks to manage an organisation by setting SMART objectives and goals so that all employees have a clear understanding of what is expected of them – this is the maxim that "what gets measured, gets managed". However, it is interesting to note that another management guru, Henry Mintzberg, was critical of the Taylorist-influenced MBO because it focused on measurable benefits and thereby overshadowing less quantifiable social benefits and invariably social values were left behind (Mintzberg, 1989).

When MBOs are not properly set, agreed and managed by organizations, either self-centred employees or employees under pressure to achieve targets may be prone to manipulate the results. This is known in academic terms as gaming, which could lead to sub-optimal performance (Smith and Goddard, 2002; Radnor and McGuire, 2004). It can also lead to a culture of short-term thinking and a focus on efficiency but not effectiveness so that attention focuses on "what gets measured, gets managed" and what does not get measured, does not matter (Johnston et al., 2002). This approach can subsequently inhibit organisational citizenship behaviour (Organ, 1988), which means that employees will focus less on the good citizenship actions that they may do in addition to the requirements of their job description.

Drucker's management by objectives approach eventually morphed into the balanced scorecard philosophy, which was a holistic interface between strategy and operational management via four perspectives: internal business processes, customer focus, financial focus and innovation and learning focus. It has been euphemistically referred to as the management cockpit. The framework was developed by Kaplan and Norton in 1992 and has been praised as the most important management tool in the last 75 years (Bourne et al., 2005).

## Old days: methodology was king

As discussed in the introduction, the emergence of management "best practices" began to take root in the early twentieth century when the focus of organisations shifted to productivity. Management consultancies subsequently developed proprietary methodologies to effectively protect their intellectual capital in a way organisations could only experience through engaging with that consulting firm.

This approach was maintained until the early 1980s. Until then, there were very few business books other than design or university programs. Consulting organizations, such as Arthur Anderson, developed and codified proprietary consulting approaches for Arthur Anderson staff, and their approach was referred to as Method 1 (Squires et al., 2003). The Method 1 books were only in designated areas and were serial number controlled in order to ensure their proprietary methodology did not enter the wider marketplace outside of their consultant's delivery. This would have also been reinforced with non-disclosure agreements, but it would not always prevent a former employee from reconfiguring the methodology for their own purposes.

Around the time that Drucker began popularising management theory, a nascent global consultancy practice, McKinsey Inc., which is arguably the gold standard consulting practice today, began their global expansion from their US base. In 1959 Hugh Parker, another graduate engineer from MIT, opened McKinsey's first international office in London and began advising major clients such as Cadburys (now owned by Kraft Inc.). Parker has been credited with globalising the McKinsey brand by bringing into the popular lexicon the phrase "to be McKinseyed" (McKinsey, 2016).

Among the advice offered to organisations in the 1960s by Parker was to improve organisational effectiveness by reducing costs and increasing revenue. The cutting of costs was achieved by cutting perceived waste and non-value adding activities. The advice to achieve revenue growth was to internationalise and restructure the organization into strategic business units in a multi-divisional form (Palmer et al., 1993). This approach was subsequently copied by other consultancy practices such as BCG and Bain. The principle of portfolio management was that good managers could manage business units in any context, and the bonus of portfolio management was that stronger performing units could cross-subsidize weaker business units and the parent company could spread its risks. Each of the consultancy practices developed their own methodological models to manage their clients' portfolios. McKinsey developed the GE/McKinsey Matrix, and BCG developed the Growth Share Matrix (BCG) and the Ansof Matrix (Mindtools, 2016).

Before the 1980s, most business books were focused on providing rules and guidelines around accepted management practices such as accounting and traditional strategic planning.

## New days: methodology is a commodity

In the 1980s, former McKinsey partners, Tom Peters and Bob Waterman, published a best-selling book entitled *In Search of Excellence* (Peters and Waterman, 1982), which McKinsey had a 50% royalty on and this paved the way for the commoditization of business books.

It challenged organisations to get closer to the customer and to benchmark their performance against the best in the industry.

During the 1950s, the effect of the Japanese economic miracle heralded a new philosophy known as quality management, popularized in print by Edwards Deming, who was one of the key facilitators of knowledge transfer from the USA to Japan (Deming, 1982). Deming was one of the pioneering consultants of the quality management revolution, which led to a successful recovery of the Japanese economy. Those principles of success were subsequently exported to organizations in the west throughout the 1980s and early 1990s, disseminated in the first instance as a result of Krafcik's work (Krafcik, 1988). On a positive note, the quality management revolution has developed into a body of theoretical knowledge with several international journals dedicated to the topic of quality management; for example, the *TQM Journal, Total Quality and Business Excellence* and *the International Journal of Quality and Reliability Management* to name but a few (ABS, 2015). Conversely, quality management has its distractors who believed that it spawned the fad of the 1980s, the quality management surge (Miller and Hartwick, 2002).

Quality management was buoyed by the success of Japanese companies in world markets. Such competition from these emergent Japanese organisations resulted in loss of market share of established organisations in the US, which were being undercut on price and out-performed on quality and reliability. This poor performance was also experienced by the organisations cited in Peters and Waterman's book *In Search of Excellence*. A criticism of this book was that it seemed to reflect the current themes facing business at that time, as some of the so-called excellent companies were no longer performing as well by the end of the decade. One of the organisations cited by Peters and Waterman was IBM, and, in 1993, they suffered a massive downturn and posted a loss of $5 billion, the biggest loss in American corporate history at that time (The Tech, 1993). The scale of the losses by the organisations cited in the groundbreaking book did not prevent Peters from becoming a management guru, authoring more books and carving out a lucrative niche in the business lecture circuit. This fuelled the charge of consultancy being perceived as either a flavour of the month or the commercialisation of management fads (Miller and Hartwick, 2002).

The dawn of the 1990s ushered in a global recession, and during this time some hitherto globally successful organisations suddenly posted record losses. In the depths of the recession of the early 1990s, Hammer and Champy published a groundbreaking book called *Re-engineering the Corporation* (Hammer and Champy, 1993). Business Process Re-engineering (BPR) involves radical change to improve organizational performance. It often involves technology as an enabler to facilitate a step change in improvement by reconfiguring organizational structure around business processes as opposed to functional departments (Mindtools, 2016). This went far beyond automation as their mantra was "don't automate, obliterate". BPR had huge potential but it became synonymous with corporate downsizing.

These early milestone books ushered in a plethora of books by business school professors seeking to monetise their research findings by distilling their academic research and codifying their knowledge from journal articles into a readily digestible form for managers and policy makers.

Bookshops and airport lounges became awash with "how-to" and self-help books that applied consulting tools that were historically the preserve of the elite consulting firms.

The explosion of the availability of these self-help management consultancy books effectively shifted management consulting from a scarcity model to an abundance model.

No matter what your business interest is, there are likely several books on how to deal with that situation. With the ubiquity of broadband Internet access, there are a variety of additional channels for organisations to quickly acquire business methodology skills. For example, business portals such as Mind Tools and Business Balls, not to mention personal YouTube videos and academic articles through Google Scholar. The role of the consultants is no longer the development of proprietary methodologies as any client can buy multiple books on the topic from the desk and have them on the desktop within days. To maintain their preeminent position as knowledge leaders, consultancy practices publish white paper position pieces that can be posted onto their corporate websites and downloaded by clients and prospective clients. These papers serve a dual objective of knowledge exchange and subtle brand marketing, a component part of the corporate marketing strategy.

## Why consultants will continue to publish their methodologies

It is not surprising for consultants that the continual publishing of methodologies as authored books is still viewed as one of the two credentials that legitimize the value of the consultant. David Norton, co-author of the balance scorecard books, once described his own books to one of the authors of this chapter as "business cards on steroids". Norton and his co-author, Kaplan, perceived the books as a means to open doors to senior leadership teams in significant transnational corporations.

If consultants or business school professors are lucky enough to see their book achieve bestseller status, they are likely to be able to charge premium fees to their clients. This is effectively the embodiment of Ricardo's theory of economic rent in that if demand for perceived scarce/valuable resources is very high, their market value will be priced at a premium (Ricardo, 1817).

## The methodology needs to be carefully managed

The codification and publication of these methodologies has become a complex business. In addition to the traditional duo of book publishing and speaking tours, authors must now also create associated websites, field books, tools, etc.

The deployment and application of methodologies must also be carefully managed. Michael Hammer's book, *Reengineering the Corporation*, is a good example of what happens when a bestselling business book is released. Many consultants and organisations saw the innovative ideas in the book to be of great interest and value. Consultants quickly synergised the concepts of BPR and began delivering services based on their unique interpretation. Very quickly, "reengineering" became a phrase associated with organisational downsizing and people being fired. The reengineering brand went from a huge success to a black mark within five years.

By contrast, the balanced scorecard body of knowledge is one that has been carefully managed over last 25 years since its inception in the early 1990s (Kaplan and Norton, 1992, 1996, 2001, 2008). Kaplan and Norton have kept their names closely associated with balanced scorecard despite the approach being licenced (or other forms of intellectual property agreements) by five different organizations over that period of time (KPMG, Cap Gemini, Gentia, Renaissance (IPO), the Balanced Scorecard Collaborative and Palladium).

As will be discussed later, they had done a good job in updating the balance scorecard concepts based upon experience, best practices and changes in the business environment.

The disadvantage of the balanced scorecard's carefully managed brand is that strong association with their names mean that as Kaplan and Norton progress into their retirement years, the concept of the balance scorecard risks falling out of popular reference. At the moment, like many models it does have limitations, but according to Bain (2016) it is still considered one of the top management tools.

The legacy of other proprietary business models has been preserved even after the death of the author. Having created the principles from the best-selling book *The 7 Habits of Highly Effective People* (Covey, 1989), FranklinCovey has done an outstanding job of developing, packaging and marketing consulting methodologies that can be delivered through their network (FranklinCovey, 2016).

## Implement best practices

Consultants are able to gain credibility and achieve critical mass through applying these widely recognized methodologies: Blue Ocean, Balance Scorecard, Five Forces, Six-Sigma and Seven S. In many cases, these are just "grey market" offerings that are similar to the published materials with minor variations to deal with local cultural or language requirements.

There is an increasing expectation on the part of clients that business improvement frameworks are enabled through software platforms and/or cloud-based resources. This potentially raises the barriers of entry for boutique consultancies and makes delivery of services somewhat more difficult for local consultants, but not impossible.

As methodologies and approaches become commoditized, and the quality becomes assured by licencing through web-based deployment, there is less need for the intellectual capability to be delivered by the large consultancy firms. Small, boutique consultancies with deep, local relationships, intimate knowledge of local customs and language and competitive rates are able to deliver methodologies that previously could only be delivered by large consultancies.

The market will still be dominated by large consulting organisations (especially for significant transformation engagement), but all other services that can conceivably be delivered effectively will be done so by local small consulting organizations.

## The consultants primary results: contact list

Consultants typically fill the role of trusted advisor. They become that channel for best practice ideas to enter the organisation. As such, once a consultant has established the trusted advisor relationship, his next task is to find related best practices to offer to his contact list.

The commoditisation of best practices makes this strategy easier, although clients are sceptical of the ability of consultants to deliver multiple types of consultant work. The opportunity and proficiency to deploy cloud-based methodologies enables IP providers an easier path to existing consultants and their relationships.

## Clients are more able than they used to be

As the average education level of management employees increases in organisations, the relationship changes from knowledge transfer to a facilitated partnering engagement. For example, with the rapid growth of MBA business school programmes, organisations in theory have the knowledge and expertise to solve their own problems. This has led to the emergence of internal consultancy departments within large organisations in both the private and public sectors. The important skills that consultants bring to the relationship are their experience and ability to integrate multiple methodologies into an appropriate solution for that organization. In addition, they can bring a fresh perspective to the problem because they are free from the cultural baggage of the organisation. In other instances, they may simply be brought in to be a legitimating exercise or a lightning rod to deflect the bad feeling when a deep change programme requires difficult decisions to be made from which the organisation subsequently has to negotiate strategic renewal. This view is supported by Matthias (2013), who summarises the rationale for buying the services of management consultants as the Four E's: expertise, externality, extension and endorsement.

## Same methodology in two different cultures provides two different solutions

Methodologies that are designed and developed to solve a specific problem can often be adjusted to address a different problem in a different environment.

As an example, the balance scorecard was developed in North America to combat the inclination of publicly traded organisations towards making short-term decisions to achieve order and earnings. The word "balanced" is intended to address the issue of balancing the short-term and long-term needs of the organisation. The "scorecard" is a holistic framework and is comprised of four perspectives that measure performance relating to finance, customers, business processes and learning and growth within the organisation. The balanced scorecard was designed as a strategy execution tool.

To develop an effective balance scorecard, one needs to do some degree of "strategy decomposition" to cascade the strategy down lower levels of the organisation. What is interesting is that this strategy decomposition process has been effective in developing work breakdown structures to be used in Third World organisations to help individuals and teams with little formal education understand the small portion of strategy/tactics that they are responsible for delivering.

## The age of integration – a case study of AT&T Canada

What has emerged in consulting is the evolution of multiple best practices into what is referred to in this chapter as "the age of integration", in which consultants add value by carefully crafting solutions that integrate elements of many best practices into the client's final solution.

The work that PM2 did at AT&T Canada is an example of how this integration should work. PM2's AT&T case study has been profiled in Kaplan and Norton (2001, 2008), but the essence is as follows.

In 1995, AT&T Canada was in serious financial trouble and employee engagement was at rock bottom. A 1995 survey of North American organisations placed AT&T Canada significantly lower than the median ranking and their financial performance reported a loss of over $300 million (Kaplan and Norton, 2001). The banks took swift action and brought in Bill Catucci as CEO in December 1995 (ibid).

On assuming responsibility for AT&T Canada, Bill Catucci, invited PM2 to provide guidance to him and his executive team in their attempts to develop and execute a new strategy.

At that time, AT&T was losing about $1 million a day. It was losing customers faster than it could attract new customers. It had structural and knowledge sharing issues as an organization, and was run as 11 separate businesses that did not share customer details, product offerings or common back-end services such as finance and information technology.

The poor performance at AT&T was caused by a combination of different factors: failure to communicate and articulate the strategy, organisational design and personnel accountability under-laps and duplication, which led to silo-based behaviours, and poor process alignment, which resulted in unproductive activities.

"On a beach in Mexico" Bill developed a strategy with five core objectives.

Bill had been exposed to the concept of the balanced scorecard through some executive training and wanted PM2 to include it in the delivery of the scope of work of the consultancy assignment. In addition, the client insisted on a number of unique approaches that did not appear in the balanced scorecard, such as weighting the strategic goals, using some light-weight lean (process analysis) tools to link strategic goals to the activities that people work on.

Based on PM2's experience with other organisations and the balance scorecard approach, PM2 was able to incorporate these unique requirements within the general framework of the balanced scorecard in order to achieve the benefits of the scorecard while implementing it within the existing structures and frameworks at AT&T.

The development of the balanced scorecard began with the creation of a strategy map (Kaplan and Norton, 2001). The strategy map for AT&T Canada is shown below in Figure 17.1. The map effectively puts the business strategy on a single page by showing in graphic form the objectives of the organisation overlaid on a cascading balanced scorecard

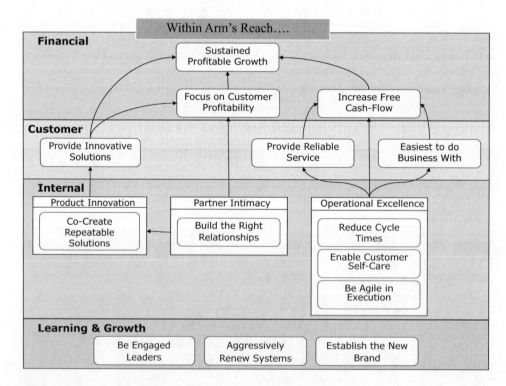

*Figure 17.1* Strategy map for AT&T Canada

with the financial perspective at the top followed by the customer and internal processes perspectives and finally learning and growth forming the foundation at the bottom of the map.

PM2 subsequently developed the strategy map by applying generic strategy tools, such as their SWOT, and partnered with the executive committee of AT&T Canada to establish weightings for each perspective and then each strategic goal. During this phase of the project, each objective was given a weighting relative to the other objectives so that the total weighting was 100%. The weighted strategy map is shown in Figure 17.2. Weightings were not a core tenet of the balanced scorecard, but when introduced by PM2 at AT&T Canada, it was seen to add to the body of knowledge. It has been referenced in several of Kaplan and Norton texts (Kaplan and Norton, 2001, 2008) as well as featured in the balanced scorecard hall of fame (Palladium, 2014).

PM2 then worked with the operational teams at AT&T. These teams reported to the executive committee, which was vital for ensuring that the balanced scorecard cascaded down to operational levels of the organisation. The aim of working with the operational team was to link the scorecard to the core processes. This was achieved by assessing the impact of each of the core processes with a score of 1 to 5 against each of the strategic objectives. The impact score was related to the weighting of the respective strategic objectives to achieve a ranking to facilitate prioritization. The ranking matrix is shown below in Figure 17.3. Assessing the impact of each core process against the strategic objectives allowed PM2 and the client to see both the alignment and core impact points. Again, this is not a core tenet of the balanced scorecard as published by Drs Kaplan and Norton, but

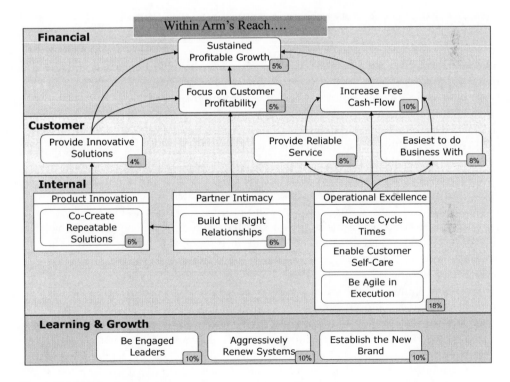

*Figure 17.2* Weighted strategy map

## Initiatives Ranked Against Strategy Map

X-pm²

| -3 year view of impact -current year weightings -meant to be relative to each other / Strategic Goals | Sustained Profitable Growth | Focus on Customer Profitability | Increase free Cashflow | Provide Innovative Solutions | Provide Reliable Service | Easiest to do Business With | Co-create Repeatable Solutions | Build the Right Relationships | OpExcel (reduce cycle times, self care, agile in exec) | Be Engaged Leaders | Agressively Renew Systems | Establish New Brand | TOTAL | Ranking |
|---|---|---|---|---|---|---|---|---|---|---|---|---|---|---|
| | 5% | 5% | 10% | 4% | 8% | 8% | 6% | 6% | 18% | 10% | 10% | 10% | 100.00% | |
| New Brand | 3 | 1 | 1 | 3 | 1 | 1 | 1 | 3 | 1 | 3 | 1 | 5 | 1.90 | 10 |
| AIN | 5 | 1 | 1 | 3 | 5 | 1 | 3 | 1 | 1 | 1 | 1 | 1 | 1.72 | 11 |
| Card | 1 | 1 | 1 | 1 | 1 | 1 | 1 | 3 | 1 | 1 | 1 | 3 | 1.32 | 12 |
| OE OM Billing | 3 | 1 | 3 | 5 | 1 | 5 | 3 | 3 | 5 | 5 | 5 | 1 | 3.54 | 1 |
| CCV | 3 | 5 | 3 | 1 | 1 | 5 | 1 | 3 | 5 | 3 | 5 | 3 | 3.46 | 2 |
| PPC | 3 | 1 | 3 | 3 | 1 | 5 | 5 | 3 | 3 | 3 | 5 | 3 | 3.22 | 3 |
| Total Billing | 3 | 1 | 5 | 1 | 5 | 5 | 1 | 3 | 3 | 3 | 1 | 1 | 2.82 | 4 |
| Enterprise Portal | 3 | 1 | 3 | 3 | 1 | 5 | 3 | 5 | 3 | 1 | 5 | 1 | 2.82 | 4 |
| Network Reach | 5 | 5 | 5 | 3 | 1 | 3 | 1 | 3 | 3 | 3 | 1 | 1 | 2.72 | 6 |
| Major Service Model | 3 | 5 | 3 | 3 | 1 | 4 | 1 | 3 | 3 | 1 | 1 | 3 | 2.50 | 7 |
| Custom Solutions | 3 | 3 | 3 | 3 | 1 | 1 | 5 | 5 | 1 | 1 | 1 | 5 | 2.36 | 8 |
| International Service | 5 | 1 | 3 | 3 | 3 | 3 | 3 | 3 | 1 | 1 | 1 | 3 | 2.24 | 9 |

*Figure 17.3* Business process/strategic objective ranking matrix

when introduced by PM2 at AT&T Canada, it was seen to add to the balanced scorecard body of knowledge.

To the credit of Kaplan and Norton, when they conducted their research on the success of the scorecard at AT&T, they saw the benefits of adapting their balanced scorecard model to accommodate these innovations. These innovations within the execution of the balanced scorecard were instrumental in featuring in the Kaplan and Norton textbooks as case studies and also becoming a member of the balanced scorecard hall of fame which features well known organizations.

To deal with poor process alignment, PM2 incorporated some simple lean tools to test the alignment between strategic goals and process. In particular, PM2 looked at the processes impact and performance. Based on the weighting of each strategic objective, the processes impact and its estimated performance score were able to identify the gap between the level of process support required to enable strategic success and the current level of process support.

Beyond the context of the scorecard, a similar approach was used to assess the viability of the recommended process improvement projects to identify the "strategic gap closing capability" for each project. In this way, the AT&T leadership was able to clearly see their strategic process gap and choose amongst possible process projects for those with the greatest impact. This, and the bill scorecard monitor, allowed them to identify the implication of changes that reduced the new customer "on-boarding" process from 27 steps in 35 days to nine steps in three days.

These lean tools also revealed the gap between the 11 product silos. Ultimately, this gap was closed by establishing a strategic objective within the balanced scorecard that targeted "multiple product customers". The only way the leadership team could achieve this objective was to break down the silos and implement changes such as sharing customer details and contacts and bundling their products.

Again, this case study demonstrated the integration of several bodies of knowledge – process mapping and value stream mapping tools – to reveal the operational gap silos and balanced scorecard tools to establish common objectives and key results.

PM2 then incorporated "HR tools" such as the role clarity model (RACI) (Mind-Tools, 2016) and effective organisation design. AT&T preferred the RACI (Responsible, Accountable, Consulted and Informed) model, or defining an individual's role in any process. By incorporating this within the above process work, PM2 in partnership with AT&T was able to redefine who is responsible for implementing what changes and what key results were expected from the individual.

At the same time the combined lean process analysis with organisation design works in order to establish how the organisation could best be designed to enable customer value streams while conforming to the regulatory requirements within the telecommunications industry.

At the time, the regulatory environment in Canada was undergoing the deregulation of the phone, long-distance, Internet and cell systems. AT&T was able to adjust the weightings of the strategic goals rapidly in reaction to changes in the regulatory environment to take advantage of opportunities and close down threats.

By creatively synergising and integrating multiple bodies of knowledge, PM2 was able to build a custom solution based on established best practices.

At the end of the project, AT&T Canada reversed its poor employee satisfaction to become a best practice of employer satisfaction. According to Kaplan and Norton (2001: 18), "The 1998 survey of 500 North American organizations showed that AT&T Canada's employee satisfaction scores were 50% higher than the average performance of the top 10 percent companies in the sample". In 1999, four years after the project begun, this money-losing business was sold in a deal worth over $7 billion, (Kaplan and Norton, 2001), proving that value can be quickly achieved through integrating existing best practices.

## Conclusion

This chapter has provided a journey through the evolution of management consulting from its early inception at the end of the nineteenth century to the present day. It shows how consultancy has evolved from the methodology being king to the emancipation of consulting know-how from the larger organizations to the boutique consultancy practices. The pervasive nature of consulting is that client solutions do not require a one-size-fits-all or even a single approach. They require the tailoring of appropriate best practice frameworks that can fit around the client needs and their organizational culture. The case study that was discussed in this chapter was a seminal balanced scorecard implementation within a large telecommunications company, AT&T Canada. The consulting assignment that used several additional consulting approaches was a resounding success that achieved a step change in employee satisfaction and financial performance. The icing on the cake was that the case study featured in Kaplan and Norton's hall of fame as a beacon of success (Palladium, 2014). Bill Catucci left AT&T after the merger and established his own consultancy practice. In 2007, Catucci was honoured by Kaplan and Norton by being recognised as a Senior Palladium Fellow (Palladium Fellows, 2016).

## References

ABS (2015). *Chartered Association of Business School, Academic Journal Guide*. Online. Available from https://charteredabs.org/academic-journal-guide-2015 [Accessed on May 31 2017].

ARWU (2016). *Academic ranking for world universities*. Available from www.shanghairanking.com/ [Accessed October 10, 2016].

Bain (2016). Available from www.bain.com/management_tools/BainTopTenTools/default.asp [Accessed August 11, 2016].

Bourne, M., Kennerley, M., and Franco-Santos, M. (2005). Managing through measures: A study of impact on performance. *Journal of Manufacturing Technology Management*, 16(4), 373–395.

Covey, S. R. (1989). *The 7 habits of highly effective people: Powerful lessons in personal change*. New York: Fireside.

Deming, W. E. (1982). *Out of the crisis*. Cambridge, MA: MIT.

Drucker Institute (2016). *Peter Drucker's life and legacy*. Available from www.druckerinstitute.com/peter-druckers-life-and-legacy/ [Accessed August 5, 2016].

Drucker, P. F. (1974). *Management: Tasks, responsibilities, practices*. New York: Harper & Row, Publishers Inc.

FranklinCovey (2016). *FranklinCovey webpages*. Available from www.franklincovey.com/ [Accessed October 10, 2016].

FT.Com (2016). *Business school rankings*. Available from http://rankings.ft.com/businessschoolrankings/new-york-university-stern [Accessed October 15, 2016].

Hammer, M., and Champy, J. (1993). *Reengineering the corporation*. New York: Harper Business.

Johnston, R., Brignall, S., and Fitzgerald, L. (2002). 'Good enough' performance measurement: A trade-off between activity and action. *Journal of the Operational Research Society*, 53(3), 256–262.

Kaplan, R. and Norton, D. (1992) The Balanced Scorecard: Measures That Drive Performance. Harvard Business Review, 70:1 pp71–9

Kaplan, R. S., and Norton, D. P. (1996). *The balanced scorecard: translating strategy into action*. Cambridge, MA: Harvard Business Press.

Kaplan, R. S., & Norton, D. P. (2001). *The strategy-focused organization: How balanced scorecard companies thrive in the new business environment*. Cambridge, MA: Harvard Business Press.

Kaplan, R. S., & Norton, D. P. (2008). *The execution premium: Linking strategy to operations for competitive advantage*. Cambridge, MA: Harvard Business Press.

Krafcik, J. F. (1988). Triumph of the lean production system. *MIT Sloan Management Review*, 30(1), 41.

Matthias, O. (2013). Developing a customisation blueprint for management consultancies to better serve their clients. DBA. University of Bradford School of Management.

McKinsey (2016). *McKinsey Alumni Centre*. Available from https://ac2.mckinsey.com/public_content/500169659 [Accessed August 11, 2016].

Miller, D., and Hartwick, J. (2002). Spotting management fads. *Harvard Business Review*, 80(10), 26.

Mindtools (2016). *Strategy tools*. Available from www.mindtools.com/ [Accessed October 10, 2016].

Mintzberg, H. (1989). *Mintzberg on management: Inside our strange world of organizations*. New York: Simon and Schuster.

MIT Libraries (2016). Available from http://libraries.mit.edu/archives/exhibits/adlittle/history.html [Accessed August 5, 2016].

Organ, D. W. (1988). *Organizational citizenship behavior: The good soldier syndrome*. Lexington MA: Lexington Books.

Palladium (2014). *Balanced Scorecard hall of fame chart*. Available from http://event.thepalladiumgroup.com/SiteCollectionImages/HOF/HOF%202014%20Logo%20Slide.pdf [Accessed August 11, 2016].

Palladium (2016). *Palladium fellows, Bill Catucci*. Available from http://event.thepalladiumgroup.com/about/fellows/Pages/WilliamACatucci.aspx [Accessed October 10, 2016].

Palmer, D. A., Jennings, P. D., and Zhou, X. (1993). Late adoption of the multidivisional form by large US corporations: Institutional, political, and economic accounts. *Administrative Science Quarterly*, 38(1) 100–131.

Peters, T. J., and Waterman, R. H. (1982). *In search of excellence: Lessons from America's best-run companies.* New York: Warner Book.

Price, M. P. (2003). Frank and Lillian Gilbreth and the motion study controversy, 1907–1930. *Frank and Lillian Gilbreth: Critical Evaluations in Business and Management*, 2, 455.

QS Ranking (2016). *Top universities.* Available from www.topuniversities.com/ [Accessed October 15, 2016].

Radnor, Z., & McGuire, M. (2004). Performance management in the public sector: Fact or fiction? *International Journal of Productivity and Performance Management*, 53(3), 245–260.

Ricardo, D. (1817). Principles of political economy and taxation. London: J. Murray.

Smith, P. C., and Goddard, M. (2002). Performance management and operational research: A marriage made in heaven? *Journal of the Operational Research Society*, 53(3), 247–255.

Squires, S., Smith, C., McDougall, L., and Yeack, W. (2003). *Inside Arthur Andersen: Shifting values, unexpected consequences.* Hoboken, NJ: FT Press.

Taylor, F. W. (1914). *The principles of scientific management.* New York: Harper.

The Tech (1993). *IBM's $5 billion loss highest in American corporate history.* Available from http://tech.mit.edu/V112/N66/ibm.66w.html [Accessed October 10, 2016].

Times Higher Education (2016). *World university rankings.* Available from www.timeshighereducation.com/world-university-rankings/new-york-university#ranking-dataset/589595 [Accessed October 12, 2016].

Wall Street Journal (1999). *AT&T to Merge Canadian Unit, MetroNet in $2.4 billion accord.* Available from www.wsj.com/articles/SB920554976587811500 [Accessed October 10, 2016].

# Conclusion

This book seeks to offer something different within the body of literature on management consulting. Since the publication in 1911 of *The Principles of Scientific Management* by arguably the first management consultant, the American engineer Frederick Winslow Taylor, books in this field have tended to fall into one of two camps. First, there is the process book. There are a host of 'how-to' books that lay out logical, sequential and rational approaches to the profession. Second, there is the psychological or behavioural book that generally presents consultancy as the opposite of rational because consultants create illusions using rhetoric and rely on impressions. Weaving together the strands of a broad set of principles to an approach to consulting or selling an underlying philosophy, we see an emphasis on headline impact: change and revolution available through the impact of a consultant as management guru.

There are excellent and highly readable examples of both types of books. Both have merit because they remain true to the core principle within the MCA definition of what consulting is: "the practise of creating value for organisations." Whether that value is delivered to clients as a result of implementing structured recommendations (process), or through a shift in the cultural values of business leaders (philosophy) is irrelevant. Value is still judged by the client. What change is brought about? More importantly, what benefits are experienced as a result of that change? Change can be fraught with danger because it invariably enters the zone of uncomfortable debate, and sometimes needs both catalysts and dampeners within the management of the change process. The consultant as change agent in any capacity requires a deft political touch and carries great responsibility.

This book also has the notion of the creation of value at its core. In Part I, there was robust academic discourse from contributors who have both experience in the business of consulting and the world of academia from universities around the world. This discussion does the essential job of bridging the gap of 'pure' published management theory with its use in a live context. It also emphasises that excellence in professional management consulting is helped by understanding that each context presents an individual reality and consultancy tools and techniques to underpin research, diagnosis and eventual recommendations that need to be tailored to the particular context. Experience alone is not always enough. In Part II, we have case studies of consultancy practise across five continents. From NGO work in Australia, public policy development in Africa and commercial clients in North America, the breadth of these examples reinforces the notion that consultancy is multi-faceted and contextual in nature. It is a discipline that is a true broad church – there really is no one-size-fits-all approach to consulting. Consultants can bring about change in diverse circumstances and these case studies provide us with examples of best practice.

The added relevance to this consideration of management consultancy comes from the higher education sector. Although entry to the profession does not require a particular qualification, unlike accountants and lawyers, it is now less common to find consultants operating without some academic foundation beyond a bachelor's degree. This may be an MBA, a qualification similar to the Chartered Management Institute's Diploma in Professional Consulting or a vocational master's degree in a specific commercial sector. The common theme is that it is rare to find top-level consultants relying on decades of experience and 'war stories' alone as the strongest element of their value proposition. This book therefore has a role where management consultancy is taught, be it as an integral part of an MBA course (as in Chapter 8) or a stand-alone course. Process and philosophy books have a role to play in teaching the discipline, but the discussion here adds much needed flavour and context to the actual delivery of consultancy work.

As we settle into the twenty-first century, we continue to experience a speed of economic, social and geopolitical change similar to other milestone periods in history. To help firms navigate the current uncertainty, management consultancy can negotiate and facilitate the change process and manage the risk so that organisations brave enough to seek out opportunities and not ignore threats will survive and prosper.

These uncertain times present challenges to not only the global business community but also academia itself. At the time of writing, the UK government is formulating legislation that would reform university teaching and research to make the research community serve the UK economy and tax payer more effectively. The reforms are set out in the white paper, 'Success as a Knowledge Economy'.[1] These reforms include the amalgamation of several research councils and the proposed changes are proving to be controversial as views have been aired that the planned changes can lead to the funding of 'pet projects' or that research will be value-laden with a vested interest. Notwithstanding, these reforms can also provide opportunities for the academic and business community. For example, applied research, such as the contributions in this book, that demonstrates economic impact can be valued more by the academic community.

As the Austrian economist, Joseph Schumpeter, wrote in the middle of the last century: "Progress means turmoil."

## Note

1 Success as a Knowledge Economy: Teaching Excellence, Social Mobility and Student Choice. www.gov.uk/government/uploads/system/uploads/attachment_data/file/523396/bis-16-265-success-as-a-knowledge-economy.pdf

# Index